TRAD
NA

Old Cawnpore
Captain Robert Smith, c.1828

ENDPAPERS
From panorama of a small British station in the Ganges:
watercolour by an Indian artist c. 1800, for James Nathaniel Rind.

FRONTISPIECE
Unknown gentleman with a hookah.
Oil by John Thomas Seton, Calcutta, c.1778.

TRADERS AND NABOBS

The British in Cawnpore
1765–1857

ZOË YALLAND

MICHAEL RUSSELL

© Zoë Yalland 1987

First published in Great Britain 1987
by Michael Russell (Publishing) Ltd,
The Chantry, Wilton, Salisbury, Wiltshire

Typeset by The Spartan Press Ltd,
Lymington, Hants
Printed in Great Britain
by Hollen Street Press Ltd, Slough

Maps drawn by Denys R. Baker

FOR
HUGO, JONATHAN AND JOANNA JANE

Contents

Illustration Sources

Collection Tom Parr, frontis; Victoria Memorial, Calcutta, 34, 35, 95; Board of Trustees of the Victoria and Albert Museum, 1, 29, 33b, 43, 165, 168, 204, 231, 284; collection Theon Wilkinson, 21, 52, 53, 63, 92, 108, 109, 120, 198, 207, 208, 238, 247, 278a; Lieutenant-Colonel P. St. G. Maxwell, MC, 25, 189, 230a, 230b, 287, 288; author's collection, 20, 23, 24, 33a, 58, 64, 81, 93, 148, 149, 156, 166, 172, 178, 184, 199, 267, 281a, 281b, 282, 285; National Portrait Gallery, 129; India Office Library and Records (British Library), 31, 41, 42, 61, 66, 82, 97, 100, 153, 159, 164, 176, 186, 211, 215, 220, 221, 226, 245a, 245b, 264a, 270a, 275, 330; BACSA records, IOR, photograph Elizabeth McKay, 73; Roy Miles Fine Paintings, 37; National Army Museum, London, 38, 236, 243, 264b, 265, 270b, 272, 274, 276, 278b, 278c; the late Mrs Noel Kilby, 113, 127, 193, 229; Hobhouse Ltd, endpapers, 122; 'property of a gentleman', 45; Leger Galleries Ltd, 47; British Library, 68, 69, 98, 182, 183; private collection of the Duke of Wellington, photograph Courtauld Institute of Art, 75; National Archives, New Delhi, 76; Lieutenant-Colonel I. A. J. Edwards-Stuart, 90; BBC Hulton Picture Library, 105; Major P. J. A. Mallaby, 200; Mrs Audrey Baylis, 203; Phillis Rogers, 218; Mrs Elfie Peppé, 196; the late Tommy Macdonald, 195; Lieutenant-Colonel T. Leahy (great-great-grandson), 138, 139; Mrs Mollie Mallaby, 232a, 232b, 289; Reggie Bason, 328; private collection, 329; W. Holmes, 268, 280; BACSA archives, IOR, 273.

Author's Note

Over the years the spelling of many words and place names has changed: I have used the earlier spelling wherever possible as being more in keeping with the times. Early letters are peppered with capital letters, which have been left in the text – as has the inconsistent spelling: sometimes, even in one letter, several versions of the same word are used, echoing the drawled vowel sounds of the English language two hundred years ago.

While respecting my Indian friends' modern preference for the 'First War of Independence', I felt it appropriate to describe the stirring events of the sepoy revolt in 1857 as the 'Mutiny'.

Indian words and words of Indian origin which found their way into everyday conversation of the English in India are in italics with a glossary at the end of the book. It is intriguing how many Indian words are now included in the *Concise Oxford Dictionary*.

The following abbreviations are adopted in the text:

ARO	Allahabad Record Office
BL	British Library
BACSA	British Association for Cemeteries in South Asia
CC	Cambridge University Centre of South Asian Studies
CL	Calcutta Library
CRO	Calcutta Record Office
DNB	*Dictionary of National Biography*
IOR	India Office Library and Records
NAI	National Archives India, New Delhi
NAM	National Army Museum
V&A	Victoria and Albert Museum
VM	Victoria Memorial, Calcutta

Acknowledgements

Work on the research into the British families in Cawnpore began nineteen years ago, in 1968. A generous grant from the Trustees of the MacRobert Trust made it possible to work in India for six weeks in 1970 and this proved to be the foundation for all subsequent research. I am greatly indebted to Stanley Sutton, Director of the India Office Library at that time, Herschel Cohn and Kenneth Wilcox who wrote ahead to India with valuable introductions and to Colonel K.K. Khanna who made all my travel arrangements in India work smoothly.

Of the many people who kindly helped me during my research in India I must particularly thank the High Commissioner, Sir Morrice James, and George Boon and Michael Stokes of the British High Commission, New Delhi, for their helpful introductions; Dr S.N. Prasad, Director of the National Archives of India, who made the archives available; Dhan Keswani who guided me and Mr Talwar who organised the typing; Dr Saletore, Director of the State Archives, U.P.; K.P. Srivastava, Keeper of Archives, Allahabad; T.K. Mukherjee, Assistant Director Archives, Calcutta Record Office; the staff at the National Library, Calcutta; and S.N. Ghosh of the Pioneer Press, Lucknow, for help with records.

India is famous for its hospitality and on that first visit and subsequent yearly visits I have been made to feel very much at home by many dear friends: Pushy and 'KK' Khanna; Pushy Tandon; Vimla and Ramesh Srivastava; Santosh and Mahendrajit Singh; Audrey and George Tinkler; Balraj and Shyama Vohra, who also generously helped with typed material from Calcutta; Wilfred and Elaine Oakley at Mirzapore, who also organised the despatch of my Allahabad records; Geoffrey Seager, Jean and Kim Butterworth at Kamaria; Anita and Vijay Rewal at New Delhi; Vijay and Nini Srivastava at Rampur; Henry Thomson at Sitapur; and Hari and Hamida Srivastava at Dabra.

While in Kanpur I was greatly helped by the following: B.N. Chopra for Muir Mill records; Clary Desouza for Elgin records and for copying photographs; Atma Prakash Gupta for access to the library of his father, the late Rai Bahadur Ram Narain; P.C. Jain for B.I.C. records; P.N. Kaul IAS and Krishna Kaul for information on the D.M.'s bungalow; Adam Muir for the generous use of a car; Canon Messenger for Church records;

Hari Srivastava for access to the records at the Chamber of Commerce; Tony West for early mill records; and S.P. Mehra who was very generous with his time and information. Since that first visit Atma Prakash Gupta and S.P. Mehra have been regular and most helpful correspondents.

I would also like to thank the following for their help with reminiscences and other material during my visits to India: Principal Abrahams; Ram Advani; Kailash Agarwal; A.B.L. Agnotri; S.P. Awasthi; T.V. Baddeley; Rameshwar Prasad Bagla; S.M. Bashir; Ira Brown; Frank Carroll; Professor Satish Chander; Bill Clarke; Gipsy and Amerjeet Dass; Denis DeCunha; Pam Desouza; Babtosh Dey, Charles and Co., Murli Dhar; George Dickson; D.N. Dikshit; K.K. Dubey; Margery Dutta; Mr Dutta, Barnett's Hotel; Mahant Onkareshwari Giri; Ram Narain Goyal; A.C. Grice; Archdeacon Harland; Queenie Hirdey Narain; Siddharth Hirdey Narain; Mrs James; W.R. Joseph; Sri Kishan; Babu Lal, *chowkidar* Cantonments Cemetery; Peter Leggatt; Monica Lehmann; Ravi Matur IAS; Macneill and Barry Ltd; Murli Manohar; M.A.C. Massy; R.K. Mehra; O.P. Mehrotra; Prem Narain Mehrotra; P.G. Moore; Shambu Nath; Dr Nigam; Father Noronha; Florence Noronha; May Noronha; Willy Noronha; Nur Sing; Pioneer Tannery; Dr Chandrakanta Rohatgi; Chunni Lal Sachdeva; B.N. Sapru; Keith Shepherd; Phyllis Sherred; Dr Maurice Shellim; Dora Shinde; Kripal Singh; Santosh and Mahendrajit Singh; Narindrajit Singh; Colonel P.P. Singh; Pami Singh; Raghavindrajit Singh; Yogendrajit Singh; Sir Padampat Singhania; Brigadier A.S. Sidhu; General Somdutt; Sonny Srivastava; Tigger Stack; P.V. Subhedar; Pyari Lal and Kanti Tandon; Jean and Fritz Thalmessinger; the Revd Henry Wilson; Kochin Wu.

I am grateful to the following UK institutions: British Library, Department of Printed Books, Department of Western Manuscripts and the India Office Library, in particular Barry Bloomfield, Martin Moir and Tony Farrington; the National Army Museum, Elizabeth Talbot Rice and Jenny Spencer Smith; the Aberdeen Library and Moira Henderson; Guildhall Library and Phillida Malling; London Spiritual Mission; the Oriental Club and R.N. Rapson; the United Society for the Propagation of the Gospel and their archivists, Mrs I. Pridmore and the Revd Ian Pearson; Robson Lowe Ltd; Scottish Record Office; County Library, Moray and Nairne; the Centre of South Asian Studies, University of Cambridge and Mary Thatcher; James Purdey and Sons Ltd; RHQ 16th/5th Queen's Royal Regiment and Colonel R.A. Bowman and Captain D.J.H. Farquharson; Lancashire County Museum; University Library, King's College, Aberdeen; and RHQ Royal Highland Fusiliers.

A large number of friends and wellwishers have helped in tracing the families concerned, in the loan and gift of books, letters and photographs, and in giving me permission to note down their memories and reminiscences. The material collected covers 1765-1947. I would like to thank members of the Maxwell and Gavin Jones families who invited me to their homes and so generously made available private family papers and mementoes for this first volume in the series: Nuna Davey, General Claude Dunbar, James Dunbar, Lady Gavin Jones, Margaret Gavin Jones, Gwyneth Huelin, Noel Kilby, Maxfield Mackay, Mollie Mallaby, Major Antony Mallaby, Iris Mainwaring, Colonel Peter Maxwell, Patience Maxwell, Valerie Maxwell, Rose Morris, Marjorie Murray, Cyril Martin-Onraët, Major Donald Stephenson, Bertha Sykes, M.R.C. Thomas, Joyce Umfreville, Linda Walker, Yolande Warner, Antony Werner, Jean Young.

The following kindly helped with material on the Mutiny; Alice Aylen with the Maltby papers; BACSA archives with additional material on Amelia Horne and Colonel Morris's papers; Reggie Bason and Iris Shepherd for new light on the Miss Wheeler story; Sir Ronald Lindsay Bt, and Humphrey and Elfie Peppé for original family letters; Richard Muir for Mrs Angelo's diary; Barbara Rogers for the original letters of Mrs Louisa Chalwin; Theon Wilkinson for Captain Rawlin's diary: also Barbara and James Anson; Alice Beeson; Major Leslie Dutton; Cecil Gash; Colonel N.H.W. Joynson; Monica Morris; Georgina Thompson; Thomas Smith; Mrs H.G. Warre; RHQ The Staffordshire Regiment; RHQ The York and Lancaster Regiment; and RHQ Duke of Cornwall's Regiment.

I would like to thank the many kind people who have helped with the illustrations: I am particularly grateful to Mildred Archer, Giles Eyre, Niall Hobhouse and Charles Greig for generous help and advice; Betty Tyer at the India Department, Victoria and Albert Museum; Marion Harding at the National Army Museum; Pauline Rohatgi, Jerry Losty and Pat Kattenhorn at the Prints and Drawings Department, India Office Library; Pankaj Dutta at the Victoria Museum, Calcutta, Sarah Wimbush at the National Portrait Gallery; and Sotheby's.

Major John Stewart was very generous with access to papers of his family's long association with Cawnpore; Colonel Ivor Edwards-Stuart helped with the ancestry of the Grants and Lord Roberts; Evelyn Battye, Salli Dyson, Colonel Leahy and Douglas Rivett-Carnac contributed to the Ravenscroft saga; Derek Hammond Giles lent some early letters written from Cawnpore; Lady Smith was an inspiration; Field-Marshal Montgomery supplied a note on his grandfather; Lord Birkenhead for extracts from his unpublished ms. on Kipling; Charles Allen, John Bannerman, Audrey Baylis, Gussie Bevis, E.S. Bishop, F. Brightman, Ewen Caldwell, A.L.

Carnegie, H. Finch, Phyllis Forster, Margaret Forster, Pop Fuller, Maisie Harrold, Richard Horsman, Charles Ker, Tommy Low, Ian MacMaster, R.N. Marsh Smith, Dr Charlie Milne, Fred Moores, Suku Morgan, Sir Frank Mudie, Dilys Owen, Major Nick Pocock, Mabel Ridsdale, Bishop Saunders, Tommy Shortis, the Revd R.G. Slater, Colonel Hamish Souter, Victor Small, E.A. Stromeyer, and C.O. Tattersall between them provided a wealth of information and significant observations.

Many other valuable contributions which will be incorporated into a sequel to this book were made by: the Revd Christopher Ackroyd, Bill Aitken, E.T.H. Alexander, Geoffrey Allen, Millie Arbor, Doris Bacon, Elsie Bambridge, Veronica Bamfield, Kathleen Bannerman, Mrs Barber, Malcolm Barnes, Charles Bassill, Jeanette Bath, J. Stanley Beard, E.W. Bell, Dr Maren Bellwinkel-Schempp, Iris Beveridge, Ruby Biddle, Dr M. Bierbrier, Major Alec Binney, W. Binns, Dr Stanley Black, Ada Blake, Jack Bolam, John and Peggy Booker, John Branford, Mrs J. Brochocha, Crystal Brown, Doreen Bullock, the Revd E.S. Butler, Colonel Valentine Cambier, Noel Carrington, Evelyn Carson, C.W. Cassé, John and Elizabeth Christie, Sir William Christie, Hilda Cobbold, Richard Collier, Margaret Cooke, Barbara Corneille, the Revd J.C. Cox, Stanley Cozens, Lord Croft, Frank Crofts, Edward Danby, Pat d'Arnaud Taylor, Sir Arthur Dash, Nest Davies, Seaton Dearden, Ruby DeCunha, Katherine S. Diehl, Dr Algy Dixon, Canon R.P. Dodd, Janet Dunbar, Edie Dymott, Eton College Library, Connie Everett, Austin Fawley, Peter Fay, May Filose, Michael Garnett, Reggie Ginns, the Revd C.G. Gordon, Perry Gordon, Yolande Gough, B.H.E. Goult, Basil Green, Angelo Grezo, Grace Hainsworth, Mrs H. Hambley, Fred Hampson, L.P. Hancox, R.L. Hards, John Harris, John Harrison, Robin Hartley, Laura Haskell, Ann Hauff, James Hepburn, Christopher Hibbert, Herb Hill, Joan Hobart-Tichborne, May Hoerder, Edith Holland, Alice Horsman, Henry Horsman, Yasmin and Shahid Hosain, General B.P. Hughes, Evelyn Ismail, Kay Jackson, Louis Jackson, Anthony Jenkins, W.W. Kemmish, Lorna Lancaster Wells, R.R. Langham Carter, Mrs Larmour, Brigadier Lewendon, Kitty Lilley, Andro Linklater, Dr Rosie Llewellyn-Jones, Major Henry Lowe, Tony Lucey, Gritze Lugg, General James Lunt, Colonel C.H.T. MacFetridge, Laura McGlashan, Philip Mason, Noreen Meadmore, Rosie Meares, Jim Meek, Patrick Mendies, Military Academy, Woolwich, Bryce Miller, Edie Milne, Peter Musgrave, Shirley Neame, Joan Nilsen, W.D. Ogilvie, Old Cliftonian Society, Wendy Orr, Major R.A.F. Page-Croft, C. Ivan Parr, 'Dippy' Peel-Yates, Sir George Pearce, M.D. Perceval, Robert Perceval, Roger Perkins, Lois Perry, Iris Portal,

Kenneth Price, Colonel A.H.M. Reade, Michael Reade, Dr R.K. Renford, Mona Richardson, Brigadier Geoffrey Rimbault, Candida Roberts, Florence Robertson. Arthur Roland Price, Lorna Rondo, Edith Royston, Winsome Rudling, Ada Rutherford, Narinder Saroop, Michael Satow, Sir Reginald Savory, T. Irvine Smith, Lady Souter, Jerry Speer, Jim Stevens, Sir Hugh Stephenson, Dr James Stevens Curl, Major E.S. Straus, Louise Taylor, Richard Terrell, Anne Thalmessinger, the Revd F.R. Thompson, Charlie Tosh, Paul Tritton, Raleigh Trevelyan, Geoffrey Tyson, Uppingham Old Boys' Association, Dr Robert Varady, Maisie Vincent, Norah Vivian, Joan Walsh, Nancy Watson, Mabel Watt, Mildred Watts, Sheila Wells, May West, L.S. White, George Whittle, Wiggins Teape Ltd, Thomas Willer, Major Idris Williams, Peggy Williams, Hector and Theo Wilkinson, Douglas Wimberley, Leonie Wylie, United Grand Lodge of England, and Mary Young.

The MacRobert Trust generously made available their private museum and Ian Mitchell the archivist, an enthusiastic collaborator, steered me through the papers during two visits to Douneside. David Beevers researched for me at the India Office Library and Mrs I.M. Flemming among Scottish records. Ann Huxley, Andrew Motion and Valerie Magill read part of the early text and offered useful advice. Louise Henry transcribed some of the taped interviews. Kanchan Rohatgi helped with the glossary, Eleanor Corey and Naval Heeramaneck gave practical advice and Marjorie Lampard helped with copy editing and made many useful suggestions for the notes and sources.

So many people have helped me over such an extended period that there may be others that I have inadvertently omitted from this lengthy list. To them I can only apologise and record my thanks again, I do, however, owe a special debt of gratitude to Herschel Cohn whose guidance in financial matters over the years made my research work and yearly visits to India possible, and I would like to thank my publisher for all his professional expertise in completing this adventure.

On a more personal level I must thank my mother for the stories of her childhood which have always fascinated me, my brother Theon Wilkinson for his never-failing help and interest and especially for the generous loan of his collection of mica paintings and other material, my nephew Wynyard Wilkinson for many valuable references in the Indian newspapers to Cawnpore traders. Within my own family I have been enormously inspired and encouraged in many practical ways by my children, Hugo, Jonathan and Joanna, and my husband Basil Yalland, and I thank them for their support and faith during its protracted progress.

Introduction

*Never to this hour can I hear the voice of the dove without feeling
myself carried back in memory to that beloved abode in Cawnpore.*
MRS MARIA SHERWOOD

This book is a tribute to a city and to the men and women who created it
and made it thrive. In the space of a hundred years Cawnpore grew from a
small army camp into an industrial city, eventually to become the Manchester of the East. The British families in Cawnpore were merchant
adventurers, ordinary men and women who went to India to seek their
fortune, whose contribution to Empire has hitherto gone unrecorded. I
have used actual source material wherever possible to build up a rounded,
general picture of them: one that conveys the kind of people they were,
their needs, their struggle to cope with life as they found it. The picture is
highlighted by the particular story of two families, the Maxwells and the
Gavin Joneses, who between them were responsible for Cawnpore becoming an industrial city.

From early times until two hundred years ago, the place where the
filthy, overcrowded, smoke-belching city now stands was a lonely stretch
of land between Bithoor and Jajmau. It was traditional rural India: mile
upon mile of flat brown earth, baked hard as a brick under the heat of the
colourless Indian sky. Scattered throughout the region were villages where
the mud houses of the peasants seeking protection against the warring
armies that had devasted the area for centuries clung closely round the
high-walled fortresses of the local chieftain. Life in the villages was governed by the seasons and had not changed for thousands of years. The
peasants were poor and hard-working, ploughing the land, driving the
cattle out to graze, cultivating the crops, always submissive to their fate
and to whichever petty rajah happened at the time to hold power over their
lives. Their attitude hid an enormous tenacity and strength of purpose:
there is a proverb, 'When the wind blows the grass must bow its head . . .'
and, like the grass, the villagers bowed before every invasion or conquest,
only to return to cultivate the land when the wind of power had passed by.

In 1750 or thereabouts, the small hamlet of Kanhpur, overlooking the
upper Ganges, 800 river miles from Calcutta, was founded, so legend says,

The Rajah's Palace, Old Cawnpore: *pencil sketch by Captain R. Gore-Roberts, 1818. 'The palace of the Rajah forms a very striking and characteristic picture of Indian scenery . . . Being evening there were few bathers at the ghauts to disturb the calm water, which as the burning sun descended reflected the ruined palace and the long line of ghauts in a mirror of glowing crystal.'*

by Hindu Singh Chandel as an act of penance for his misdeeds and in honour of Lord Krishna.[1] 'The imposing façade of the palace he built, reflected in the swiftly flowing river, contrasted sharply with the mud houses and narrow lanes of beaten earth where 3,000 people lived and toiled. Whole families worked in the fields from morning to night tending the tall feathery *bajrah,* the dhal creeping close to the ground, and the brilliant yellow mustard. Others drove their herds of thin cattle and goats to nearby scrubby jungle and ravines to graze, returning in the evening with bundles of firewood and baskets of dung. The boatmen cast their nets in the shallows of the river for fish and cultivated melon and cucumber on its sandy banks. In the hamlet itself, all menial tasks of fetching and carrying were the duty of the *chamars,* the untouchable scavengers, When the sun went down, dusk fell swiftly. The cows were milked, the fires lit, the simple evening meal prepared and a light blue haze hung low over the little village. The rhythm of everyday life was regularly interrupted by the excitement of *mela* days when people in their best and brightest clothes made their way to the riverside temple to celebrate the gods, to bathe and pray.

In 1770 this way of life was affected dramatically by the arrival of a small detachment of the Honourable East India Company troops, campaigning with the Nawab of Oude against their common enemy, the Mahrattas. The force had been sent from Calcutta to guard the ford over the River Ganges into the territory of the Nawab. The men camped beside the hamlet of Kanhpur, on 'a dusty treeless plain, cut into ravines by torrents of rain'. Officers had to find their own accommodation and houses were built on prime sites along the river frontage, stretching over a distance of six miles. Behind them were long straight rows of crude huts where the soldiers were housed, and behind those again huddled the huts and crowded bazaars of the thousands of camp followers who served the needs of this little force. Attracted towards it, looking for work, came the *chamars* and labourers from the outlying districts.

Here, eight weary days' march from Calcutta, the soldiers carried out their military duties, living in leaking ruins of huts, dying of sunstroke, rum and boredom. The camp grew rapidly until it became the largest military encampment in northern India, a base camp in the Mahratta Wars. It attracted to it traders of all descriptions: men to build boats and bungalows, to supply grain and liquor, shopkeepers, auctioneers, all in their own ways opportunists, all living off the needs of the troops.

Village Life: *Company painting on mica*

Thirty years later, with the Cession of 1801, Cawnpore for the first time became British territory. The East India Company's civil servants arrived to take up their duties, to impose Company law and order and to administer the complexities of assessing and collecting revenue from the land. Endless quarrels took place between the civil and military authorities who both resented the sharing of power. Many of their squabbles had to be resolved by reference to Calcutta. The civilising of Cawnpore was achieved only gradually.

The Mahrattas were defeated, peace came to the interior and the ladies started to arrive from England to join their husbands. They exerted their influence to make Cawnpore as English as possible. Social amenities were created for their amusement: the Assembly Rooms for balls and parties, a theatre, a racecourse, a school, and finally a church. The residents became settled and affluent, a corporate feeling was established and Cawnpore enjoyed 'palmy days'. The decision to bring the railway to Cawnpore, connecting it with the port of Calcutta, seemed to make its future as an important prosperous town certain.

Within the bounds of Cawnpore, as if by will power, the British kept Indian influence at bay. All around the city, however, there was a dark shadow. Decadent, fabulous Lucknow, capital of the Kingdom of Oude, last remnant of the Moghul Empire, was a hotbed of intrigue. Only the River Ganges separated Cawnpore from Oude. Twelve miles to the north of Cawnpore, at Bithoor, the defeated leader of the Mahrattas, the ex-Peishwa of Poona, with his adopted son, Nana Sahib, lived out his life in exile. In the Districts there was no tradition of established Indian landowning families to exert a stable influence. The shadow was menacing.

Cawnpore was affected by government policy in the wider sphere. The introduction of liberal laws and education was misunderstood and viewed with suspicion. The annexation of Indian States was deeply resented. When Oude was annexed, the feeling of discontent and disquiet began to be felt throughout northern India, from Delhi to Calcutta, and led to the terrible events of the Mutiny in 1857. The Mutiny overwhelmed Cawnpore, it destroyed all that had been established in the past eighty years and swept away almost the entire European population. The ordeal in Wheeler's entrenchment, the massacre at the boats, the slaughter of the women and children at the Bebee Ghur made the name of Cawnpore notorious.

Less than twenty years later Cawnpore re-emerged as a busy prosperous city. Among the many mill hands and technicians who flocked from Lancashire to Cawnpore to take up work offered by this expanding, confident boom-town was my maternal grandfather, who with his wife arrived in 1882 to join the newly established Lalimli Woollen Mill. He found new schemes afoot to start large cotton mills, tanneries and sugar refineries; houses, mills and factories were under construction; roads were being built and railway sidings developed. He and his family settled down to enjoy the social life and contribute thirty-seven years' work to this promising industrial city.

When I was a small girl living in Cawnpore, I woke every morning to hear the hooters of the Elgin Mills calling the men of the first shift to work. As the sound died away with a downward note, suddenly running out of

Workers at Cooper, Allen, c. 1930

puff, the hooters sounded from Muir, New Victoria, the Lalimli, Cooper, Allen – all the great mills of Cawnpore vying with one another to call their men to work. When they called, the men set out from overcrowded lanes in the bazaar, from modest brick and concrete quarters in mill estates and from outlying villages, some as far as ten miles distant. The workmen converged in thousands towards the mill gates, their heads in winter wrapped against the chill morning air, some carrying bags of food or a black umbrella. Many rode bicycles, knees apart, white dhotis flaping. The mills were the life force of Cawnpore and Cawnpore was the mills.

My father was the Elgin director, having joined the firm of Begg, Sutherland & Co., Managing Agents, in 1912. Each morning he was driven to the mill in his red Fiat. The double gates were thrown open by the imposing figure of the gatekeeper. Gurkha *chaprassis* in khaki uniform, puttees wound round their legs, brass badges winking at belt and turban, stamped to attention and saluted smartly. Someone took my father's topee and attaché case; the verandah *chick* was held back and my father disappeared into his dark green office. His desk stood in the centre of the room. Overhead the blades of the punkah flipped slowly round. Papers were in baskets, kept from blowing about by paperweights. On the wall was a framed picture of an old-fashioned gentleman with fluffy white moustaches: 'Hugh Maxwell•who started the mill'. My father was proud that Elgin was the first up–country cotton mill in India.

Years later I found myself wondering about the men who had built the

Elgin Mills, 1916

mills. Who were they? Where had they come from? Why had they chosen to come to Cawnpore? So it came about that I started a search, a treasure hunt, a pilgrimage into the past to discover what I could about this place called Cawnpore and the men and women who had once lived there.

In tracing the background of these early pioneering families, the contemporaries of my grandparents, I found that it was the history of Cawnpore itself that emerged. I learnt that Cawnpore is a creation of the British, an unique example of how they adapted to the ways and conditions of life in nineteenth-century India. Cawnpore's progress from being an army camp to becoming the Manchester of the East followed no preconceived plan for expansion; events took place piecemeal and pragmatically in response to the circumstances of the time.

This book tells the story of the *early* history of Cawnpore, the period from 1765 until the Mutiny, when the first British families, adventurers, traders and merchants, attracted by the opportunity offered by the army camp, came to Kanhpur and created a city. Ultimately many prominent families emerge to play their part, but in those far-off, pre-Mutiny days it was the link between the Maxwell family and the Gavin Joneses that was the vital factor in the growth of the city.

Hugh Maxwell: Bourne & Shepherd, 1870

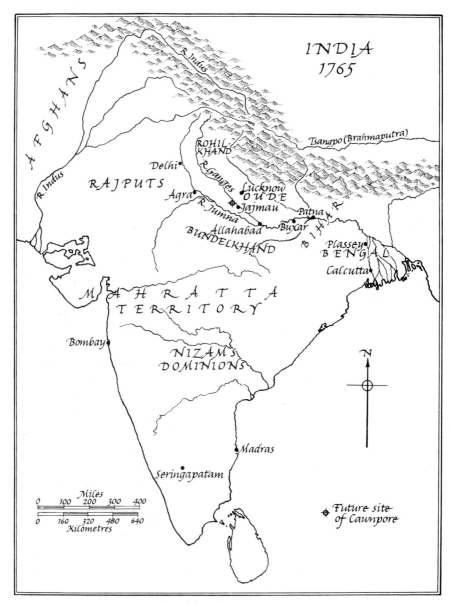

The Moghul Empire, founded two hundred years earlier by Muslim invaders, once stretched across northern India and the whole area of the Ganges basin. It included several kingdoms with their own princes and rulers who owed allegiance to the Emperor, Shah Alam II; the two most powerful were Bengal and Oude. By 1765 the Moghul Empire was in collapse, and the Mahratta armies terrorised central India. Only the kingdoms of Bengal and Oude retained something of their former splendour.

I

Cawnpore Becomes an Army Camp
1765 – 1800

The Camp at Jajmau

On 26 May 1765 General John Carnac[1] wrote to the Select Committee of the East India Company at Fort William, Calcutta, informing them that the troops under his command had put the Mahratta army to flight and set up camp on the heights of Jajmau, overlooking the Ganges, a few miles down river from the hamlet of Kanhpur. He headed his despatch 'John Carnac, Brigadier General, Colonel in the Service of the United Company of Merchants trading to the East Indies in the Provinces of Bengal, Behar and Orissa, and Commanding Officer of their forces upon the Bengal Establishment', and his curious mixture of ranks reflected the strangeness of the East India Company's own status in India. It was, as Macaulay describes it, 'an anomaly': a company formed by unpretentious London merchants, gambling a few hundred pounds on the success of a voyage. It had been trading with the East Indies since 1601. It was now firmly established at its trading posts at Madras, Bombay and Calcutta. Fort William, Calcutta, the original trading post of the Company in Bengal, was the most profitable.

In 1765 Company affairs in India were controlled by a Select Committee of four under a President, who was Governor of the Presidency of Fort William. The Directors of the East India Company, operating from East India House, London, were solely responsible for the affairs of the British trading in India. For a century trade between the Company and the country powers had been peaceful; but competition for trade with the French Compagnie des Indes Orientales led to both the English and French Companies enlisting private armies of Indian sepoys, officered by Europeans, to protect their lives and their trading bases. Inevitably, the protection of trade led to military contests.

It was common knowledge that the Directors were thoroughly alarmed at the adventuring into the interior of India by the Company's troops. They were interested only in trade, not in territorial expansion, but they were separated from their servants in the East by months of travelling time and had no real control over them. The man on the spot had to act as each situation demanded and according to his own judgement. Effective power was with the Company men in India.

In Bengal resentment against the East India Company and their trading practices led in June 1756 to the incident of the Black Hole of Calcutta, when the Nawab of Bengal, determined to be master in his own house, threw the English out of the city. Clive[2] avenged the disaster at the momentous Battle of Plassey in 1757 and the Company found themselves in a position to become rulers of Bengal. Seven years later a direct clash took place between the Moghul authority and the East India Company. Sujah Dowlah, Nawab of Oude, had come to the aid of the Nawab of Bengal, taking the fugitive Emperor with him. Together they raised a huge army to oppose the small, newly formed Bengal Army.[3] A long-drawn-out campaign ended in a decisive victory for the Company forces at Buxar in 1764. The Battles of Plassey and Buxar were the turning points in the Company's history in India; the victory at Buxar made it certain that the Company would assume the authority of government in Bengal.

The Nawab of Bengal disappeared; Sujah Dowlah fled up-country to seek help from the Mahrattas to fight again. The Company forces followed him closely up the Ganges. The Mahrattas had marched from the Rohilla country down the banks of the river to meet the army commanded by General Carnac, but when Carnac advanced the enemy would not face him. After the exchange of a few shots 'the dastardly Morattas galloped off the field'.[4] Sujah Dowlah, incensed at their cowardice and treachery, realised 'dejectedly' that there was nothing left for him to do but swallow his pride and make friends with the Company.

Sujah Dowlah approached Jajmau and in May 1765 presented Carnac with a petition. Translated from the Persian, it strikes the courteous, elaborate note that was to typify negotiations between the Company and native states.

It is known all over the World that the illustrious Chiefs of the English Nation are constant and unchangeable in their Friendship which my heart is fully persuaded of. The late disturbances were contrary to my inclinations, but it was so ordered by Providence; I now see things in a proper light, and have a strong desire to come to you alone, and I am persuaded you will treat me in a manner befitting your own Honour. You have shown great favours to others – when you became acquainted with me, you will see with your own eyes and be thoroughly sensible of my attachment from which I shall never depart while I have life.[5]

Sujah Dowlah, accompanied by his officers and a guard of 400 horsemen, came in person to the camp at Jajmau to treat with the British and offer them

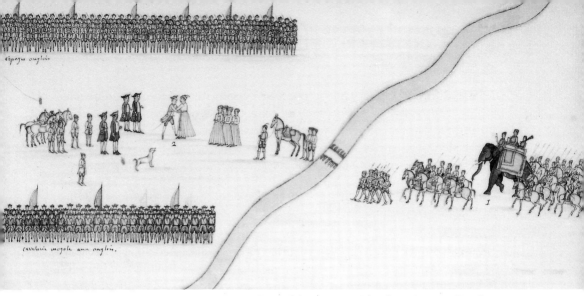

Detail: General John Carnac meeting Sujah Dowlah at Jajmau. Colonel Jean Baptiste Gentil, a French soldier in the service of the Nawab 1763–75, commissioned an Indian artist to record the cordial meeting of Carnac (accompanied by his dog) and the Nawab. While ranks of 'cipayes anglois' and 'cavalierie mogula auz anglois' looked on, the Nawab's entourage with elephant approached from Oude to cross the River Ganges by bridge of boats at Jajmau ('djaharemahou').

his allegiance. He was an imposing figure, noted for his amazing strength: his soldiers boasted that he could lift a man in each arm. 'Carnac attended by his staff and the several Company officers proceeded to the banks of the river to receive him. Here they all dismounted from their horses and the Nawab Vizier alighting from his *palkee* embraced the General, who met him with every mark of respect and presented him each with a *nuzzer* according to their rank.'[6]

Carnac was able to report to the Select Committee not only a military success but the prospect of an amicable peace. From the Company's point of view, an alliance with the Nawab might do away with the need for further military activity in Oude – thus appeasing the Directors – while safeguarding and consolidating their recent gains. It seemed an admirable opportunity and Carnac was careful to recommend taking it:

> *John Carnac, Jajemau, to Lord Clive, President and Governor of Bengal.*
> If we can make a friend of Sujah Dowlah, which I really believe we may, provided we use with moderation our success and do not urge him to despair, I am firmly of the opinion that he, from the extreme regard in which he is held throughout the Country even in his present distress, will prove a much better security to our frontier than any one we can put in these Dominions in his room.[7]

Lord Clive had sailed from England in 1764 to take up duties as Governor of the Presidency of Fort William for the second time. England was on the point of losing her American colonies. Her great rival and adversary in

Europe, in the East Indies and on the seas, was France. There were French trading posts in India at Pondicherry, Chandernagore, Karikal and Mahé. On his eleven-month-long voyage to India Clive pondered the events which lay ahead. Writing home to Thomas Rous, the Chairman of the Company, in April 1765, he said:

I must now enter with you into the Politicks of India. . . . We have at last arrived at that critical Conjuncture, which I have long forseen, I mean that Conjuncture which renders it necessary for us to determine, whether we can, or shall take the whole to ourselves.

Suja Dowla is beat out of his Dominions; We are in possession of them, and it is scarcely a Hyperbole to say that the whole Mogul Empire is in our hands. The Inhabitants of the Country, we know by long Experience, have no Attachment to any Nabob whatever, their Troops are neither disciplined, nor commanded, nor paid as ours are. Can it be doubted that a large Army of Europeans would effectually preserve to us the Sovereignty, as I may call it, not only by keeping in Awe the Ambition of every Country Prince, but by rendering us so formidable, that no French, Dutch, or other Enemy could ever dare to molest us?

. . . Our Troops you will hear are at this time, above half way to Delhi – A March I highly disapprove of. I mean absolutely to bound our Possessions, Assistance and Conquests to Bengal, never shall the going to Delhi be a Plan adopted if possible to be avoided by me, and you may depend on my putting a Stop to it. . . .[8]

On his arrival in India, Clive travelled up to Allahabad where he met General Carnac and the Nawab of Oude to discuss the terms of a settlement. His instructions from the Select Committee were to establish a friendly relationship with the native powers with a view to the extension of trade. Clive, for his part, believed that the way to protect the Company's trading rights in India was with arms: 'What is it, then, can enable us to secure our present acquisition or improve upon them but such a force as leaves nothing to the power of treachery or ingratitude.'[9]

However, in negotiating the treaty with the Nawab of Oude, he had instructions from the Select Committee that revealed a rather different attitude: first and foremost, the Company was interested in trade; it was keen to have peaceful relations with the native powers because they benefited trade; and it was not concerned with territorial expansion or displays of military force except in so far as these things protected trade:

We think Sujah Dowlah should be reinstated in full possession of all his Dominions with such limitations only as he must see are evidently calculated to the good of his country and happiness of his People. Retaining possession of any of his strongholds may be deemed a necessary pledge of his fidelity; for our part we would rather consider it as a source of future contention and an un-necessary Burden to the Company, unless it is proposed one day to resume the thought of extending their

...le, accompanied by his four sons, holds General Sir Robert Barker ...nce between them. Captain Gabriel Harper, in command of the ...appears behind them. Tilly Kettle, Fyzabad 1772.

...t Cawnpore which is to be enclosed by a ditch until ...to be properly fortified.'[13]

...ince of Corah on the frontier of Oude, situated on ...er could sometimes be forded, was a camp of great ...s not long before the Nawab asked the Company ...received information of 'the intended march of the ...nce of Corah and from thence to Allahabad'.[14] He ...requested the troops of the 3rd Brigade, who were ...to proceed with all possible expedition to his ...first Company troops arrived in the new camp.[15] ...ing the Treaty of Allahabad, Cawnpore took on ...frontier post in a country full of enemy forces and

Lord Clive, attended by General Carnac, receives the grant of the Dewani of Bengal from Shah Alam the Moghul Emperor. Detail from Benjamin West, London c. 1818.

Dominions – A measure very opposite to the sentiment in which we left the Proprietors and Court Directors. . . .

It will be necessary however that your Lordship obtain a full grant in the strongest terms for carrying on a free trade through his Dominions, with the privilege of establishing Factories wherever we think proper – to which shall be annexed contiguous lands and districts as may be found necessary to the convenience and support of the settlements. . . . But the keeping of strongholds and protecting our Commerce by Military power is a measure concerning the expediency of which your Lordship will judge from a further enquiry into Circumstances.[10]

The result of Clive's inquiry appeared in the treaty signed at Allahabad on 16 August 1765 by the Nawab of Oude, the Nawab of Bengal and the English Company and approved by the Moghul Emperor. Although Company forces had defeated all three native powers, it seemed expedient to treat them differently: to make a friend of the Nawab of Oude, and to conciliate the Emperor, at the expense of the Nawab of Bengal. Clive nominally upheld the authority of the Moghul Emperor by assigning to him

three provinces that had been part of the Kingdom of Oude, on condition
that he resided in one of them, at Allahabad. The Nawab of Bengal forfeited
the little power he had left. He retained his title, but the Company took over
the Dewani or sub-rule of Bengal, which empowered them to administer
the revenue. Part of the taxes were to be paid to the Emperor, and part used
for the defence and administration of the province.

The Nawab of Oude was more fortunate. Although he had lost three
provinces to the Company, the bulk of his kingdom was restored to him to
be a buffer state against the Mahratta forces which were terrorising central
India, gaining in strength as the Moghul Empire collapsed. The Nawab and
the Company promised mutual assistance against their common enemy and
the Nawab agreed to defray the 'extraordinary expense' if the Company
troops were used in his defence. By the terms of the treaty, the British troops
were to withdraw from all the dominions of the Nawab except his fort at
Chunar.

The Select Committee was torn between desire for this foothold in Oude
and nervousness about an acquisition that was difficult to justify. Their
disquiet was expressed in the following resolution:

> It is not surprising that the Vizier should hesitate upon ceding the fort of Chunar Gur
> to us in perpetuity . . . indeed when we consider the positive orders of the
> Company not to extend their territorial possessions we are in doubt whether we
> ought to have accepted it . . . but the evident advantages resulting from our having
> it in possession renders it of too much consequence . . . if therefore we can bring the
> Vizier readily to consent to our maintaining a garrison there and to withdrawing his
> own, with his permission to hold it while the troubles in the country or the interests
> of the Company make it expedient, it is all we can desire to obtain from him.[11]

This rather tentative resolution concluded a treaty that marked a
momentous advance for the Company. Company men had first come to
Bengal to trade; the defence of that trade had drawn them on to military
power; when they accepted the Dewani of Bengal it became apparent that
fighting had led them into government. Clive had laid the foundations for
the British Raj.

The treaty had significance, too, for the history of Cawnpore; indeed, it
marked the beginning of British Cawnpore. For it was in fulfilment of the
clause providing for the defence of the Nawab against the Mahrattas that
British troops stationed themselves near the village of Kanhpur. The names
of Oude and the Company were formally linked for the first time, at the start
of an association which would bring both prosperity and catastrophe to the
future city of Cawnpore.

ABOVE *Clive: e*
RIGHT *Indian m*
From an album
Nawab of Oude

Sujah Dowlah, Nawab of Oud
by the hand, signifying the allia
Company's troops in Fyzabad

In the Nat
1770 in a
Fyzabad, t
of the N
possession

Cawnp
Mahrattas
dominate
Compan
mutual
Nabob's
Harper
Cawnpo
few tro
Battalio

*Every N

and cavalry will remain
after the rains, when it is
Cawnpore, in the prov
the Ganges where the riv
strategic value, and it wa
for support there. He had
Mahrattas into the Provi
set out for Cawnpore and
already on the march,
assistance'. As a result the
In the five years follow
the character of an isolated

The Emperor, Shah Alam, attended by Sujah Dowlah, Nawab of Oude, reclines in his tent at Allahabad while General Sir Robert Barker explains the military manoeuvres taking place before him. Tilly Kettle, London c. 1781.

unreliable allies. The Company was trying to maintain the allegiance of the Nawab of Oude and of the many petty rajahs under him, and to foster a friendly association with the Moghul Emperor at Allahabad, while at the same time fighting the Mahrattas and countering their attempts to entice away the Company's allies. The officers in the district – often quite junior men – had an impossible job. The Commander-in-Chief, Sir Robert Barker, reported that 'the Mhorattah Arms have struck a panic into the whole area'.[16] In this atmosphere, the sympathies of the Emperor and the Nawab, to say nothing of lesser chiefs, would veer to the Mahrattas, and the Company officers were faced with the task of regaining them. Moreover, keeping the loyalty of great men was not their only problem. When the advance detachment of Company troops first reached Cawnpore, led by

Captain Robert Brooke,[17] they found the area disturbed by petty intrigue among the native chiefs.

Brooke had simultaneously to pacify the area and to prepare for a campaign against the Mahrattas. Like many Company men, he had to do his job without the help of up-to-date instructions or money to pay his troops. In a report to Sir Robert Barker on 2 February 1771, made from the camp at Tulchay, Brooke wrote:

A few days ago I marched the detachment to Cawnpore, the Mahrattas being then expected, and being preceded to it by the Vizier and his son, I wished myself to wait as long as possible out of the works, knowing the rebellious disposition of the Rajahs in this country, and how apt they would be to rebel upon the smallest appearance of my force not being able to keep the field. My conjecture proved just; all the country was under arms and securing their mud forts by additional defences. Immediately upon finding this, and receiving certain intelligence of the Mahrattas having suddenly marched towards Delhi, I left two companies in the line and proceeded immediately against the first zemindar who had rebelled, in the fort of Tullcherry [sic]; a place which had often been beseiged but never taken. . . .

My sepoys are in great distress, having about four months pay due to them; and I myself am as badly off, being obliged to fortify my post at Cawnpore and lay in provisions and stores for to sustain an attack of thirty days, without the smallest advance having been made to me.[18]

If Cawnpore was to be used as a buffer between Oude and the Mahrattas, the encampment had to be fortified. Captain Brooke undertook the work at the Nawab's request. He was to render the works 'strong and mutually assisting . . . the situation being so eligible for the defence of both the Corah province and his own Territories'.[19] It is probable that Brooke's ditches and earthworks formed the site of what was later to be the Cawnpore Magazine, built on rising ground close to the outskirts of the village of Kanhpur, and with easy access to the river. These fortifications were the nucleus of the new station, and justified the appearance of the word Cawnpore on the map of India. It was sometimes spelt Cawnpoor, Khanpore, or Kanhpore, but by about 1785 the drawl of eighteenth-century speech had settled the name as Cawnpore.

The Nawab was impressed by Captain Brooke's work on the fortifications, as Captain Harper reported on 22 March 1771:

On the Vizier's return to this place from visiting the post occupied by Captain Brooke and his own troops at Cawnpore, he could not avoid making a comparison between the English and the Hindustan mode of fortification, and paying many compliments to the abilities of Captain Brooke in this particular branch. He has often mentioned to me his concern at having no place of strength . . . where he could on any emergency lodge his family and treasure, and

Lord Clive, attended by General Carnac, receives the grant of the Dewani of Bengal from Shah Alam the Moghul Emperor. Detail from Benjamin West, London c. 1818.

Dominions – A measure very opposite to the sentiment in which we left the Proprietors and Court Directors. . . .

It will be necessary however that your Lordship obtain a full grant in the strongest terms for carrying on a free trade through his Dominions, with the privilege of establishing Factories wherever we think proper – to which shall be annexed contiguous lands and districts as may be found necessary to the convenience and support of the settlements. . . . But the keeping of strongholds and protecting our Commerce by Military power is a measure concerning the expediency of which your Lordship will judge from a further enquiry into Circumstances.[10]

The result of Clive's inquiry appeared in the treaty signed at Allahabad on 16 August 1765 by the Nawab of Oude, the Nawab of Bengal and the English Company and approved by the Moghul Emperor. Although Company forces had defeated all three native powers, it seemed expedient to treat them differently: to make a friend of the Nawab of Oude, and to conciliate the Emperor, at the expense of the Nawab of Bengal. Clive nominally upheld the authority of the Moghul Emperor by assigning to him

three provinces that had been part of the Kingdom of Oude, on condition
that he resided in one of them, at Allahabad. The Nawab of Bengal forfeited
the little power he had left. He retained his title, but the Company took over
the Dewani or sub-rule of Bengal, which empowered them to administer
the revenue. Part of the taxes were to be paid to the Emperor, and part used
for the defence and administration of the province.

The Nawab of Oude was more fortunate. Although he had lost three
provinces to the Company, the bulk of his kingdom was restored to him to
be a buffer state against the Mahratta forces which were terrorising central
India, gaining in strength as the Moghul Empire collapsed. The Nawab and
the Company promised mutual assistance against their common enemy and
the Nawab agreed to defray the 'extraordinary expense' if the Company
troops were used in his defence. By the terms of the treaty, the British troops
were to withdraw from all the dominions of the Nawab except his fort at
Chunar.

The Select Committee was torn between desire for this foothold in Oude
and nervousness about an acquisition that was difficult to justify. Their
disquiet was expressed in the following resolution:

It is not surprising that the Vizier should hesitate upon ceding the fort of Chunar Gur
to us in perpetuity . . . indeed when we consider the positive orders of the
Company not to extend their territorial possessions we are in doubt whether we
ought to have accepted it . . . but the evident advantages resulting from our having
it in possession renders it of too much consequence . . . if therefore we can bring the
Vizier readily to consent to our maintaining a garrison there and to withdrawing his
own, with his permission to hold it while the troubles in the country or the interests
of the Company make it expedient, it is all we can desire to obtain from him.[11]

This rather tentative resolution concluded a treaty that marked a
momentous advance for the Company. Company men had first come to
Bengal to trade; the defence of that trade had drawn them on to military
power; when they accepted the Dewani of Bengal it became apparent that
fighting had led them into government. Clive had laid the foundations for
the British Raj.

The treaty had significance, too, for the history of Cawnpore; indeed, it
marked the beginning of British Cawnpore. For it was in fulfilment of the
clause providing for the defence of the Nawab against the Mahrattas that
British troops stationed themselves near the village of Kanhpur. The names
of Oude and the Company were formally linked for the first time, at the start
of an association which would bring both prosperity and catastrophe to the
future city of Cawnpore.

ABOVE *Clive: engraving by W. T. Mote.*
RIGHT *Indian marigold: by an Indian artist.*
From an album presented to Clive by the
Nawab of Oude, Sujah Dowlah.

Cawnpore Camp

In the National Archives of India the first mention of Cawnpore occurs in
1770 in a report dated 2 May written by Captain Gabriel Harper from
Fyzabad, the then capital of Oude; 'The day before yesterday two Battalions
of the Nabob's★ Sepoys with two guns marched from hence to take
possession of Cawnpore.'[12]

Cawnpore was to be a military base for the protection of Oude from the
Mahrattas. Indian politics at the end of the eighteenth century were
dominated by fear of these marauders. In the Treaty of Allahabad, the
Company and the Nabob had undertaken to defend each other against this
mutual enemy, and the Company kept themselves informed when 'the
Nabob's troops began to gather at Cawnpore. On 16 June 1770 Captain
Harper reported from the camp on the bank of the Ganges opposite
Cawnpore that 'His Excellency [the Nawab] marched from Lucknow with a
few troops and arrived here yesterday making two long marches. A
Battalion of Sepoys, four guns and about twelve hundred matchlockmen

★Every Nawab was familiarly dubbed 'Nabob'.

Sujah Dowlah, Nawab of Oude, accompanied by his four sons, holds General Sir Robert Barker by the hand, signifying the alliance between them. Captain Gabriel Harper, in command of the Company's troops in Fyzabad, appears behind them. Tilly Kettle, Fyzabad 1772.

and cavalry will remain at Cawnpore which is to be enclosed by a ditch until after the rains, when it is to be properly fortified.'[13]

Cawnpore, in the province of Corah on the frontier of Oude, situated on the Ganges where the river could sometimes be forded, was a camp of great strategic value, and it was not long before the Nawab asked the Company for support there. He had received information of 'the intended march of the Mahrattas into the Province of Corah and from thence to Allahabad'.[14] He set out for Cawnpore and requested the troops of the 3rd Brigade, who were already on the march, 'to proceed with all possible expedition to his assistance'. As a result the first Company troops arrived in the new camp.[15]

In the five years following the Treaty of Allahabad, Cawnpore took on the character of an isolated frontier post in a country full of enemy forces and

Officer of the 2nd Bengal Infantry Brigade, typical of the first officers to reach Cawnpore. Tilly Kettle, c. 1773.

Warren Hastings in civilian clothes, c. 1800: engraving by H. Robinson after Sir Joshua Reynolds. Warren Hastings came to India as a young Writer in 1750 and rose to become one of the Company's most able administrators. He was appointed in 1772 to be Governor-General of Bengal.

now being struck with the appearance and strength of the post fortified by Captain Brooke at Cawnpore, renewed his wishes of having a place of strength in his own territories.[20]

The Nawab's lines however, proved too difficult to fortify except, according to Harper, 'at a great expense, owing chiefly to the number of heights in the neighbourhood which are too extensive to be included in the lines, or to be secured by advanced works', and the project was abandoned.

The difficulties mentioned by Captain Harper suggest that the Nawab's troops were camped at a little distance from Captain Brooke's men and close to the old fort at Jajmau. The chance situation of these two camps was probably responsible for a peculiar feature of Cawnpore, remarked on in years to come by every traveller: 'the great extent of the Cantonment'[21] that stretched for seven miles along the bank of the Ganges. The two straggling encampments, facing the river and served from behind by the bazaar huts that quickly sprang up to cater for the needs of the soldiers, became the outline plan for the future city. Many of its later ills, such as the overcrowding of the bazaars and the difficulty of urban development, sprang directly from this beginning.

The Company's servants were not the only people short of money. The Company itself was in such desperate need that in 1772 the Directors negotiated a loan from the English Government for one-and-a-half million pounds. In return, the Company agreed to the Regulating Act, which brought its affairs for the first time under the control, albeit indirect, of Crown and Parliament. Warren Hastings[22] was appointed the first Governor-General of Bengal with power over all three Presidencies: Bengal, Bombay and Madras. Reports from him and from the Council in Calcutta were to be shown to the Government within fourteen days of their arrival in England.

Because the Company was short of money it was slow to pay the Emperor his promised revenues. He therefore decided to shift his allegiance once again to the Mahrattas, handing over to them the provinces assigned to him by the Company and in due course being installed in Delhi as a puppet king under Mahratta domination. His old ally, the Nawab of Oude, seeing in his defection and the Company's need for money an opportunity to regain his three lost provinces, approached the Company and offered to buy them back for fifty lakhs* of rupees, provided the Company would make available their well-trained army for his defence.

The British agreed to the Nawab's proposal and in 1773 drew up the Treaty of Fyzabad to record the transaction in which they promised that the Nawab 'shall by no means and under no pretence, be liable to any obstructions . . . from the English Chiefs, Gentlemen of the Council, and by the Company, nor shall it ever be broken or deviated from'.[23]

As it transpired, the Treaty of Fyzabad did not remain unbroken for long. In the meantime, however, the Company troops promised to the Nawab were cantoned at posts on the frontiers of Oude; one of them at Cawnpore. Here a brigade encamped, consisting of two battalions of Europeans, six battalions of sepoys and one company of artillery. Their expenses were calculated at two lakhs and ten thousand rupees, payable by the Nawab. All these men were cantoned in conditions so primitive that they were only marginally better than those on the march. Calcutta, with the delights of society and civilised existence, was 800 miles away by river. It might have been another world.

★100,000 rupees make a lakh. Before the Mutiny, the rupee was the equivalent of two shillings and a lakh was worth £10,000. There were originally so many varieties and weights in rupees that the rupee was standardised in Bengal, Behar and Orissa as the *sicca* rupee in 1793.

Behind the Camp

The first brigade of Company soldiers arrived in Cawnpore in 1774. They had marched the long overland route from Calcutta, bringing with them all their equipment and provisions, and attended by a vast army of servants and a bazaar department.

Their approach to Cawnpore was across a wide, sandy plain. Here they experienced an enduring feature of Cawnpore, commented on by many travellers – the dust: 'The ground becomes parched to a cinder, all vegetation is destroyed, the tread of horses, camels, and bullocks, loosens each day a certain quantity of dust upon the surface which raises into the air in the form of a thick cloud, which not only hides the sun but envelopes the whole station in mid-night darkness.'[24] Captain Brooke's fortifications were all but complete; below the immensely thick, turreted walls of the Magazine, flat-bottomed boats containing the arsenal were moored, alongside them two hospital boats for the sick.[25] Beyond, apart and self-contained, was the village of Kanhpur, the small mud houses dominated by the imposing palace built by Rajah Hindu Singh, the founder of the original hamlet.*

The brigade settled down at Cawnpore, their tents pitched in rows like streets. Behind, at a little distance, the great huddle of camp followers massed together as best they could.

Besides the women who follow the fortunes of officers and private soldiers there is a mixed multitude of different denominations, termed the bazaar people, consisting of all pursuits, some exercising particular callings and making themselves useful, while others accompany the army merely with a view to plunder: and yet even these straggling marauders are of material service to the great community upon which they depend by searching for the concealed grain and bringing what they find to market, with other provisions obtained in a similar way.[26]

The encampment at Cawnpore was intended to be temporary but the Nawab of Oude continued to request the services of the Company brigade to assist him against his hereditary enemies, the Rohillas, and Warren Hastings used Cawnpore as an official cantonment. In 1778 he assembled a large force there – 6,600 fighting men led by 103 European officers, attended by 19,000 servants and a bazaar department of 12,000 – to march across central India, 'through hostile and unknown regions, from the banks of the Ganges to the western coast of India'[27] as part of his strategy against the Mahrattas.

*Fifty years later Lieutenant de Wend (see note 65, p. 303), exploring Cawnpore, commented that the Rajah's palace was 'the only building of any consequence I could ever find'.

The first bungalows at Cawnpore, 1790. Watercolour by James Blunt, a surveyor.

Gradually the outlines of the camp changed. The tents were replaced by crude, shoddily built huts. No one planned the erection of proper buildings or the design of a permanent cantonment because it seemed unlikely that the troops would remain for long. However, ten years after the original garrison had arrived, Company forces were still in Cawnpore. William Hodges, the portrait painter, on his way to seek work at the court of Oude in 1783, wrote in his diary '. . . I . . . proceeded to Cawnpoor, a large military station on the Ganges. This is a cantonment for a brigade, amounting, on the war establishment to ten thousand men; and may be considered a great encampment, the men living in huts with their families instead of tents.'[28]

The troops were housed in huts of a kind dictated by the need for haste and the Company's impoverished circumstances. 'The approaching season demanded that the troops should be sheltered immediately, and I have given the necessary orders for doing so with all expedition and with as little expense to the Company as possible,' wrote Eyre Coote, the Commander-in-Chief.[29] The walls were made of matting, with door and window frames

Army Encampment: *watercolour by James Blunt, c.1790.*

of soft yellow mango wood, which was devoured by white ants every rainy season. The roofs were constructed to a common Indian pattern, crossed bamboo poles thatched with elephant grass, called a '*chhappar*' by the local people and a 'chopper' by the British. Each year the ravages of the climate made the huts almost uninhabitable.

It appearing by a report of the state of Cantonments at Cawnpore that the publick buildings there are in a ruinous condition, the Commander in Chief has ordered the Assistant Quarter Master General in the field to give an estimate of the expense necessary to put them in proper repair. In the meantime, the General has ordered the hospitals to be made habitable for the sick. They were represented by the Commanding Officer at Cawnpore to be in so bad a state that the men's lives were endangered in them.[30]

One survey begins, 'These barracks were repaired last year but they are again in bad condition',[31] and, goes on to list defective standards, doors, windows and 'choppers' in the barracks of every battalion.

The Commander-in-Chief, Major-General Stibbert, writing to Warren Hastings in 1784, remarked that 'a considerable saving would have accrued to the Company if, instead of the present temporary barracks, small brick ranges with terraced roofs had been erected at Cawnpore for the soldiers; and when that station was fixed on in 1778 for a Cantonment, could I have foreseen that it would have continued so for the period it has, and that the expense for repairs would have been so large and constant, I certainly should have proposed that mode.'[32]

The officers' living conditions were a little less harsh, although still primitive. They had to provide their own lodgings and built bungalows at selected sites overlooking the river. These were consequently scattered and far apart and it was necessary to hire *chowkidars* to protect them. 'Whoever pays the *chowkidars* is secure, whoever neglects to hire them, is plundered.' There was danger not only from thieves but from wolves. It was reported in 1785, that 'The vicinity of Caunpore has been for some time infested by wolves. These savage animals . . . not only frequently carried off children, but actually attacked the sentries on their posts. Three of these monsters attacked a sentinel, who after shooting one and dispatching another with his bayonet, was overpowered by the third and killed at his post.'[33]

The bungalows for the officers were very simple affairs, built of

Bangla, Cawnpoor: *sketch by Captain Robert Smith, c.1828. 'The house was built of cucha brick, and thatched, but being whitewashed inside as well as out had a neat appearance; it contained a large room in the centre 30 feet by 20, approached and lighted by no less than ten doors which were generally kept open for the free circulation of air, excepting that blinds called cheeks, were hung up to keep out the insects, and other flying vermin in the evening. In front of the house was a raised puckah platform called a choubootra which it is usual to have watered and chairs were placed in the evening to smoke cheroots or the hookah, and where I used often at night have my bed taken to sleep, as the most elevated and coolest spot in the compound.'*

sun-baked mud bricks with walls of considerable thickness for the sake of coolness. The plan of the bungalow was a large central room to serve as eating and sitting room, with rooms at each corner for sleeping. The whole was covered with a thatch that came low on each side giving the building the appearance of a beehive. The space between the corner rooms was left open as verandahs, somewhere to sit in the evening. Furniture was of the simplest: straight-backed chairs, tables and beds arranged well away from the walls to avoid termites. Clothes and possessions were kept in boxes. The cook house and 'necessary' were in the compound near the outhouses.

Fresh meat and vegetables were scarce, the climate was debilitating and the death rate was very high. For much of the time there was no official duty and the men had to find their own amusements.

As the practice of feeding beef, mutton pork and poultry was not then introduced, their tables were very poorly supplied; even vegetables were not to be had; though an article indispensably necessary in this climate. These inconveniences were aggravated by a constant routine of irregularity. After dinner it was the usual custom to go to sleep, in the hottest time of the day; for this every party was awakened in the evening, to partake of a supper, which protracted a drunken sederunt till a late hour of the next morning. Midst continued repletion, and frequent irregularity, the climate operated with fatal influence . . . late hours and hard drinking induced gaming which prevailed to a degree ruinous to many individuals.[34]

It was not an easy way of life for the officers. On the one hand they found themselves severely limited by the scarcity of goods and on the other caught by the protocol of Eastern customs. A young surgeon, whose pay and allowance amounted to £900 a year, about the same as a captain in the Army, complained that it was impossible to convey an idea of the extravagant manner in which life was lived.

Though the real necessaries of life are remarkably cheap, yet our expenses nearly equal our incomes. My servants alone, and I am thought an economist, stand me above £200 sterling per Annum. It is indeed the heaviest expense we occur, as no person under the rank of Captain can keep less than 30 servants. Many have twice that number. Our allowances here are much greater than in Bengal as we are paid by the Vizier whose country we are protecting.[35]

The soldiers spent their time very idly. Apart from drill every morning and dismounted drill in the evening, there was absolutely nothing for them to do except sit on their charpoys and play cards or while away the time drinking cheap over-proof arrack, three pints for a rupee. 'There was a great deal of drinking and men dying every day from the effects of drink.' Cholera, dysentery and sunstroke took their toll. 'Deaths amounted to two or three every twenty-four hours. Those that died in the day we buried at

The Begum Sahibah: *Charles Smith, Lucknow 1786. This Indian lady dressed in fine mustard chiffon, leaning against red velvet cushions, was perhaps the* bebee *and 'faithful companion' of one of the early Europeans at Lucknow or Cawnpore.*

sundown, and those that died in the night we buried at 5 a.m. We soon got used to it.'[36]

The first army chaplain on a tour of duty up-country reached Cawnpore in 1780. Before that, the soldiers themselves had buried their dead. The chaplain's first duty was to baptise the children born to soldiers in the camp. The number of European women in Bengal was so few that many of the Company men took Indian *bebees* and lived Indian-style with a zenana. Up-country the shortage of marriageable European women was even more acute. A contemporary wrote scornfully from Cawnpore: 'Most of the

European women here are mere adventuresses from the Milliners' shops on Ludgate Hill and some even from Covent Garden and Old Drury. They possess neither sentiment nor education, and are so intoxicated by their sudden elevation, that a sensible man can only regard them with indignation and contempt.'[37] It is not surprising that many men set up house with an Indian *bebee*.[38] While the liaisons in well-to-do circles between officers and Indian ladies of respectable families were generally longstanding and tender relationships, the keeping of native women among the junior officers and private soldiers created many problems, in particular over the upbringing of the children, many of whom were abandoned to the care of their mothers.

On the first baptismal return from Cawnpore, only fathers' names are given, indicating that the mothers were native and unmarried. On a roughly scribbled list the chaplain recorded the names of twenty-five children baptised on 18 June 1780; the following day he baptised eighty-nine. It was the hottest time of the year and the scene in camp must have presented a ludicrous side. The chaplain was so short of time that the entries on the first day omit the ages of the children, but on the second day he noted five adults (perhaps some of the soldiers' *bebees*), and children varying in age from infancy to twelve years. Some men brought two or three children with them for baptism. Orphans were given cruelly comical surnames, such as Rupee, Burma and Dhoby.[39]

Drinking, gambling and sexual licence were by way of compensation to the soldiers for living in highly unpleasant surroundings, a life that was dangerous and idle by turns. A further compensation was the men's vision of themselves as part of a network of British enterprise and military success that spread all over the world. The Company maintained the troops' morale and fostered their sense of closeness to 'home' with reports of the latest events in Europe. When the Mahratta fortress at Gwalior fell in 1780, the Board issued this Minute with instructions for a royal salute and three volleys from the troops to be fired at each station of the Army. It was a form of political advertising:

News of the prosperous course of the British arms opposed to the united strength of France and Spain is to be made known at every military station of the army, that all may participate in these events so favourable to the interests of the British Empire and to the honour of the British name. While such occasions of mutual felicitations are afforded us from home, the operation of the Hon. Company's forces during the war in which they have been engaged with the Mahratta State have contributed no less to raise our nation's reputation in India and to prove that no accumulation of difficulties nor combination of enemies can produce any other effect on the power of the British nation than to display the innate vigour of its constitution, and to excite the spirit of its subjects to a more animated exertion.[40]

Sir William Blair and his wife seated outside their bungalow at Cawnpore: John Zoffany, Cawnpore 1786. The Blairs' elder daughter, Jane, plays one of Handel's sonatas at the square pianoforte while the younger daughter, Maria, plays with a cat held by a young Indian girl.

In this frame of mind, the less dissipated of the officers at Cawnpore carried out their duties and took their exercise in the winter months, riding, or going out with a gun into the surrounding district to hunt small game. There in the fields and villages they conversed with the ryots, observing their wretched state and the harsh measures employed by the officials of the Nawab to extract revenue and collect grain. Since the beginning of Moghul times the collection of revenue had been organised by Amils who were responsible to local governors. Three-quarters of the public revenue came from the land. Revenue was also collected at *gunges* on merchandise in transit. 'Almost every petty Raja in all the great lines of communication had his toll platform for the purpose of collecting transit duties on all merchandise passing through his territory, whilst cesses [taxes] were levied on all the products of agriculture and home manufacture, as well as on the exercise of all kinds of trade and handicrafts . . . sweetsellers, grocers, shop

keepers, weavers, fishermen, toddy and date trees were all taxed.[41] The
Rajah was subsequently taxed by the Amil, who in turn paid the revenue to
the Nawab Vizier.

People who could not pay their taxes borrowed what they owed from the
money lenders – the *shroffs* – and some families were indebted to *shroffs* from
one generation to another, passing on an ever-increasing debt to their
children. To the Indians, the system was sanctioned by time-honoured
practice and hitherto by the compliance of the ryots. To English eyes,
however, the impossibility of ever getting free from such claims seemed
unfairly oppressive on the ryots: their remedy was that in debts outstanding
for fifty years, the debtor should pay part of the sum and be forgiven the rest.
Here was an opportunity for the officers to re-organise the *gunges* to their
own advantage while at the same time indulging a love of efficiency and
taking the part of the underdog. The difference between the Eastern and
Western attitudes to justice and debt were immense: both sides misunderstood each other.

The Officers and Gentlemen who are at Cawnpore and Futtyghur . . . and other
places, by different Means act very tyranically and oppressively towards the Amils
and Ryots and Inhabitants, and to those who require a Dustack they give it with their
own seals affixed and send for the Amils and punish them.
    If they say anything the Gentlemen make use of but two words, one, that it is for
the Brigade, and the second that it is to administer justice. . . . The Gentlemen have
established Gunges for their own Advantage. . . . The collections of the Customs
from all Quarters they have stopped and collect them at their own Gunges. . . .
They have established Gunges where there never were any, and where there were,
those they have abolished. . . . Major Briscoe has established a Gunge which is
rented out for Rs 45,000 and has stopped the Ghauts round about. . . . The
Merchants coming from Cashmere and Jehanabad and bringing shawls and other
goods and spices etc. from all Quarters he ordered to his Gunge and collects the
duties from the Amils. . . . From this conduct at Cawnpore, Futtyghur etc. the
Duties from the zillahs of Cora and Ihtawa are destroyed and occasions a loss of three
Lacks [sic] of Rupees. . . . In this country formerly, and even now, whatever is to be
received or paid among the Zemindars, Ryots and Inhabitants of the Cities . . .
neither those who can pay, or those who cannot, ever make any excuse to the
Shroffs, but when they could pay they did. In old Debts of fifty years whoever
complain to the Gentlemen they agree that they shall pay one quarter and send
Dustack and sepoys to all the Amils. . . . They send for every Body to do them
justice, confine them, and say they will settle the business. So many and numerous
are these calamities.[42]

On the other hand the English found the Nawab's attitude strangely
frivolous. Gabriel Harper, who had been appointed to the Court of Oude to
act as an intermediary for the Company with the Nawab, reported, 'Sujah
Dowlah continues . . . the most idle life imaginable. His chiefs are forbid his

presence and consequently much disgruntled, very few of the officers of his household have admittance to his Durbar and none without particular leave. He spends his time in childish amusements in his garden amongst his women and in the company of two or three favourite eunuchs.'[43]

Gabriel Harper and the officers and gentlemen at Cawnpore shared the Westerner's belief in his own power to determine his fate. Sujah Dowlah lived a fatalistic existence dictated by the Eastern experience of life lived in unpredictable and apparently uncontrollable circumstances. A modern psychologist has pinpointed this distinction:

Westerners measure time by action and outstanding actions are recorded as history. In contrast, India has never produced a written history. The Hindustani never troubled to make detailed chronological records of their national development, for they lived in a time domain characterised by a changeless sense of ever-becoming. To Westerners, Indians may seem lacking in urgency. Their universe, world, and social order are eternal; personal life is only a sample of a succession of lives, repeating themselves endlessly. Transmigration of souls and perpetual re-birth make meaningless any quantitative view of a particular period of time. Life, infinitely recycled, makes history less significant, and an individual's biography is merely a transient moment in the process.[44]

This fundamental difference in outlook was to bedevil relations between Oude and the Company for as long as the Company's Raj lasted. It led eventually to the annexation of Oude in 1856, and so to the Mutiny, in which the legacy of resentment and incomprehension played a significant part.

The First British Traders in Cawnpore

Trade between England and India was in the strictest sense vested in the East India Company. No British subject either abroad or at home could embark on it, except with the express permission of the Company, while the commerce of foreigners was forbidden. Ships known as East Indiamen were commissioned by the Company for their trade with the Far East. The commanders and officers of the East Indiamen, by an indulgence of ancient practice, were allowed to occupy a certain proportion of tonnage freight free, according to their respective ranks. This privilege of private trade was very lucrative. Captain Eastwick, an eighteenth-century mariner, noted that 'the gains to a prudent commander averaged from £4,000 to £5,000 a voyage, sometimes perhaps falling as low as £2,000, but at others rising to £10,000 or £12,000 and three or four voyages assured any man a very handsome fortune.'[45]

The captain of an East Indiaman with a view to taking full advantage of the privilege granted him by the Company, would generally come to an agreement with a shopkeeper in Calcutta to buy his goods on arrival. The 'Europe shop keepers' in Calcutta, many of whom also had auction rooms, so that they were both buyers and sellers, were in a very favourable position, and permission to proceed to India to reside in Bengal for the purpose of private trade and to set up as a Europe shop keeper was keenly sought and granted only by licence.

Petitions 'praying permission to proceed to India' [46] were considered by the Court of Directors. If the sponsors were approved, a sum in security was stipulated, often as much as £500, and a bond drawn up by which the trader was 'held and firmly bound unto the United Company of Merchants of England trading to the East Indies'.

For information on the state of the market, the pages of *Oriental Commerce* were full of statistics and advice to would-be traders. [47] The largest imports into Bengal, after treasure, were wines and spirits – it was a thirsty country. Glass, cutlery, carriages, hosiery, malt liquors, oilman's stores, saddlery, woollens and metals were all high on the import list. Of the goods exported from Bengal by far the largest in quantity was indigo, used for dyes. A long way behind came raw silk, piece goods and cotton.

Advice on articles suitable for the Bengal market reveal the life of those times. Men wore boots on all occasions: in the hot weather they were made of hessian. Furniture had to be solidly built to stand up to the extremes of climate. Candles were supplied with shades to protect the light from the insects, and elaborate crystal lustres and girandoles were in demand for entertaining. Letters were written with transparent quills sharpened by penknives; billiards, backgammon and battledore were played to pass the time, and children's toys were mostly made of tin. It seemed that every household used Raspini's dentifrice and best Windsor soap.

Most money was to be made in consumer goods. There was always a demand for perishable goods because 'whether sold or not, if the inhabitants do not consume the climate soon does!' Permission to trade privately in such goods was given so sparingly by the Company that determined men found another way: they signed on as a crew member of a Company ship, and while the vessel was refitting in Madras or Calcutta they jumped ship and 'ran the country'. On the *William Pitt*, an East Indiaman that made the voyage to India in 1786, out of a crew of 133 the captain had to record that 29 members had 'jumped ship' at Bengal. The Company was alarmed at the number of illegal immigrants.

The frequency of desertion of persons in different stations from the freighted ships in our service make it necessary that some effectual means be adopted to prevent the like in future . . . the persons so leaving their ships remain in India and procure appointments, sometimes in preference but always to the prejudice of those who proceed thither with our permission.[48]

The Company acted firmly to protect its own interest. An edict went out in the *Calcutta Gazette* requiring all persons to register their names and occupations and give both the name of the ship on which they came out and of its commander and the year of their voyage. The result was that, almost without exception, the entry of each man into India could and still can, be checked.[49]

In Cawnpore the first traders were those attracted to the Army camp to supply its many needs. Indian merchants, tradesmen, servants flocked to serve the soldiers. William Tennant, Chaplain to the Company, visiting Cawnpore in 1798, noted how the establishment of a European cantonment attracted to it both trade and a large labour force, and improved the amenities of the district.

No inconsiderable portion of the pay of the army reverts to the same source from which it was drawn, to the farmer for his cattle, grain, and vegetables, and to the artificer for his labour. Hence agriculture in the vicinity of Caunpore has profited by the stimulus of an European market and high prices. Not only Indian corn, but gram, barley, and wheat are cultivated to an extent equal to the demand. Turnips cabbage and European vegetables, are at this season in great abundance, not only in the gardens of officers, but in the fields cultivated by the natives. Grapes, peaches with a profusion of fruit, have long since been supplied by the Europeans.[50]

Calcutta shopkeepers were also keen to exploit the opportunities provided by this new market. Some sent Europe goods, as they were called, up river; others, more venturesome, decided to go themselves, and set up in trade in whatever commodity seemed most profitable. Their prospects were not entirely rosy, for they faced a number of drawbacks. The region round Cawnpore was not yet British territory and therefore was not subject to the Company's jurisdiction: there could be no legal redress there for civil or criminal cases. It was the obvious refuge for illegal immigrants – those who had 'jumped ship' – and for men in trouble with the Company or the law. The Company consequently sought to restrict such traffic with a strictly applied system of passports. Every trader, ambitious to go up country, had to apply for one, unless he were country born. In December 1793 John Shepherd petitioned for a passport, being as he said, '. . . desirous of obtaining the permission of Govt. to proceed to Cawnpore with an Investment of Europe Articles to be disposed of there and at the intervening Stations of the Army. My conduct in this Country has been such, as I trust, gives me hopes to look up to the Protection of Govt. and I feel confident the Hon. Govn. Gen. in Council will grant the indulgence I most respectfully solicit.'[51]

Some of the adventurers were reported to be enrolling themselves in the Mahratta armies or attaching themselves to the fabulous court of Oude, and so a strict watch was kept at the stations through which travellers had to pass to reach the interior.

The legal traveller, when he had obtained his passport, had then to find a way of reaching his chosen destination. His possibilities were limited by the climate, the difficulty and strangeness of the terrain, and the distance: from Calcutta to Cawnpore by river was 800 miles. There were three ways of travelling: by dak, by marching, and by river. Marching was only practicable in the cold weather and was not really a civilian option. A voyage by river was best arranged during the rainy season when the river was in full spate. Travel by dak could be undertaken at most times of the year but was very slow and uncomfortable. The ordinary traveller had to choose between the river and the dak. Travelling by river was cheaper and more comfortable, but it had its hazards, as the Revd F. A. Dawson discovered: 'The

A budgerow on the Ganges: Company painting on mica.

voyage up the Ganges is a far more dangerous affair than that from England to Calcutta – I had the misfortune to lose my baggage and stores, the vessel having capsized in a heavy squall. Two of my servants were drowned, but I happened at the time to be in another vessel ahead.'[52] John Stewart, writing in 1785 from Cawnpore, where he had arrived to take up his appointment as surgeon in charge of the Sepoy Hospital of the 3rd Brigade, had a less disagreeable experience:

After a voyage of four months on the river Ganges arrived safely at this station. The length of this voyage will astonish you as our distance from Calcutta does not exceed a thousand miles but the windings of the river and the necessity of having our boats dragged the greatest part of the way by men, partly accounts for the length of the voyage. Indeed our party consisting of six gentlemen and two agreeable ladies, was so happy that we were in no haste to dissolve it. We were each supplied with three boats for ourselves, our servants and baggage and had each an allowance of about £20 per month to defray the expense of them which I assure you was scarcely sufficient such was the style in which we travelled.'[53]

The dak consisted of a palanquin – an oblong box supported by poles. Inside the traveller lay full length, with his baggage in boxes piled on top of the roof. The traveller was carried by eight bearers who were changed every ten miles. A hundred miles could be covered in this way every twenty-four

The palanquin and bearers camp under a tree on one stage of the journey by dak: Company painting on mica.

hours and the journey from Calcutta to Cawnpore was reckoned an eight-day journey. The bearers kept up their jog trot all through the night while the traveller lay full length on a comfortable couch. At night the palanquin was accompanied by armed guards with torches, to keep off thieves and wild animals.

Once they had made the journey up-country, the traders had to find suitable premises and warehouses with access to the river. They were then ready to advertise their new businesses in the Calcutta papers. This notice sent from Cawnpore on 21 April 1796 appeared in the *Calcutta Gazette* only two weeks later:

Mr George Birch, an old Resident in India, and many years in this part of the country, begs leave to acquaint his Friends and the public in general, that he proposes to transact business at this place on COMMISSION, at the established rates that the Agency Houses charge in Calcutta, either in the purchase or sale of goods not prohibited by Government.

He will also undertake to receive Packages and Parcels of all kinds and forward them up or down the Country by Land or by Water, at a moderate compensation for his trouble. Mr B is conveniently situated for this kind of business; his House being close on the Banks of the Ganges, with good Godowns and a safe Ghaut to land goods and load Boats at. He requests the favour of those that may honour him with their commissions to be full and explicit in their instructions, and they may rest assured, strictest attention will be paid to them.[54]

GEORGE BIRCH

George Birch was one of the earliest traders resident in Cawnpore. The first official list of traders is dated 1804, but it is quite probable that the census was incomplete. Against each man's name was entered the place of his birth, the year in which he had arrived in India, his trade and the manner in which permission had been granted him to travel up-country.

FIRST CAWNPORE RESIDENTS (NON–OFFICIAL CIVILIANS) TO BE RECORDED, 1804.

Edward Willson England. . . . Merchant 17 years Came up-country by a pass from Lord Cornwallis 7 July 1798 and in 1801 had permission by a public letter from Marquis Wellesley to reside up the Country
Andrew Mackintosh North Britain Merchant 1789
Robert Bailie Ireland Trader 1777 Govt. of Bombay
John Hunter Great Britain Merchant 1801
Matthew Featherstone Head Clerk Pay Office 1783 Sir John Shore
James Murray England Trader 1785 authorised by Col. Scott in Lucnow [sic]
James Gowan Londonderry Monthly writer 1786
Joseph Tracchino Corsica Tavern Keeper 1779
Archibald Finlayson Stirling in North Britain Trader 1796[55]

Most of these early traders concentrated on the sale of Europe goods brought up river from Calcutta, but one of them, Robert Bailie, discovered a line of business that seemed more profitable – the hire of boats and the buying and selling of bungalows to military men as they passed through the station. When a detachment arrived in Cawnpore, the officers had to rent or buy bungalows at whatever price they were available. When orders came for the detachment to take up field duties, the officers then had to sell their houses for whatever they could get. It seemed that Mr Bailie was on to a good thing, but he rapidly encountered difficulties.

Many of the officers heavily overdrew their pay and went off for field service owing him large sums. Because Cawnpore was outside the Company's jurisdiction, he had no means of redress. Furthermore, his backer in Calcutta, Mr Joys, who had financed his venture, was waiting for repayment of the money and began to believe that Robert Bailie intended to abscond with it. Mr Joys sent an official complaint to the court in Calcutta and lengthy proceedings followed.

In vain Robert Bailie protested, 'Unless your Hon. Board will be so humane as to interpose the same authority in my favour, and oblige these gentlemen who are indebted to me to do me justice it will be out of my power to pay my creditors immediately, though I have double the sum due to me that I owe, exclusive of my stock of trade, boats etc . . . I beg leave to observe to your Hon. Board that when I have applied for my property to many of the gentlemen who owe me money these years past, I have been insulted by some, and others have put me off with pay and *batta* bills.' Robert Bailie was ordered to Calcutta and his passport and licence revoked by the Governor-General in Council. On 2 September 1788 he appealed to the Commander-in-Chief, Lord Cornwallis, not to act on the order:

If I am sent away . . . it will be impossible for me to Collect my Debts . . . besides the irreparable injury I will suffer by being removed from this place where my Effects are, in Bungalows, Boats and shop goods; I should lose the hiring of my Bungalows to the Brigade coming up, and my Boats to the Brigade going down, if your Lordship will out of your great humanity order a Committee to inspect into my affairs here, they will find double the property I owe. . . . I sent the Account of twelve thousand rupees, I could have sent a schedule of above Thirty thousand I shall collect in before the end of this year.[56]

Fortunately, Bailie's appeal came at a time when the Commander-in-Chief was concerned about 'a proper spirit of military subordination' in the Army, the lack of which he attributed to 'habits of dissipation and expense'. Lord Cornwallis intervened on Robert Bailie's behalf, publishing a bulletin in the *Calcutta Gazette*:[57]

Mr Bailie has stated that he is rendered incapable of doing justice to others, by finding it impracticable, by any means in his power, to recover certain sums that are due to him by Military gentlemen, of whose names and debts he has transmitted a list, accompanied with an application for assistance to Lord Cornwallis as Commander-in-Chief.

Lord Cornwallis, on perusing that list, has seen with much concern that the greatest part of it consists of the names of Subaltern Officers, and he is sorry to say that he could not avoid receiving a very unfavourable impression of their private conduct from this observation. Because, knowing as he does that their allowances are superior to those of similar rank in any other Army in the world, and that those allowances are found amply sufficient, by men of common prudence, to supply all reasonable wants of gentlemen in that early period of service, he is obliged to conclude that their debts can only have been contracted by dissipation and extravagance.

Such being Lord Cornwallis' sentiments, he would be conscious of a criminal neglect of duty if he did not interpose his authority as Commander-in-Chief, to endeavour to put a stop to practices which are hurtful to society and ruinous to Military discipline.

It is no part of his intention, nor is it his province, to enter into any examination of those accounts, but he gives this public notice, that he has recommended to Mr Bailie to apply to the Supreme Court of Judicature for legal assistance in the recovery of the debts that are due to him by gentlemen who are now stationed within the Provinces, and that he has also assured him, that if he finds it necessary to repeat his complaints against Officers now at the field stations after three months from this date, he will remove such Officers immediately, and appoint them to the Regiments within the Provinces, that they may be amenable to any decree which he may obtain against them in the Supreme Court.

As a result, Robert Bailie[58] was able to exact what he owed and pay his own debts. His reputation and livelihood were safe, and he returned to Cawnpore to prosper. His name crops up in the records from time to time, but only in such minor matters as a complaint that excessive customs dues had been charged on a pair of Calcutta boots. Meanwhile, trade such as his had been firmly established at Cawnpore, and now, with the protection of the Commander-in-Chief, it was on a more secure footing.

2

John Maxwell Comes to India
1786 — 1800

━━━━

His Home in Scotland

Eight years before the first English soldiers camped at Cawnpore, John Maxwell was born. The story of the important connection between the Maxwell family and Cawnpore begins with his birth in Scotland. His father, Mr John Maxwell, was the Minister of New Machar, a small village some ten miles to the north-west of Aberdeen. John Maxwell the younger was born at the Manse on 24 November 1762.[1]

New Machar was a rural parish and its Manse was surrounded by the fertile agricultural lands of two or three country mansions and small farms. In winter, when the trees were bare, it was possible to see great distances across the low hummocky hills to the valley of the Don, to Benachie and the Grampians remote in the background. Few visitors passed that way. The Church was the centre of a simple social life as well as the religious life of the countryside, and the Minister commanded the respect of all. Twice a year there was a season of communion, each lasting three weeks, and people came to the church from far away, riding in carts and wearing their best clothes. The mill at the Manse had to provide for their needs and was busy all day long, grinding grain to make flour to be baked into bread.

When John Maxwell was ten, the pattern of his life was abruptly changed by his father's sudden death. The Minister died on 7 March 1773, aged about fifty-five years, and was buried in the churchyard close to the porch of his church. As the only son, young John Maxwell grew up in the knowledge that his mother and six sisters would depend on him for support in the future.[2]

The family moved to Aberdeen and made plans for his education. He was to go, as his grandfather had done, to Marischal College, one of the two universities in Aberdeen at that time. It was usual for boys to enter at the age of fifteen or sixteen and to remain for four years. The College records give John Maxwell's age as fourteen when he joined and his residence lasted only

New Machar Church, 1970

three years, which suggests that there was an urgent need for him to start earning his living and that money for his education was limited. At the age of seventeen, his schooling over, he had to find himself a career.[3]

Every man who took the decision to seek his fortune in India, leaving his home and family, often for ever, and facing great uncertainties and danger, must have been given the idea by some circumstance that made the venture seem attractive. In 1788 Barbara Maxwell, one of John Maxwell's sisters, married Alexander Burnett, Quarterly Deputy Commissary General, Honourable East India Company's Service, who was described as 'late of Bengall in the East Indies'. The Burnett family lived at Elrick House, the big house in the neighbourhood of New Machar Manse. It is possible that at Elrick House John Maxwell's imagination was first stirred by stories of the fabulous East.[4]

In the six years that passed between John Maxwell's leaving Marischal College and setting sail for India in 1786 nothing is known of his activities. It is likely that, as a first step, he went to London. There is just one clue. Years later, when he drew up a will, he referred to his old and worthy friend 'Martin of Lloyd's Coffee House' – possibly Adam Martin, son of Robert Martin of Aberdeen, who obtained his Master's degree at Marischal College in 1780.[5] John Maxwell turned to commerce. Countless Scots left their country to seek their livelihood abroad. They took with them a toughness learnt in that harsh environment, a sense of clan brotherhood, a respect for learning and a stern sense of duty to God. They were successful pioneers the world over.

That a man could be identified by his surname at Lloyd's Coffee House is an indication of the smallness and intimacy of the group who met to do business there. In 1774 Lloyds moved to the Royal Exchange in London. Here young men such as John Maxwell met to exchange ideas, discuss politics, and to hear the latest news from the commanders of the East India Company's ships: which ones had docked; what cargo they carried; the prices obtained for the merchandise; which vessels were lost at sea, and whether by storm or enemy action.

John Maxwell resolved to go to India. He decided to take the chance of setting up as a Europe shop keeper in Calcutta. First he sought introductions to business connections in Calcutta. Then he obtained a licence through a London contact who would plead his cause with the Company men and guarantee his good behaviour. Eventually his efforts were successful and he was given an introduction to a trader, Alexander Davidson, who had been established for two years as a shopkeeper in Calcutta and who now invited him to become a business partner. John Maxwell sailed for India on the *William Pitt*, an East Indiaman commanded by Captain Charles Mitchell. It was March 1786.[6]

The Voyage Out

As soon as it was established that John Maxwell would sail for India on the *William Pitt*, preparations for the long voyage were begun. A travellers' guide advised the voyager to equip himself before leaving England with a considerable outfit: many dozens of shirts, all of calico, since this was said to be cooler than linen; some of fine quality and frilled; while about four dozen were required with sleeves to the hips to do double duty as sleeping shirts. On the voyage a boat cloak and pantaloons were considered indispensable. Velvet stocks, which tied with ribbon, and fine linen neck handkerchiefs were all the fashion and unobtainable in India except at huge cost.[7]

At such time of parting each member of the family presented their dear one with a keepsake; some gift lovingly worked or devised, to recall the donor to his remembrance in the distant land for which he was about to sail. These precious possessions probably included a Bible, a portable wooden box to serve as a writing desk and a Persian grammar and dictionary to study on the voyage.[8] Family gifts could not, however, lessen the immense distance that would separate him from everything familiar. For John Maxwell, like many such young men, the anxious, hopeful parting was a final one: he was never to see his home or family again.

The *William Pitt* was one of the fleet of East Indiamen chartered and freighted by the East India Company. Besides the usual complement of seamen – mates, boatswains, quartermasters, a purser, a gunner, a surgeon and many ordinary seamen – a sailing vessel in the eighteenth century carried tradesmen to supply her needs on the voyage: carpenters, coopers, caulkers, sailmakers, cooks, an armourer, a butcher for the livestock and several servants. Rates of pay varied from £10 per month[9] for the Captain for the fourteen-month round trip, to 20 shillings per month for the seamen. The passenger's fare was £100, and this secured a seat at the Captain's table.

The crew embarked at Gravesend, but John Maxwell and other passengers joined the ship further along the estuary, in the Downs, because it took several days to load the cargo and provision the vessel for the long voyage: 'Ship's Log 9 March 1786. Strong gales from the NW with snow. Received on board 50 casks of provisions for the ship's use and sundry other stores. Employed stowing them in the hold and about the rigging. Also received on board a boatload of private trade.' When everything was ready the Blue Peter was flown from the foretop masthead as a signal for the passengers to go aboard. From the beach they climbed into small dinghies which were rowed out to the ship. The sides of the vessel towered above them, ropes were thrown down on the sheltered side and, at the height of the wave, the passenger caught hold of one and ascended by a rope ladder. On deck, all hands were preparing to cast off. The ship was now ready for sea and the wind sufficiently fair. The Captain wrote in his log, 'From London towards India.'

For a ship's passenger the journey out was four or five months of enforced idleness in uncomfortable conditions, suspended between his old life and the new. John Maxwell spent the greater part of the voyage below deck in his cabin, which he shared with five or six other passengers. Here it was too dark to read; the air, which entered through one porthole and a scuttle and then only when the sea was calm enough to allow them to be opened, was suffocating and rank; the noise was tremendous. John Maxwell's trunk served him as table and chair and held his pewter basin. It contained all the worldly goods he wished to take with him.

There now began the long monotony of the voyage. Surprisingly, food was abundant and provided in some variety: joints of mutton and pork,

OPPOSITE *Ship's log: voyage of the* William Pitt, *1786.*

Courses	K	F	Winds &c	Tuesday the 1st day of Augt	17
			Throughout Variable Breezes with Rain at times. Delivered last of the Honble Company's Cargo. Bent the Foresail & Topsail. Received on Board Water, Started it in the Forehold the Spritsail Topsail. Caulker Caulking Fall. Entered on Board Wm Gowland, Wm Merritt, Wm Mitchell Thomas Wilcocks Seamen, Confined Thomas Smith Quarter in Irons for Striking the Fifth Officer		
Wednesday	2d		Land & Sea Breezes with fair Weather. Received on board 120 Recruits on account of the Company, Passed for Bengal. & 15 Chitts of Water. Washed the Gun Deck, Blacked the Bends, & bent the Mainsail and Main Topsail		
Thursday	3d		Variable Winds throughout with frequent Squalls & heavy A.M. Cleared Hause Unmoored Ship, & hove in to half Cable on the Best Bower. Received on board Passengers Baggage. Employed Starting of Water and clearing Ship for Sea		

	D		MD	Lat D	K.Lo	Lo.in	Bearing & Dist

Courses	K	F	Winds &c	Friday the 4 day of Augt	17
			Fresh Breezes & Cloudy Weather. At 7 A.M. weighed with the Land Wind, stood out into 10 fm & came to with the Best Bower, the Flagstaff bearing NWbW distance about 3 Miles Off Shore. Employed receiving on board Passengers Baggage &c Hoisted in the Boats Run from the Ship David Fostine, John Smith Saul Kier, James Willson Seamen & Wm Muirhead Quarter Master — This Log ends at Noon		

curries and pilaus, chickens and ducks, and on Sunday, turkeys and hams. On arrival at Calcutta passengers were entitled to complain and report the Captain if he kept an inadequate table. Chairs and tables were strapped to staples in the deck, and the passengers rested their plates on green baize cushions intended to stop them from slipping. The crew fared less well on a diet composed chiefly of salt junk (meat) except for one occasion when there was an enormous sea pie made of albatross and sea fowl taken with hook and line. On Sundays there was some interruption of the tedium. The Captain held divine service and Mr Begbie, the Purser, assembled a few people in his cabin' where, 'we read the Bible and were afterwards regaled with gingerbread and a glass of wine or cherry brandy.'

The weather improved once the ship had rounded Spain. The log records 'pleasant breezes and fair weather with smooth water'. The tradesmen worked on deck: the sailmakers repaired the old sails, making awnings and tarpaulins from them; carpenters shaped new spars; caulkers caulked the water-way seams; while the seamen were set to work washing the decks, disinfecting the lower deck, washing the beams with vinegar, and tarring and blacking the rigging. One of the seamen, William Dingwell, must have struck up an acquaintance with John Maxwell for he jumped ship at Calcutta and went to work as clerk to Davidson and Maxwell and eventually followed John Maxwell up-country to work for him in Cawnpore (see page 112).

The ship was crowded with Irish recruits to the Company Army who lived below deck in extremely cramped conditions, and were never far from mutiny. To keep them busy, they were given an odious task, otherwise reserved for convicts and paupers, known as 'picking oakum', unravelling old pieces of rope and picking out the loose fibres, which were used for caulking seams.

Several deaths at sea were recorded among the recruits and crew. Petty theft was rife; the first night aboard a young midshipman found his greatcoat and hammock had been stolen. Theft was punishable by flogging. On 30 March 1786 the Captain called a consultation of officers and punished George Dawson, a recruit, at the gangway with a dozen lashes for theft. A dozen strokes of the cat o' nine tails was the equivalent of 500 lashes on shore, but even this punishment did not deter others from thieving. When the crew failed in their duties they were subject to 'mastheading' – sitting aloft on the main yardarm, far above the sea, sometimes for hours at a time.

Once round the Cape, the weather and climate were tropical and there were frequent thunderstorms. The log records: '. . . hard gales, excessive heavy squalls and following sea, shipt much water.' But the worst of the

First view of Madras: Fort St George.

voyage was over. The first sight of India was the approach to Madras, which came in view at daylight on 24 July. As the *William Pitt* drew into Madras Roads she fired the customary salute of nine guns; the same number was returned to give her permission to proceed into the harbour. The ceremony stirred the hearts of the passengers; so did the proud sight of seven of the Company's ships riding at anchor: the *General Goddard, Fort William, Ponsborne, London, Worcester, Middlesex* and *Vansittart*. It was exciting and reassuring to see the evidence of British enterprise spread so far.

At Madras the *William Pitt* took on food and water, received some more recruits, delivered the Company's despatches and set sail again for the run up the coast to Calcutta. The approach to Calcutta was a different matter from the entry to Madras harbour. Where the waters of the Ganges met the Indian Ocean the currents were treacherous, and underwater there were drifting sandbanks. No ship dared proceed in the Sandheads without a pilot who sounded the unchartable waters with a line and lead every few yards. The *William Pitt* made the passage without accident and on 14 August 1786 moored at the buoy off Diamond Point. The five months' voyage was ended and the passengers gave thanks to God for bringing them safely thus far, 'and returned sincere acknowledgements to the divine Providence which had watched over so many lives in so long a course across the fathomless and pathless deep'.

The passengers transferred into a *budgerow*, a small covered boat, to complete the sixty miles upriver to Calcutta, looking out all the time for their first sights of this new country. Until a much later date, with the building of the Suez Canal and the coming of the Indian railways, the route to the interior of India was via Calcutta. These first impressions of the city, of the Indian people and their customs, of the way the English lived in Calcutta were common to every European who eventually made his way up-country.

The first sight of Calcutta was at Garden Reach. Here on the right bank

A gentleman dressing, attended by his head bearer and other servants. Illustration by Charles D'Oyly, The Europeans in India, *1813.*

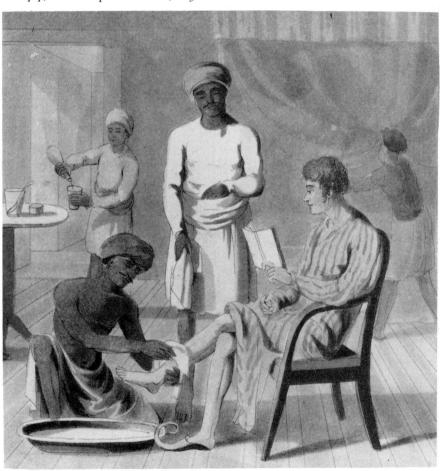

were tall elegant houses, like villas, with porticoes and shuttered windows, set in gardens laid out in English style, sloping down to the river. It made a picturesque scene crowded with a variety of boats from the largest Indiaman to the smallest country craft. At a bend of the river the whole city of Calcutta 'burst upon the eye'.[10] There was a considerable fortress, an Esplanade and beautiful and regular buildings. The evidence of the Company's activities in India was everywhere. Calcutta was unmistakably a busy and prosperous centre for trade. John Maxwell stepped ashore at the Customs wharf, which extended from one end of the fort to the other. There was no outer drawbridge, no sentries on duty, no stopping of baggage. Immense piles of goods of various sorts, imports and exports, lay stacked along the front of the wharf. There were novel and curious sights all around him – Indians bathing decorously and gracefully in the river without removing their clothes; palanquins being carried through the streets; Englishmen out walking, protected from the sun by immense umbrellas, called *chattahs*, six or eight feet wide. A sedate gentleman with what appeared to be the head of a snake in his mouth proved to be smoking an innocent Bengal hookah.

John Maxwell was conducted to the Europe shop of Alexander Davidson where he was warmly welcomed and shown upstairs to a spacious suite of apartments. Here he was greeted by a bewildering number of servants and that evening, in contrast to the hardships of the voyage, experienced 'the luxurious and effeminate ways of an Indian life', being put to bed by servants. This was his first night in India; tomorrow he was to start a new life as a partner in Davidson and Maxwell, Europe shop keepers of Court House Street, Calcutta.[11]

Europe Shop Keeper, Calcutta

Court House Street was wide and elegant, in the heart of residential Calcutta. It took its name from the old Court House that stood at the head of the broad thoroughfare, facing the Esplanade with a view beyond it of Fort William. It was a promising site for a shop. Court House Street ran parallel to the river where many ships rode at anchor. The long line of Writers' Buildings, where the Company's book-keeping work on all imports and exports was carried out, connected the Customs House wharfs with Old Court House Street. It was a comparatively simple matter for goods once cleared of Customs to be delivered to Davidson and Maxwell. Their range of commodities, revealed in newspaper advertisements, was wide.

Have just received in commission some REAL CONIAC BRANDY that they can venture to recommend to their friends. It was bottled in France and is allowed to be the best that has been in this country these many years.[12]

Old Court House Street, Calcutta 1778: *engraving by Thomas Daniell,* Views of Calcutta, *No. 9. In a key to this picture William Hickey identified No. 10 as the Library and No. 11 and No. 12 as 'A Europe Shop, that is where all the Europe articles are sold'. It is possible that Davidson and Maxwell were at No. 11.*

Men who came to India were gambling on a quick fortune. It was rumoured that there were so few trades-people in Calcutta that in ten years it was possible to take home £25,000. But in that climate they were staking their lives. Gambling fever entered into everything. Considerable properties, houses and estates, were disposed of by lottery. Davidson and Maxwell offered unusual merchandise for raffle rather than auction:

India Gazette, 3 May 1790: An Elegant NEW EUROPE CHARIOT AND PHAETON (brought out by one of the last Ships) To be Raffled for, at the warehouse of Davidson and Maxwell by Forty Subscribers at one hundred rupees each. The highest of three throws, Doublets, to win the Chariot, and the lowest the Phaeton. NB. The Carriages may be seen at the Warehouse.

They rose to every opportunity that presented itself. In August 1790, the peak sales time of the year, they filled the entire first column of the *India Gazette* with advertisements for an extraordinary selection of goods: 'D and M have purchased and will expose for sale in a few days a very capital and choice investment of Europe Goods brought out in the *Princess Amelia*, Captain Millett.' The long list included 'Jews Beef and Tongue, Boots, shoes and Half Boots from Rymer, Doubled Barrelled guns from Mantons, Pistols by Wogden, fashionable buttons, Shoe and knee buckles, Coffin furniture, Ironhoops, Rod Irons and Ironmongery, Medicines and Medicine Chests, Haberdashery and some elegant Millinery'.

Nor were they slow to see the possibilities of supplying the military outposts up-country, where men starved of English goods would pay large sums for luxuries. Davidson and Maxwell sent boats on the first and fifteenth of every month to the upper stations on the Ganges as far distant as Cawnpore and Fatehgarh. They would engage a *budgerow* and freight it with luxuries such as raspberry jam, pine-cheese and English pickles, which fetched excellent prices. A jar of preserves that sold in London for four shillings could fetch as much as twenty-four and was seldom sold up-country for less than sixteen shillings.[13]

Trade for Davidson and Maxwell proved profitable. They were fortunate to set up in business at a time when attitudes towards private enterprise were broadening. The Governor-General, Warren Hastings, gave a lead to this view; he did not believe the Company trade would suffer as the result of open competition.

. . . I insist upon it, as a fixed and uncontrovertible principle, that commerce can only flourish when it is equal and free. . . . When commerce is left to itself, it will correct its own evils. The private merchant, ever quick-sighted to his interests, will only maintain a competition whilst a profit is to be derived from the trade; and so long as he derives a profit, the Company ought to derive one also.[14]

THROUGH THE NORTHERN PART OF
INDIA, KASHMIRE, AFGHANISTAN, and
PERSIA,
AND INTO RUSSIA,
BY THE CASPIAN SEA;

Containing the Route from Calcutta to Kashmire—
Sketches of Hindoo Mythology—and an abrevi-
ated History of the ROHILLAHS, Shujah-ud-
Dowlah, and the Sicques.

Embellished with a correct Map, explanatory
of the Route.

BY GEORGE FORSTER,

In the Civil Service of the Honourable East India
Company.

This Work will be comprized in two Volumes,
in Quarto, of an elegant Type, and upon superfine
Paper. A certain number of Copies only is intended to be published in India; which will be at the disposal of
MESSRS. FERGUSSON, FAIRLIE, AND CO.

DAVIDSON and MAXWELL,

BEG to inform the Public, that they have now
for Sale, at their Warehouse, all the

C L A R E T,
BROUGHT OUT BY
MR. JAMES CHIPPENDALE,
AND FROM THE FOLLOWING HOUSES:
STOCKDALE,
CARBONELL,
CHATFIELD,
BROWN and WILKINSON,
URQUHART,
PAXTON and ROSS,
MICHIE,
RAIKES, and
ALLAN and SMITH.

All of which, from having been approved by the
first judges in the settlement, they can venture to recommend to their Friends.

DAVIDSON and MAXWELL

BEG to inform the Public that they have just
received an Invoice of PARMAZAN and
other CHEESES,—and
CONFECTIONARY, consisting of
Raspberry Jam—Current Jelly, in large Jars.
Scarlet Strawberry Jam.
Apricot and Quince Marmalade.
Preserved Raspberries.
Brandy Fruits and Hoffman's Ratafia.

Advertisement.

MR. JONES, of Cawnpore, begs Leave to inform the Gentlemen in Bengal, his AGEN-
CY COMMISSION WAREHOUSE, and AUC-
TION ROOM, continue their respective Branches, separately, for ready Money, or Accepted

SALES BY AUCTION.

To be sold by public Auction,

By MOUAT, and Co.

At their Auction-room,

On WEDNESDAY next, the 17th Instant,

A VARIETY OF

Europe and Country Goods,

Particulars will be mentioned in Wednesday's Paper.
Hand Bills will be published.

To be sold by public Auction,

By MOUAT and Co.

At their Auction-room,

On WEDNESDAY next, the 17th Instant,

(Precisely at Twelve o'clock.)

FIVE PIPES OF

MADEIRA WINE,

OF A REAL GOOD QUALITY.

Musters may be had at the Auction-room.

MOUAT, and Co.

HAVE NOW EXPOSED FOR SALE,
AT THEIR WAREHOUSE,

A Consignment of

THE BEST HYSON TEA,

AND

NANKEENS,

BY THE RESOLUTION.

FOR SALE,

BY MOUAT, and Co.

LONDON Particular Madeira, Seven years in India, at per dozen, Sicca Rupees,   25   0
London Market ditto, Four years ditto, per pipe, —   —   —   450   0
Madeira, of a very good quality, Three years in India,   —   —   250   0
Ditto, ditto, per dozen   —   —   16   0
Ditto, ditto,   —   —   —   14   0
Royal Coniac Brandy, per dozen, — — 12   0
Ditto in Casks, per gallon,   —   2   12
Old Jamaica Rum, per dozen   —   10   0
Ditto in Casks per gallon,   —   2   0
French Claret, of a good quality. per dozen, 14   0

Advertisements from the India Gazette, *15 March 1790.*

SALES BY AUCTION.

To be sold by public Auction,

By EDWARD GARDNER,

At his Auction room,

This Day, MONDAY, the 15th of March,

THIRTY maunds of Indigo Seed, of an excel-
lent quality,
Five pipes of real good Madeira,
A pair of square Looking-glasses, 3 feet 3 in. by 1
foot 11 in. in gold burnished frames,
A pair of oval ditto, 2 ft. 5 in. by 1 ft. 8 in.
A silver-mounted Fowling-piece, by Kotland,
Cloths and Cassimeers, of fashionable colours,
Jockey and half Boots,
Glass-ware,
Plain Hunting Saddles,
Wines and Liquors.
And a variety of other ARTICLES.

FOR SALE,

By Messrs. FERGUSSON, FAIRLIE, & Co.

MADEIRA WINE,

OF THE FOLLOWING QUALITIES,

The produce of the Estate of

DONNA GUIOMAR:

	S. Rs.
Old Madeira, at per pipe,	350
A few pipes of London Particular, at per ditto, -	450
London Market, - -	375
India Market, - -	300

An Allowance will be made to Persons who purchase a Quantity.

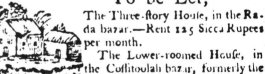

To be Let,

The Three-story House, in the Ra-
da bazar.—Rent 125 Sicca Rupees
per month.
    The Lower-roomed House, in
the Cossitoolah bazar, formerly the
Court of Requests.
The large GARDEN-HOUSE at Kidderpore,
at present occupied by CHARLES GRANT, Esq.
The House to the Eastward of the Play-house,
ately occupied by Captain Forbes.
The House adjoining to the Bankshall, the Property of Andrew Hunter, Esq.

AND

The HOUSE to the Northward of Cutcha Goody
Gaut, with six large commodious Godowns, at
present occupied by Mr. LA BEAUME.

ENQUIRE OF

Messrs. FERGUSSON, FAIRLIE, and Co.

Shopkeeping was John Maxwell's first venture in India, but it had been dictated by expediency. He had aspirations to a more intellectual career; the fact that the library was next door to Davidson and Maxwell gave him the opportunity to enter into an association with a circulating library. In 1788 Messrs Cock Maxwell and Co., Calcutta, put forward a proposal for establishing a library at Berhampore. They planned to circulate books to Dinapore and Cawnpore, provided that sufficient numbers of interested subscribers could be found; the subscription rate to be eight sicca rupees a month, as it was in Calcutta. In particular they hoped to attract 'gentlemen in the medical line . . . with approved ancient and modern authors, on medicine, surgery, anatomy and chemistry'. However, it seems their ideas were ahead of their time because in 1790 the library of Messrs Cock Maxwell in Old Court House Street was up for sale.[15]

This slight clue – that, in spite of the apparent success of Davidson and Maxwell both in Calcutta and up-country, John Maxwell attempted to enter another field through the library – is all we have to go on, but the indication seems to be that he was trying to rise above shopkeeping. His efforts were at last successful: in 1798 he was appointed Editor of the *India Gazette* – a leading newspaper in Calcutta – and he left shopkeeping for ever.

India in the 1790s was still very much a man's country. The number of European women in Calcutta was so few that every spinster and widow was snapped up at once, no matter how limited her charms. 'The number of European women to be found in Bengal and its dependencies cannot amount to two hundred and fifty, while the European male inhabitants of respectability, including military officers, may be taken at about four thousand.'[16] In the circumstances it was inevitable that many Englishmen should adopt the Indian mode of life, setting up a zenana or keeping an Indian *bebee*. Advertisements in the newspapers offering houses for sale referred discreetly to the need to house a Hindustani friend or provide for a 'Black Family'.

House for sale. The small Upper-roomed Garden House, with about five biggahs of grounds, on the road leading from Chowringhee to the Burying Ground, which formerly belonged to the Moravians; it is very private, from the number of trees in the grounds, and having lately received considerable additions and repairs, is well adapted for a Black Family. Apply to Mr Carnac. March 1788[17]

John Maxwell followed this practice. Two children were born to him in Calcutta: a daughter, Agnes Isabel,[18] and a son, Adam. In the baptismal records, Adam is described as illegitimate while Agnes is registered only under her father's name, implying that both children were born of a native mother. On the page in 1793 on which Adam's baptism is recorded, of forty-five baptisms entered, eighteen are of illegitimate children. Adam's Eurasian birth was to be of great importance to the Maxwell family. To prevent the exploitation of the country the Company had drawn up laws prohibiting Europeans from owning more than a small amount of landed property. These laws did not, however, apply to children born of European fathers and native mothers before November 1793. Adam came into this category, known as 'country-born', and was thus able eventually to acquire land in the Cawnpore district.

The British in India adopted many Indian customs, altering their way of life to suit the conditions and climate and morality, but on one point they remained resolute: their children must be sent 'home' for their education. There were good reasons for this practice: the mortality rate among children was very high, and there were yet no facilities for their education in India. But more than that, it was a deep instinct. Although the fathers were cut off from the things they loved most, it seemed vitally important that their children should grow up knowing England as their home. The tradition was established that English children born in India should be sent away to be brought up by relatives in a strange country, sometimes when they were as young as four, but certainly no older than eight. To make it possible, their parents endured great financial burdens and years of anguished separation from them.

Agnes Maxwell sailed for England in 1792, when she was only three years and four months old, accompanied by a native servant called Rose. Six years later, when he was four, Adam too sailed for England. It is likely that the two children were brought up by John Maxwell's unmarried sisters. It must have taken him great courage to part with such young children and to commit them to the long and perilous voyage. However, he was no longer alone in India: soon after Adam's birth, an entry in the marriage register states that John Maxwell married Prudence Stewart in August 1794. At the time of the marriage there is a Robert Stewart, carpenter and coachbuilder, listed as living in Court House Street, and it seems possible that it was his daughter whom John Maxwell married.

Editor of the *India Gazette*

John Maxwell had been married for four years when he took up his appointment as Editor of the *India Gazette* in 1798. His pleasure in his new appointment was counterbalanced by the departure of Adam for England and by his wife's death later that same year. The Editor recorded her death in his newspaper on the following day: 'Prudence, wife of John Maxwell, died

9th May 1798.' The brevity of the announcement seemed to demonstrate his attitude to misfortune.

Sudden and frequent death was familiar to everyone in the East. The forms of death played a prominent part in the continuing lives of the bereaved. Undertakers advertised huge slabs of marble, capable of holding the longest inscriptions, and swathes of black velvet and satin for mourning. South Park Street Cemetery, where Prudence Maxwell was buried, was a much-visited recreation ground for European Calcutta: 'Obelisks and pagodas are erected at great expense; and the whole spot is surrounded by as well turned a walk as those you traverse in Kensington Gardens, ornamented by a double row of aromatic trees which afford a solemn and beautiful shade.'[19]

Familiarity with death did not make it easier to bear. The extremes of the Indian climate do not give that sense of the renewal of life that comes with the cycle of the seasons in a temperate region. Many Europeans in India have felt deprived of that certainty and confidence. John Maxwell must have looked back to that other funeral in New Machar, which had marked the end of his childhood, and measured his achievement since then. He had come to India with such high hopes, to find himself now isolated, a widower, separated from his children. Nevertheless, he had established himself; he had made a little money; he had some good friends and his health. The solution he found to his unhappiness was to throw himself into his work.

At the end of the nineteenth century, the Indian press in Calcutta was still in its infancy. Calcutta's first newspaper had appeared in 1780, set up by James Hickey and known as *Hickey's Gazette*. The *India Gazette* followed later that same year. It consisted of two sheets of about 20 × 12 inches, and came out every Monday. It contained news of the arrival of the latest ships, official communications from the Company, and the reported movements of the various regiments. There were no reporters as such, but members of the public wrote in, describing events of interest, and extracts from their letters were a regular feature. Much space was given over to the Calcutta social scene: descriptions of the balls, theatricals and musical evenings, recording who had attended, what they had worn, what toasts were drunk and how the apartments had been decorated. As far as the libel laws permitted, both public and private figures were taken to task. Literature was represented by clumsy verses occasionally submitted by readers or by extracts from English papers. Whenever a ship arrived the different newspapers vied with each other to be the first to procure the precious bundle of English papers and print the latest European news. One page was devoted to advertisements, both private and commercial.

South Park Street Cemetery, Calcutta, c. 1980.

Publications such as this found a ready market and by 1799 there were seven newspapers being published in Calcutta. Yet despite their contemporary popularity, these papers have been hardly judged by historians. James Mill said, 'In the early portion of its career, the Indian press had been left to follow its own courses, with no other check than that which the law of libel imposed. The character of the papers of early days sufficiently show that the indulgence was abused, and that, while they were useless as vehicles of local information of any value, they were filled with indecorous attacks upon private life and ignorant of public measures.'[20] This is unjust. For while the papers evidently fulfilled an important local need, the editors and proprietors had a limited range of material and they were working under the eye of government at a time when the Company, nervous of the Napoleonic threat and anxious for the security of its foothold in India, was highly sensitive to criticism. Their life was to become more difficult still.

John Maxwell's editorship of the *India Gazette* coincided with the appointment of Richard, Lord Wellesley as Governor-General in 1798.[21] Wellesley took up his appointment, pledged to maintain peace. His vision of India was not of an amicably run trading concern, however, but of an empire with himself at its head. His government was autocratic and formal and he would not tolerate public criticism of his policies. From the moment he arrived in India he was determined to reform private manners.

The first hint of this to affect the press was the introduction of a measure increasing the cost of postage on newspapers sent outside Calcutta. At a time when postage was still paid on delivery, the editors saw that their readership would be limited to the well-to-do. The *India Gazette* protested: 'The great and sacred privilege inherited by the people of this country of a free press may be invaded in various ways . . . we know of none so subtle, so little likely to arouse indignation, but at the same time, so efficacious in its tendency as a gradual advancement of the price of the commodity, so as to draw it imperceptibly from the hands of the great mass of the people and confine it to the few who are opulent and idle . . .'[22]

Matters soon grew worse. The Company had always been sensitive to the presence of the French in India. Now, with Napolean's armies advancing in Egypt, the activities of the French adventurers known to be in the south of India, serving Tippoo Sultan* and the Nizam of Hydrabad, convinced Wellesley that he must go to war with Tippoo in Madras. Mr Bruce, the Editor of the *Asiatic Mirror*, published some comments on the comparative

---

*Tippoo Sultan, the 'Tiger of Mysore', was the son of Haidar Ali, a Muslim adventurer who had conquered the state of Mysore, which had originally been Hindu.

Marquess Wellesley: oil by Robert Home, Calcutta c.1801. Appointed Governor-General 1798. Wellesley had a vision of India that was not of an amicably run trading concern but of an empire with himself at its head.

strength of the European and native peoples. Wellesley took exception to the article, considering it 'thoroughly mischievous and exposing public security to hazard'. He wrote to the Commander-in-Chief, Sir Alured Clarke, in April 1799: 'I shall take an early opportunity of transmitting rules for the conduct of the whole tribe of editors; in the meantime if you cannot tranquillize the editors of this and other mischievous publications, be so good as to suppress their papers by force and send their persons to Europe.'[23]

Facsimile of letter from John Maxwell, Editor of the India Gazette, 1790.

Within a month regulations were issued restricting the publication of newspapers in Calcutta. No newspaper was to be published until it had been previously inspected by the Secretary of Government; no papers were to be published on Sundays; and all editors and proprietors had to declare themselves to the Secretary of Government. The penalty for offending against any of these regulations was immediate embarkation for Europe. The regulations marked the end of a free press in Calcutta.

The censorship was stringent, but the editors had little choice but to accede to the regulations. None of their letters of acknowledgement of the orders expresses anger or frustration; several are subservient in tone. One editor pledged 'I will in every respect conform myself to the directions of government', and another group stated that 'we consider it a duty incumbent in us to comply in every respect to the Regulations of Government.'[24] Even so, they must have been alarmed and disappointed by the limitations placed on their craft. John Maxwell's letter, headed Editor of the *India Gazette*, No. 7 Larkin's Lane, Calcutta to Secretary Barlow, 17 May 1799, is correct and formal, revealing nothing of his opinions.

It is significant that after a brief period, when he took over from the unfortunate Bruce as Editor of the *Asiatic Mirror*, John Maxwell left Calcutta for good and went up-country to seek his living in a different field. The reasons behind his decision are uncertain. What is clear is that he left Calcutta at a time when official interference with private citizens was increasing, and that he settled outside the jurisdiction of the Company. It seems probable that he resented the restrictions on his speech and independence and deliberately sought an occupation and a home where he could be his own master.

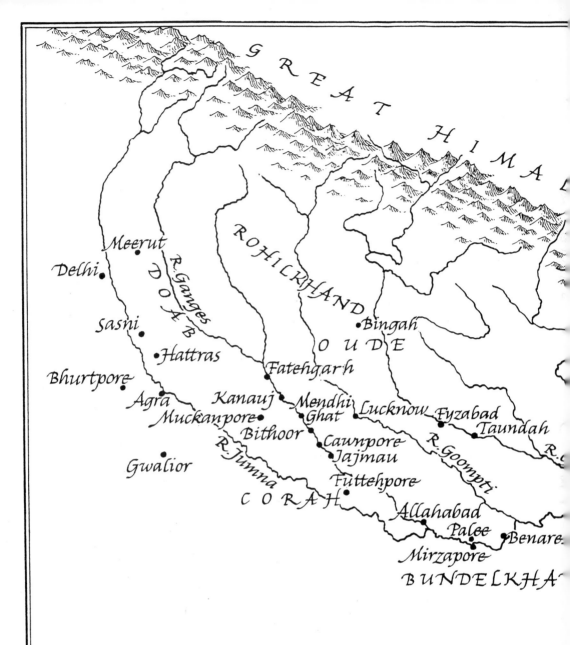

GREAT HIMAL

Meerut

Delhi

DOAB

R. Ganges

ROHILKHAND

Sasni

Hattras

Bhurtpore

Agra

Muckanpore

Kanauj

Bithoor

R. Jumna

Gwalior

CORAH

Bingah

OUDE

Fatehgarh

Mendhi Ghat

Lucknow

Fyzabad

Taundah

R. Goompti

R.

Cawnpore

Jajmau

Futtehpore

Allahabad

Palee

Benare

Mirzapore

BUNDELKHA

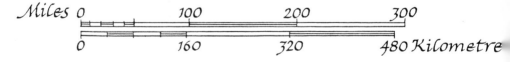

Miles 0   100   200   300

0   160   320   480 Kilometre

'If you take the trouble to look at the map of Hindustan you will see the place where many younger Brothers are punished for making their appearance so late in the world. Cawnpore is situated in that long neck of land between the Ganges and Jumna about one hundred and fifty miles above Allahabad and as far below Delhi. The country for some part of the year is very pleasant but the Westerly winds which prevail in April, May and June and blow over the burning sands of Tartary render it so unsupportably hot that a European cannot expose himself for a minute without doors from nine in the morning till five in the evening but at the risque of his life.'

SURGEON JOHN STEWART

N
I B E T
A Y A N
R A N G E
Dinapore
Patna
B I H A R
R. Ganges
B E N G A L
Serampore
Calcutta

3
Cawnpore Becomes British Territory
1801–1804

The Cession

When Lord Wellesley took up his post as Governor-General in 1798 there were two threats to British supremacy in India: in the South, Tippoo Sultan, ably supported by the French, and in central India, the Mahrattas, whose bands of cavalry terrorised a huge area. Tippoo was defeated and killed at Seringapatam in 1799, and the Governor-General appointed his own younger brother, Arthur Wellesley, the future Duke of Wellington, as Governor of Seringapatam. Then, with the same determination to have things done his way which had brought the Calcutta editors to heel in 1799, he turned his attention to subduing the Mahrattas.

The five leading Mahratta chiefs had quarrelled among themselves. Their nominal head, the Peishwa of Poona, had fled to Bombay, leaving Scindia of Gwalior the most powerful. Scindia's men were divided into two armies, that in the north was commanded by a Frenchman called Perron and was centred on Delhi where the aged, blind Emperor of the Moghuls, Shah Alam II, was kept in custody by the Mahrattas.[1] Adjoining this territory was the state of Oude. It was here Wellesley decided to take action.

Under the Treaty of Fyzabad in 1773 the revenue from the provinces of Corah, Allahabad and Rohilkhund went to pay the upkeep of the Company troops in Oude. But the internal administration of the state was medieval. On the one hand the court was reported to be fabulously rich and splendid. At the wedding of the Nawab's son in 1795, the young bridegroom was said to be 'covered with jewels to the amount at least of two million sterling', and two tents alone cost fifty thousand pounds. An eye witness described the procession to the wedding reception as 'grand beyond description'.[2] At the other extreme, the Nawab was months in arrears in paying both his troops and those of the Company, whom he had agreed to support. The result was a breakdown in discipline. It seemed to Wellesley that in waging war against the Mahrattas he should be able to rely on a stable administration in Oude,

Marquess Wellesley and his suite, at the Nawab of Oude's breakfast table, watching an elephant fight, Lucknow: Charles D'Oyly in The Europeans in India, *1813.*

Wellesley's camp at Cawnpore, 1802: watercolour by Mrs Ward, the Chaplain's wife.

and the regular payment of his troops. The simplest way of ensuring that was to take over the running of the province himself.

I am satisfied that no effectual security can be provided against the ruin of the province of Oude until the exclusive management of the civil and military government of that country shall be transferred to the Company under suitable provisions for the Nawab and his family.[3]

The breaking of a treaty seemed a small price to pay for security in time of war. In the event, he split Oude in two – half he left to the Nawab providing he disbanded his troops; the other half, consisting of the provinces of Corah, Allahabad and Rohilkhund were 'ceded' to the Company. These provinces became known as the Ceded Provinces, and Cawnpore, in the province of Corah, became for the first time British territory in 1801.

Richard Wellesley was Governor-General for seven years. With Arthur Wellesley acting as Governor of Seringapatam and another brother, Henry Wellesley, appointed Lieutenant-Governor of the Ceded Provinces,[4] this powerful family changed the East India Company from a trading concern into an empire. Cawnpore was only one of many accessions dating from this period and the Treaty of Fyzabad was not the only casualty. The Cession caused great and lasting discontent in Oude: the unfortunate Nawab had been forced to sign away the very territory which Sujah Dowlah had bought back from the Company for half a million pounds. His helplessness in the matter was hardly disguised by the elaborate manner in which he was eased of his possessions. All the etiquette and protocol which Wellesley believed in was observed. A report from the *Calcutta Gazette* of January 1802 gives some idea of what was involved.

On the 17th the Nawab Vizier, attended by his five younger sons, accompanied by the British Resident at his Court, by the Chief Officers of his Court, and by many of the principal inhabitants at Lucknow (from which city the Nawab Vizier had come to meet the Governor General) arrived in the vicinity of Cawnpore, and encamped on the bank of the Ganges opposite to that Cantonment. The Nawab Vizier was accompanied by a large body of troops.

On the 19th His Lordship received in his tents the visit of the Nawab Vizier, the troops of the station being drawn up in line for the reception of the Nawab Vizier; a royal salute was fired on his Excellency's arrival at the Governor General's tents, and on his departure. The Nawab Vizier was attended on that occasion by his sons, and by many of the principal Officers of his Court.

On the 20th the Governor General returned the visit of the Nawab Vizier at dinner in his tents.

On the 22nd the Nawab Vizier and his sons were present at a Ball given by the Governor General in his tents, when the Governor General presented to the Nawab Vizier two large State tents, ornamented with embossed cloth of British manufacture.

When the ceremonies were over, Cawnpore found itself for the first time under Company administration and within the jurisdiction of the Calcutta Presidency. Civil administrators began to struggle with the procedures for the collection of revenue and other everyday matters, while the town filled up with soldiers preparing for the great attack on the Mahrattas. In the background of this activity, the Mahratta chiefs Scindia of Gwalior and the Peishwa of Poona were to have special significance for Cawnpore's history. In the state generally, bitterness festered against the high-handed treatment of the Nawab of Oude.

Company Administration

The Cession of 1801 that gave Cawnpore to the Company had been justified by Wellesley because of the anarchy prevalent in Oude: in taking over three provinces, he hoped to ensure the regular payment of the revenues to finance his troops, and to safeguard the tranquillity of the territory in the district around Cawnpore – a district without roads, bridges, public buildings or any civil amenities.

The first East India Company civil servant took up his duties in Cawnpore in March 1802. Mr Welland[5] was appointed to fulfil the triple offices of collector of revenue, magistrate and judge: a superhuman task. His instructions were to decide all civil cases according to his own judgement; excused formal reports, he was merely to keep a diary of them in the Persian language, and to assume charge of the revenue.

On his arrival at Cawnpore Mr Welland rented a modest bungalow for 100 rupees per month. It was constructed of mud with a '*chuppered*' roof – in no way a safe place for the treasure. The revenue was collected in the form of silver coin which presented practical difficulties: bullock carts laden with rupees had to be escorted from the district into Cawnpore and then carefully guarded. His first action therefore was to authorise the building of a pucka bungalow of burnt brick which would fulfil all the purposes of his authority. It combined his own residence, a *cutcherry* where civil law suits would be heard, a treasury for the reception of collected revenue, a guard room for the sepoys who protected the building, a lockup cell, and a record room for the innumerable files which had already begun to collect.

The walls were two feet thick, the doors and window-frames made from seasoned wood, secured with brass and iron bolts, the inner windows glazed and the outer windows protected by Venetian shutters. As a safety precaution the Treasury chests were bigger than the openings for doors and windows.

Most of the new Collector's time was taken up with ordering the Company's principle source of income in these provinces – the collection of revenue from the land. Landlords were taxed on the yield in crops that their land was likely to give. Mr Welland was instructed to make inquiries 'with a view of ascertaining a proper basis on which to assess the land revenue'.[6] In the past the revenue had been collected by the Amils of the Nawab of Oude. They had applied no particular system, but had demanded revenue in proportion to the exigencies of the times, regardless of the actual holding or income of any landowner. 'Provided they got their revenue, it signified little how or from whom.' This arbitrary practice had contributed largely to the chaos in Oude that Wellesley wished to counter. As Welland began his own assessment, the prospects for ordered prosperity looked gloomy:

The subjects in this part of the country are in the most abject poverty. Let the face of the country be examined, and there will hardly be a manufacture found, or an individual in such circumstances as to afford the payment of a tax; the whole is one desolate waste, in which tyranny and oppression have hitherto universally prevailed.[7]

Yet Mr Welland was so confident of the benefits of British government about to be conferred on the people that, despite the depressed state of the district, he assessed its capacity at an extraordinarily optimistic figure. Moreover, he made his calculations on a basis as groundless as the Nawab's had been. The income received by the Nawab of Oude was stated in round numbers to have been twenty-two lakhs. Welland was too over-burdened with work to make the slightest inquiry as to the productive resources of the country; he accepted the Nawab's rent-roll 'which was simply a statement of the amount he [the Nawab] and his subordinates were able to screw out of the people'[8] and added two *lakhs* of rupees to the annual demand.

Welland overlooked the fact that there were particular reasons why the assessment in Oude should be lower, more flexible and more carefully calculated than elsewhere. The soil in general was inferior to that in the Lower Provinces, the seasons more uncertain and the crops 'liable to damage in a greater degree from drought and unseasonable rain, from frost, locusts and frequent hail-storms'.[9] The instability of the climate became grimly apparent in 1804 when after two years of exceptionally fine harvests there was a serious famine. As a result, landowners failed to pay the taxes demanded of them. In July 1804 the Collector reported that numbers of landholders had absconded[10] because the harvest had failed and they could not pay their taxes. There seemed no likelihood of the balance of what they owed being recovered. Welland strongly recommended that Government should put up any such defaulting estates for auction. The following year the Council reluctantly agreed.

Welland and subsequent Collectors were generally motivated by the desire to establish an equitable assessment and then to apply it with justice. But they were severely hampered both by the size of the district and by their ignorance of its customs – a combination which made them dangerously dependent on the native officers employed to implement the system, and thus vulnerable to deception. If these officers failed to explain either the revenue or British legal procedures, the landholders were liable to find their estates sold around them, with no means of redress that they could understand. Robert Montgomery who was Collector of Cawnpore in 1848 made a detailed study of the early revenue problems:

The landholders were little acquainted with our Revenue Regulations and were in many cases through the chicanery of the Native Officers kept in perfect ignorance of the penalty hanging over their heads. It was the interest of the Native Officers to blind the people on this point, and purchase the Estates on the day of sale on their own account. . . . The Collector addressing the Board details the villany of one Rammohun Ghose, Tulseeldar of Shioolee [native revenue officer] who was convicted on the clearest evidence, of having reported many Zumeendars to have absconded who were at the time actually present in their villages. The Zumeendars on being questioned why they concealed themselves from the Government Peons said, they had done so by order of the Tulseeldars. They likewise stated that no advertisements were ever put up in the villages, and that they were ignorant of the sale, till the purchaser came to take possession. In other cases it was proved that the Tulseeldar promised to purchase the Estate, in the name of the Zumeendar's relation, instead of which, he purchased it for himself, in the name of his own friends.[11]

To the unfortunate people of the *Doab*,[12] it seemed that they had merely exchanged one kind of oppression and injustice for another. The sale of lands near Cawnpore took place on a massive scale. In 1841 the Collector recorded: 'In no district has there been such a rapid and extensive change of landed property as in Cawnpore!'[13] In the next thirty years at least three-quarters of the landed property of the district changed hands. This wholesale transfer of property had two harmful results: it created an undesirable landowning class, for the only people who could afford to buy estates at the assessed revenue rates were wealthy speculators who usually sought to make their profits not from agriculture but from lending money to their new tenants; at the same time, the transfer of property destroyed the landed families with hereditary rights who were accustomed to exert a benevolent and stabilising influence on the villages. The district felt their loss over a long period of time, and it is possible that their absence accounted partly for the violence of the mutiny of 1857 in Oude.

By 1821, Government had become aware of the disruption their revenue system was causing, and appointed a Commission to remedy what injustice it could. This Commission reversed the sale of a number of villages but, as ever, its members were hindered by their lack of understanding of local practices and the peculiar tenures of the country. The British approach to revenue had worked on the assumption that the structure of an English village, based on the position and responsibilities of a squire and his tenants, was directly equitable with the workings of an Indian village. The Commission began to realise that the two cultures simply could not be compared. 'The privileges of the managing land-holders being at present but imperfectly understood, and those of the cultivators never having been directly recognised, it is impossible satisfactorily to pronounce upon them.'[14]

Clearly it was difficult for the Commission to effect a just settlement for communities whose rights it did not understand. Moreover, its members realised the harm that had been done, and the impossibility of merely putting the process into reverse. 'It can scarcely be doubted that our public sales must, in most cases, have so broken assunder the whole construction of the village communities within the estate sold, as that the mischief consequent upon them will be very imperfectly corrected by the mere restoration of the former Malgozars [men responsible for the rent collection].'[15] Nevertheless, the Commissioners and individual Collectors could make some improvements.

One of the most energetic of the early Cawnpore Collectors was Henry Newnham, who took up office in 1812.

[He] commenced by clearing the District of a party of corrupt and intriguing public servants. By the removal of these prople and their relatives, he at once opened up sources of information, which had hitherto been blocked up. He proceeded into the interior of the District, and held personal communication with the people, not as heretofore through the medium of the Native Officers. He seems quite to have gained their confidence and affection; he restored where possible, many of the old and injured Zumeendars to their Estates and by a judicious reduction and equalization of the Revenue, and a proper selection of representatives to the different communities, he formed a settlement which for a period of 12 years stood well, and was collected without distressing the people.[16]

Newnham's settlement was the fourth since the Cession. Each one was a reduction on the last, and each was intended to be permanent. They were abandoned in turn as being too severe to be practicable. It became clear that the revenue question was too complex to be resolved by one man's estimate. In 1872, seventy-one years after the Cession, the Collector, Mr Halsey, reported that the just and workable settlement, which Wellesley had assumed the Company could introduce at once, had still not been achieved: 'The cultivator, so far from thriving under our rule, is still in the same state of abject poverty he was described to be in 1801; and the proprietor has been in a chronic state of transfer ever since the commencement of the century.'[17]

It is hardly surprising that many of the Company's civil administrators of this period made an indifferent job of their offices: they were faced with a massive and extraordinarily complex task, for which they had little formal training. As a missionary complained: 'The men who were to undertake the important offices of judges, magistrates, collectors and ambassadors were considered sufficiently qualified for their duties if they were versed in the mysteries of the counting house, wrote a legible hand, and understood book keeping by double entry.'[18]

Mr Welland, the first Cawnpore Collector, very probably had an exhausting first year in office, battling not only with the intricacies of the revenue, but with all the crime and civil complaints in the district too. In 1803, however, the administration of the revenue was separated from the maintenance of law, and a combined judge and magistrate was appointed for the Cawnpore District. The offices of judge and magistrate continued to be fulfilled by one man until 1827.

The Magistrate's early reports convey an impression of Cawnpore as a dangerous frontier town, frequently vulnerable to attack from several directions. 'In this district the roads leading to Delhi, Agra and the Dekkan have always been infested by Mounted Robbers who come over the Mahrattas Provinces and conceal themselves in the Jungles which are on the border of these districts.'[19] It was a custom among the landholders on the Mahratta side of the river to harbour thieves and share in the property they plundered. In 1803 the Magistrate wrote to Government requesting guard boats to patrol the river and prevent the crossing of raiders and thieves. He suggested each boat be manned by five or six sepoys and stationed near the principal ghats and be 'continually during the night moving within certain limits so as to prevent as far as possible all persons from going to and fro from dusk in the evening till sunrise'.[20]

He required guards for the bazaar, for the treasury, for the escort of treasure, for the jail which was 'only of mud and there are upward of 100 prisoners confined in it',[21] and for attending the working parties of convicts employed on Government business. Government authorised Captain Richard Hodgson of the 11th Native Regiment to raise a Police Corps of six companies. Until the corps had been enlisted and drilled, the Magistrate employed temporary *jamaders* and *burkandases*.

The unfortunate Magistrate was trying to do his job under the most difficult circumstances. He could not rely on the arrival of any communications or funds; the Mahrattas were in the area; the landholders were nervous and unconfident, and if the crops failed he feared the peasants would resort to plunder. He reported disaster after disaster to Government: 'an outrage has been committed by gangs of banditti . . . the dawk [post] has been stopped and opened three successive days'; on the outskirts of the town a daring raid had been carried out – 'a desperate attack was made by a party of dekoits on a Hackery loaded with Dollars which had only a few hours previously arrived in the Chupper Mahal';[22] five men were killed and seven badly wounded. The robbers made off with two-thirds of the treasure and the Magistrate was shocked at 'the enormity of the offence'. Affairs in his own office were no easier: he was 'destitute of stationery'; the boat in which Government regulations for the period 1793–1802 were being sent to Cawnpore was sunk; and once his records were in order, a number were found to have been destroyed by white ants.

The Magistrate's life was further complicated by the delicate relationship that existed between the civil and military authorities. Prior to the Cession all matters concerning the British in Cawnpore had come under the jurisdiction of the commanding officer but after 1803 three powers – two civilian and one military – had to apportion responsibilities between them. It was a situation with infinite scope for conflict and the local people were quick to take advantage of it. When an Indian woman named Betsy complained to the Magistrate that the soldier she lived with had beaten her severely, the soldier's commanding officer voiced his disapproval of what he regarded as interference in army affairs:

. . . fifty such cases as these and even worse, happen every day amongst the Europeans and their Women and I never knew of their going beyond the Company or Troop in which they happen. I recommended it to her [Betsy] in the morning to lay her complaint before Captain Abercrombie to whose Troop the Soldier belongs, who is possessed of ample authority to give redress; but it seems she has preferred stating her case to you.'[23]

Even in times of mutual danger, areas of responsibility remained undefined and open to dispute. When he heard a rumour of a Mahratta attack the Magistrate prepared for action. 'Intelligence has this day arrived of a very peculiar nature. It says 15 or 20,000 Cavalry belonging to the Mahratta Scindia are headed by a Monsieur Fleury a Frenchman . . . his orders are to destroy the Dewaub to the very gates of Allahabad.'[24]

The Magistrate took steps to put the Magazine into some state of defence. Working enthusiastically with the Military authorities, he brought in quantities of grain and encouraged individuals to lodge their public property within its walls. He wrote to Government to arrange a concerted plan and a signal, but the official response was merely to commend him for cooperating with the commanding officer, while pointing out that such arrangements were in the province of the Collector! Disputes and misunderstandings such as these between the civil and military authorities were to characterise Cawnpore affairs for the next twenty years.

The Company's main source of income was from the collection of land revenue, but there was a further lucrative source of income which as traders they understood well – the long-established practice of exacting customs dues on goods in transit. Aware of 'the great extent of the Ceded and Conquered Provinces and the importance of not subjecting the commerce of those provinces to any unnecessary restraint or impediment . . .'[25] a Collector of Government Customs, Mr Robert Grant, was appointed in 1803 to Cawnpore's Customs House with deputies at Etawah, Allahabad and Bundelkhand.

The Customs House was a tall, imposing building with lofty rooms,

warehouses, offices, guard rooms, outbuildings and courtyards. It stood a little back from the river, fronted by two long wharfs. Here a great crowd of boats and craft of all sizes were tied, those with goods in transit alongside one wharf, and those with goods for landing at Cawnpore against the other. The wharfs were gay with bunting and a tall flagstaff proclaimed that this was the most important gathering spot in Cawnpore for all traders.

No goods could pass the Customs House without paying duty and obtaining a pass or permit to proceed further. Similarly no goods for sale in Cawnpore could be landed without paying Town dues and obtaining a permit. A 'great assembly' of merchants attended the office waiting for their passes and meeting their boatloads of goods to clear them of customs. The busy office had to issue permits in three languages, Persian, English and the Nagree script, while keeping a careful inventory of all goods and passes issued. It was the making out of 'permits' which gave the Customs House the name of Permit (or in the local speech, Permutt) Ghat which is still in use today.

The scene at the wharfs was an immensely busy one. Piles of goods stood on the bank, huge weighing scales were constantly in use, carpenters opened chests, blacksmiths hammered them shut again, coolies carried bales and boxes on their heads into the warehouses where goods were deposited for fifteen days waiting to be claimed. After that time if unclaimed they were confiscated. Armed men guarded the store rooms and inspected and searched the goods coming ashore. Smuggling constantly took place but only, it seems, on a modest scale; four shawls were discovered among a mass of imported goods; bags of sweets were found to contain small pieces of valuable lace. On all the roads round the city to a radius of four miles barriers were set up where people coming in were searched. One man was found to have hidden fifteen strings of corals in his loin cloth.

The Company levied a duty of 5 per cent on imports and $2\frac{1}{2}$ per cent on exports of all articles of trade. The Collector of Customs got $2\frac{1}{2}$ per cent commission, 5 per cent commission on town dues and one-fifth of the value of all confiscated articles.

Duty was levied at different rates. A list of duties collected at the Cawnpore Customs House in the month of December 1806 shows that by far the biggest single item was raw cotton, and this attracted the highest rate of duty. Indigo, cotton piece goods, sugar and iron all produced a high return. Other commodities which passed through Cawnpore but in much

OPPOSITE *Robert Grant, Collector of Customs, Cawnpore: according to family tradition painted in Calcutta by John Zoffany, c.1783.*

Weighing cotton: Company painting on mica.

smaller quantities were silk, salt, country paper, jaggery, (a crude form of sugar) ghee, saltpetre and spices and utensils of brass and copper. The total sum of duties collected for that month amounted to Rs 22,651, 13 annas, 3 pies.[26]

Collector of Customs was a lucrative appointment and open to many abuses. The records are full of complaints from private individuals whose personal property had been mistakenly taxed, but at times the complaints were more serious. In 1806 Mr Grant was admonished for want of consideration, 'harassing the Merchants without cause'.

The merchants in Cawnpore bought their cotton from the village cultivators in the Agra district. In order to send the cotton down river a pass had to be obtained at Agra and duty paid; the growers needed money for this duty before they could supply the cotton. This money was advanced by the money-lenders in Cawnpore. Once the cotton had come into Cawnpore the merchants sold it and repaid the money-lenders: it was a complicated system of economics and any hold-up caused a total stoppage.

The following is a translation of a complaint from Gocoolchund Inderjeet and other cotton merchants:

Ruins of the Customs House, 1970.

From the commencement of the Hon'ble Company's administration to the present day, cotton purchased by us has passed under the Rowannah [passes] we have obtained; now, the officers attached to the Cawnpore Custom House refuse to allow our cotton to pass. They require of us to take out Rowannahs from Cawnpore, and to pay the Duties there from the beginning. The Mahajens of Cawnpore who advanced us money to enable us to pay the duties at Agra, now demand the same back again and the Cawnpore Beoparees, who purchased the Cotton from us, refuse to pay us the full cost, but deduct the amount of the Duties from it. Under these circumstances the whole of the cotton is stopped. . . . We entreat you to take our case into early consideration and preserve our credit and reputation.[27]

Government took up their case and suggested the merchants should go personally to state their case at the Courts in Cawnpore and obtain redress 'for no order of Government warrants an Injury to a Merchant by the Collection of Double Duties on his Goods'.

The Customs House continued until 1833 when the department was closed down. Its ruins still remain. The river has receded and the elegant old building, now used by squatters, stands forlornly some distance from the water's edge as if brooding over the scene of constant bustle and commerce it once knew.

4
Cawnpore: Army Headquarters
1804–1822

The Mud War

> Cawnpore is the principal depot for the Bengal Army, containing
> seldom less than ten thousand troops, including a regiment of His
> Majesty's Light Dragoons, and one or two of infantry, besides the
> company's artillery with seapoy corps. . . . It is likewise the Headquar-
> ters of the army, the Commander in Chief residing there.[1]

In 1803 Cawnpore became the base camp for the 'Mud War'. What had once
been a temporary camp was now the headquarters of the greatest army
mobilised by the Company in India. This army was commanded by General
Lake whose specific task was to crush the power of the Mahrattas in
northern India. In this huge up-country cantonment – the largest in India –
the Company's seasoned native troops led by Company officers were joined
by British infantry and cavalry from the King's regiments. Together they set
out from Cawnpore to break the power of the Mahrattas.

Lake's objective was to expel the Mahrattas from the Moghul cities of
Delhi and Agra and to destroy Scindia's almost impregnable stronghold at
Gwalior. In order to do so, many forts held by independent chiefs had first to
be defeated. These forts were made of earth, with walls often 50 feet high,
and 200 feet thick at the base. They were protected by ramparts and bastions
and a deep encircling ditch that made them difficult to assault. It was the
attack on these mud forts that gave the campaign the name of the Mud War.

Every soldier who fought in this Mud War passed through Cawnpore at
one time or another, and so did all the military equipment: the artillery, the
ordnance, the transport animals, the food rations and the medical supplies.
General Lake took up his headquarters in Cawnpore and here he made plans
for his attack. News came that Scindia's army, which was rumoured to be
twenty times the size of the British, and led by the French General Perron,
was preparing to meet them. It was the time of the monsoon rains and

Lord Lake and his son at Fatehgarh, 1804: oil by Robert Home.

unheard of to move an army in such conditions, but the monsoon had failed and Lake intended to take the Mahrattas by surprise. His troops marched out of Cawnpore in the middle of August. A young officer, Lieutenant John Pester, kept a diary of the campaign:

Cawnpore 15 Aug. 1803 Got up this morning an hour before daybreak, and saw my tent and baggage all laden on the camels and bullocks. At gun fire we paraded, wheeled into line, and then by sections backward on our left, at six we marched out of cantonments, the drums and fifes playing the Grenadiers' March – officers and men in the highest spirits possible.[2]

The army was so cumbersome and the heat so great that a day's march covered only nine or ten miles. The gun for marching fired at 3 a.m. before it was daylight and the camping ground was reached before the sun became too ferocious. Conditions on the march were often appalling. The palanquins carrying the officers went very slowly. If the wind blew out the flaming torches it was too dangerous to proceed owing to numerous wells in the road. 'During the march of an Army when no lights are allowed, men, horses, and elephants are destroyed by falling into wells.'[3]

The Europeans had their packs carried for them, but the natives carried their own. Rations for the native troops consisted of half a *seer* (about 1lb) of rice daily. The European soldiers lived on biscuits, salt beef and rum. The officers fared better, but everyone suffered alike from the intolerable heat. In order to sleep they had to move their bedding from couches on to the floors of their tents, and Pester records an evening so hot that the wax candles on the table at dinner actually melted and sank down on to the cloth. The thermometer stood at 125°F.

Despite the conditions and the war, the officers took every opportunity to hunt, gamble and dine well. Their hunting dogs, terriers and greyhounds, travelled with them, and in the early morning on off-duty days, or, astonishingly, in the evening after a day's fighting, they rode out with their grooms. 'We killed seventeen brace of partridge, six brace of hares, five peacocks and a brace of fine deer. Home in time for breakfast at 12, face and hands peeling.'[4]

In the evening it was customary for the officers to dine with each other in turn. After a battle the celebration dinner was particularly noisy. Following the fall of the fort at Sasni, in February 1803, Pester describes a memorable meal: 'A glorious evening. 14 honest gentlemen within its walls. Three dozen and a half of claret, and proportionate quantities of Madeira – every one sang his song, and this was as gay an evening and terminated as pleasantly as any I ever passed in my life. We concluded by breaking our

First Bugle: *watercolour by John B. Bellasis, c.1822.*

candle shades, pranks which too often finish our drinking parties in this quarter of the globe.'⁵

Men brought to war many of the qualities which they displayed in their sport – pride in winning a good fight; great personal courage; a sense of camaraderie; and an acceptance of death. One of the most hard-fought battles of the campaign was the fight for Delhi. Scindia's troops comprised 17,000 men with 100 cannon; the British army numbered 6,000 with eight guns. Lake's troops had marched eighteen miles and were near exhaustion but he chose to take the initiative and attack at once. The advancing line of the Company's army was raked with shot and grape but the soldiers went forward without taking their muskets from their shoulders. At 250 paces from the muzzles of the enemy guns came the order to fire. The volley was followed by a cheer; to the sound of drums the men rushed forward for the bayonet charge. The air was filled with shot and smoke and the sounds of

Siege of Sasni: watercolour by Lieutenant St Aubin, frontispiece to Pester's book. Lake's\army prepares to attack the mud walls of the fort.

trumpets and bugles and officers hollering, when all of a sudden Scindia's men broke and the battle was over. General Lake [6] entered the captured city to visit Shah Alam, who received him graciously and, embracing him, called him his 'saviour'.

After the battle Pester inspected the General Hospital Tent:

The scene was truly shocking. About 30 surgeons were absolutely covered in blood, performing operations on the unfortunate soldiers who had their arms and legs shattered in the action, and death in every shape seemed to preside in this assemblage of human misery. Numbers were fainting, and even dying under the operation; others bore the pain with as much fortitude as they had evinced in the early part of the day, gallantly executing that duty in which they had received their wounds. In one corner of the tent stood a pile of legs and arms from which the boots and clothes were not yet stripped off . . .[7]

In Pester's regiment, the 1st Battalion of the 2nd Native Infantry, of the original eighteen officers, only three were left fit for duty. For five weeks the troops had not changed their 'fighting coats', the tattered and filthy uniforms of which they were very proud, nor had their clothes off their backs to sleep.

General Lake, on whom a barony was conferred in 1804, had successfully taken Delhi and Agra. He concluded his Mud War campaign in 1805, tying up the Mahrattas in an uneasy series of treaties and truces. The fighting, however, did not stop. Company forces found themselves with another enemy, the gangs of Pindaree horsemen – robber bands who had been employed by the Mahrattas in return for the opportunity of plunder – 'rather like poachers keep dogs', as one Englishman described it. Having dealt with the poachers the Company now had to deal with their dogs. For twenty years Cawnpore remained prominent as a vital base camp from which expeditions set out to attack the many great fortresses which were in the hands of the Pindarees or likely to afford them assistance.

Before and after each expedition the troops encamped at Cawnpore. The contrast between the dangers and hardships of life at the front and the gaiety and sociability of leave in Cawnpore was recorded by one of the soldiers who travelled back and forth. John Shipp was a workhouse boy who had joined the army in England when he was nine years old, and arrived in India at eighteen to serve in Lord Lake's army as a drummer boy. For outstanding bravery he was granted a commission by Lord Lake himself.

Shipp records the abrupt juxtaposition of peace and war. On one occasion after the fall of Hattras, in 1817, a siege made memorable by a chance hit on the enemy's magazine which blew up the whole fort, . . .'we saw a hideous sight. Heads, bodies, and shattered pieces of bodies lay scattered indiscriminately among guns, swords, spears, colours, and all the debris of the ruined fort.' Yet shortly afterwards, when his regiment returned to Cawnpore, 'the station slipped back into its usual gay manner of life when there was no fighting to be done. There was nothing but parties, balls and suppers and such like until many were bored, and most in debt.'[8]

It was not long before the troops were under marching orders again. Just before their departure, Shipp took part in some amateur theatricals in the presence of the Governor-General, Lord Hastings. 'There were farewell dinners in all directions, and to end the festivities we produced an amateur dramatic entertainment. I played Lord Dubberley in *The Heir at Law* and Lord Minikin in *Bon Ton*.'[9]

Soldiers thought nothing of travelling great distances from the scene of war when leave was due to them in Cawnpore. Twice Shipp covered over 400 miles cross-country, alone, once to marry the daughter of a conductor[10] in the Cawnpore Commissariat and the other time to spend some leave with her. 'Cawnpore was a gay place just then, and I was so occupied with festivities of one kind and another, during the whole of my eight or ten days leave, that I was quite worn out when the time came for me to return.'

When the officers came back to Cawnpore on leave, they found themselves caught up in high society. The presence of the Commander-in-

Chief and very senior army officers created a social circle where entertainments were lavish and occasionally splendid. Few ladies, however, were yet available to play hostess and those who arrived up-country mostly lacked grace and culture. Pester was very scathing: he found them 'plain, proud and ignorant; attempting the airs of gentlewomen, though it is more than probable that previous to their arrival at our markets most of them could not boast a change of dickies twice a month.'[11]

Henry Martyn, the fiery evangelical missionary, a Cambridge scholar who was for a short time chaplain in Cawnpore, also had some very critical comments to make. He complained that at one dinner party none of the ladies knew the tune of the 145th Psalm well enough to join in and sing it and his hostess had never heard of the poems of Cowper although a copy was available at the library. He was a serious-minded man and found many aspects of Cawnpore society obnoxious. An entry in his diary reads:

Went to a large party at Mr G's [probably Mr Grant, the Collector] to dinner, and sat down with 56 people, officers and ladies of the station. I repented of having gone, and would rather be preaching to my beggars. The splendours of these entertainments does not dazzle me as it once did. I looked along the crowded table, and could not with the utmost stretch of charity believe that they were serious. They staid dancing till late in the morning; I escaped immediately after dinner. December 1809.[12]

A special event, which was duly reported in the Calcutta papers and

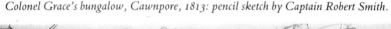

Colonel Grace's bungalow, Cawnpore, 1813: pencil sketch by Captain Robert Smith.

outshone all others, was the masked ball given by Colonel Tetley in 1814. The invited élite from the town and outlying districts numbered as many as 120 people. On that occasion there were fancy dresses, firework displays, 'sumptous *nauch* girls and exquisite champagne'. The magnificent supper was served in five tents to seat the guests. The tents were gaily decorated with devices and mottos, carrying the names that made every man's heart beat a little more proudly. Wellington: Hastings: Clive: Coote: Wellesley: Achmuty: Gillespie: Cornwallis: and then, nearer home, Lake and Laswaree. It was a time when society's heroes were her generals and each military victory was a matter for congratulation in which every Englishman felt he shared. In this outpost of British civilisation Colonel Tetley was determined to make his mark. He presided over the toasts, dressed (in somewhat dubious taste) in a gorgeous Persian costume, which he claimed to have been the property of the Moghul Emperor, Shah Alam.

The toasts were:

1st 'The King.'
2nd 'The Queen; the pattern of chastity and ornament to her Sex.'
3rd 'The Filial Prince; may he never know sorrow.'
4th 'The Duke of York and Heroic Army.'
5th 'The Duke of Clarence and Invincible Navy.'
6th 'Lord Wellington, Prince of Vittoria, may his career be always bright.'
7th 'Our liberal employers, the East India Company.'
8th 'Earl Moira and India's happiness.'
9th 'Mrs Grant and Ladies who honoured us with their Company.'
10th 'Old England for ever. Huzza!'
11th (By Colonel Grace) 'Our noble host Colonel Tetley.'
12th 'The Royal House of Timur.'[13]

At a late hour the company dispersed, delighted and gratified by the hospitality.

Society at this period was sharply divided, with little social contact between officers and the men. They were even buried in separate cemeteries. The troops at Cawnpore were housed in barracks, ten ranges of buildings fifty yards apart. Each thatched range consisted of one large room with four small rooms at the corners, surrounded by a verandah. These four small rooms were allotted to the sergeants with European wives, while the long room was used by the privates, corporals and their wives and children. The soldiers' pay was sufficient to allow them to employ native servants.

Sweeping changes had recently been introduced to ensure that only men of good character were enlisted, but previously the reputation of men in the armed forces had been very low. 'Every ship, hulk and prison, was swept of the very dregs of the metropolis of England, to supply the army and navy.'

Many of the new recruits were Irishmen; the more fortunate ones were accompanied by their wives, lively simple women, who quarrelled and fought in the great public barrack rooms and swore with the best of them.

Day began at Gun Fire and the bugle called the men to parade. Drill over, the men returned to barracks where they 'lay and read' on their cots or played cards or took refuge in the oblivion of liquor. The barrack rooms where the majority of soldiers lived were an amazing sight. They were crowded with privates and corporals with their womenfolk and children, many orphans, all living in the minimum of privacy – no family possessed more than a bed and a chest for their few belongings – and the cramped conditions in that terrible climate provoked quarrels and jealousies which often led to blows. The talk of bazaar prices – the soldiers' wives did their own shopping – was of rupees and 'puckers' (pice). The latest goods to arrive at the Europe shop were eagerly discussed: 'There is a man in the great bazaar who has some of the elegantest artificial flowers I ever saw in my life; there you may buy Europe sash ribbons of all colours and as good as new, in 2 or 3 shops. O you must go!'[14] Conversation was a mixture of current slang and Indian words for things in everyday use. The sergeant's room was his 'berth', his bed a 'chopper cot'. Wearing a cap and sash he would sit outside in the doorway stitching a 'gooderie' while his wife sat on a 'mora' plaiting some fine lace upon a worked muslin gown. The many young boys ran wild round the barracks, getting up to every form of mischief. They played cricket and skittles outside the barracks and teased the pelicans which came to scavenge near the kitchens. Babies were frequently quietened by the men giving them a mouthful of liquor – there were cases when it silenced their cries for ever. Once a month dances were held and then the soldiers' wives vied with one another to wear the most sensational white muslin gowns, flounced and trimmed round the waist with ribbon, their shoes coloured, hair dressed with flowers and feathers, beads round their necks and carrying fans.

There was no church in Cawnpore but Sunday services were held on the parade ground half an hour before sunrise. The regiment marched to the place, band playing; the soldiers' wives dressed all in white, wearing caps instead of bonnets, stood in their places carrying painted umbrellas. Higher ranks all came in carriages until the square was covered with vehicles. The congregation stood the whole time and nobody thought of anything but how soon the service would be over.

On Sunday after the church parade the men went along to the bungalow of the Paymaster. Here he presided over the large iron chest containing the rupees, the *circar* (native accountant) sat in the corner weighing the rupees and the sergeant wrote down the accounts. A few of the more serious-minded men would join the chaplain, Henry Martyn, at his bungalow to read the Scriptures and sing psalms but the great majority took their pay and went straight to the canteen to spend it on drink. The canteen was open all day, with a sentry on duty to see that no liquor was taken outside. 'In those days drink was the rage in India.' Some men went to the lengths of making a 'bishop', a sort of mitre-shaped bladder that fitted inside their shirt and trousers. It would hold about eight drams, which they were able to smuggle out of the canteen and sell at a good price to other men. These were known as 'Gun Fire tots' because they were sold at Gun Fire. The women were equally involved in smuggling liquor.[15]

We had a woman named Paddy Burns, called 'the old tin kettle'. She had a Tin Baby made with a wax face. This she would take into the canteen at evening and mimick a cry, and then give it a little grog. The child's body held more than a gallon. She would get the men to get many rupees' worth for her, and she used to then fill the child. When full she would mimick the cry and say, 'Ah, I must take the young devil to its mother, I suppose' and out she would go by the sentry. This she would sell at 4 annas per dram in the night – when it only cost her one anna. When men had been drinking in the day, they would pay any amount for it in the night.[16]

Soldiers' misdemeanours were inevitably linked with alcohol. They committed their worst crimes under the influence of liquor and took refuge from their shame at the resulting punishment in more hard drinking. Flogging was the most widespread form of punishment used in the services at the time. When John Shipp found himself in charge of the congee house – the guard house – in cantonments, the experience helped to make him passionately opposed to flogging. He believed that the soldier found the practice so degrading that after he had suffered it once, his spirit might be permanently broken and the only course open to him would be to drink himself to death. One soldier, twenty years old, was sentenced to receive 150 lashes for a first offence. 'From the day he was flogged until the period of his death, I can venture to assert he was never two hours sober.'[17]

However, Shipp believed that capital punishment was a necessary part of military discipline. He cites the instance of a young soldier who attacked an officer while drunk, and was sentenced to public execution by shooting, in front of the whole regiment. Fully aware of the awful pathos of the ceremony of execution, he described it as a warning against strong drink.

The regiments, both of which were European, then formed three sides of a square, of which the shooting party, with coffin, formed the other. Scarcely was this accomplished, when we heard the dismal sounds of the muffled drum, and the doleful notes of the band playing the Dead March in Saul . . . [the condemned man] entered on the right flank of the square, and passed along the front of the line to the left, the soldiers resting upon their arms reversed, that is, muzzle down, and with their two hands upon the bottom of the butt. The sobbing of many of the men could be distinctly heard, and some could not even look on him. . . . The Native troops turned their backs on him as he passed, and many of them wept aloud. . . . He knelt down by the side of his coffin, and prayed for a short time. . . . The criminal's eyes were then bound, and his death warrant read. . . . When the shooting party came to the 'present' every eye was turned from the dreadful scene but, at the well-understood signal, six or more of the men fired, and he instantly fell, five of the shots having lodged in his heart. . . . A whisper then went through the ranks, 'He's dead, he's dead.' The army broke into file, and every man passed him at slow time. This was a ceremony more afflicting than most people would imagine.[18]

Death in all its forms was ever-present, whether on military service or from drinking and boredom, from sunstroke or from a fatal disease such as cholera. In India divine retribution could take immediate and direct effect. The knowledge of this lent a heightened awareness and influenced how men lived. Cawnpore was witness to it all. War was 'a jubilee' and the men marched out in high spirits for each adventure.

Soldiers were called to live a curious dual life, dividing their nature into the part fit for fighting and the part better suited to finer, less crude feelings and activities. Shipp described this as 'a kind of heroism of the soul, which a soldier must nurse and cherish, and which, added to a love of his country's glory and honour will at all times bear him through his perilous services. There is also, unquestionably, a time when vent may be given to the softer feelings and sensibilities, and the heart may be permitted to melt into sweet sympathy.' All through the wars against the Mahrattas and the Pindarees, for the men who fought with the Company army, Cawnpore was the place for 'sweet sympathy'.[19]

John Maxwell's Good Fortune

Early in 1800 John Maxwell left his appointment as Editor of the *India Gazette* and in 1806 became Agent to the Army Contractor in Cawnpore. Tantalisingly few facts are known about his life in the period between Calcutta and Cawnpore. The only official reference to him during this time described him as 'indigo planter, Taundah'. Taundah was up-country near Fyzabad, the old capital of Oude, a centre of the weaving trade and noted for the fine quality of its muslins.

What is certain is that at Taundah Maxwell learned all about the processing and manufacture of indigo and the buying and selling of raw cotton, practical knowledge which he was able to put to good use once he

An indigo factory

became established at Cawnpore. Indigo and cotton were two of the major exports from India. Indigo had been grown and manufactured in Bengal since the end of the eighteenth century. Cakes of indigo, obtained from steeping the indigo plant in water and processing the precipitate, were in great demand in Europe for the beautiful dyes they made. Raw cotton and cotton piece goods were also destined for the European markets – valuable trade at the time of the Industrial Revolution.[20]

To modern eyes the transition from newspaper editor to up-country planter seems strange and impractical. That John Maxwell made it so successfully indicates both the country's enormous potential and his own energy and good management. Life on an indigo estate was very different from his Calcutta existence, but it was not entirely alien to him. It operated on a quasi-feudal system which was not unlike the pattern of his early life in Scotland. On the indigo estate, the ryots rented their land and were given their seed by the landlord. They cultivated it under his overseeing, and once a year carts full of the harvested indigo trailed up to the manager's house for the lengthy and delicate business of processing, on which everybody worked together. As a boy, John Maxwell had witnessed a similar procession of carts every year when the whole neighbourhood trooped into

New Machar for the season of communion (see page 57). In both countries master and men were dependent on each other for their existence, and were united against the common enemy of a harsh and wearying climate.

The Scottish minister's son took to farming indigo and dealing in cotton with marked success. Taundah was in an area largely unexplored by Englishmen and outside the Company jurisdiction. Without the reassuring network of Company administration, the planter's life was both lonely and dangerous, often forty miles from the nearest European in a district terrorised by bands of robbers. Of necessity many planters lived in houses like small forts, with high walls, locked gates and armed servants at every entrance.

On the estate life for a common planter seeking to establish himself was also extremely hard. He lived surrounded by the crops; he rode out and inspected them twice a day; he measured them; he oversaw the sowing and the harvesting and the processing. In the hot weather he did five hours' work before breakfast to avoid the worst of the sun; spent the hottest part of the day inside with the accounts, and in the evening rode round the fields again. And all this work would come to nothing if the rains were late or insufficient. For a man to make money in indigo needed both hard work and good luck.

Mr Longcroft, an indigo planter in that District of Oude confided these hazards to a friend visiting him. 'He said that one or two successful seasons would indeed enable him to leave India, but that such an expectation generally proved delusive, an indigo planter in those parts being subject to a succession of unfavourable years, in which the produce was so disproportioned to the extent of cultivation as barely to reimburse his expenses. The want of an adequate supply of water to compensate the deficiency or irregularity of the rains seemed to be his chief inconvenience.'[21]

John Maxwell was lucky not only in the timing of the monsoon, but also in some friends he made in the district, Major and Mrs Paton. He had been very short of European companionship: his wife, Prudence, had died in Calcutta; of his two children, Agnes was probably also dead, Adam was at school in Scotland. He does not seem to have married again, although a daughter, Frances, was born to him in 1803.[22] Mrs Paton, whom he later described as 'an old and most particular friend of mine' and 'a very clever sensible woman', stood godmother at the baptism of little Fanny Maxwell. It was a fortunate friendship for John Maxwell. He was over forty, he had served his apprenticeship in the district; and the time had come for him to consolidate his success and return to something like civilisation. The Patons provided the opportunity. They were posted to Cawnpore where Major

Paton was to be Deputy Adjutant-General, and in a position to support John Maxwell's application for the job of Agent to the Army and Military Store contractor – a very useful appointment at Army headquarters. It was confirmed on 11 December 1806.

During the delightful cold weather months John Maxwell travelled to Cawnpore. He made the long, hazardous journey through the Vizier's dominions by palanquin. Little Fanny and her ayah travelled in another palanquin, carried in turn by eight of a group of twenty-four bearers; they were accompanied by hordes of servants and baggage and armed retainers. Everything they might require for their journey had to accompany them and the extent of their retinue was immense.[23]

When they reached the Ganges they had to wait for the ferry to take them across the river. Standing on the Oude bank, glad to relax their limbs after travelling for hours in the cramped space of the palanquin, they viewed the whole extent of the station of Cawnpore. The river front was a long line of handsome ghats with steps leading down to the water's edge, the onion domes and conical roofs of many temples beside them. The river was full of shipping, large sailing vessels known as 'the fleet' that brought soldiers and cannon balls and matchlocks and gunpowder up from Calcutta were tied against the bank-the shifting sands of the Ganges made it impossible to anchor. The crude square-sailed boats, laden to the water line with bales of cotton which projected over the sides, clearly indicated the wharfs of the busy Customs House Ghat. Trees softened the outline of the cliffs and here and there among them peeped the thatched roofs of the officers' bungalows. On a high plateau beyond, the endless lines of soldiers' huts stretched away in regular rows. To their left were the heights of Jajmau where Carnac had once received the Nawab of Oude, while to their far right was the huge solid Magazine and beyond it the Palace of Old Kanhpur.

Crossing the Ganges was a major feat which took considerable time and careful planning. Ferries were ordered, wooden flat-bottomed boats which took the majority of passengers and their possessions or charges across the river. These were pulled by men with ropes where the stream was low, and in the deep fast cuttings the oarsmen rowed with short quick strokes to try to cross the current before it carried them too far down stream. The larger animals swam and their attendants swam with them, holding onto their tails and shouting encouragement and directions. Eventually the whole party crossed the river and re-formed their cavalcade. In this manner John Maxwell made his grand entry into Cawnpore.

Cawnpore had a very pleasing, established air about it to the traveller from the District. The bungalows were set back from the road in neat

View of Surseya Ghat, Cawnpore: drawn by S. Prout from a sketch by Captain R. Elliot, RN, c.1822. The view of the Magazine peeping over the top of the trees is artist's licence: the Magazine was in fact out of sight further upstream.

compounds, usually with a circular driveway which allowed conveyances to enter by one gate and leave by another. Walls were well maintained and beside them were planted shady trees which provided a green and cool look to what had once been a dust bowl. But away from the 'gentlemen's residences' roads were mere lanes just wide enough to allow two carriages to pass; they were seamed with ruts, ankle-deep in dust and after rain quite impassable. In the centre of the town the long blocks of barrack buildings and the innumerable lines of the sepoys' huts were separated by the open parade ground from the Great Bazaar where the Indian merchants lived. Few Europeans ever ventured into it.

The houses in the street were chiefly built of mud, bedaubed with cow dung, having no windows towards the streets, and doors so low that a child of ten years old could scarcely go in without stooping; and as to a chimney, there was no such thing. The streets were so narrow in most places, that, as the old saying is, two men might shake hands across the way; and before every door there were filthy gutters and puddles, which are never cleaned, except by some chance shower of rain. The houses of the richer people were but little more convenient than those of the poor, only that they were much loftier, some being raised to the height of three or four stories; they had also little windows towards the tops, which, however, a man could scarcely put his head through; with here and there a balcony or railed gallery on the outside, in which the master of the house, in an evening, is accustomed to sit and smoke his pipe.[24]

The Patons introduced John Maxwell to all the notable residents in Cawnpore, calling in the evenings either in palanquins or buggies at each house in turn. On Sunday they attended a private service held at the General's bungalow which was conducted by the missionary, Henry Martyn. John Maxwell was interested to meet him and afterwards drew him into conversation and they talked 'on eternal things'. [25] The main event of each day, however, was the spectacle provided by the evening drive, when the European residents paraded for exercise and gossip. Local people of distinction, in an amusing variety of equipage and costumes and conveyances, went along most evenings to the Sepoy Parade.

There were officers in their plumed hats and gallant uniform, riding for their lives, with the *sais* panting by their sides, bearing in their hands the *chowries* by which they defended the heads of their horses from the hosts of flies which always tormented them, elephants with their splendid howdahs; curricles and gigs, bullock coaches laden with dames and babies; now and then a string of gawking camels; and in great numbers, the open tonjon bearing the European lady in her elegant evening dress and lace cap or veil, serving as a bonnet.[26]

Two ladies in a ton-jon: by an unknown Indian artist.

Henry Martyn was a familiar figure, driving with a companion in his gig. 'He never looked where he was driving but went dashing through thick and thin being always occupied in teaching Hindustani by word of mouth or discussing some text of Scripture.'[27]

Cawnpore was well served with shops, several being run by Europeans. Mrs Paton probably took her little goddaughter to see 'the Great Europe Shop'. 'One side was set out with caps and bonnets, ribbons, feathers, sashes, and what not. On the other side were all kinds of necklaces, gold earrings, bracelets, coloured shoes, and many other things. Then there were dolls and toys of all kinds. In the verandah also were many kinds of gaudy palanquins and fine furniture; even wheel carriages adorned with gold.'[28]

It was not long before John Maxwell bought a large house and settled down to make his new life at Cawnpore. The appointment of Agent to the Army Contractor included the valuable contract for supplying rum to the troops. Rum was made at a distillery on the fringe of Cawnpore, at Jajmau. While his duties as Agent meant he had to live in Cawnpore, John Maxwell was determined to put to use the knowledge he had gained of indigo and cotton. He had retained his factories at Taundah and within a few months of arriving in Cawnpore had prospected sites which would be suitable for erecting indigo vats and cotton presses. His scheme was to work these through managers. He quickly ran up against the Regulations, which restricted the amount of land a European might hold to fifty *bigahs*. Letters went to and fro between John Maxwell, the Cawnpore Collector and the Board of Revenue.

In compliance with the Regulations respecting the purchasing or renting of houses or lands in the Ceded Provinces by Europeans not in the service of the Honourable Company, I have to request that you will do me the favour to apply for the sanction of Government to my holding a Bangalow [sic] and Garden, which I bought at this station, as well as a spot of ground for an Indigo Manufactory at Mokunpore, which I had rented previous to my knowledge of the Regulations on this head – I have also to solicit permission to rent two pieces of ground, for the purpose of erecting Indigo works at the villages of Kakoopore Pergunnah Sorrajepore and Maharajepore in the Pergunnah of Selimpore; the quantity of ground I require at each of these places does not exceed 150 yards square, and I have the honour to forward to you, for perusal, Rageenamahs from the proprietors, which I beg you will have the goodness to return.[29]

The Collector at first refused to give the necessary permission, objecting that the ground on which the 'Bangalow' stood was more than fifty *bigahs*. John Maxwell got round that obstacle by explaining that 'one fourth of what is included in the measurement consists of Ravines and broken ground, which can be no manner of use to any person, being an entire bed of Conker without the least vegetation on it, and inclosed with the garden solely to prevent their being made a nuisance. . . .'[30] Over the important matter of acquiring land on which to set up factories he found he had a very useful way round the Regulations; he could buy land in the name of his son, Adam Maxwell. Adam, being 'country born' before the 1793 restriction was introduced, came into the category of people entitled to hold land in their own name. This allowed John Maxwell to take advantage of the many estates that failed to pay their taxes and were put up for farm. As landowners defaulted, finding the new Company revenue policy too harsh, many absconded and John Maxwell was one of the few Europeans who, through this loophole in the law, was able to increase his holdings and acquire many villages that eventually stretched the whole extent of the Cawnpore District from Kanauj to Jajmau.

There are many references to John Maxwell's property in the revenue records of that period. In 1814 the Cawnpore Collector reported one such example:

Mahomed Ewuz having made a practice of embezzling the revenues of Mahowedpore Bija and Nahurghatty as well as of Muhla, and other estates for the past 3 or 4 years I determined to bring him to punishment and to this end I pushed the law against him in support of my demands. Preferring however selling his estates to going to Jail, he thought proper to make them over to Adam Maxwell by deed of sale who duly discharged the balances as under written, the recovery of which was entirely hopeless.[31]

John Maxwell's will lists cotton presses and go-downs at Jajmau, indigo factories at three villages near Kanauj, considerable property in indigo and cotton near Taundah and the rum distillery at Jajmau.[32] The overseeing and control of these many ventures took great skill; they were organised from his office in the compound of his bungalow. Here, regularly, there was a long procession of visitors asking John Maxwell to loan them money. Colonels, captains, ensigns, surgeons, merchants, even Mrs Grant, the Collector's wife, all came to borrow money.[33] He in his turn borrowed money from an Indian *shroff* (banker), one Beharee Lall, setting a precedent that was to be followed for the next hundred years in Cawnpore–English enterprise backed by Indian money.

Maxwell's office was in two sections, one to deal with bills written in Persian and the other for bills written in English. The English writer or clerk was Mr Samson who earned Rs 100 a month.[34] There were grass mats on the floor and jars of quills on the desk. Red ink was made by mixing gall with vinegar; a large pot of sand stood by the huge ledgers to be used for blotting. Entries in the ledgers covered a wide variety of subjects. Orders were placed for boatloads of firewood and molasses to come from up-country for the distillery, with casual labour employed to unload it at the landing stage. Indigo seed was brought from Taundah – indigo was a comparatively new venture in the Cawnpore District – and when the seed arrived duty had to be paid twice over, once to the Vizier and again at the Customs House.[35] A good atmosphere must have prevailed among the men who worked for John Maxwell. One entry reads 'Iman [sic] for Holi': Holi is an important Hindu festival and by giving a small bonus to his workers on such occasions John Maxwell expressed his respect for their way of life.[36]

Cotton was grown 'abroad', in the District near Agra. It was loaded on to boats, 'rude barks,[37] which were steered with the minimum of effort, gliding swiftly with the current and avoiding the many shifting sandbanks until they reached Cawnpore. At the Customs House wharfs the bales were brought into the town by the cotton brokers or merchants who sold them to men such as John Maxwell. It was a job he undertook personally because the brokers were capable of many tricks : 'One of the principal frauds of these brokers and native cotton dealers was that of exposing the cotton, spread out on cowdung floors to the nightly dews, and then weighing it early the next morning in a moist state to the receivers. This occasioned great loss in the weight when it became dry.'[38] The only way to prevent this was to make unexpectedly early visits to the broker and test handfuls of cotton against the cheek. With an honest dealer the cotton felt perfectly dry.

At the go-down the cotton was spread in the sun to dry and then combed out. In the screw house coolies pressed the cotton and 'screwed' it into bales, secured with iron bands and twine and gunny until it was tightly packed and ready to be shipped to Calcutta.

One of the early lists of Cawnpore traders gives John Maxwell as the only European to employ other Europeans. William Dingwell, the sailor who had travelled to India with Maxwell on the *William Pitt*, was in charge of the cotton presses; R. W. Finch at Muckampore was 'assistant to Maxwell' and John Sago at Marajpore was 'from Malacca and in the employ of Maxwell'. These managers of indigo estates led very lonely lives, only very occasionally seeing a visitor from Cawnpore, a long day's ride, but it speaks well for John Maxwell that they were content to remain in his employ. The estates themselves were set on high ground and well defended. The approach to the village was blocked by a jungle of bamboo and enormous sinister-looking cacti bushes. The walls beyond were nine feet thick and high enough to incorporate loopholes for matchlocks. When money had to be sent to the estates, John Maxwell had to arrange for armed sepoys to guard the bullock *hackery*.

One matter to which John Maxwell gave great importance, later remarked upon in the official *Gazetteer*, was the need to build as many wells as possible. The lands of the Cawnpore District only needed water to make them fertile. The extent of Maxwell's wells was considerable. When Sir George Nugent, the newly appointed Commander-in-Chief, and his wife made an official visit to the station in 1811 they dined with John Maxwell. Lady Nugent mentioned the subject of the wells in her diary:

At 8 we dined with Mr Maxwell, the heat extreme today. Mr Maxwell told me upon the subject of wells, he has no less than 2,500 open at present. On his indigo plantation, there are often double that number. Just now I am sure there must be many required, for the ground is as hard as flint.[39]

Having at last achieved success John Maxwell sat for his portrait to a miniature artist. He looks out at us with an air of guarded intelligence, and it was this combination of shrewdness and warmth of heart that had made him one of the wealthiest and most respected inhabitants of Cawnpore.

'Liquor! This Baneful Traffick'

*India was an elegant country – you'd always a fine thirst upon you
and the means of quenching it immediately at hand.*[40]

Company troops had barely set up camp at Cawnpore before an official rum distillery was established. The conditions of the soldiers' service in the East made many of them depend on liquor for survival. What concerned the civil and military authorities was how to prevent the men illegally procuring liquor of such inferior quality that it would endanger their health and be available in quantities that threatened the peace of the community. There were huge sums to be made in the traffic of liquor smuggled up the river by traders. A gallon of Bengal rum cost Rs 1 but would be sold illegally to the soldiers for Rs 4 or 5. The Acting Collector of Cawnpore wrote to the Board of Revenue warning them that ' . . . Bengal Spirit of a very strong nature, perhaps 20 degrees above proof, is brought up in large quantities by a great variety of people, who whether European, Bengalees, Portuguese or the native born of English, may be classed as is frequently done under the term of *Up-Country Trader*, and that the quantities which these people import and dispose of secretly and by stealth is one cause of intoxication. . . .'[41]

William Kelly, 'an unhoused European',[42] was a typical example of how a man came to be drawn into selling liquor illicitly. When caught selling rum to the troops and arrested and charged, he pleaded ignorance. Kelly was a native of Dublin, twenty-six years old, and had come to India in 1811 as a personal servant to Major-General Hugh Stafford. He accompanied the General up-country and remained with him two years in Cawnpore. In 1813 he was discharged and entered the service of the Nabob of Oude as coachman and huntsman. He left the Nabob's service at his own request and returned to Cawnpore to sell up his property and return to Europe. It was during this period that he was tempted into smuggling rum. The Magistrate was lenient and discharged him, provided he left Cawnpore at once for Calcutta.

People such as William Kelly, not resident at Cawnpore, were difficult to prosecute. The answer seemed to be for Government to license certain distilleries and sutlers, to provide a controlled outlet for good liquor. The Commanding Officer Cawnpore, Colonel Wood, wrote a thoughtful report in 1808:

I beg to state it as my opinion that the health of the European soldiery has been very much injured by the facility with which spirituous liquors have been obtained, particularly at this station, and this opinion is not only founded on my own experience in the command of a European regiment, but has also been confirmed by the sentiments on the subject of medical persons and officers who have resided much longer than myself in India. I am however inclined to believe that it will not be possible wholly to prevent this baneful traffick, and where no good spirit is to be purchased the soldier will I am convinced find the means of purchasing bad, whatever may be the distance at which it is sold. For which reason therefore I beg to recommend to the Board of Commissioners the measure of establishing regimental canteens, which should be placed entirely under the control of the Commanding Officer of each regiment. The liquors might be supplied by the Army Contractor, and should consist of good beer, wine, brandy, and the best arrack, and for which the sergeant of the canteen or sutler might be made to pay to government a certain tax collected either on the liquors at the time they were delivered by the contractor, or on a licence granted to the sutler for that purpose. . . .[43]

The Collector doubted the propriety of a Revenue Officer's licensing shops for the sale of spirits. Two sutlers' shops were nevertheless established on a licence from Government. One was in the lines of the European cavalry corps at a licence fee of Rs 5 a day, and the other in the European infantry lines at Rs 9 a day. No other shopkeeper was authorised to sell liquor. Some years earlier the Army Contractor had set up a rum distillery at Jajmau. When John Maxwell became the Army Contractor, he also took over the job of supplying the sutlers, adding rum to the other commodities in which he traded.

The licensing system proved difficult to administer. It failed to prevent abuses. Countless cases came up before the Magistrate. A shopkeeper named Thomas Tolly, 'this notorious seller of liquor',[44] was accused of illegally selling liquor. The charge against him stated that 'crowds of soldiers from morning till night were seen frequenting the house of Tolly and that they were plied with liquor by Tolly and his *Chowbook Sowar* Kaleh Khan [literally a rough-rider, but in this context his bodyguard and chucker-out]. That the Europeans, when they went into the house, were sober, but that they came out in a state of inebriety.' Tolly denied the charge and claimed the soldiers came for the amusement of cockfighting, and that he never plied them with liquor. The Magistrate raided the shop next door to Tolly's, broke through into his house, and seized '8 or 10 cases of Bengal rum bottled off in English bottles and with the cork marked Cogniac Brandy [*sic*] which however would not pass current with me until I had compared the liquor with Mr Maxwell's rum and I found them to be one and the same'.[45]

As far as the European community was concerned, the Magistrate had little scope for authority. If a European trader found himself in court for illegal activities, he was likely to be punished with a fine. Government imposed a limit on the size of the fine, and forbade Magistrates to imprison offenders if they would not, or could not, pay. The traders took advantage of the Magistrate's lack of effective power and the confusion that existed between areas of responsibility held by civil and military authorities. As the then Commander-in-Chief complained in 1813:

The European shop-keepers in general at the station of Cawnpore, had for a length of time past indulged themselves in a latitude of conduct and expression not merely indicative of the most perfect independence, but evincing such a total disregard to the control and authority of the Commanding Officer and even of the Civil Power, as made it in his Excellency's opinion extremely doubtful how far any admonition conveyed under his individual authority would prove effectual to the purpose intended.[46]

When he overstepped the maximum fine of Rs 500, the Magistrate was forced to make a refund to the guilty party. The court's ultimate check on European civilians was still that with which Wellesley had threatened the editors of Calcutta: the cancellation of their licence to remain in India and deportation to England.

In 1812 the Magistrate protested that unless Government allowed heavier fines to be imposed, 'the European shop keepers in Cawnpore would with impunity continue the sale of liquors to the European soldiers, many of whose lives had been paid forfeit to the improvident use of it.'[47] The official medical report on the case against James Duhan for selling illegal spirits declared that the deaths of at least four out of five of the young soldiers who died in hospital in India were occasioned by the free use of 'ardent spirits'. To this anarchic state of affairs the Governor-General was eventually alerted. He ordered the Cawnpore Magistrate to remove any such transgressors from Cawnpore and to withdraw their licence to remain in India.

This was a power which the Company seems to have been reluctant to put into effect. James Duhan was seriously warned three times but was at length allowed to remain in the country.[48] It seems that Government 'forebore to proceed to the extreme measure of revoking Mr Duhan's licence in consideration of his large family and the ruin which might probably entail upon their affairs'.

The enforcement of the law was made more difficult by the disagreement and misunderstandings between the authorities involved. The Collector, mindful of his revenue, felt that the issuing of a licence came within his jurisdiction. The Colonel commanding the Station, concerned for the health of his men, believed the control of the sutlers should be his responsibility. The Magistrate, well aware of the breaches in law and order that went hand in hand with the sale of liquor, considered the authority to issue licences lay with him. They did their quarrelling on paper, dashing off letters to each other and to the Council in Calcutta, loaded with references to orders and regulations.

The volume of paperwork was so great that it obscured the real basis of the dispute. The baffled Collector on one occasion had to write to the supplier of rum, John Maxwell, to ask him to explain his official position:[49]

April 1813 Cawnpore Collectorship: A question having arisen in a case before the Magistrate whether I can grant a License to the sutler in Cantonments for the sale of liquor Manufactured by you, another arises, how far are you authorised to sell in wholesale to the sutler, I beg that you will inform me of the nature of your distillery and how far you may consider yourself entitled to dispose of liquor to individuals. It being intended to refer the question stated by the Magistrate, I have taken the liberty of begging this information as I cannot at present trace in the records of this office anything relating to your distillery.

John Maxwell's reply defines his own role but sheds little light on the place of the authorities:[50]

The Distillery at Jagemow [Jajmau] was established so far back I believe, as 1786 or 1787 by the Contractor for victualling the European troops, and has been carried on from that time to the present, by the different contractors for victualling, with the exception of some intervals when other arrangements for the supply of Rum were in force – during the last seven years it has been under my management part of the time as agent and latterly as Contractor – on my receiving charge of the Contractor's concerns as Agent in 1806 I found that in order to prevent spirituous Liquor being sold to the Soldiers the Sutler was required by the Regulations for his shop to purchase the spirits he furnished from the contractor, these Regulations still exist, and under the authority of them, and with the sanction of the Commanding Officer I have supplied the sutler of this Station, and of Meerut ever since.

The authorities' dispute came to a head over the case of Daniel Clarke, 'a mere boy of 11 or 12',[51] who was found to hold a sutler's licence, to the outrage of the Commanding Officer. It seems that Daniel's father had been a merchant at Cawnpore with a half share in selling spirituous liquors under licence from the Collector. When Clarke died, leaving a widow and five children, Mrs Clarke raised a loan and bought the concern outright. She continued to trade for two years without complaint. When she also died, the children and the profit from the shop were entrusted to Mr Foley, writer at the Customs House, the mortgagee, who, as the licence was in the name of Clarke, put forward the eldest son as the nominal licensee, despite his extreme youth.

The Field Commander, General Champagne, on discovering Daniel Clarke's age, ordered him to stop selling liquor, and set up a protégé of his own in Clarke's place:

Finding the person under whose name a licence has been granted by the Collector to sell spirituous liquors within the limits of Cantonments an *improper one*, I endeavour to rectify the evil by procuring an Englishman who has long been in the country and whose conduct in the public service has been noticed and rewarded by Marquis Wellesley when Governor in India. This man I ordered to take charge of the liquor shop at Cawnpore giving timely notice to the deposed person to part with his property and to cease selling liquor.

Mr Hill, the man whom General Champagne appointed, started selling liquor before the Collector had granted him a licence. The Collector promptly issued a warrant for the seizure of his stock, while Daniel Clarke continued in business. An absurd situation then arose, with the Collector giving instructions for Clarke's shop to stay open and the General sending troops with orders to close it. The Collector refused to issue the General's protegé with a licence. The General would not allow the official holder of the licence to operate it. The Magistrate chose to uphold the letter of the law and took the collector's part: 'It is not in any way provided that you shall take away the licence of any individual because you wish the appointment of another person, or that you should render the operation of that licence nil and void by the total suppression of the sale.'

While these furious letters flew back and forth, Government was losing revenue. To settle the matter, the Vice-President in Council, with great tact, intervened. He reprimanded the General for interfering and confirmed Daniel Clarke as licensee for the term of the licence. Thereafter it was to be issued to the General's applicant.

Government might settle one dispute, but relations between the civil and military authorities in Cawnpore continued so strained that in 1811, to stop this squabbling, Government felt obliged to move the entire civilian administration out of the army's way – to Bithoor, half a day's arduous ride away. In vain the Collector protested against the dangers of the move. Bithoor was so close to the Nabob's dominion that dacoits – robber gangs – might easily attack and rob the Collector's Treasury and 'succeed in carrying off into the Nabob's country sacks of rupees e'er intimation of the robbery could reach Cawnpore'.[52] Large sums of money, often seven or eight lakhs of rupees, were kept in the Treasury for the payment of troops and the Collector wanted a regular battalion of troops to guard it. He argued that the move would provoke great expense, and an extra battalion would cost Rs 17,000 a month. Most of all he resented the enormous inconvenience of his office being twelve miles from the focus of his work. Everybody in Cawnpore, whenever they needed the help of the Collectorate, would have to drag there in carriage or bullock cart, at walking pace over unmade dirt tracks, shaken, jolted and choked with fine dust. But Government was adamant and from 1811 to 1819 the civil affairs of Cawnpore were conducted from Bithoor. This continued until the arrival of Bajee Rao, the ex-Peishwa of Poona.[53] His exile to Bithoor in 1818 caused the recall of the offices back to Cawnpore, where they were established at Nawabganj, at the edge of the old village of Kanhpur, and as far from the military cantonments as possible.

Home Life of the Maxwell Family

John Maxwell's house in 1806 stood in extensive grounds overlooking the river. It was a bungalow with thick walls of sun-dried brick and covered with a thatched roof so steeply pitched it looked like an untidy beehive. The house closest to it, on the other side of the public road leading to the bathing ghat, was a more modest affair.[54] It belonged to Richard Nann, a silversmith long established in India, who lived there with his daughter Elizabeth.[55] John Maxwell formed an attachment to Elizabeth Nann and to all intents and purposes she became his wife. Together they enjoyed the settled domestic happiness that had until then eluded him. Elizabeth Nann bore him four sons, Peter, Hugh, David and James.

Under the shaggy eaves, the half-lit verandahs were strewn with large toys. Rocking horses, wooden carts, baby carriages proclaimed a household of many 'baba logue'.[56] Indoors a profusion of toys and books littered every room. When the weather was too hot for the children to play in the garden they were forced to remain for hours inside and roamed from room to room, amusing themselves and the tribe of servants who were in constant attendance. Each boy was accompanied by two servants whose duty it was to see that his little charge got into no mischief, came to no physical harm, was never bored and kept out of the way of the grown-ups. A genuine affection existed between the servants and their small masters.

All morning the four young boys played in the darkened house, wearing the scantiest of clothes. In the hot afternoon they rested and slept, but at the approach of evening they were woken from their siesta, bathed and dressed in all their finery and escorted into the garden to play. In the stables they loved to be lifted on to the back of the big 'Europe horse' – highly prized by their father because it had come from England. In the outhouses where the carriages were kept, the saddles and bridles hung on hooks, and there were huge bins of grain and cakes of rough soap. Further on were tethered the sheep and cows kept for meat.[57] Everywhere the hens pecked and squawked and the boys would throw them wheat and bajrah grain.

Europe Horse: Company painting on paper.

The Ganges, flowing below the house, was a source of endless fascination for the children. Ferry boats plied backwards and forwards to the Kingdom of Oude. There were buffaloes swimming across, elephants being scrubbed with bricks and douching themselves with water. Men on light rafts kept afloat by empty gourds crossed half under water, apparently unafraid of the crocodiles sunning themselves on the far banks. On festivals and holy days the boys sat on the wall and watched the crowds going down to the river. They bought sweets from the sweetmeat man and cheap gaudy paper toys from the toy seller and threw coins for the beggars. They grew silent and solemn when the funeral parties chanted their way to the burning ghat and laughed and clapped their hands when the monkey man passed by with his drums and – on long ropes – his monkeys dressed in skirts and hats. Each day they absorbed the exhilaration of the strange contrasts and inequalities of life in India.

The evenings when John Maxwell drove out for dinner and their mother entertained friends in her own apartments were for the children the best time of all. They were left alone with the servants; supper of '*pish-pash*'[58] was served at the undersized nursery tables, presided over by the old ayah, the Buriah Ayah, who was in charge of everything and everyone. 'The Buriah Ayah was very old and quite grey, she was wont to sit on the floor with the children lying or sitting beside her. . . . The Buriah was born at old

Cawnpore, a native city close by to the cantonment, but she could tell nothing of her age, except that she was very very old and had lived there before the Sahib Log had come.'[59]

At last the children shut their eyes and snuggled down under the thin covers. The candles in glass sconces cast huge shadows on the walls, but the light did not penetrate to the corners of the room. Outside, on the river bank, the jackals began their nightly howling. The Buriah Ayah fanned the children and sang them a lullaby, all the while gently kneading and massaging their little limbs. The texture of her hands felt soft and dry; the bangles on her arms jingled and a faint smell of coconut oil and jasmine came from her grey hair, strained back under the cotton sari.

> Ninni baba ninni,
> Muckan roti chinee;
> Muckan roti hogiah
> Chota baba sogiah.★

And so the Maxwell boys slept, the old myths and legends told them by the ayah colouring their dreams.

It was a large and amiable household. With business prospering, John Maxwell needed more help and in 1811 he arranged for Adam to return from schooling in Scotland. With Adam came Alexander Burnett, his cousin from Elrick House, the 'big house' at New Machar. Burnett was to become John Maxwell's trusted confidant. Fanny Maxwell, the only girl among this family of boys, was a great favourite with everyone, so much so that she remained in India until she was twelve. The four boys the ayah had sung to sleep were born within five years of each other and were outwardly very alike, but it was Hugh, John Maxwell's third son and fourth child, who was to inherit most of his father's ability and energy and to carry on his concerns.

Every European in India was aware of the possibility of sudden death. There were dangers everywhere: any journey was fraught with the possibility of a meeting with dacoits or wild beasts; disease, the climate and over-indulgence took a severe toll even in a settled domestic life. For every man returned to England with a fortune, many lay dead, buried in up-country cemeteries. This consciousness informed the lives of men such as John Maxwell, whose whole existence seemed to depend on a benevolent deity: despite all their efforts, a hailstorm or the failure of the monsoon could ruin their crops; a sudden chill or fever might end their lives. Consequently

★Sleep little one, sleep,
  You shall have buttered bread and sugar;
  When the bread and butter are all gone
  Little baby will be fast asleep.

The ayah entertains the baba logue: watercolour by a Patna artist, c.1820.

they took every opportunity to secure their hard-won achievements, both in property and in worldly wisdom, for their children. The last letter John Maxwell wrote to his daughter Fanny (see Appendix 1), then at school in England,[60] was full of fatherly advice, given with an eye to the unforeseeable future:

I suppose that you have already acquired all the more solid parts of female education, and that your attention will now be required to the ornamental, such as music, dancing and drawing – if you find you have any talent for the latter, but without that I think it a waste of time to try it. Do not forget what you have already learnt and let me especially request the greatest attention to your reading with propriety, writing and spelling correctly. I hope you will always keep up an intimate correspondence with your aunts, to whose kindness you have been greatly indebted.

The year 1816, in which John Maxwell had written to Fanny, was particularly unhealthy. The hot winds had continued much longer than usual. For week after week the 'bangalow' had been shut up against the great heat. Each morning before the sun got up, every outer door of the house and every window was tightly closed. All the interior doorways and venetians were left open and the private apartments were screened by curtains of grass partially covered with green silk, which looked like fine wire work. It helped to keep the heat out but it reduced the house to almost total darkness. Mr Maxwell worked at his accounts, Elizabeth Nann lay upon a sofa, trying to make the effort to read, while the children played in their nursery, their attendants in a state of perfect apathy, chewing paun. There was no sound 'but the monotonous click click of the punkah or the melancholy moaning of the burning blast without, with the splash and dripping of the water thrown over the *tatties*'. At six the wind generally dropped, the *tatties* were removed and the doors and windows of the house opened. The family then took an airing in the carriage or walked about the garden.[61] The evenings and nights were so warm that they brought no real relief. The family sat out on the *cherbutra* sipping brandy and water and watching 'the glorious appearance of the heavens and the brilliancy of the starlit nights at Cawnpore',[62] fanning themselves and wondering when the first welcome rain would fall.

After a bad drought, torrential rains followed. The combination of the two bred an epidemic. In Cawnpore, eight or nine soldiers were buried daily. Once a man had caught fever, his chances of recovery were not great. Outside the towns there were no hospitals or official care. Everyone kept his own supply of medicines, which he prescribed for himself and his family as he thought necessary. Chests of medicines were among the imported articles available in the Calcutta Europe shops. To anyone reading the advertisements now, the efficacy of most of the medicines seems dubious. 'As elegant and genuine as if procured from Apothecaries' Hall: Tinctures of every Description, Extracts, Pills, Plaisters, Ointments.'[63] Even in towns where there would be four military surgeons to a Brigade, the drastic medical practice of the period seems as likely to have hurried a patient on to death as to have held him back.

A feverish patient was treated with an emetic to make him perspire; frictions were applied and saline draughts given. It was usual for four or five ounces of blood to be taken from the arm to reduce the blood pressure and an enema, administered to 'discharge those vitiated morbid humours' consistent with the modern practice, all too often proved 'ineffectual'.[64]

Sick people seem to have endured such treatment with great patience. A contemporary recorded something of what he suffered in a very matter of fact way: 'Taken suddenly ill with the prevailing epidemic fever, had 30 leeches applied to my head and was given a strong emetic which kept me vomiting the greater part of the day; wound up with 'rattling' pills at night. Rather weak. . . . Severe cold pains in chest and difficulty in breathing. 40 leeches applied to my chest; feet in hot water.'[65]

John Maxwell was suddenly taken ill, a month after his letter to Fanny. He was gripped by a high fever, his whole body and skin burning as if on fire and he tossed restlessly, only half sensible of the people around him. Elizabeth Nann bathed his face and hands with vinegar and applied cool compresses to his head. The children were forbidden to make a sound, the whole house held its breath. Elizabeth Nann sat beside the sickbed day and night and servants took it in turn to beat away the flies with a *chowry*.[66] His last conscious action, on 23 December 1816, was to draw up a codicil to his will. Fever and ague continued for four long days and nights until he became exhausted with the struggle. On 27 December 1816 he died.

There was little time to arrange the funeral. Because of the heat a body was often buried at sunset on the day of death. The bereaved family had a short time to choose from a variety of funeral equipment. One undertaker's stock ranged from a coffin 'covered with black Boglipore,* nails, lining and bearers to carry the body to the ground, grave digging and attendance on the funeral' for Rs 32, to a teak wood coffin 'made in the best manner, with an inside shell covered with superfine broadcloth, inside lined with silk, a mattrass and pillow; a complete set of the best furniture, breastplate, glory,[67] and urn, handles, escutcheons, angel drops, gilt lace etc; hearse and mourning coach, and use of the best velvet pall; plume of feathers, grave digging and attendance'[68] for Rs 400. He also supplied silk hat bands, crepe, scarfs and monuments.

*A town in Bihar, famous for the weaving of silk and cotton fabric.

John Maxwell's taste, or that of his family, lay at the simpler end of the scale. He was buried in the Kacheri Cemetery, the oldest of five cemeteries in Cawnpore, and still in 1816 unhallowed ground. At a time when both grief and social standing were indicated by ornate and lavish tombs, rising to temples and obelisks, John Maxwell's is a plain tablet, topped with marble, into which the lead lettering was so deeply cut that even after 150 years of monsoon rain, the words are still legible today.[69]

HERE REST THE REMAINS OF JOHN MAXWELL ESQ.RE

A Gentleman many Years Resident in India,
Who was born at New Macher in Aberdeenshire, on
the 28th Day of November A.D. 1762, And
Died at Cawnpore December the 27th
A.D. 1816
in the 55th year of His Age.

To pleasing Manners
And an Agreeable Exterior
He added the best qualities of the Heart
and the clearest conception of the Mind
and an affectionate and Dutiful Son
A fond and indulgent Parent
A kind and generous Brother
A warm and steady Friend
In every change of Circumstance, in
every vicissitude of Fortune, He uniformly preserved
The equanamity of Temper so becoming a
Man and Christian so rarely met with in the World.
Misfortunes could not sour his Disposition
Prosperity could not Corrupt Him
His Integrity was Unimpeachable
His perseverence Indefatigable
Charity and benevolence marked all his Actions
And influenced all his Opinions
He constantly Preserved the Respect and Esteem
of the Community to which he belonged
And the Love and attachment of A Large
Circle of Friends.

By the terms of John Maxwell's will (see Appendix 2), everything he owned was to be sold and the bulk of the proceeds equally divided between his children. The only exception was the house and grounds once owned by Richard Nann which now became known as the Jenannah – this is a rustic pronunciation of the Persian word *zenana*. Elizabeth Nann continued to live in this house with an income from John Maxwell's bequest. There was provision also for John Maxwell's sisters, and for his nephew and executor, Alexander Burnett. The gift of Rs 2,000, four times the price of Elizabeth Nann's bungalow, to his 'old and faithful servant Manshee Bhagwana' suggests a highly valued relationship between master and servant.[70]

In Maxwell's will all business affairs and the well-being of his young family were entrusted to Alexander Burnett, rather than to Adam Maxwell. Alexander Burnett, born in 1790, good-looking, charming and with the heritage of Elrick House behind him, seems to have earned the complete confidence and affection of John Maxwell, who was a shrewd judge of character. But John Maxwell could not foresee the exceptional changes which were about to affect the social stability of Cawnpore, nor that Burnett would become infected with the widespread gaming mania which would ruin him in a madness of opportunism.

Burnett began the task of realising the extensive property:[71] the process eventually took six years. Hundreds of chests of indigo were shipped to London, thousands of maunds of cotton went on the market. He organised the sale of John Maxwell's personal possessions; among the goods left unsold were a pair of plated girandoles valued at Rs 900 and twelve dozen bottles of Malmsey wine at Rs 50 a dozen – indications of the lifestyle of a very prosperous man. Both Burnett and Adam Maxwell exercised their option to buy some of the property for themselves and the rum contract was renegotiated in Burnett's name. During this period Adam Maxwell and Alexander Burnett formed the firm of Maxwell and Burnett to carry on the extensive business in cotton, indigo and rum established by John Maxwell. They also acted as up-country agents for Calcutta firms.

At the same time they attended to the daily affairs of Elizabeth Nann and the four young boys. Now that the small bungalow was to be her home, it was redecorated. Walls were replastered, balustrades strengthened, tailors stitched new ceiling clothes, 2,500 bundles of straw arrived in boats at the bottom of the garden from across the river to rethatch the roof. Glass was fitted in the windows, chintz covers made for the sofas, the cane chairs rerattaned, the *hackery* and buggy repaired, while hundreds of new earthen pots were bought for the garden. In the account books, references to the growing children are frequent; eight pairs of shoes, eight pairs of socks, new clothes for the children, pillow cases, the barber to trim their hair, silver forks . . . no detail was too small to be omitted from the inventories.

Sketch believed to be of Alexander Burnett, c.1810, perhaps by one of his sisters at the time he went out to India to join John Maxwell at Cawnpore.

Gradually John Maxwell's sons grew up. Each of them intended to go to England in due course, to be brought up in Scotland by John Maxwell's unmarried sisters. Hugh, David and James did go, but Elizabeth Nann could not bear to part with all her children, and kept her eldest child, Peter, with her. So it was that Hugh Maxwell, although the second of the four boys born to Elizabeth Nann and John Maxwell, found himself fulfilling the part of an elder brother.

5
Unprincipled Extravagance
1822–1832

―――

The Decline and Fall of George Ravenscroft

Three years after John Maxwell died the war against the Mahrattas came to an end and the Mahratta leaders capitulated one by one. By the middle of 1819 the Governor-General, Lord Hastings, had completed the work Wellesley had set out to do. Vast tracts of land in central India had been directly annexed by the Company, and many small native states now acknowledged its overlordship. For the first time in twenty years peace came to the central plains of India . . . 'the peasants actually have reappeared in thousands like people come out of the earth to claim and re-cultivate lands that have been fallow for twenty years.'[1] Everywhere the villagers acclaimed the Company Raj for restoring peace.

Cawnpore, which had come into existence to support war, floundered over the transition to peace. Social amusements, such as the theatrical entertainments and the race meetings that had at one time been no more than interludes in the more serious business of waging war, now became the main antidote to boredom. It was a town of quarrels and gossip, and of values that got out of proportion. Without the restraints which a time of war exerts, the sense of opportunity went to men's heads like champagne laced with brandy. A gambling frenzy seized Cawnpore; the most serious-minded and respectable individuals behaved as though possessed. It took ten years for the town to emerge from this unsettled period.

The story of George Ravenscroft is a moral tale of his times. It demonstrated both the strengths and weaknesses of the administrative system, and shows up some of the characteristics of Cawnpore society – its inter-relatedness, for instance: everyone was in debt to everyone else, and if

OPPOSITE The Misses Ramus: *watercolour copy by J.H.S. Mann after the Gainsborough portait destroyed by fire at Waddesdon in 1890. Louisa Ravenscroft's beautiful aunts, painted by Gainsborough and Romney.*

one amateur banker failed, the entire town might be ruined. The story is an example too of the prevalent gambling mania. It was widely believed that fortunes were to be made if only enough capital could be raised to back a venture; and in the meantime one could live extravagantly on the expected profits.

George Ravenscroft was described by a contemporary as the handsomest and most athletic man in India.[2] These were not his only attributes. He was one of a new kind of Company servant, who arrived in India at the beginning of the nineteenth century believing it to be a land of infinite potential. Here a man might fulfil a marvellous destiny: in the position of a Collector his work could improve the lives of thousands while bringing glory to the Empire and honourable profits to the Company. The successful Collector might feel considerable satisfaction. Ravenscroft arrived in Cawnpore to take up the Collectorship in this state of mind. He had been sixteen years in India and it was his fourth such post;[3] but his fervent idealism remained untempered by practical consideration.

When Ravenscroft became Collector of Cawnpore, the Collectorate was still twelve miles outside Cawnpore, at Bithoor. Here Ravenscroft and his wife Louisa,[4] a society beauty with a large private income, set up their home. With the greatest enthusiasm Ravenscroft threw himself into his new job, writing passionate letters to Government on the subject of agriculture.

The celebrated Sully calls agriculture one of the breasts from which the State draws its nourishment. That great man could not possibly have given us a more happy simile. Your lordship's discerning mind will point out to you in an instant the aptness of this simile to the source of wealth in India, from whence springs for the most part the revenue of the State.[5]

He himself assiduously cultivated the art, experimenting with varieties of cotton, inventing a hoe plough, and passing on his opinions to Government for the edification of both hemispheres. Clearly he judged these experiments to be part of the many-sided responsibilities of Collectorship: he ended one letter 'Bonus Civis, Bonus Agricola!' He was even more passionate on the subject of the revenue. He seems to have regarded everything to do with Government as sacrosanct, and accordingly his attitude is zealous almost to fanaticism. He referred on one occasion to 'this sacred depository the record office', and complained about the worthiness of his fellow civil servants. 'In so short a period after my arrival I regret the necessity of drawing your serious notice to the conduct of the Treasurer of this office, but the duty which I owe to the Public Interests and to the Government is paramount to all consideration of a lenient nature.'[6]

In the light of later events, his righteous prosecution of offenders makes pathetic reading. 'In those cases in which an embezzlement of the public money shall be brought to proof, the Board may depend on my exposing the parties implicated to their notice, and they will I trust make a signal example of all public Robbers who seem generally to have marked out the Government as a fair object for plunder.'[7] Government response to his complaints was cool. But for the next five years Ravenscroft continued happily as Collector. He was a man of principle, known and liked for the easiness of his temper; he earned a good salary and lived a life of strict economy.

The long-drawn-out campaign against the Mahrattas had ended with the surrender of Bajee Rao, the Peishwa of Poona. When the Peishwa was settled in exile in Bithoor in 1818 and the Cawnpore Collectorate moved from Bithoor back to Cawnpore, Ravenscroft set up his new offices at Nawabganj, at the extreme western end of the station. Now the pattern of his life changed; the impact of Cawnpore society, the recent death of his wife Louisa and perhaps the influence of Charlotte Fitzgerald, whom he had married in 1820,[8] all seemed to have prompted lavish living.

The Cawnpore residents were amazed at the display of wealth and style and at the manner in which their Collector lived. He affected the most exquisite Indian costumes, rich velvets embroidered in silver. His rooms were filled with elegant furniture, 'beautiful cut wood sofas with chintz bedding and pillows',[9] expensive oil paintings in handsome carved gilt frames, including one of the Duke of Wellington,[10] and time-pieces from the well-known clockmaker, Hare of London. At dinner his guests sat round a huge toonwood table with brass paws, and drank from 'richly cut champagne glasses'. After dinner the men gathered in the library and were provided with hookahs with long silver mouthpieces tipped with gold, such as only the Nawab of Oude used. The library was filled with a large collection of leather-bound volumes proclaiming the range of George Ravenscroft's interests: there were books on philosophy, chemistry, agriculture, the classics, the arts and politics as well as collections of anecdotes.

After two years of princely living, rumours that all was not well with the Cawnpore Treasury began to filter through to Government. Instructions reached the unsuspecting Magistrate that the Company books must be examined. Ravenscroft begged for time to adjust his accounts, but the position was hopeless. He had embezzled large sums of money from the Treasury. The news was received by the citizens of Cawnpore 'with astonishment little less than despair'.

Ravenscroft wrote to Henry Newnham, the Magistrate, asking for help, in terms as flowery and as consciously high-minded as ever:

'I have been rained down with villainy, and if the Board make a blaze of the matter, the money will be lost to the government; but if they . . . allow me two months all will be repaid. I depend on your friendship in going out to meet the Board. It is in my power to put a pistol to my head, but I consider it more manly to endeavour to make some restitution for my errors, and finally (if all else fail) to undergo the sentence of the law.'[11]

Newnham, together with an officer called Major Cunliffe, agreed to act as Ravenscroft's trustees. Their motives for doing so were not merely sympathy for Ravenscroft's predicament. His misfortune had reverberations throughout Cawnpore, for he had been cashing the bills drawn on Calcutta Agency Houses through Mr Foley, the local banker.[12] This was the same Mr Foley who was involved in the case of Daniel Clarke the sutler. Foley was Head Writer in the Customs House and carried on a private banking business, obliging the officers of the regiments stationed in Cawnpore by encashing their bills. If Foley were now to become bankrupt on Ravenscroft's crash, his ruin would bring down many of the officers of the station with him.

It soon became apparent to Newnham and Cunliffe that Ravenscroft's ruin was the result of his adventures in trade; he had stopped recommending advantageous schemes to Government and started trying them out for himself. These adventures were made disastrous by Ravenscroft's character, which was credulous and unbusinesslike. They reported:

From the confused and scattered state of Mr R's concerns we have hitherto obtained but little insight into them but we conceive we are fully justified in asserting that the simple source of Mr R's misfortunes is traceable to his being drawn into merchantilist speculations originally with a view to assist an individual named James Smith, alias James Greenfield Doubleday. Messrs Cruttenden, Mackillop and Co apparently willing to avail themselves of the official influence of a gentleman in the centre of the cotton countries, aggravated the first entanglement into vast embarrassment by the facility of a credit which must astonish by its amount. . . .[13]

James Smith, alias James Greenfield Doubleday, was the villain of the piece. He had met Ravenscroft's wife, Louisa, on a trip up the river in 1816 when he had done her some kindness, and in return she introduced him to her husband. It is a measure of Ravenscroft's gullibility that he did not discover sooner the character of his new friend. After the crash, his trustees quickly found it out. 'Our enquiries lead us to know he was a deserter from the *Lord Duncan*, employed by Mr Havell as a feeder of hogs at Dinapore, then confined in jail in Calcutta where to those who attend the Supreme

Court he is well known, and lastly we find him a most practised swindler.'[14] Ravenscroft saw none of this. Out of feeling for his lately deceased wife, he took Smith into his house, and when Smith offered to run a factory which had belonged to Mrs Ravenscroft and which she had used as a retreat,[15] he accepted. From that time Ravenscroft's fate was settled. Smith's intention was to get Ravenscroft deeply into debt and then to transfer the assets to his own name, claiming that he was Ravenscroft's creditor. Then Smith planned to sue him for 'his' money, forcing Ravenscroft to choose between exposure and ruin.

His method was transparent flattery. He called Ravenscroft 'the most generous and manly hearted of men', and signed his letters 'yours ever, the unutterable and sincere' and 'thine the faithful'. He led him on from speculation to speculation with a mixture of threats and promises: ' . . . if you let this opportunity pass over, all your prospects will be lost . . . let me once more intreat you not to doubt my veracity, and if you do not support the indigo with all your might immediately, all the shining prospect before us will be blasted.'[16] So, against all reason, Ravenscroft let himself be drawn on, as he later explained to the Solicitor General.

Dear Sir, I am induced to lay before you the whole circumstances attending the important connection between Mr Smith and myself. The result of this communication will show to you the very great injury I have sustained and the losses which I have incurred from the day he received my protection and support.

In 1816 Smith came up to me an absolute beggar . . . I took him under my roof, fed and supported him. He then was sent to one of my factories . . . which he has now possession of by a fictitious Bill of sale. When the first year's manufacture of about 600 Maunds of Indigo was brought down by Smith to Cawnpore for which I had advanced about Rs 25,000 it was not without threats and promises I could get my property out of his hands, as he well knew I was fearful of exposure, and I was induced to offer him 10% Commission on his own exorbitant valuation of Rs 140 per Maund. . . . After having despatched the Indigo I was induced in an evil hour to commence speculations to an enormous extent in cotton and salt petre, the whole of which was entrusted to Smith, and I built large screw houses and a saltpetre laboratory, and allowed Smith a good bungalow and garden for his residence.

The whole of these he retains possession of in deeds of sale, made out in his own name for the sake of keeping my name out of sight and kept them as if they were his own, without ever dreaming of a fair valuation and set off against his own demands. Besides allowing Smith [various commissions] I took him in as half partner in the Indigo concern in 1817. During the whole of this partnership, not a single rupee has been advanced by Smith but the whole outlay has been mine.

GEORGE RAVENSCROFT. Cawnpore.[17]

He speculated against the explicit warnings of Mackillop, the senior partner of Cruttenden and Mackillop and a close personal friend, whose letters over a period of two years reveal Ravenscroft's astonishing naiveté in commercial matters. 'You write about matters you really know nothing of . . . no man in his senses would send cotton to *China* as a speculation. . . . You talk of Lacks of rupees as if we had them at our command – we have no such things, nor are Lacks in Calcutta at present. . . . I write to recommend selling, if you can, all the goods you have in Cawnpore.'[18]

The inevitable resolution of these confused economic exploits slowly became clear. Ravenscroft received a letter of warning from the Cawnpore Chaplain which revealed Smith's plan.[19] 'Little Smith, who has been with me, is I apprehend, much inclined to work your ruin.' He had showed the Chaplain several confidential letters which referred to various commissions and pecuniary transactions, and told him that he had submitted copies to the appeal judge. He declared his intention to swear a debt of 1½ lakhs against Ravenscroft and have him arrested in Calcutta. Soon after, Cruttenden and Mackillop, through their Cawnpore agents Maxwell and Burnett, started legal proceedings to reclaim the balance of Ravenscroft's account. When Ravenscroft could not borrow more, he used the Treasury funds; as his debts grew he dipped deeper into Government money. It was at this point that Government started asking questions about the Treasury books.

The fortunes of many people were threatened. Two senior Indian employees at the Treasury absconded and it was found they had made use of public funds. Senior Indian bankers had been drawn into helping Ravenscroft. An indigo planter of unsavoury reputation, John Jones,[20] had entered into Smith's schemes to appropriate the best indigo and pass off the poor variety to 'Mr R.'. Messrs Maxwell and Burnett were responsible to Cruttenden and Mackillop and called on the unfortunate Mr Foley, demanding all his property be mortgaged to pay his debts. Mr John Hay, the tailor and auctioneer, once described by Ravenscroft as 'the only honest shopkeeper in Cawnpore',[21] had lent him money and wondered if he would ever see it again. In fact the whole society of Cawnpore watched the outcome of events with sympathetic anxiety.

The Company servants worked diligently to try to sort out the affairs, fearful for 'the honour and high character of the service; the confidence of Government in that service; and the hope of rescuing the national character from any degeneration in the eyes of the native population.'[22] Everything depended on what Ravenscroft would do next. He could put a pistol to his head; he could stand trial and face ruin and ignominy; or he could run for it. For a time he remained indecisive, answering official communications with pleas for more time to sort out his affairs, or excuses that he was too debilitated by fever to comply with orders. When the final notice of criminal proceedings for breach of trust and embezzlement was served on him, desiring him to proceed to Calcutta, he, accompanied by his second wife and their infant son, was already in the territory of the Nawab of Oude, and outside the jurisdiction of the court. When the full extent of his crime could be assessed, it was found he had appropriated from the Treasury the enormous sum of Rs 274,853.00 (£27,485).[23]

For a time Ravenscroft was lost to the authorities despite orders to secure him issued throughout Oude. An appeal was made to the Nawab to direct his officers 'to apprehend Mr R wherever he may be found within the limits of your Majesty's territories'. Rumours circulated that he had left the country and taken refuge in the foothills of Nepal, or 'having embarked on a small Boat he was drowned on his passage across the stream'.[24] Government discounted them as having been put about by Ravenscroft himself. Then one report came in which seemed to deserve more credit. It indicated that Ravenscroft was indeed dead, murdered by a gang of dacoits in a village called Bingah, and buried there; and that several servants had been wounded in the attack, though his wife and son had escaped.

The nearest place of any size to Bingah was Secrora. The commanding officer at Secrora tried to trace this report. After several days two men came forward and swore on the Koran that they were eye-witnesses to the attack and murder, and that they had seen Ravenscroft buried. Government was not satisfied; they were shocked at such 'an atrocious outrage on the person of a British subject'[25] and suspicious that this was just another ruse to help Ravenscroft escape justice. They ordered a full inquiry to be made at the site of the murder in Bingah.

The court of inquiry camped on the banks of the River Raptee. It was two months since the murder of Ravenscroft had taken place. The court's first action had been to disinter the body to try to identify it as Ravenscroft's. The handsome monument over the grave was demolished, the corpse dug up and examined, but the 'body was too decomposed for positive identification. However from the appearance of the grave clothes, stained in several places apparently with blood, the Court conceive it to be the body of a man severely wounded and in the way Mr Ravenscroft is said to have been. The court remark that the body has a large beard.' The corpse was replaced in the grave and the earth thrown back.

In this incongruous setting, in the open air, under the neem trees, where the ring doves cooed and the grey tree rats chased each other, in sight of the Rajah's fort, and surrounded by fields of indigo, for five days witnesses were called and questioned carefully. At last the full story could be pieced together.

After his flight from Cawnpore, in his desperation, Ravenscroft had gone to the friendly Rajah of Bingah, whom he had previously met on a mission. 'The Rajah made over to him a portion of land for tillage, and a suitable place in a mango grove, about a mile from his fort, to build a house upon. He built one after the Hindoostanee fashion, with bamboos and grass from the adjoining jungle.' The house was constructed round a courtyard, the rooms all facing inwards, and with only two entrances; the main entrance at the front of the house and at the back a small door leading into the bathing room.

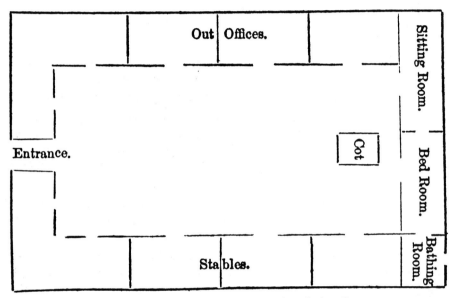

The plan in Sleeman's Journey through the Kingdom of Oude *(1858).*

The Rajah gave Ravenscroft some villages in farm, and he settled down to cultivate indigo, and, no doubt, to indulge his passion for agricultural experiment. The Ravenscrofts appeared to be comfortably established in their life as outlaws: Mrs Ravenscroft even made several social trips to Secrora and Cawnpore; and, Government later found to its horror, officers on leave came to stay with them from time to time. The Rajah was friendly, although, as it transpired, his eldest son was not.

On the night of the murder, 6 May 1823, Ensign Platt from Secrora had been staying with the Ravenscrofts on a hawking trip. It was the hot weather: while Mrs Ravenscroft and her child slept in the bedroom, Ravenscroft was sleeping on a cot in the open courtyard and Platt had pitched a tent at a little distance from the house. The court noted the following statements:[26]

Ensign Platt. Between about 1 and 2 o'clock in the morning I was awakened by a terrible noise and immediately got up and ran out of my tent towards the house from where the noise proceeded, but on my way I was attacked by 3 men armed with spears who wounded me in 4 different places, having no weapon in my hand wherewith to defend myself. I was obliged to run and providentially escaped them.

But the attackers were not primarily interested in Platt, and the centre of the furore was inside the courtyard.

Dulgunjun, Taylor. On awakening I perceived the courtyard filled with men armed with spears; the reflection from the torches was so bright that it appeared like day light.

Reports estimated the number of men as anything between fifty and a hundred. Clearly the unarmed and exposed Ravenscroft had no chance of survival, despite his reputation as a practised and athletic swordsman.

Emandy, Syce. I was sleeping in the stable on the night of the attack when I saw the thieves rush upon the late Mr Ravenscroft, who immediately called out to me by name, 'Emandy bring me my sword and shield!' I was in the act of carrying them to my master when I was intercepted by the thieves; they continued to spear my master until they drove him out of the courtyard.

Another witness, Juggoo, a syce, confirmed the story: 'As they attacked, the dacoits were shouting, "There's a man run here from Secrora to settle amongst us. This is a murderer and a thief."'

Mrs Ravenscroft, warned by the general hubbub and by her husband's shouting to her, managed to escape with her child and two servants through the bathing-room door. Meanwhile the noise of the attack had woken the Rajah's servants; shots were fired from the fort as men came to help Ravenscroft. The dacoits plundered what they could find and disappeared, leaving Ravenscroft dying, four of his servants and a boy murdered, and eighteen servants wounded. Ensign Platt found Ravenscroft lying on a charpoy on which he had been placed by the Rajah's people; he was groaning terribly but could not speak. 'I found that he had been wounded by spears apparently in 17 places and was bleeding most profusely.' Platt did what he could to bind up the wounds but Ravenscroft lay insensible until he died, two days later. Ensign Platt, with the help of his hawker, washed the body and buried it. While the hawker held the prayer book, and another servant held a large umbrella over his head, Platt read the burial service over the grave – 'the most painful ceremony'.[27]

So much the court of inquiry discovered, but they learnt it with difficulty;

OPPOSITE *Mordaunt Ricketts,* HEICS: *painted at Lucknow by an unknown artist. The decoration of a miniature of the King surrounded by a double row of pearls was probably designed by Robert Home. As Resident of Lucknow Ricketts assisted in getting Ghazi-ud-din-Haidar recognised as the first King of Oude. In gratitude the decoration in the portrait was conferred upon him – the first by an Indian King on an officer of the Company. Ricketts married Charlotte (*BELOW, *modelled in wax by David Morrison, London, c.1831), widow of George Ravenscroft.*

the circumstances surrounding Ravenscroft's death were as confused and mysterious as his financial dealings. Ensign Platt, anxious that no one should know that he had visited a wanted man, had returned to his regiment without reporting the murder. Mrs Ravenscroft, thankful to have escaped, went quietly to stay with friends and said nothing. As it was, the court could find no trace of the murderers, although it was generally believed that the Rajah's eldest son had hired the dacoits, fearful that Ravenscroft would usurp his lands and position.

Mrs Ravenscroft continued in friendship with the Rajah of Bingah. She married the Resident of Lucknow, Mr Mordaunt Ricketts, but tragedy still followed her. The Ravenscrofts' little son was drowned in the water tub of a bathing room into which he had been locked for some naughtiness. As for poor Ravenscroft and the attitude of Cawnpore, a kind of epitaph had already been given him in the report of Newnham and Cunliffe. 'The confined society of his countrymen at Cawnpore will always look with anxiety to the fate of a too generous and infatuated man, who has been an enemy to no one but himself.'[28]

Burnett & Co. Fail for Nine Lakhs

The possessions of John Maxwell were so considerable that it was not until 1822, six years after his death, that the trustees were able to wind up the estate. At last, when everything was complete, Adam Maxwell and Alexander Burnett found themselves very rich young men, able to please themselves. Adam returned to England, but Burnett, convinced that the opportunities in India were too good to leave, remained in Cawnpore. He began to look for others to share in his schemes. In much the same way that an Indian trader working in the United Kingdom today hopes to send home for his brothers and cousins to join him in his new venture, so Alexander Burnett persuaded Robert Maxwell Dunn and William Cleugh to come out to India from Scotland. One of John Maxwell's sisters had married the Rector of Aberdeen Grammar School; Robert Maxwell Dunn was their son.[29] William Cleugh was a writing master at the school and a close friend of the Maxwell family. Now these three men entered into partnership to form Burnett & Co. This company undertook the management of Adam's estates in his absence. Responsibility for paying the revenue on the estates was accepted by two Indian bankers who were also the bankers and treasurers for Burnett & Co. So, despite the break in the old partnership, the affairs of Maxwell and Burnett remained closely intertwined.

The two young men had acquired their wealth at an unfortunate time. The gambling mania that had ruined Ravenscroft was still prevalent, yet nobody seemed ready to profit from his example, least of all Alexander Burnett. 'From the time that Mr Ravenscroft made such a figure in his speculations here, there appeared to have been a general emulation to imitate the same course. . . . [In 1822] . . . the firm of Burnett & Co darted into existence, in such a style, that a determination to outvie all other speculators seemed their ruling principle.'[30]

The little that is known of Alexander Burnett's personal life suggests that he was something of a gambler and not entirely scrupulous in his dealings. The dazzling vision of so much wealth had turned his head in a way that John Maxwell had never imagined possible; but the times were exceptional. Burnett's business interests stretched far beyond the Cawnpore District and many of his journeys took him through Fatehgarh. He never married but in Fatehgarh he formed an association with a woman called Harriet Gibson and a daughter, Barbara, was born to them. He fondly imagined that this daughter would one day be a much-sought-after heiress. He was utterly confident in his abilities and the value of his possessions. He had a controlling interest in five indigo factories, cotton presses and cotton houses in four different places, two rum distilleries, and various other house properties. Altogether he reckoned his assets to be eleven lakhs (£110,000).[31]

The public reputation of Burnett & Co. did not apparently stand so high. One of their concerns was the contract for supplying rum to the Commissariat which had formerly been John Maxwell's. The Collector suspected them of illicit dealing and ordered a party to search the distillery at Jajmau. Burnett and his partners were sufficiently confident to defy the Collector's orders, and allow the party to inspect only part of the premises, as the *darogah* in charge reported:

On the 17th July Mr Burnett and Moonshy Bugwan Doss came and directed that we should not be allowed to have access to the Distillery, giving particular instructions to his people not to permit our entrance into the Distillery and told us that we were only entertained to watch at the Distillery outside.

After having endeavoured to obtain access to the Distillery without effect, we took our station outside in front of the principal entrance and Gate to prevent any Rum or other spirits being removed from the Distillery without your knowledge and permission or without a pass being previously obtained from you to cover the same. . . . The Distillery has 5 gates from which any person may easily enter and procure rum without our noticing it.[32]

The Collector could not prove any malpractice, and Burnett & Co. were let off with a caution. They continued to act as though money and commercial opportunities were infinite. The special Revenue Collector appointed to sort out the disastrous finances of these years was astounded by such behaviour:

The extravagance, unprincipled extravagance of that period surpasses description. . . . There was no want of money. Little care was taken to provide equivalent returns for advances made, and the unprincipled as well as the imprudent went on as if this state of things could last. The money does not seem to have been laid out in improvements . . . the fiscal value of no estate was advanced; and precisely as advances were supplied with perfect heedlessness as to the results, so were they received with no other than fraudulent intentions, or non-payment in any shape. . . . It is indeed to me a matter of astonishment the way in which so much money thrown into circulation has been wasted.[33]

Like many of their competitors, Burnett & Co. had grown too large too quickly. It was only a matter of time before disaster overtook them. In the spring of 1827, just four years after the Ravenscroft scandal, Burnett & Co. crashed. They failed for nine lakhs of rupees (£90,000), and their mortgagees and creditors quickly moved in.[34]

The Collector, fearful for his revenue, wrote to Government:

I have the honor to Report . . . the unfortunate circumstances of the failure of Burnett & Co, Merchants and Indigo Planters at Cawnpore and that Fergusson &

Co have taken possession of their papers and Effects under a Warrant from the Sheriff on a Judgement Bond for sixteen lacks of Rupees. Cruttenden & Co have also a Judgement Bond for three lacks; there are besides Debts to a great Extent due to Natives and Europeans for money.[35]

Everyone involved tried to salvage something from the disaster for himself. There were large stocks of rum at Jajmau, and the Collector wondered if he should seize them in lieu of revenue before the creditors claimed them. The two Indians who had been Burnett & Co.'s bankers, and legally responsible for the payment of revenue on Adam Maxwell's lands, were nowhere to be found, though the Collector issued a 'process by Sowars and Peons for their apprehension and for the recovery of the balances' – some Rs 25,000.[36] At Muckanpore, the principal indigo factory was reported to be under a state of siege. Fergusson and Co. demanded the right to take over charge, while the Native Creditors surrounded the factory clamouring for their dues. The factory manager, Mr Sago, had been in charge for nearly twenty years, ever since John Maxwell first came to Cawnpore. He refused to deliver up the factory or its contents, regarding them as still the property of Burnett & Co., and not to be despatched until paid for.

The whole position was greatly complicated by the fact that many of the villages and estates involved actually belonged not to Burnett and Co. but to the absent Adam Maxwell. Though they were heavily mortgaged, they could not legally be seized to redeem Burnett's debts, as the Collector of Cawnpore reported; 'Although the factories are mortgaged to Fergusson & Co. by Burnett & Co., the warrant of the Sheriff nor of the Judge cannot interfere with Mr Adam Maxwell's lands for the payment of the debts of Burnett & Co.'[37] Nevertheless, they remained so heavily involved that the only other member of the Maxwell family then in India, Peter Maxwell, could do nothing to free them. He did, however, at the age of nineteen, take over the running of the Muckanpore indigo factory from the recalcitrant but loyal Mr Sago. In the end, Sago had reluctantly handed it over to Fergusson & Co., though he flatly refused to work for them. 'Young Mr Maxwell' was appointed in his place, which at his age seems to indicate that he was a capable young man.

None of the original partners remained on the spot to sort out their affairs. Robert Maxwell Dunn and William Cleugh, finding themselves responsible for huge debts they could not meet, fled to Serampore, the Danish settlement beyond Calcutta, where they were outside the reach of the law. Nothing more was heard of the unfortunate Alexander Burnett. He disappeared into obscurity as quickly as he had 'darted into existence'.[38] The crash ruined him. He was declared insolvent and by the end of the year he was dead. No official record of his death exists; it is possible that in desperation he took his own life. In 1825 he had drawn up a splendid will, a very different document from the sober assessment of property made by John Maxwell. Again and again Burnett referred to 'good and lawful' money as if by repeating the magic formula his fortune would be secured for ever. The inventory of his remaining possessions included a mahogany table and a handsome glass dessert service, but of the eleven lakhs of rupees a mere Rs 116 were found in bank notes in his desk.[39]

When Adam Maxwell heard the news of Burnett's crash he returned to India at once and with Peter Maxwell's help set about the difficult business of rescuing the family estates. The Maxwell lands were out in the District, centred round Mendhi Ghat and within easy distance of Fatehgarh – an area noted for the toughness and individuality of its European inhabitants. This was because at the time of the Cession, in 1801 Government had offered an amnesty to any European adventurers who were illegally officering the Mahratta armies. It was in Fatehgarh, the furthest point from Company administration at that time, that most of them had settled to make their living in indigo.

Many of these planters, living isolated lives in the District, had become both independent-spirited and 'brahminised', adopting Indian customs and ways of life. In times of trouble the planter had no one to look to for help but himself. 'It is well known, that in days of yore, a body of well trained *latti-wallahs*, formed an essential part of an Indigo Planter's establishment.'[40] An incident which well illustrates this independence of spirit was recounted by Emery Churcher, a planter of Fatehgarh and related in marriage to the Maxwells. He had been denied possession of a village awarded him in a court of law and could not resist taking personal action:

I could not stand the challenge and decided to take forcible possession. I sent word to the estate tenants that they were to attend at my house next morning. They did so, armed in the usual way with clubs, swords and matchlocks. . . . I started at the head of my little army, which consisted of about 200 foot, and six horsemen. When we had approached to within 150 yards of Mowat, the skirmishing began. Desultory fire from both sides went on for a short time, but as no progress was made, and there were no casualties, I got impatient and shouted to the men to storm the village. They rushed forward, yelling as they went, with myself and the other horsemen at their head. We entered the village, but our opponents had decamped, and we were left in peaceful possession. We had obtained a bloodless victory.[41]

It was not surprising that these planters regarded the official administration as bureaucratic and interfering, while in the comparative order of

Cawnpore the planters seemed autocratic and overbearing. Adam Maxwell shared this difficulty. He was trying to maintain the family estates at a time of general economic distress. On every side there arose 'a systematic evasion of payment, resistance of process, and a general character of contumacy'.[42] So serious had the state of the revenue collection become in the Cawnpore District that a special Deputy Collector of Revenue, Mr Reade, was appointed. Mr Reade went about his task with an inflexible sense of duty to Government. It was his intention to select the estates of the most notorious defaulters, put them up for sale and, by making a severe example of a few, gain the willing obedience of the others.

Adam Maxwell stood the recorded proprietor of thirty-one villages. The revenue due from these was a yearly Rs 41,316.13.3 (over £4,000). When Reade took over there was an outstanding balance due to Government of Rs 12,637.11.3 (£1,263). Mr Reade made full inquiries:

The account of the property is exceedingly simple. Mr John Maxwell the father of Adam Maxwell who was a European purchased several villages at the public auction sales in the name of his son Adam whose other parent was a native. His private purchases were made in the same way, principally in liquiding of debts due to him from the Zamindars incurred by them in connection with Indigo concerns.[43]

Mr Reade found that heavy arrears were due for years preceding and he formed the opinion that Adam Maxwell was a rogue, whose defaulting was due to extravagant living, mismanagement and neglect of his estates. 'It is my firm belief that the systematic default in which Mr Maxwell has been permitted to persevere with impunity, has encouraged the other Zemindars of the Districts to with-hold payment of the dues of Government and that it is absolutely necessary to make an example of him.'[44]

How far Adam Maxwell was being genuinely dishonest, and how far his disputes with Reade were the natural product of their incompatible outlooks – Reade's the zealous, British official, and Adam Maxwell's the easygoing Anglo-Indian – is difficult to determine. It is certain that John Maxwell seems to have trusted his eldest son less than his nephew, but it is also true that following Burnett's crash the estates were so entangled that Adam was, in effect, fighting for his livelihood. It seems he used every possible method to delay paying the revenue he owed.

Adam Maxwell wrote protesting to the Commissioner of Revenue at Allahabad that the Collector had singled him out unfairly; he begged for more time to pay, pleading the extenuating circumstance of hailstorms and sudden disease among his cattle; he made 'oblique and malignant attacks' on Reade's character. Reade wrote reports patiently answering each of Adam Maxwell's assertions point by point with his own version. He accused

Adam Maxwell of merely trying to gain time to plunder the new crops in order to liquidate the previous year's debt and cited 'the most flagrant attempts have been made by Mr Maxwell's people . . . *to compel* the Ryots to pay in advance. I have heard that the cattle of some of the Ryots have been seized and in one instance sold outright.'[45]

Mr Reade's inexorable diligence had its effect. The Commissioner of Revenue directed that Adam Maxwell's estates be put to farm. One Kullulooddeen Khan became the farmer for a period of twelve years. He paid down to Government all the outstanding balances and agreed to pay Adam Maxwell a small allowance of Rs 256 (£25) a month. Mr Reade was complimented by Government.

From the Commissioner of Revenue to Government.
I consider it due to the Deputy Collector Mr E. A. Reade to take this opportunity of bringing to the notice of the Board the satisfactory manner in which he has resisted all the efforts of Mr Adam Maxwell to oppose him in his zealous exertion to reform all the abuses which have so long existed in the fiscal management of the District of Cawnpore.[46]

At the time of the foreclosure, Reade was convinced that the measures were fully justified, but within a few years Government considered that they had perhaps been over harsh. However, Government's reconsideration of the case came too late to help Adam Maxwell. Seven years after the estates had been put to farm the collector reported: 'The Proprietor sank under the Pressure of the existing *Jamma* [the assessment for revenue].'[47] Adam Maxwell died in November 1838, his death almost certainly brought on by the anxieties of his situation. He was buried in the same grave as his father, but for him there were no eulogies, only the brief message, 'Adam Maxwell born October 30 A.D. 1793 and died November 30 1838.'

A less extravagant glimpse survives. On the death of a Cawnpore merchant, Henry Orde, in 1824 his effects were auctioned. Goods were keenly bid for by traders such as John Leonard Jones, John Kirk, and Robert Foley. Indian traders, officers from the regiment and sergeants competed for such personal effects as boots and buff leather gloves. Adam Maxwell also attended the auction. He is the only person listed as Esquire; his purchases were barely serious: four bottles of eau de Cologne, four phials of cinnamon, two bottles of Wright's Bitters. . . .[48]

6

A New Corporate Feeling
1833–1838

Cawnpore Free School

At the time of Ravenscroft's embezzlement, Cawnpore boasted the largest society in India outside Calcutta. It was made up of several distinct groups. The '*grand monde*' of Cawnpore consisted of the Company civil servants, 'the aristocracy of India', the military garrison – many of whom were senior officers, men of high rank and large incomes – and two or three prosperous indigo planters. Unlike most up-country stations, however, Cawnpore had other British residents, 'who form a second circle; the owners of shops and farms, coach-makers, bakers and tailors, to whom it must be a much more desirable place of abode than a smaller station, since it affords them the advantage of society'.[1]

Society had its disadvantages too. In Cawnpore it was hierarchical, jealous and quarrelsome. Its very size allowed factions to form, even beyond the natural groupings which already existed. The main division, perhaps an inevitable one, lay between the civil and military parties, but these were further subdivided: there were two kinds of civilians – the Company officials and those who were trading on their own account, men like the Maxwells. And there were two kinds of military men – the Company's troops and the King's troops temporarily posted to India. There were many causes of contention between the two sorts of regiment. Officers in the King's troops had the privilege of holding army rank far above their regimental ranks; thus a captain in the King's troops ranked as a lieutenant-colonel in the Company army. Senior Company officers who prided themselves on their knowledge of warfare in India found themselves junior in rank and pay to comparative youngsters fresh from England. This was the cause of a good deal of jealousy and unpleasant feeling.

In 1822 the famous regiment of the 16th Lancers had recently arrived in Cawnpore, full of their exploits and successes at the Battle of Waterloo. With their dark blue cloaks and scarlet and white plumed lance caps as they swanked on parade they inflamed the jealousies of the other regiments. One Lancer officer, Lieutenant Lowe, summed up his new surroundings: 'On becoming acquainted with the society of the place, I find it is divided into several parties. I shall be disappointed if the quarrelling is not productive of fun.' He gleefully described[2] such an incident at a ball: 'A Bagatelle Club was endeavoured to be established, but broke down after two balls. Mrs Nicol, the wife of a Colonel, at the first ball flew into a violent passion because she was not handed to supper by the proper person. The Company's Officers sided with the Colonel's lady and were very national.'[3] The result was that one half of the European community was not on speaking terms with the other.

Such incidents seemed enjoyable and trifling to Lieutenant Lowe but they marked deep differences of attitudes and method beginning to make themselves shown in Cawnpore society. It was a fact of military life and, to a lesser extent, of life in the Company's civil service, that men were continually at the mercy of fresh postings. Their stay in any station was temporary and they usually treated their surroundings as an impermanent backdrop to a travelling life. Cawnpore, however, was not typical. When the Governor-General, the Marquess of Hastings, visited Cawnpore in 1814, he stayed with the Collector, and remarked on his house and grounds as something unusual:

Took up my residence at the house of Mr Grant the Collector. It is an elegant bungalow and the grounds are laid out with a degree of taste not common in India where individuals always looking forward to translation to a better post cannot be expected to lay out money on beautifying a precarious possession.[4]

Mr Grant's care for his property was symptomatic of a growing awareness of their surroundings felt by the Cawnpore residents, and particularly by the civilians. They began to think of themselves as individuals first, and as servants or (in the case of planters) tenants of Government second; and therefore they came to look on Cawnpore not as the site of temporary accommodation and short-lived duties, but as their home. When they felt that amenities were lacking, they now raised private subscriptions among themselves to fill the needs of their community. Eventually, Government help for any project would be sought, to place it on a permanent and financially secure footing, but the initiative and original backing for each scheme came from the residents. One of the earliest of these schemes was the Cawnpore Free School.

The first attempt to deal with the problem of schooling for children in Cawnpore had been made by Maria Sherwood as early as 1808. Maria

Frontispiece from Mrs Sherwood's The History of Little Henry and His Bearer. *The scene, with the exception of the exaggeration of the distant hills, is typical of the view from the Sherwoods' bungalow at Cawnpore.*

Sherwood is famous for her book *The History of Little Henry and His Bearer*, which has been translated into many languages and read by children all over the world. Her husband was Paymaster of the 53rd Regiment of Infantry; Captain and Mrs Sherwood arrived 'with the fleet' in 1808 and lived in Cawnpore for five years. It is often said that European women in India found so much time on their hands that they took either to gossip and flirting; or to drinking; or to religion and good works. Certainly Maria Sherwood found comfort for her troubles in her active Christian faith. She was by nature inclined to be serious, and the ever-present threat of sudden death, the loss of several of her children, and the influence of the missionary Henry Martyn, who was a close friend, combined to guide her towards philanthropy. In Cawnpore this took the form of a school for children of the Regiment.

No provision was made by Government for the instruction of soldiers' children, many of whom were the children of European soldiers and Indian women. If their father could not afford to send them to England they ran wild about the barracks, getting up to all sorts of mischief.[5] At a dinner party one evening their case came under discussion and Mrs Sherwood offered to start a class in her bungalow. Her husband agreed to lend his clerk to assist and she began to hold daily classes for children aged from eight to twelve.

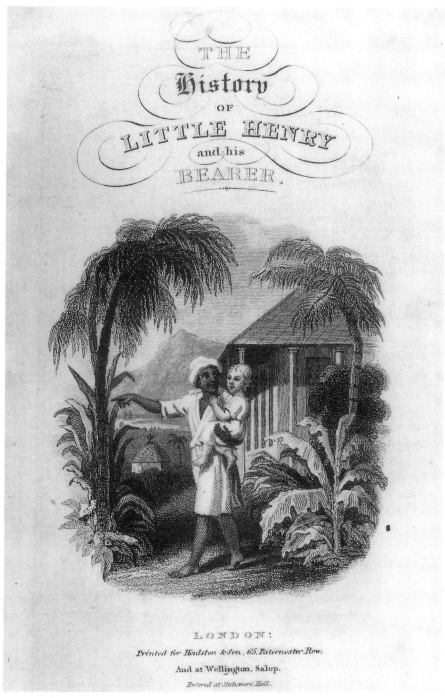

THE

𝔥𝔦𝔰𝔱𝔬𝔯𝔶

OF

LITTLE HENRY

and his

BEARER.

LONDON:

Printed for Houlston & Son, 65, Paternoster Row,

And at Wellington, Salop.

Entered at Stationers' Hall.

The title page of Little Henry

The children who came daily to her school, with their glossy black hair braided and knotted on top of their heads, wearing white muslin dresses, red shoes, gold earrings and necklaces of cornelian, were taught their letters, and sewing and Christian stories. Mrs Sherwood tried to convey Christian morality to her pupils by telling them stories, but these children, who had never known England, would ask on hearing them, 'What is a barn?' 'Do they walk out at noon without a *chatta*?' 'Are they not afraid of serpents in the grass?' So she gave her stories an Indian setting, using the sights and sounds of Cawnpore. These were published in *Stories from the Church Catechism* and give a wealth of detail about Cawnpore.

After the Sherwoods left Cawnpore nothing significant changed about schooling. The well-to-do sent their children to school in England or engaged a sergeant to teach the '3Rs' to them at home. There was no education for the families of the military nor for the 'second circle' of residents. The leaders of Cawnpore society, with their growing awareness of themselves as part of a community, were conscious of their responsibilities to that community, and they decided to establish their own school. The Cawnpore Free School opened in 1820.

A subscription was raised and each subscriber paid Rs 69 per month. From among the subscribers a managing committee was formed. The Chaplain, Mr Williams, who was also a member of the Society for the Propagation of the Gospel (SPG), was appointed in charge of the day-to-day running of the school. He became Secretary of the committee and also Treasurer until somebody else could be found to take on the job. Major-General Thomas, the head of the army commanded from Cawnpore, was elected to be President of the Free School. The school house was centrally situated near the Grand Parade; while its main purpose was to provide schooling for children of the British residents of Cawnpore, the Chaplain was keen to include classes for Indian children and even a few adults who might benefit from a Christian education. The emphasis of teaching was on English grammar and arithmetic and the syllabus included an outline of general history.

The Free School Committee was an uneasy cross-section of Cawnpore society. The President, General Thomas, had two rather thin nieces for whom he was trying to find suitable husbands, which explained his friendliness to the officers of the 16th Lancers. The civilian subscribers to the Free School, however, found him officious and hidebound. He invariably linked Government and military, confessing to feeling 'a general superintending responsibility attached to my situation in all that concerns the military interests of Government connected with the community of the station under my command!'[6] He brought this attitude to bear on the school; and this the civilians deeply resented.

After two years the Cawnpore Free School had proved its usefulness to the community. They now applied to Government for official recognition of 'an Establishment of much public utility'.[7] They forwarded a letter of appreciation from the Bishop of Calcutta who had donated Rs 150 and asked government for financial support which would give the enterprise a 'prospect of permanence'.[8] Government agreed to a contribution of Rs 400 per month to add to the private subscriptions. When this became known General Thomas felt an even more proprietary interest in what he now saw as a Government enterprise. He made his views known to the committee. 'The Major General . . . considers it particularly his province to protect and guard that part of the fund which Government has so liberally subscribed, and which amounts to four fifths of the whole.'[9] The civilian subscribers, on the other hand, viewed the school with different eyes, regarding it as 'a private design which has been seconded and approved by Government'. The difference between these attitudes was bound to lead to a dispute.

Some subscribers were critical of the fact that the funds of the school – which now amounted to nearly Rs 4,000 – were out on private security instead of being invested in Government paper. They questioned the sums of money paid by the school to the SPG for missionary books and tracts sent from Calcutta. Matters came to a head and a full-scale row broke out over the appointment of a new headmaster.

Major-General Thomas, who had been away from Cawnpore on field exercises, returned to learn that 'a mere sojourner, a particular individual but just arrived at the station who nevertheless felt himself at liberty to call on the secretary for a meeting and finding this demand not complied with, resorted to the singular absurdity of prevailing on two other individuals to meet him in a self elected committee when they adopted a string of resolutions, completely to the subversion of the existing order of things'.[10] Several important motions were proposed and carried by those present: that a man *not a member of the Church of England but a Baptist*, recommended by the sojourner, should be made headmaster; that two senior civilians be invited to become subscribers; and that one of them should relieve Mr Williams of his additional post of Treasurer. Evidently Mr Williams regarded this last proposal as a personal slight, though he made no objections at the meeting. Instead, in the established manner of committee intrigues, he went straight to Major-General Thomas to complain of the affront to his dignity and threatened resignation.

Thomas was horrified by every aspect of the meeting: he deplored its informality, he declared its motions inadmissable on the grounds that so few members could not authorise them; he took Williams's part over his removal from the post of Treasurer, accusing the other subscribers of 'unfeeling flippancy' towards him; and he was not convinced by the qualifications of the proposed headmaster. He compiled a report, headed 'Observations on Some Recent Illegal Proceedings at Cawnpore' and sent it to the Adjutant-General, requesting him to bring the matter to the notice of the Commander-in-Chief, and with his permission to the Governor-General in Council. In the meantime he disallowed the offending motions, and froze the Free School funds.[11]

The civilian subscribers believed that the dispute was no business of Government, and were reluctant to appeal to higher authorities, but they felt obliged by Thomas's action to report their version of events. This report clearly reveals their new vision of themselves as individual men, at home in their own community.

The affairs of this institution, which had its foundation in private bounty and is indebted for its permanency to individual activity and benevolence, are therefore now exclusively administered by the orders of the officer commanding the station. A higher assumption of authority and a more glaring invasion of private rights than involved in this proceeding, could not, we conceive, be alleged.[12]

They refused to have their local school project blown up by official handling into being a weighty and solemn matter of state. 'If a slight degree of informality could be alleged, there surely was no call for that strict precision and regard of form which might be requisite in affairs of the state or in the transactions of a public body.'[13] And they pinpointed the heart of their grievance: that Major-General Thomas should consider that his military position made him in some way a Government overseer, instead of one among many other private residents of Cawnpore. In conclusion they requested that Government would not 'afford their countenance to the unjust and irregular interference of Major-General Thomas, but direct that officer to limit the exercise of his command to those affairs for which it is specifically ordained.'[14]

There was no final solution that Government or any one else could provide to the dissension. Tempers gradually cooled; Mr Grant, as Chairman of the troublesome meeting, resigned his seat on the committee and cancelled his subscription; Mr Williams was persuaded to remain as Secretary but within a short time he was taken ill and died, exhausted by quarrelling. The school went through a difficult time. Bishop Heber found little to praise when he visited it in 1824.

Bishop Heber: oil by Thomas Phillips, RA, c. 1822.

It has an excellent house, with good school-rooms, an English master and mistress at a large salary, and a Persian *monshee*, but I found it attended but by few European and half-caste, and still fewer native children, in deplorable want of books and other similar supplies, and with a master who had apparently been brought in as a party measure, who was previously altogether inexperienced in the improved system of education . . . he taught them to write a fair hand, and to work ridiculous and useless sums in fellowship, the double rule of three, and this was all his ambition.[15]

However, the official report to Government in 1826 listed the whole number of scholars as 154, divided into departments studying in English, Persian and Hindi. The school survived all the early problems and became a permanent part of the town life. It marked for the Cawnpore residents a turning away from the reckless behaviour of the last few years to a more sober assessment of their common aims and needs as a community. Thus when the next opportunity for community action occurred, Cawnpore society had learned to be a little less factious and jealous. It came about in 1837/38 – the year the monsoon rains failed. The Cawnpore residents recalled it as the 'year of the famine'.

It was not possible to live in India without being dominated by the seasons. The violent extremes of the climate were forces which exerted total influence over the lives of those who suffered them. In the hot weather the heat was often so intense that it seemed astonishing that anything could survive. During April, May and June, the hot dry winds which carried the dust storms turned Cawnpore into a dust bowl. 'People lose their way on the plains, and everything is full of dust – books, dinner, clothes, everything.'[16] This continued until the end of June. Then, day after day, everyone watched the skies for the first glimpse of the storm clouds that would bring the deluge of the monsoon rain. It was too hot to move, almost too hot to breathe; even the birds sat motionless with wide open beaks waiting, waiting, for the first drop of rain. When at last the monsoon 'broke' with torrential rain, a great shout went up from the bazaar, men and women ran out into the streets to feel the cool rain bucketing over them, rejoicing in the goodness of the gods who had saved them for another year. Streets and gullies were awash with rain, rivers foamed through the dry beds of the ravines, the bare dusty plains turned miraculously overnight into green fields, the drooping trees sprouted new growth, the cattle lifted their heads.

The terrible cycle of the hot weather relieved by the monsoon was an experience people endured year after year, now as then. But it became more a calamity when the monsoon failed. In the year of the famine there had been no rain for a year and a half in the districts round Cawnpore. Throughout recorded history India has depended for survival on its agriculture, and the agriculture has depended on the monsoon rains. When the monsoon failed, there was famine; with little artificial irrigation the crops withered, animals died and all cultivated land became a dust bowl. The result was starvation for thousands of peasants. In 1838 the situation was most severe in the villages and fields of the outlying districts, where there was no possibility of famine relief. In a desperate search for food the dying poured into Cawnpore.

Mrs Ashmore, the wife of an army officer, remembered it clearly:[17]

The multitude of beings, who had been able to earn a scanty subsistence in the fields during other years, were at this time thrown out of employment; provisions became extravagantly dear; the failure of so many crops deprived them of subsistence, and wretchedness succeeded: it was then that thousands of these poor creatures sought the towns, and were seen crowding every avenue to the cantonments. Cawnpore was filled with them: those who had youth and health brought in their aged and infirm relatives – poor disabled creatures, who had for many years never left their hovels; disease and famine rendered them scarcely able to crawl along the parched roads under an almost vertical sun.

In September 1837 the Civil Magistrate, seeing this great influx of destitute poor into Cawnpore, sent round an appeal to all residents for donations and support. He formed the Cawnpore Relief Society, financed entirely by local subscription. The Society tried to meet the disaster by creating work for the able-bodied, repairing the roads and the parade ground, and building a large tank or reservoir. They provided free food for women and children with young families and set up a hospital for the sick. But the Relief Society could not cope indefinitely with the large numbers of famine victims, and the Secretary appealed to the Governor-General for Government aid. 'Private charity may do much to allieviate individual suffering but the relief of hundreds for an indefinite period comes only within the means of government.' He stated that Rs 1,500 had been spent and 1,300 men women and children supported. Government agreed to help and pay for the roads and works of 'general utility'.[18]

Government employed every man woman or child who liked to do the semblance of a day's work, knowing that this was wiser than charity. Those who were too ill to work were taken care of by subscriptions. The ladies of Cawnpore decided to devote the proceeds of their sales of work towards financing a female orphanage, for girls whose parents died in the famine. An officer of the 16th Lancers commented, 'In that dreadful famine hordes of wretched famished Bundelas[19] flocked into Cawnpore, and very liberal subscriptions were collected to feed them; great numbers, however, perished from hunger, and mothers offered their children for sale for one rupee each: several were bought by very well-intentioned persons, to be

Famine memorial: Company Bagh Tank, 1970.

educated and converted to Christianity.' The girls who were to be trained as ladies' maids lived in the Savada Koti – a house which became notorious twenty years later, in the Mutiny.

Whether it was in organising the famine relief or work parties to support the new orphanage or serving on a committee to supervise the Free School, the residents of Cawnpore had now become thoroughly established in their community endeavours, capable of articulating their needs and initiating projects to fulfil them. This created a pattern of self-help that continued in varied forms until Independence in 1947. It was the antithesis of the thinking that led to the welfare state: men with ruggedly individual personalities took upon themselves the responsibility for the needs of their community. Those who had most to give gave generously, in time as well as money, and Government was only brought in when it became absolutely essential.

The Famine tank still exists in the grounds of the Agricultural College, a witness to the community spirit of Cawnpore residents long departed. In the shadow of a huge mahogany tree whose branches reach out over the tank stands a simple monument on which this inscription is carved:

To afford employment to the starving poor this tank commenced with the voluntary contribution of the Civilians and the inhabitants of Cawnpore and was completed from the funds of the British Government at an expense of 12,000 Rupees, exclusive of the labour of the prisoners and the four flights of steps under the superintendence of L. C. Wilson Esq. Magistrate. A.D. 1837–1838 the year of the famine.

The orphanage building, the Savada Koti, did not long survive the Mutiny. A broad flight of stone steps conjuring up the picture of a large bungalow with spacious rooms and shady pillared verandahs, is all that remains on the plain beyond the old racecourse.[20]

It is the Cawnpore Free School that proved to have the most far-reaching and beneficial effects. It was a lasting witness to the new sense of corporate feeling in Cawnpore. After the Mutiny the Cawnpore Free School was transferred to the SPG and renamed Christ Church School. Eventually it emerged as Christ Church College and became affiliated to the University of Allahabad, and it continues to this day.[21]

Cawnpore through Official Eyes

For the Europeans living in India every aspect of life seemed to have dual facets. They lived in India for the whole of their working lives, influenced by things Indian, and yet they were English, their roots were in English ways and they would one day retire to England – God willing. The climate in Cawnpore strengthened this awareness: the cold weather months were as near perfect as man could wish, the hot ones almost unbearable.

India offered the Europeans dazzling opportunities for achieving wealth and acquiring power and reputation, but always at the risk of early death. Living among foreigners the English took care to behave circumspectly before the Indians, which led to a certain formality and stiffness in their manners, but when they were 'off-duty' they sometimes behaved so unconventionally that they became considerable 'characters'. This duality of life could be felt in any situation; it was almost as if the Hindu gods exercised their influence over the lives of people in India. One form the duality took was the complacency of the inhabitants of Cawnpore about their good fortune in the life they lived there, and the rather supercilious distaste shown for it by visitors from Calcutta or those newly arrived from England. This was true in 1840 and it was equally true in 1940. Certainly the Eden sisters found Cawnpore a 'semi-barbarous place'.[22]

Emily and Fanny Eden had lived with their brother, George Eden, the second Lord Auckland, for many years. When he was appointed Governor-General of India in 1833 the two sisters naturally accompanied him to manage the domestic side of his duties. All three were unmarried, a devoted close-knit family who moved in the highest society, on terms of personal friendship with the prominent Whig families.

In October 1837 the Governor-General left Calcutta to tour the Upper Provinces. He was to be away from Calcutta for two years and intended to halt frequently so that he could meet the native rulers of the states through which he passed. Emily and Fanny Eden went with him, sketching, keeping a careful journal and writing many letters to friends and family in England, describing 'the great journey'.[23]

They arrived in Cawnpore to hold a series of official functions, both for the European inhabitants and for the Nawab-now the King-of Oude. The young Prince of Orange went with them. Emily wrote in her diary: 'We made one of our grand entries into Cawnpore, or rather *on* to it; for there is no particular Cawnpore visible. But we drove over a miniature plain to our tents.'[24] The entry into Cawnpore was as splendid as it could be made. Two regiments of cavalry and two of infantry, along with a tribe of officers, were sent to meet the Governor-General's party, who were welcomed into the town with guns firing and bands playing. Lord Auckland and his staff rode in and Fanny followed on a white Arab pony. Emily kept the Prince of Orange company in an open carriage until the horses refused to pull the carriage over a bad pass; whereupon they took to elephants.

Fanny Eden's diary: camp scene, Cawnpore 21 December 1837.

As soon as they reached the town the official reception began. For the people of Cawnpore this was a rare, exciting and nerve-racking occasion: the Governor-General represented the highest in power and rank that India held. Before such a visit the officers inspected their uniforms minutely and their ladies planned every detail of the dresses they would wear to catch the attention of the great family. But while the occasion was unusual and distinctive for the Cawnpore inhabitants, for the Edens it was a tedious repetition of other functions in other towns: a duty to be got through, but by no means a pleasure.

G [George, the Governor-General] had his levée an hour after we arrived, and we had our party the same evening, for this is one of those dreadful large stations where there is not a chance of getting through all our duties if we lose an hour's time.

It was lucky we had the large tent pitched, for there were between 200 and 300 people at our party. Luckily I thought a dance might be made out, which the Prince of Orange likes, and they had battened the floor of the tent till it was smooth; so the dancing went on very well.

It was the more essential, because, with every chair and sofa assembled from all the other tents, we could not make up a hundred seats, so it was necessary to keep part of the company constantly dancing.[25]

Indeed almost the entire European population of Cawnpore was contained in the tent, and would not have missed being there for anything. One of the guests was Fanny Parks, who arrived late. 'We lost our way in a ravine from a dense fog; when we reached the tent the whole station was assembled there, quadrilles and waltzing going forward.'[26]

The guests were eager for the chance of a few words with the Edens, but Emily was defeated by the problem of remembering so many names and faces. She recognised one or two Calcutta faces without being able to put a name to them and concluded, 'I see it is one of those crowded stations where it is better not to fatigue a failing memory by any attempt at names.'[27] Fanny Eden took a downright dislike to Cawnpore: it is only fair to note they were visiting in the 'year of the famine' when conditions were exceptionally bad; nonetheless, her rejection of Cawnpore was emphatic.

Of all the ugly Indian stations I have yet seen, this is the very ugliest – a dead flat of course – but not one single blade of even brown grass to be seen – nothing but loose brown dust which rises in clouds upon the slightest provocation. I have a notion that I really could not live here, but as other people do that may be a delusion.[28]

Emily Eden too, a sensitive, refined woman, used to a more regulated state of affairs, was inwardly appalled at its lack of fastidiousness; above all, at the willingness of its inhabitants to compromise with the makeshift. The absence of a church up-country gave rise to incongruities which she recorded. They spent Christmas Day in Cawnpore and she confessed herself to be feeling 'Indianly low'. The servants had hung garlands at the doors of the tents and assembled to give her '*Burra Din ka salaams*', but she deeply resented the contrast between an English family Christmas and this. The church service took place in a tent and Emily was conscious of kneeling on the spot where visiting dignitaries had sat for their festivities. It all seemed unnatural.

Emily Eden was unusual in continuing to find the country and its customs alien. Most of India's European inhabitants adapted their lives to fit the country so that each became almost part of the other. Yet, perhaps because of her aloofness, she observed and recorded the experiences around her and her reaction to them with insight and humour.

The most splendid event of the Edens' Cawnpore visit was the entertainment of the King of Oude's son and heir.[29] It was considered politically expedient to treat the king with the utmost courtesy and ceremony: his court at Lucknow was one of the most magnificent and luxurious in India – a place of inlaid marble floors, pillars studded with diamonds and emeralds and rubies, and fountains spouting in every room. To maintain British prestige, the Edens' entertainment of the Prince of Oude had to compete on the same level. The Governor-General gave a breakfast party for him, and strict formality was observed.

Fanny Eden went to George's room to see how her brother was faring with his preparations and found him putting on 'his very goldest coat, star and ribbon, and cocked hat'.[30] He was in a frenzy of indignation at the thought of having to appear in such regalia, at this unseemly hour of the morning and, to make matters worse, riding on an elephant!

The heir-apparent of Oude was camped five miles outside the town, and the two parties were to process towards each other on elephants. British ADCs were sent off at intervals to accompany the Prince's party: at seven o'clock four aides went all the way to his camp; half way two senior officers met him, and another was dispatched when he was a mile from the Governor-General's tents. The full encounter between the Prince and the Governor-General took place on the edge of the encampment. Everyone was on an elephant and at the 'shock' of their meeting many of the howdahs were broken. The Governor-General embraced the Nawab and the visitor got into the howdah of the visited and in this friendly fashion they arrived. Speeches were made, and compliments and presents exchanged. Then they all sat down to a magnificent breakfast prepared by the Edens' French chef.

G[eorge] sugared and creamed the Nawab's tea, and the Nawab gave him some pilau. Then he put a slice of buttered toast (rather cold and greasy) on one plate for me, and another for F[anny], and B[Macnaghten]said in an imposing tone, 'His Royal Highness sends the Burra Lady this, and the Choota Lady that,' and we looked immeasurable gratitude. At the end of breakfast, two hookahs were brought in, that the chiefs might smoke together, and a third for Colonel L[ow], the British Resident, that his consequence might be kept up in the eyes of the Lucknowites, by showing that he is allowed to smoke at the Governor-General's table. The old khansamah wisely took care to put no tobacco in George's hookah, though it looked very grand and imposing with its snake and rose-water. George says he was quite distressed; he could not persuade it to make the right kind of bubbling noise.[31]

It all went off very well. The Prince of Orange was astonished at it, wondering that so splendid a repast could be produced in the 'middle of the desert', as he called Cawnpore.

Soon the Governor-General continued his tour. Once they were in the countryside, beyond the reach of the Cawnpore Relief Society, the sights of famine and distress were 'perfectly frightful'. Starving people followed the camp, children with bones sticking through their skins, without a rag of clothing, women who looked as if they had been buried alive,' their skulls look so dreadful',[32] begging for food. Every evening the camp distributed food sent to them from Oude, feeding 200 regularly. Inevitably, however, there was the despairing thought that no matter how much food was given, many were beyond help and the situation was hopeless.

Emily Eden was very aware of the incongruities of their situation: she constantly deflates the pomposity of officialdom and pokes fun at the absurdities of her own position. She debunks herself playing the foreign visitor – not so different a beast from the modern tourist – looking at ruins, reporting strange native customs and longing to be at home. When visiting the ruins of the ancient capital of Kanauj, a thought came to her of the whole position reversed, with the Indian people behaving in England as presently the English behaved in India. It was an idea almost visionary and at least astonishingly ahead of her time.

Perhaps two thousand years hence, when the art of steam has been forgotten, and nobody can exactly make out the meaning of the old English word 'mail-coach,' some black Governor-General of England will be marching through its southern provinces, and will go and look at some ruins, and doubt whether London was a large town, and will feed some white-looking skeletons, and say what distress the poor creatures must be in they will really eat rice and curry; and his sister will write to her Mary D at New Delhi and complain of the cold, and explain to her with great care what snow is, and how the natives wear bonnets, and then, of course, mention that she wants to go home. [33]

Every evening when they sat down to dinner, with the band playing and all the pomp and circumstance of their life about them, their hearts sickened to hear the cries of the starving children outside the tents. Emily and Fanny would exchange glances, sit up a little more stiffly in their chairs, chins lifted, and make a brave effort to think only of their official duties.

7

Cawnpore in its Palmy Days
1838–1847

―――――

'No Indian Station Can Rival Cawnpore'

The decade from 1837 was a golden age for Europeans in Cawnpore. The Mahratta threat had been contained. A feeling of confidence and security and success pervaded the stations, and their inhabitants got down to enjoying the pleasures and benefits of a comfortable peace. They no longer felt they must behave like pioneers at a frontier outpost; instead, they could attempt to impose a conventional order on their lives, and aspire to a civilised existence in as close an imitation of life in England as was possible, given the heat, the dust and the disease.

An important part of this new existence was the arrival in significant numbers of European women. Hitherto, the voyage round the Cape had been thought too long and hazardous for them, and the interior of India too dangerous; women such as Maria Sherwood who accompanied their husbands were the exception rather than the rule. Now, coinciding with the dawning of the Age of Victoria at home, they arrived – the wives, fiancées, daughters, nieces and cousins of men stationed all over India.

The Cawnpore they found was thoroughly established. Cantonments, where the Europeans lived, was spread over ten square miles; it included over 300 well-built elegant bungalows set in some of the finest gardens in India; seven European shops and four native shops; barracks for 7,000 troops: these had altogether a population of 50,000. The original bazaar which had served the first camp was packed tight into an area of 600 acres. Here were forty-two streets and the homes of nearly 60,000 people, the main business being fifty Indian banking houses. Old Kanhpur, 'now much fallen into decay', was still a village of 3,000 inhabitants, according to statistics given by Robert Montgomery in 1849.[1]

The coming of the ladies had two important aspects. First of all, the single ladies – the 'fishing fleet' – were in search of husbands, and they brought with them an implicit demand for a stricter moral code which would uphold

ANGLO INDIANS.   PLATE J.

DRAWN BY W. TAYLER ESQ.ᵣ BENGAL CIVIL SERVICE.   LITHD BY J. BOUVIE

THE BREAKFAST.

The Breakfast: *illustration from W. Tayler's* Manners and Customs, *Calcutta c.1842. While the meal was rice and fish, in every other way the Victorian memsahib tried to live as close an imitation of life in England as possible.*

marriage. John Maxwell, in his will of 1816, had anticipated the changing moral climate. He left his property between his children, who were all illegitimate, with the proviso that it should pass to *their* children only if they were born in wedlock. The second notable aspect about the ladies' arrival was that there was nothing for them to do. The men had the country to administer – bridges to build, cases to try, parades to attend – but entertainments had to be devised to keep the ladies occupied.

Just as the community had felt the lack of a school, and had filled the need through private subscriptions, so now it wanted a central place of public entertainment, and began to build, by the same method, Assembly Rooms and a theatre. These two imposing stone buildings stood facing each other on the highest ground in the centre of Cantonments, the focal point for Cawnpore society.

Among the ladies who came to Cawnpore at this time was Miss Emma Roberts. She had accompanied her sister and brother-in-law to India and spent two years 'up-country', much of it in Cawnpore. She was a talented essayist and had published a couple of books. With the eye of a practised observer she described the new Assembly Rooms.

The Cawnpore assembly-rooms are extremely handsome; those apartments devoted to dancing and the supper are built in the Anglo-Indian style, being divided down the length by two rows of pillars, leaving a wide space in the centre; sofas are placed between the pillars, and floods of light stream from the wall-shades and chandeliers. The floors are boarded; no common circumstance in India, where the depredations of the white ants are so much dreaded.

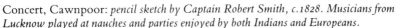

Concert, Cawnpoor: *pencil sketch by Captain Robert Smith, c.1828. Musicians from Lucknow played at nauches and parties enjoyed by both Indians and Europeans.*

None, save those who have danced upon a mat covering a *chunam* floor, can truly appreciate the luxury of boards; and the English belle, swimming through a quadrille on a warm summer evening, can form no idea of the fatigues which her Indian friends are undergoing, while performing the same evolutions upon a clay ground, the thermometer up to a hundred, and in a perfect atmosphere of mosquitos. . . . The natives look on in surprise, wondering that the *saibs* should take so much trouble, since professional persons are to be hired in every bazaar to perform for their amusement.[2]

It was typical of Cawnpore society that the subscription balls at the Assembly Rooms were badly attended, yet the private balls attracted a galaxy of beauty and fashion. Society was more dependable about going to the theatre. Amateur theatricals had been popular in Cawnpore since the days when John Shipp played the parvenu Lord Dubberley. They were sufficiently in demand to warrant the building of a proper theatre – or, at least, a theatre that was intended to be proper. At that time in India, if you wanted any sort of building erected, from a church to a hospital, you offered an engineer officer an appropriate sum to do it for you. In this case Lieutenant Burt undertook the construction of the theatre for Rs 30,000, and build 'a long oval, surrounded by a colonnade of pillars of the Roman Doric

Our Theatricals: *illustration from* Curry and Rice *by Captain G.F. Atkinson, Bengal Engineers, c.1856. Amateur theatricals were popular among the men.*

order'.[3] But he was not so well versed in acoustics as he was in decorative architecture. The theatre was opened in 1829 and Emma Roberts was asked to compose a commemorative prologue to the first play.

> Where late a jungle spread its tangled dells
> And panthers lurked within the forest's cells;
> Where still in troops the famished jackals prowl,
> And the wolf bays the moon with dismal howl;
> . . . A Doric structure meets the spell-bound eyes. . .[4]

The theatre was ornamental from the outside but the interior was unsuitable. The seats with heavily carved wooden backs, were all on one level and with the many doors left open for circulation of air the spectators had little chance of either seeing or hearing what was going on upon the stage. The plays which occupied this unsatisfactory building were performed, understandably, more in the spirit of entertainment than out of love for the dramatic muse. Emma Roberts certainly enjoyed them.

Much taste and talent is usually displayed in the scenery and dresses, and with one drawback – the performance of female characters by the fiercer sex – the Cawnpore theatricals are really delightful. Though sometimes an ambitious aspirant may insist upon tearing passion to rags in lofty verse, such exhibitions are comparatively rare; light farces and gay comedy are usually preferred, both by the actors and the audience.[5]

After the play it was customary to end the evening with a supper and ball. There was a tremendous scramble of palanquins and carriages outside the theatre and the audience was conveyed across the road to the Assembly Rooms, accompanied by their servants to attend their needs at the supper table. Young Lieutenant Beaumont Johnson of the Artillery wrote home to his mother: 'Ball after ball, dinner after dinner is all the go here. Late hours and fearfully hot weather begin to tell on our complexions and sickly faces in the morning appear on parade.'[6]

Beyond the theatre the road led to the racecourse. On this road, known as 'The Course', the whole town turned out for its evening drive with a highly cosmopolitan selection of vehicles and horses. Often as many as a hundred 'equipages and charioteers' attended, joined by the Company civil servants from Nawabganj, over four miles away. It was much the same evening drive as when John Maxwell went with the Patons, and Maria Sherwood had seen Henry Martyn dashing through the crowds in his gig, but now the drive was bordered by big shady trees and well watered in the dry season. It skirted a broad plain which was bounded on one side by the native city where the mosques and minarets of the temples gave it a picturesque setting.

Magazine Bridge, Cawnpoor: *pencil sketch by Captain Robert Smith, c.1828.*

Once a week the band of the King's Dragoon Regiment played at the band stand and the carriages drew up 'two or three deep' in a circle around it to listen to the music and exchange gossip. The young officers dismounted and lounged from carriage to carriage to pay their respects to the belles of Cawnpore – for a brief moment it was possible to forget that they were in a foreign land.

The Anglo-Indian community, especially the military, took their horses seriously, paying large sums for European and Arab animals and racing them at every opportunity. The Cawnpore race meeting, held in the cold weather, drew large crowds. It continued on alternate days for three weeks. The race funds were ample and attracted crack horses, many being brought great distances to compete. The more serious races were interspersed with hack races, in which even the most amateur could try his luck. One of these was the Cheroot Race in which riders rode with lighted cigars. Bets were settled at the Assembly Rooms afterwards. Emma Roberts noticed that at the races, as in so many aspects of life in India, the European population aspired to an image of Englishness and achieved a curious blend of the familiar with the exotic:

These races form a very amusing scene, the male spectators, with a few exceptions, appearing in masquerade; for the object being to divest the meeting of all military shew, the young men endeavour to imitate, as nearly as their wardrobes will permit, the dress and appointments of English country gentlemen, farmers, and even rustics: rather a difficult achievement, where there is so little opportunity of keeping up a stock of plain clothes . . . round hats and jockey caps are at a premium, and native tailors are employed to manufacture facsimiles of uncouth garments from all sorts of materials.[7]

For most of the spectators, the occasion was merely a social event, but prestige and often large sums of money were at stake for others. Gambling was a recurring problem of Indian life. Many young men were constantly in debt from betting on horses, cards, dice and cock-fighting. Lieutenant Lowe reported a craze for cock-fighting. 'A pit is formed in the compound, and meeting established every Saturday. The birds brought are good, and betting is very high – 25 Gold Mohurs – £50 – is a common sum to have depending on a battle. A Lt in the Infantry had the other day 64 GM's on one cock and won his money.'[8]

It was this gambling mania and the want of a church which so shocked Emma Roberts about Cawnpore society. There was little she felt she could do about the church but she created a sensation in London with a despatch to the *Asiatic Journal* in which she described the conditions prevailing in Cawnpore.

Gambling is indulged in by the idle youths in the station to an alarming extent, two quinea points at short whist and 100 quineas on the rubber is not unusual, especially in those seasons when there are no balls or parties to divert the attention of the young men. The want of a public Library is severely felt. Had the Government established Libraries at the headquarters of Districts, they would have been of incalcuable benefit to the very young cadets sent out to fill the vacancies in the Indian Army.★[9]

Letter-writing played an important role in counteracting boredom and in keeping in touch with 'home'. The connection with 'home', which the British in India never forgot, was maintained in many little ways. Young officers were sent copies of *Punch* and the *Spectator* and the *Illustrated London News* by thoughtful aunts; parents in England had daguerrotypes made of themselves to send out to their sons; and long letters passed to and fro, from home full of family news, the latest in politics and fashion and scandal, and from India attempting to convey something of the new country. Beaumont Johnson wrote home: 'Nobody can imagine the delight of an English letter, or the disappointment of those who do not receive one. Happy am I that as yet I do not know the latter sensation. . . . Oh gracious, how hot it is – there is a stream large enough for water-cress all down my face.'[10]

Another letter conveys the impression of a bored young lady, made

★Eventually a Library was provided. The original meeting and reading room for young officers at Cawnpore is the central room around which the present Cawnpore Club is built.

languid by the heat, racking her brains to find something to say, and stringing together unconnected lumps of gossip which speak volumes about the station.

Plowden left Harriet at Kaurnaul where he bought a very nice bungalow for her, but he has been leading a very wild life here. He attached himself to a Widow about ten years his senior, used to ride with her every day, drive her about all day, he gave her a Ball and then rode 16 miles out in order to ride with the widow for half an hour. Harriet will do more than scold him when they meet.

I have got such a beautiful Arab horse. I ride it every evening and very often in the mornings. Henry gave Rs 800 for it. It is still reported that our Regiment will go to Goruckpore next month. Colonel Arnold of the 16th Lancers has been dangerously ill. He burst a blood vessel in drinking soup at dinner, part of it went the wrong way and such were the injurious effects from it, that he was very nearly gone. He is recovering slowly by the last account, but it is felt that a repetition of violence or momentry passion may occasion a relapse.

Mr Gwatkin the painter is here. One of the spinsters in our Corps is to be married soon. There are no less than six in our Regiment.[11]

The soup on which the Colonel choked was probably delicious. In material things the European community lived pretty well, for the gardens were full of delicacies. Cawnpore was famous for its grapes and peaches; the finest melons, oranges, mangos, limes and guavas were available, while in the cold weather months all the English vegetables were grown. Emma Roberts said that 'these gardens, intermixed with forest trees, give Cawnpore a very luxuriant appearance: it is an oasis reclaimed from the desert, for all around wastes of sand extend to a considerable distance.'[12]

Altogether, the inhabitants felt that they lived in a desirable town, which was as full of society and interest and amusement as any place in India and, indeed, some renowned English resorts. Lieutenant Lowe of the Lancers celebrated its character in verses he wrote to the tune of *Hare and Hounds*, which he could be prevailed upon to sing after a particularly excellent dinner:[13]

> If England can boast of its Cheltenham and Brighton,
> Its Margate and Ramsgate, and fifty towns more,
> I'll show, as the subject's so easy to write on,
> No Indian station can rival Cawnpore.
>
> The sun's rather hot, sir, but where is it not, sir?
> We're paid to be broil'd, so you mustn't feel sore,
> The roads are so dusty, one gets rather crusty,
> Still there's no station can rival Cawnpore.
>
> In our society there's such variety,
> Balls, plays, and parties, they're seldom a bore,

At dinners well stewed you may eat to satiety,
And drink Hodgson's Pale Ale, with the spins* of Cawnpore.

When on the course,† sir, you show off your horse, sir,
Or ride by some belle, till the night become noir,
You'll find for a lark, sir, no time like the dark, sir,
A good deal of fun, may be had at Cawnpore.

The Lancers are here, with their well-whisker'd faces,
The conquests they've made I could never relate,
They brag of their Arabs and talk of the races,
I fear they'll be dished when they start for the plate.**

Civil Servants who've come all parts of the country
Boldly avow, indeed one of them swore,
For dancing, and dressing, for sky,†† and caressing,
No Indian station can vie with Cawnpore.

Then fill, fill your glasses, a health to the lasses,
I'll propose as a toast, the fair girl we adore,
Your wine quickly take, sir, let there be no mistake, sir,
The lov'd one whether absent or now in Cawnpore.

The Church: Grace and Good Feeling Come to Cawnpore

Before the nineteenth century the East India Company regarded missionaries with suspicion and distrust. Some members of the Company were activated by respect for native customs and the caste system, or by fear of the repercussions if they were interfered with; others by reluctance to disturb a comfortable status quo. They believed that missionaries, with their attempts to civilise the natives by preaching Christianity, stirred up discontent at best and revolt at worst.

This view was put forward by a Member of the House of Commons. 'I leave it to those who are versed in moral calculations to decide what will have been gained to ourselves by giving them Calvinism and fermented liquors; and whether predestination and gin would be a compensation to the natives of India for the changes which will overwhelm their habits, morals

---

*Spinsters.   †The evening drive.   **One of the races – the Merchants' Plate.

††Skylarking, amateur races.

and religion.[14] In the event, missionaries were held partly responsible for the Indian Mutiny.

As a result of this distrust, the first missionaries in the Calcutta area were forced to operate from the Danish settlement at Serampore, outside the Company's jurisdiction, and the military stations often went unvisited by chaplains for periods as long as sixteen years. The kind of life lived at the stations was fiercely secular, and unfettered by the more rigorous sort of

Henry Martyn: from a framed picture which hung at the Parsonage, Kanpur, 1970. For eighteen months Martyn was Chaplain to the Military Forces in Cawnpore. An evangelist, he translated the Scriptures, preached to the beggars, and set up a Church bungalow.

Christian morality. However, at about the beginning of the nineteenth century, a wave of evangelism inspired young Englishmen to go out to India as missionaries and show the natives the blessings of progress, Christianity and education. Henry Martyn was one of these men.

He arrived at Cawnpore from Dinapore in 1809 to take up his duties as chaplain to the military forces. While at Dinapore this brilliant, dedicated young scholar had translated the New Testament and the Book of Common Prayer into Urdu. At Dinapore he had met and made friends with the

Sherwoods, and it was to their bungalow he was carried in his palanquin when he came to Cawnpore at the beginning of the hot weather, half dead from heat exhaustion. He rapidly discovered that the Europeans were in as great a need of Christian guidance as the native population. To begin with, there was no church.

Henry Martyn felt his first task therefore was to persuade the authorities to sanction the building of a church. His efforts were only partly successful. The thatched bungalow next to his own, used as a go-down, was converted into a place of worship.[15] The inner walls were taken down to make one large room which was furnished with pews, benches, a pulpit and a reading desk. This church bungalow was to serve the infantry and artillery barracks close by, though it held only a small proportion of the men at one time, and it was a year and a half before it was ready for use. At the far end of Cantonments he eventually secured the use of the riding school as a church for the cavalry. In the meantime he continued to preach to great numbers in the open air at several services a day, exhausting himself and hastening the onset of consumption.

Off duty, he tried ceaselessly to introduce a spirit of piety and serious-mindedness to the Cawnpore populace. He seems to have met with much puzzlement, which he confided to his diary.

Sept 18 1809 General . . . has never been very cordial, and now he is likely to be less so; for while we were walking up and down together, I reproved him for swearing; though it was done in the gentlest way, he did not seem to like it. It was the first time he had been called to order for some years, I suppose. 'So you are giving me a private lecture,' said he. He then went on in a very angry and confused manner defending the practice of swearing: 'God judges of the heart, and sees there is no bad intention.'[16]

He had more success with the native population. Laboriously he taught himself the Indian dialects and, with the help of some Indian friends, translated the New Testament into Persian and Arabic. He was constantly preoccupied with this work, to the neglect of more common cares. His great object was to bring the message of Christianity to the natives and to this end he set up schools where Christian books could be introduced.

Mrs Sherwood describes his plan: 'To hire a native school master, generally a Musalman, to appoint him a place and pay him an anna a head for each boy whom he could induce to attend school':[17]

It was held in a long shed in the cavalry lines. The master sat at one end like a tailor on the dusty floor; and along under the shed sat the scholars, a pack of little urchins, with no other clothes on than a skull cap and a piece of cloth round the loins. They had wooden imitations of slates in their hands, on which having first written their lessons with chalk, they recited them with wide-open mouth, being sure to raise their voices on the approach of any European or native of note. In these schools they were in the way of getting a few ideas. They often got so far as to be able to copy a verse on their wooden slates. Afterwards they committed to memory what they had written. Who that has ever heard it can forget the sounds of the various notes with which these little people intonated their 'Aleph Zubbur ah-Zair a-Paiche oh,' as they waved backwards and forwards in their recitations? Or who can forget the vacant self-importance of the school master, who was generally a long bearded dry old man, who had no other means of proving his superiority over the scholars, but making more noise than ever they could make?[18]

At first Henry Martyn did not trust his command of the Hindu language enough to venture preaching to the native people, though he longed to do so. But through the small circle of Indians who worked on his translations with him, news of this strange Englishman reached the bazaars, and every Sunday crowds of beggars gathered on the high ground (now known as Kacheri Hill) near his bungalow. Martyn distributed alms, giving each one an anna and a little rice. The authorities kept a careful eye on him in case he stirred up trouble among the yogis and fakirs. At last he summoned up courage and, standing on the *chabutra* in his garden, preached to the beggars. 'I told them (after requesting their attention) that I gave with pleasure the alms which I could afford, but wished to give them something better; namely, eternal riches, or the knowledge of God, which was to be had from God's word; and then producing a Hindustani translation of Genesis read the first verse and explained it word for word.'[19]

Henry Martyn remained in Cawnpore for only a year and a half. At the end of that time his consumption was worse and his strength was exhausted. On 30 September 1810 his bungalow church was opened for the first time to public worship. The regimental band played, the congregation was considerable and Martyn preached on Exodus xx 24: 'In every place where I record my name I will come unto thee and bless thee.' The text is from the great chapter telling of Moses coming down from Mount Sinai and giving God's Ten Commandments to the people. Martyn started speaking in a faint voice but, gathering strength, seemed as one inspired. In the afternoon he preached for the last time to the natives before leaving for Calcutta.

Captain and Mrs Sherwood were among the small group of friends who gathered at the river bank to watch his departure. He was so emaciated, worn out with overwork and ill with consumption that they realised they would not see him again. But the sadness of the parting did not trouble Henry Martyn; he felt that he had made a beginning. It was only a little but it was something. He recorded in his diary, 'I feel something of thankfulness and joy.'[20] Two years later, in the Middle East, where he had gone to preach Christianity, he died.

Twenty years after Henry Martyn's departure, Cawnpore continued its godless existence. Despite various efforts on the part of the inhabitants, no church had been built. Many people felt the lack of it: a church, preferably large and solidly built in the Gothic style, was a visible index to the piety and prosperity of its congregation; it had a semi-official function. Partly for this reason the Cawnpore population considered it the business of Government to build the church. They would build their own theatre and assembly rooms for their entertainment, and a school for their education, but they conceived it the duty of Government to look after the welfare of their souls. Further, any attempt to begin building was paralysed by petty quarrels between the military, the clergy and civilians, and for some time there was no external help.

The Bishopric of Calcutta was created in 1814. The see was enormous, extending beyond the Indian sub-continent, and the Bishop had under him archdeacons at Madras, Bombay, the Cape of Good Hope and Sydney. Not surprisingly, he never visited the tiny part of his diocese which was Cawnpore. The first incumbent to do so was Bishop Heber, who spent two years touring the Upper Provinces, reaching Cawnpore in 1824. He found the arrangements for services exactly as they had been in Henry Martyn's time, in a 'thatched but convenient bungalow'. Government had sanctioned the building of two churches but on a scale of 'so rigid inspection and economy' that no one could be persuaded to undertake the contract. One of the residents, Mrs Ashmore, did not agree with Heber about the convenience of the buildings. The services in the hot weather were kept very short and held at daybreak, but 'although punkahs were kept in motion the whole time, and every attempt made to keep the building cool; before the conclusion of the service the heat was generally perfectly intolerable'.[21]

So, the absence of a central, cool church was a disincentive to piety. Some felt shamed by the nature of the buildings used: a riding school which fulfilled a secular function six days a week, and a bungalow which had been a storage place for spirits.*[22] The incongruity was emphasised by the reverence with which the natives regarded their own sacred places. But the religious climate of Cawnpore did not seem beyond hope to Bishop Heber – or if it did, he met it as a challenge.

At the end of his visit Bishop Heber, with his 'whimsical caravan' of

---

*Captain Robert Smith in his journal says: 'The Church is an old bungalow, in which in former days many a jolly carousal has been held, but . . . is now raised to the dignity of a religious edifice, to the no small astonishment of the natives.'

helpers, servants and bodyguard, set off for other parts of his diocese, leaving Cawnpore uplifted but still without a church. It remained for the great church builder Daniel Wilson to galvanise the station into action twelve years later. He became Bishop of Calcutta in 1832, and set about running the diocese like a crusade. Within four years twenty churches were in the process of being built; another ten, and the Cathedral of St Paul's in Calcutta, were to follow during his episcopate. But to conquer Cawnpore proved no easy matter: in 1835 Bishop Wilson complained to Government:

I have the honour of informing the Government of Agra that a most deplorable want of a Church accommodation has long existed at Cawnpore, the most important probably of all the stations in either Presidency. By my last account from the Rev Chaplain the European population was 3,010. . . . An inconvenient bungalow at one end of Cantonments accommodated 400, inconvenient, I mean, from its low roof and the excessive heat during the 7 or 8 summer months. In the Lancers Lines at the other or Western end, there is nothing but a wretched unseemly Riding School, so filthy in order during the rainy season, and so hot in the warm, and inconvenient and unsuitable in all weathers, that last year 800 men (the usual congregation) were for eighteen Sundays prohibited by the Brigadier from attending church.[23]

Bishop Wilson had persuaded the residents to undertake the building costs of the church, if Government would provide the site and build a small bungalow to act as a chapel. He petitioned for the land. Several suitable sites

Travellers and Peasantry in the Kingdom of Oude: *engraving from a drawing by Bishop Heber, published 1827. Bishop Heber with a suwarree of forty-five sepoys travelled in this manner from Cawnpore to Lucknow, the road so ill-defined he had repeatedly to ask his way.*

were available but Bishop Wilson proceeded cautiously; he was aware that 'no limits can be assigned to the possible objections of Brigadiers'.[24] His correspondence with the officers of Cawnpore on the subject of a building site justified his fears. Brigadier Churchill was helpful in suggesting a central plot near the theatre – it was open waste land that had previously been used for camping by troops passing through – but it transpired that he had written without first consulting his commanding officer. Brigadier-General Stevenson was outraged and wrote strongly to the Bishop. 'Brigadier Churchill having without my knowledge or sanction communicated with you on the proposed site for a central church and church bungalow at Cawnpore, it becomes necessary that I should inform you for the information of the Hon Governor General that I have many and strong objections to the Spot selected for the central church.'[25]

· The usual long dogmatic letters passed back and forth, involving most of the interested bodies in Cawnpore, until suddenly the quarrel took a more personal form, and settled on the head of the Revd E. White, one of the two chaplains at Cawnpore. Ever since Henry Martyn chaplains had had to contend with the domination of the station by its officers; the European population took its religious and moral tone from the station commander, and it was not easy for an army chaplain to rebuke a brigadier for his conduct.

So, when White received a letter from Brigadier Churchill requesting to know, in the event of the church being built on óne of the notional sites, what size congregation it should be made to contain, he was provoked beyond the bounds of official courtesy and took the opporunity of enjoining upright behaviour on senior officers:

The maximum of the evening congregation would depend not only upon the site of the church, but upon the sentiment and example of the officer who may chance to be in the command of the station. If happily he be a man mindful of his duty to his Maker, obedient to the first article of war, and zealous in promoting the moral and spiritual good of his fellow creatures; if he does all in his power to prevent the desecration of the sabbath, the circulation of untold imprecations in the spread of vice and profaneness; the maximum of the evening congregation probably will be the third of the whole population of Cawnpore.[26]

On receiving this letter, the Brigadier complained to the Commander-in-Chief who in turn complained to the Governor-General in Council, applying for the removal of the Chaplain. The Bishop wrote to Mr White, urging him to 'peace and submission' and begging him to apologise. 'Make no explanation, enter into no particulars; but in a candid manner express your regret if anything has unintentionally given him offense. You perceive,

Christ Church: c.1930.

dear sir, what an amazing deal of trouble a slight omission of etiquette has occasioned.'[27] His intervention was ineffectual, and the Chaplain was dismissed from Cawnpore.

It seems as though these internal quarrels would delay the building of the church indefinitely. The Bishop decided that he must change his tactics: polite letters and formal approaches had achieved nothing; he must take Cawnpore by surprise, and publicly shame the inhabitants into building the church.

He arrived unexpectedly at the station on a Saturday night in January 1837. Word of his visit spread, and a large congregation came to hear him preach next morning. He had the reputation of being an eloquent and dramatic speaker, capable of moving his listeners to tears at their unworthiness and of filling them with awe for the penalties of sin. Now he was determined to give them an utterly compelling performance which no quarrelsome officer or tight-fisted resident could resist. From his pulpit he mourned the removal of Mr White; he denounced the conduct of immoral regiments; and he declared his intention of laying the foundation stones for two churches before he returned to Calcutta. Before then, he intended to ascertain whether there was 'any grace and good feeling in Cawnpore or not'. He then left the Cawnpore populace to contemplate his warnings and departed on a visit of a few days to Lucknow. He returned to find that his plans had worked and the inhabitants were pliant and conciliatory. The Bishop responded by carrying out his official duties with energy.

In a period of hectic activity he visited temperance societies, regimental schools, hospitals and the orphanage; conducted confirmations and an ordination; consecrated for the first time Cawnpore's four large burial grounds; administered the sacrament and preached sermons in English and Hindustani. Wherever he went, subscriptions and collections poured in, and by the end of his visit the plans for the churches were settled. The larger of the two, Christ Church, was built in the centre of Cantonments, near the theatre, and St John's Chapel two miles to the east, near the newly built station library. Bands played and the whole population gathered to watch the foundation stones being laid.

You should have seen the ceremony yesterday of laying the first stones. The immense throng of people – all the soldiers drawn out – all the officers – all the gentry – and thousands of natives! It would have done your heart good. A numerous masonic lodge assisted. The senior Civilian laid the stone at the church, and the Brigadier at the chapel. I was almost killed with the exertion of addressing, perhaps, three thousand people in the open air, I contrived, however, to make them hear.[28]

Three years later, in January 1840, Bishop Wilson was in Cawnpore again, this time to consecrate Christ Church. In his opinion ' . . . nothing can be more beautiful than this church. The whole edifice is simple, appropriate and ecclesiastical; by far the finest in India after Delhi.'[29] It was an imposing Gothic building, dominating the surrounding area with its 100-foot tower surmounted by four corner pinnacles. It seated 800 people and had cost Rs 32,402 to build, two-thirds of which was raised by private subscription; the other third came from the Church Building Fund. Now that there was a church in Cawnpore the residents felt their town had received the seal of respectability.

8

Reforms . . . and Repercussions
1847–1856

Robert Montgomery in Cawnpore

There are times in history when a single event seems to symbolise some great and intricate movement; one change, though it may not be the first or the most important, sums up an era of transition. Such an event was the decision to combine the government of all three Presidencies of India under one man. Lord William Bentinck[1] became the first Governor-General of all India in 1833.

This new concept, the huge united sub-continent of India, caused the English Government to examine its conscience about the function of the British in India and about the suitability of the Company to oversee this function. The British concluded that they had a moral duty to this strangest of all empires. They earnestly wished to improve the lot of the Indian and the governing system of the country, and they were convinced that their own ideals and methods were the best in the world. Bentinck began the process of consciously introducing these blessings to India in an energetic programme of reform.

In an attempt to create a native governing class who would understand both the British and Indian points of view and mediate between them, Indians were no longer automatically debarred from Company posts. 'No native . . . shall, by reason only of his religion, place of birth, descent, colour or any of them lie disabled from holding any place, office or employment under the Company.'[2] English was introduced as the official language in the law courts and in education. Hitherto, business had been hampered by the use of hundreds of different dialects, and this single act of the introduction of a common language bound the country together as never before. Censorship of the press was abolished. Bentinck also had sufficient nerve to tackle two problems which his predecessors had always shirked for fear of offending the native population: suttee – the burning of Hindu widows on their husbands' funeral pyres, and thugee – the strangulation and robbery of travellers. These practices had their origins in religious observance, but horrified the humanitarian instincts of all good English liberals. Despite protests from Brahmin leaders and those Englishmen who did not believe that European morality was necessarily superior to the long-established customs of India, Bentinck abolished them.

The spirit of radical reform that caused these changes was carried the more quickly from England because of the improvement in communications. For generations the route to India had been by sailing ship via the Cape. The journey had lasted about three months, which put both the orders of the Directors in London and British public feeling six months away from the Governor-General in Calcutta and yet another month or so from the up-country stations.

Now this pattern was permanently changed by the use of steam ships in conjunction with the overland route via Suez: in 1836, the Government at Bombay received London despatches in a record time of sixty-four days. The new feeling of the proximity of India to England emphasised the sense of British responsibility. Within India, too, distances were reduced. Experiments were made with steamers on the Ganges, and work began on the extended feat of engineering which was to be the Grand Trunk Road. Its metalled surface was to cover 1,500 miles and to form the 'backbone of India'.

Of all these changes it was probably the Grand Trunk Road which had the most far-reaching effect on the development of Cawnpore. Previously the great highways of India had been the rivers, where transport was cheap if slow, and Cawnpore owed a considerable part of its prosperity to its place on the Ganges. The only roads were the ancient paths linking villages, and the dusty, rutted tracks beaten out by armies, which were often impassable for several months of the year. A fast road, usable by large numbers of people at all times of the year, would bring benefits to the whole community, and especially to the army. It would help facilitate trade and all political communications with the Supreme Government in Calcutta. The road was begun in 1833 and reached Cawnpore in the late 1830s, with the result that the town continued to receive all the advantages of a well-placed commercial centre.

The making of the road was a huge undertaking which took forty years to complete. Large gangs of convicts were employed to lay the chunks of limestone, well watered and then beaten, until a very hard surface was achieved. They worked in unison, 'letting all their battering rams fall at the same time, with a noise like thunder'.[3] The road ran straight for miles and miles. Work on the surface was not all that was entailed: the road had to be

Cawnpore on the Ganges: *published by Johnson's, London 1857. This sketch of Cawnpore, probably published in response to the sudden interest in Cawnpore following the massacre, shows the theatre with its imposing Doric columns. However, the sketch clearly dates from about 1830 since it does not include the tower of Christ Church.*

nents.   6 Ghaut.   7 Mahomedan Temple.   8 Commandant's Residence

The Grand Trunk Road: c.1930. The metalled surface between wide dusty sidewalks, planted with fine avenues of trees, stretched 1,500 miles from Calcutta to Peshawar.

built on a slight embankment to protect it from floods and every natural obstacle that it met had to be crossed and every river and chasm bridged. All its length, lines of trees were planted to provide shade. At last, one continuous highway of 1,500 miles was formed. It extended from Calcutta through Cawnpore and Delhi to Peshawar, the extreme north-west frontier station at the entrance to the Khyber Pass, the gateway of Central Asia. Kipling described it very well.

Then for the first time in history wheeled carriages rolled across the land, and the map of India began to shrink. The Grand Trunk Road developed a life of its own: marching regiments behind the blare of trumpets and cheerful brass bands, wedding processions with jangle of bells and laughter and ribald jokes, a trail of scarlet litters; holy men pacing sedately from shrine to shrine; trade-carrying carts, drawn by horse or bullock, travelling twice their normal distance in a day on the smooth hard road.[4]

The volume of traffic on the road was enormous. In the year 1846/7 a stretch outside Cawnpore was used by, among others, 17 regiments, 62,000 *hackeries*, 13,500 camels, 29,000 bullocks and 565,000 foot passengers – to say nothing of the sheep, goats, elephants and horses. The cost of maintenance work on the road was correspondingly high. The whole thickness of metalling had to be renewed every six years, and bridges were constantly being destroyed by severe floods or found to have been built by a dishonest contractor who had substituted ashes and mud for lime. The estimated cost of repairs was Rs 500 (£50) per mile every year, and a network of agents and executive officers came into being to oversee the continuous work. One of those who became involved with it was Robert Montgomery, who was appointed Collector of Cawnpore in 1846. He was one of the new breed of Company men, deeply committed to their work and convinced of its value; upright, God-fearing, men of action and integrity. The letter his father wrote him on his departure for India set the standards:

As the time approaches which must separate us for many many years, suffer your attached father to give you some hints for the guidance of your future conduct. . . . Remember your Creator in the days of your youth . . . never lie down at night without asking forgiveness for the errors of the proceeding day . . . never go in debt, never play or gamble . . . be sure always to associate with persons of the best character and conduct . . . never have dealings with the idle or vicious. Finally I beg you not to be careless, nor to put off whatever might be done now. Procrastination is the thief of time.'[5]

The advice was very largely followed. Montgomery arrived in India in 1828 and served in the Upper Provinces till he was posted to Cawnpore in 1846, where he remained for four years. It was for him a time of intense hard work and quiet domestic pleasure. In addition to his Collector's duties, he found time to research and accumulate the mass of facts and figures which make up Montgomery's *Statistical Account of Cawnpoor*.[6] It was an immense achievement and, as anyone who has endured a hot weather in Cawnpore will know, a remarkable feat of will power. The report gives the complicated revenue history of the district; details of the crops grown and the rights of tenants; a census of the Indian inhabitants (see Appendix 3) and the kind of house they lived in; a description of the drainage and the postal system – every facet of administration was included.

Among the many claims on his attention, Montgomery had to deal with the protection of travellers and property on the Grand Trunk Road as it passed through Cawnpore. When he arrived in the district losses were very high. Travellers and merchants with goods put up for the night in the small groves of trees at the road side. Weary after their day's journey they slept soundly and their unprotected goods offered a tempting prize to the thieves

Sir Robert Montgomery and Sir John Lawrence: frontispiece of vol. VII pt. 1 (Mutiny correspondence) Punjab Government Records.

who swarmed along the Trunk Road. Few of the robberies were reported, the travellers preferring to accept their loss rather than suffer detention by the police and separation from their party.

Montgomery's solution was to provide carefully patrolled resting places at regular intervals. Within a year, the value of property stolen was reduced from Rs 2,350 to Rs 346.[7] Montgomery noted that robbery with violence was rare. This had not always been the case. Since the fourteenth century, Thugs[8] had terrorised the roads, strangling travellers as an act of worship to the goddess Bhagwan. They threw a knotted handkerchief round their victims' necks and garrotted them, burying the bodies at the roadside or throwing them down a well. An estimated 1,000–1,500 victims were disposed of every year, but because travelling conditions were dangerous and because the Thugs seldom hurt Europeans, the British were not troubled by the existence of these gangs of religious fanatics until the late eighteenth century.

The suppression of thugee was one of Bentinck's first reforms. Between 1826 and 1835, in different parts of India, 1,562 Thugs[9] had been caught and hanged. At their trial many became informers, and by their evidence it was possible to break up the gangs and stamp out the practice almost entirely. The Thugs had no remorse about their activities; many confessed to hundreds of victims, and went to the scaffold cheerfully praising their goddess: 'Bindachul ka jae! Bhawani ka jae!'

By the time Robert Montgomery took charge of the Cawnpore District, thugee had been effectively stopped. But now, in pursuing his measures for the protection of travellers, he encountered a new offshoot of thugee, – a sect known as the Tusma-Bazees. They were a gang of gamblers who frequented the busy roads and any suitable large gathering, particularly at fairs. Their technique was to start a game of Tusma-Bazee among themselves until an interested crowd collected; then they would challenge a passer-by to try his skill. They usually won large sums. Curiously enough, the game they played had been taught them by an English soldier. About 1804, 'one Creagh, a private in a King's Regiment stationed at Cawnpore,' taught three Indians the art of thimble-rigging;[10] now what had begun comparatively harmlessly became a cover-up operation for murder and robbery. This evil, too, Montgomery stamped out. He was a notably energetic and successful Collector – probably the most distinguished Cawnpore ever had. Physically he was short, stout, soft-spoken and round-faced, so much so that he was dubbed 'Pickwick' by his friends. But beneath the mild exterior was a 'lion-like strain in his courage'.[11] He went on from Cawnpore to serve as Commissioner of the Lahore division of the Punjab, eventually becoming

Sir Robert Montgomery KCB, Lieutenant-Governor of the Punjab and Member of the India Council.

The group of men who governed in the Punjab – the two Lawrence brothers (Henry, the hero of the Lucknow Residency, and John, destined to become Viceroy of India in 1863) and Robert Montgomery – became a model for integrity and administrative excellence. Years later Sir John Lawrence was asked what system had been applied in the Punjab that it should have been so successfully governed, and he replied, 'It was not our system. It was our men.'[12] The men were the system. They made British rule what it was, bad or good. In the era of progress heralded by Bentinck's appointment, men of Montgomery's quality and dedication seemed by their personal successes gloriously to vindicate the capacity of the Company to govern. But the Company's role in India was drawing to an end.

Bentinck, with the radical reforms he introduced, at a time when new methods of communications made such measures doubly effective, had set in motion powerful forces that would change the concept of government and lead eventually to self-rule and independence from the British Raj.

Indigo Planters

When Lord Bentinck became Governor-General in 1833, he found that India's public debt stood at over £3 million, and he took every measure possible to effect economy and increase income. Ironically, part of his programme was to expand opium cultivation into new districts. It fell to that energetic Deputy Collector, Mr Reade, to launch and watch over this new venture in Cawnpore. The man he turned to was Peter Maxwell. Only three years previously Mr Reade had heaped bitter accusations upon Peter Maxwell for evading taxation, linking his name with that of Adam Maxwell. But Peter Maxwell, with his thorough knowledge of the District, was clearly an excellent choice, and by 1847 he had earned the good opinion of Robert Montgomery, who described him as 'a most respectable landed proprietor'.

Peter Maxwell was joined in India in the 1830s by his three younger brothers. Hugh, David and James had been at school in Scotland. For all three of them, their life's work was to be in India, but those brief years in Scotland with their father's people confirmed in them their tough northern ancestry. They returned to India to take up their father's interests.

Their arrival coincided with a time of great change – the liberal reforms introduced by Bentinck, the greatly improved communications and the new breed of Company men. It was also a time of change within the Maxwell

Silhouettes of the three Maxwell boys taken in Scotland

Hugh Maxwell, Edinburgh, 1825

James Maxwell, Aberdeen 1827   *David Maxwell, 23 March 1827*

family circle itself. With the death of Adam Maxwell, the confiscation of his estates and the sale of the family home in Cawnpore, the fortunes of the family seemed to have reached their nadir. It took over twenty years of quiet hard work, but the united efforts of John Maxwell's four remaining sons, aided by a little luck, reversed the trend, until they were in a position of such strength that not even the Mutiny destroyed them.

They were helped by two pieces of good fortune. In 1837 the law preventing Europeans from owning landed property was changed; and in 1835 Peter Maxwell was appointed Deputy Opium Agent in charge of the new venture of growing poppies in the Cawnpore District. For many years opium had been grown in India as a Company monopoly and shipped to China in exchange for tea and silk, to bolster the Company's finances.

All four brothers were indigo planters. They planned their resources carefully. Twenty-five years earlier John Maxwell had taken up a central position at Cawnpore and settled trusted managers in each of his indigo concerns. The four young Maxwells spread themselves further, exercising the strength of family bonds. The River Ganges, the highway for trade, was the key to their plans. Starting from their established assets in the Cawnpore District Peter Maxwell was to continue to run his own estates at Muckanpore while acting as Opium Agent to Government – a useful connection to maintain. The other family estates round Mendhi Ghat were to be run by the youngest of the boys, James Maxwell. A little further north was Fatehgarh, a garrison town on the river with facilities for sending and receiving goods. David Maxwell was to settle there, one of the circle of influential indigo planters, to attend to the business side of their commercial affairs.

Hugh Maxwell ventured further afield. He spent the years of family reconsolidation based on estates in the Mirzapore District. This was a long way removed from Cawnpore but strategically a most valuable choice. Mirzapore was half way to Calcutta, on the River Ganges at the furthest point which large steamers could reach. Before the Mutiny Mirzapore was one of the leading commercial and manufacturing centres of Upper India; caravans loaded with goods from all parts of India converged on it and as many as fifty steamers at a time lay at anchor at the ghats. Here Hugh Maxwell made contacts with business interests from Calcutta and here destiny brought the Maxwell family and the Gavin Jones family together.

The solidarity of the family slowly began to have its effect. Government was more interested in revenue than in strict justice; having succeeded in making an extreme example of Adam Maxwell it was now ready to take a more lenient view. The balance outstanding to Government at the time of

Adam Maxwell's death was reduced by good management to a mere Rs 291.7.3 – a narrow enough margin between success and failure.[13] The threat of sale of Maxwell property was annulled and in 1840 a revised settlement was made on reduced terms. Gradually the Maxwell brothers regained all their land and villages, and – what was even more important – the reputation for financial stability that John Maxwell had created many years earlier.

In 1838 Hugh Maxwell became established at a modest indigo factory at Palee, twenty miles across the river from Mirzapore. Nearby was the flourishing and prosperous estate of Babcha (Bubcha), owned by a man from Calcutta called John Benjamin Jones (JBJ). The first member of the Jones family to come to India had been a master in the Pilot Service who settled in Calcutta about the same time as John Maxwell.[14] JBJ, his only son, was orphaned at the age of one when his father was drowned. The young widow married again and JBJ grew up in India in the care of his Portuguese grandmother and was educated at Serampore by the distinguished missionary Joshua Marshman.[*][15] In 1816 JBJ married Frances Palmer,[16] the daughter of a wealthy merchant. The young couple lived in Calcutta where JBJ worked as an assistant at the Agency House of Palmer & Co. in Old Fort Street. His progress at Palmer & Co. and his rise to comparative prosperity is indicated on the baptism certificates of his children, where he is described successively as 'assistant, book-keeper' and 'writer'. By the time his fifth child was born he was in a position to give up trade and he lists his occupation as 'gentleman'. This financial independence enabled JBJ to take his family up-country and in 1830 he settled as an indigo planter in the Jaunpore District.

. . . In those prosperous days when indigo had no rival the planters made large fortunes and lived in palatial homes like princes. Christmas week in the delightful cold weather, when work was finished for the season, used to be the time for the gathering of the clans. Planters were wont to meet and make merry. Babcha used to be the rendezvous for the annual gathering. Visitors from surrounding factories, Jaunpore and Benares flocked to the factory and magistrates out on tour joined in the festivities and enjoyed the shooting, hunting and big dinners and the utmost cordiality and good fellowship prevailed. It was not an unusual sight on such occasions to see a score or more of guests sit night after night at the hospitable table. . . .

Those were the days when the prestige of the Englishman stood high with the

*He had an interesting and unusual upbringing and education in the Danish settlement, free from the laws of the EIC, influenced both by his grandmother's devout Catholicism and the advanced ideas of the missionaries. From his grandmother he learnt fluent Portuguese and French and under Marshman he studied the classics, Hebrew and Persian and formed the habit of study that he maintained all his life.

natives and the pledged word of the Sahib was as good as a bond. The planters then formed a link that kept in touch the natives and rulers of the great 'Company Bahadur'. The zemindars lived in cordial amity with the Planters, as it was their mutual interest to do so, for large sums in advances were disbursed through them to the villagers for the cultivation of indigo. The people were contented and happy and loud in their proclamation of gratitude to the 'Sircar Bahadur' for the pax Brittanica which had brought peace and security to the land where for centuries tyranny and chaos had reigned.[17]

On many occasions Hugh Maxwell joined hunting and shooting parties arranged from Babcha, ending the evening with a convivial dinner party there. When Charlotte, the Joneses' eldest daughter, arrived out from schooling in London, the roses of the English climate still fresh on her cheeks, he found her charming. She was just seventeen. Hugh Maxwell's visits to Babcha became more frequent; he courted her all through the beautiful cold weather months, finding an excuse, after inspecting the crops on his estate, to call at the big house and take Charlotte for a ride.

On a clear, cold morning in February 1839, in the brief period of spring in India when the trees are in new leaf, Hugh Maxwell rode over from his estate at Palee to wed young Charlotte Jones at Babcha. Up-country weddings[18] had to wait for the occasional visit of a clergyman. On the day of the marriage at Babcha, there were also the two youngest Jones infants, Charlotte's brother and sister, to be baptised. The christenings were held first, with Hugh Maxwell and Charlotte Jones each acting as godparent to one child. The baptisms were performed in the drawing-room and Hugh Maxwell stood sponsor for JBJ's eleventh child, a boy who was christened Gavin Sibbald Jones.[19] Hugh Maxwell was twenty-nine; his godson, who was also to become his brother-in-law, was three.

The marriage ceremony followed later in the day. Many friends attended, travelling from great distances to celebrate the double event, with all its feasting and toasting and jollity. No one could guess the momentous events that would follow from the formal link between these two men; yet this simple domestic ceremony, a marriage and a baptism, was what brought together all the strands of the pattern that was to prove vital in the emergence of industrial Cawnpore.

Life on an indigo estate had a charm of its own; it was a peculiar mixture of hard work and good living. Planters lived in magnificent houses, unusual in

OPPOSITE *Charlotte Jones: oil painting, possibly by her father, JBJ, c.1828. She wears a yellow satin dress with a blue sash and holds up a necklace of pearls as big as a bunch of grapes. The necklace was said to have belonged to her Portuguese great-grandmother.*

India in that they were often two storeys high, set in parklike gardens. The drive up to the house might meander between hedges of roses and through grounds dotted with flowering shrubs, clumps of bamboo, and here and there great banyan trees with wide-spreading branches.

In essence, it was like the manor house in feudal times. At a little distance was the factory, with the long line of steeping vats built in a series of steps, rather like an ornate idea for a swimming pool, with the squat boiler chimney at the far end and the outbuildings for the drying house and pressing of the cakes beyond. Close by were the bungalows of the assistants who supervised the different operations. All round were the flat cultivated fields where the indigo grew and beyond the fields rose the mud walls and outlines of two or three villages whose livelihood was closely linked with the prosperity of the estate. At various periods and in different districts the methods of liaison between villagers and estate for the cultivation of indigo varied. The relationship was susceptible to abuse. Much depended on the character of the estate manager, but one method that was mutually advantageous and widely practised was the growing of '*khoski*' indigo. Under this system the indigo was cultivated by the villagers in fields they had rented from the local zemindar. Once in possession of the fields, the villagers would enter into a contract with the planters to grow indigo for them. Against this promise advances were paid. The villager was able to pay his rent to the zemindar, cultivate half his fields with indigo and the other half for his own purposes. An atmosphere of respectful contact prevailed. The assistants spent much of their year overseeing the work in the fields. It was a routine familiar to the Maxwell brothers and to the Jones family.

To rise before the sun, eat his *chota hazri*, make sure the factory ploughmen are ready to go to work, inspect horses and bullocks, and see that they are fed, mount his horse and go over all the indigo cultivation, is the daily employment of an Assistant. This may take him five hours or more; he returns via his factory *zerats* [home cultivation] and gets under shelter from the sun by 11 a.m. After breakfast he allows himself, in the hot season, a siesta till 3 p.m. takes a bath and cup of tea to freshen him up, and goes to the office to look at the accounts, and settle any matter that may be in hand. It is nearly sunset before all this is accomplished, and time to remount his horse and ride round and inspect the work done since the morning.[20]

In November the entire estate had to be measured so that the next year's cultivation could be estimated. 'With a book and pen in his hand, accompanied by a boy holding a bottle of ink, the Assistant rides from field to field, while men with nine-foot poles measure the length and breadth of them, calling out the number of poles in a sing-song voice: *Now lugge, now*! (nine poles, nine!) when another voice takes up *Dass, han, dass*! (ten, yes,

Bringing in the carts of harvested indigo; drawn by Goodry Dass.

ten!) or whatever the poles may be.'[21] There followed the sowing, and then the arrangements for processing the plants. It was harvested in midsummer. 'If rain has fallen at the propitious time – by the end of June – the plant is nearly ready to cut, and early in July the factory presents a very busy appearance. Carts arrive in hundreds, laden with indigo, which are backed, and the contents emptied into the vats.'[22] It was a hard-working life, and the end result was by no means assured. The planter was at the mercy of the monsoon and other incalculables. At times, owing to lack of rain, the plants had to be sown twice and three times over; either the ground was too hard to plough, or when the young indigo was up grasshoppers attacked it. Worst of all, when there was a run of bad luck the labour force took fright and refused to sow in future years.

The most difficult and exhausting part of the year was the steeping of the indigo in a succession of vats:

We are still manufacturing; working regularly 6 vats a day. This morning I am making my 37th boiling. We steep by time. You will see by the hours the vats ought to have been opened last night what constant vigilance is required.

1st Vat, 9.30 p.m.; 2nd Vat, 10.45 p.m.; 3rd Vat, 12 midnight; 4th Vat, 2.15 a.m.; 5th Vat, 4.45 a.m.; 6th Vat, 6.30 a.m.

We got on all right till the 2.15 and this went wrong. The punka coolie could not read the clock and we all fell asleep in the verandah – at 3.45 I woke to hear them

The estate manager's house, Birdpur House; watercolour by Annie Larpent, daughter of William Peppé, Senior, c.1868.

opening the 2.15 vat – after knocking about all day you cannot expect the peons to watch well at night, especially when this kind of thing has been going on for a month.[23]

The best cakes of indigo were a fine violet-blue, but the colour varied in each day's manufacture. The state of the plant when cut, the weather – not enough rain at the growing season, too much rain at the cutting season – and the care observed in the various stages of manufacture, all contributed to the final quality. The prizes for good-quality indigo were high. So were the hazards in achieving it.

The dried indigo was packed in chests and sent to Calcutta, where it was sold by one of the celebrated indigo auctioneers such as Moran & Co. The sales were held in a long room something like a store-room. The auctioneers were famous for their cold beef salads and draught beer tiffins. The chests of indigo were generally sold by tens, having previously been sorted by the brokers so that the colours might run as evenly as possible. 'To sell ten chests does not take two minutes; the bidding is so brisk, the great object of intending purchasers being to catch the auctioneers ear first with the final bid; this is shouted out by half a dozen men at the same time, for they know to a rupee what the batch will go for, and when it comes to the final bid, the scream for precedence is bewildering.'[24]

Once the indigo was despatched to Calcutta, the planters settled down to a pleasurable winter. For the established planters the loneliness of their situation was mitigated in part by their hospitality, which was famed throughout the country. They had the time, the means and the inclination to entertain with the greatest bonhomie. The cost of living was cheap: eight roasting fowl for a rupee, a small lamb for four annas. Country-bottled beer could be procured from Calcutta if bottles were sent down by boats, or the beer bought in casks at Rs 4 to Rs 5 a dozen. No English beer was drinkable since it took three to six months on the voyage round the Cape. If a man got up a case or two of beer, immediately all the neighbourhood assembled to 'give him a party'. Wild goings on were not uncommon. Bets would be taken on horse races that started from the upstairs drawing-room of the manager's house, twenty feet above ground, down a narrow flight of stairs, over a course of five miles to be covered by four horses. A man thought nothing of riding forty miles for a party.

Large house parties gathered in the cold weather at the big house. Those who could not be accommodated in the house itself were provided with well-equipped tents in the grounds. During the day hunting and shooting parties were arranged. They started at dawn, following jackals with horses and dogs. Then, after a large picnic meal, the company changed its sport and began a shooting party.

There must be an end to all things, and so, alas! it was with our breakfast. Cigars were duly lit, the elephants called for, and guns and ammunition handed up to our servants, who had their seats behind us on the howdahs. About one hundred men were in waiting, each having a stick with which to beat the grass and jungle, and a pair of wooden clogs to protect his feet from thorns. Besides these beaters, there was a small detachment on our flank outside the heavy grass, carrying certain baskets provided with bottles, tumblers, etc. and we realised the fact that no man need thirst whilst he kept this little group within hail. It was not long before the game began to rise, and by evening we had a splendid bag of hare, partridge and quail. [25]

At the end of the day's hunting everyone gathered at the great house for a dinner party and the evening's entertainment began. Dinner was served in the large central hall which blazed with lights from candles in wall sconces and elaborate table lamps. The main course was invariably the celebrated up-country speciality of saddle of mutton. In the cold weather months a log fire burned in the fireplaces at either end of the room and the bare wooden frames of the pull-punkas cast flickering shadows on the high ceilings.

The guests seated at the table were attended by numerous white-coated servants, those of the master of the house and nearby bungalows, and also the personal servant who had accompanied each guest. With a tremendous

Tent Club at Tiffin: *by Percy Carpenter, published as a lithograph by Day & Son.*

air of importance the *khitmatgar* stood behind his master's chair, extracted from the many folds of his cummerbund silver salt and pepper pots and the cutlery for the place setting, and with the air of a conjuror placed them before his master. This was an admirable custom; it allowed the host to entertain in large numbers, providing the best in food and drink, with the certainty that his guests' other needs would be cared for.

These meals were a strange mixture of the splendid and the primitive. Emma Roberts remarked, 'It will easily be perceived that there is an air of barbaric grandeur about these feasts, which reminds a stranger of the descriptions he has read of the old baronial style of living.'[26] The planters enjoyed them just because they were less elegant and formal than the fashionable *burra khanas* in Calcutta. At the end of the meal, the ladies retired and the men settled down to their hookahs and cigars and their stories. There were anecdotes of famous horses and bets that had been won and lost, stories of feuds and jealousies between planters who had quarrelled over their precious water supplies. One of the planters was a retired sea captain, who was famous for fighting his battles again at the dinner table, with tumblers, wine glasses and plates representing the enemy, the shore and his own ships. The wind was always represented by a tumbler full of beer.

Our Burra Khanah; *from* Curry and Rice *by Captain G.F. Atkinson, Bengal Engineers.*

At last the men rose from the table to join the ladies. The fiddler struck up and dancing began. They danced the spin and the quadrille and many country dances to tunes such as 'Ho Maggie, Hi Maggie, Hi Maggie Lauder' and 'De'il tak the hindmost says Duncan MacCallaghan Laird of Talli Ben Jo', in which the whole company joined in the chorus. They kept it up until the early hours of the morning.[27]

Young Gavin Jones grew up on his father's indigo estates where he experienced this pleasant way of life. He was the eleventh child of a family of fourteen children and this large family circle was dominated by the tall, handsome figure of JBJ. Gavin learnt to ride and swim and shoot with JBJ's heavy duelling pistols. Often he would ride out with his father to inspect the estates or, accompanied by a faithful servant, stop at the villages to greet the elders who invariably, in their kindly way towards young children, made much of him and spoiled him with forbidden delicacies. On musical evenings he played the flute and sang in a fine Welsh voice but he was not the musician his father was, nor the artist. Gavin's skill lay in his hands: very early in life he started carving in wood, a hobby he perfected and enjoyed all his life.

The boy had no talent at figures, but was in every other way intelligent

John Benjamin Jones: oil painting by Nathaniel Hartnell during the period 1826-29 when the Jones family lived in Lambeth. This portrait of Gavin Jones's father was found after the Mutiny damaged with bullet holes and slashed with sabre cuts, lying in a field, probably looted at Fatehgarh from the house of John Moore Jones.

beyond his years, keenly observant, puzzled and intrigued by Indian customs and what his father called 'the peculiarity of the native character'.[28] (It was this awareness which was to save him in the Mutiny.) In the evenings the children looked on at the big dinner parties, occasions when the green dessert service, said once to have belonged to Warren Hastings, was used.

Our father was in his element at these festivities and being a good raconteur he kept the party amused and lively with his anecdotes and humorous jokes. And music, singing and dancing was kept up to late hours. I still retain a distinct recollection of these gatherings and we children came in for a good share of the attention from the visitors and enjoyed the romps and petting bestowed on us.[29]

This delightful way of life came to an end for the Jones family ten years before the Mutiny. JBJ had entered into partnership with Fergusson Bros., a firm of Calcutta merchants, in a new venture, the establishment of a sugar works at Ranjpore, near Babcha. Machinery was imported from England and America, the help of expert sugar manufacturers from the West Indies was sought but in 1847, before the work could be completed, the Union Bank of Calcutta failed. Fergusson Bros. went bankrupt. All JBJ's money was with the Union Bank and, faced with crippling debts, he was forced to sell his indigo estates and the property in Calcutta that stood in his wife's name. He cleared himself of debt but he never recovered from this setback. He moved to Allahabad where he died four years later.[30]

Gavin Jones was twelve years old at the time of the crash. His father's financial ruin put an end to the enchanting life Gavin had known; it probably contributed to the seriousness and aloofness of his manner; it also limited his formal education. He had intended to train to be an engineer but with no money behind him this had to wait. He went with his mother to live in Calcutta and here he had what education they could afford. In 1853 his mother died of cholera and now John Moore Jones, Gavin's eldest brother, became head of the Jones family. It is perhaps significant that in both the Maxwell and Jones families for two generations the children had to make their way without a father's help.

The Peishwa and the Nana Sahib at Bithoor

Close to Cawnpore were the towns of Bithoor and Lucknow, both steeped in Indian heritage, both casting an uneasy shadow over Cawnpore's well-ordered prosperity and 'Englishness'. Bithoor, some twelve miles from Cawnpore, lay in the ancient heart of the Hindu holy lands. Its influence conflicted with the Muslim authority at Lucknow. At Bithoor Brahma is specially reverenced. After the act of creation he offered a great public sacrifice; by chance the pin fell from his divine slipper and was fastened by his devotees into one of the steps of the principal ghat. Pilgrims from all over India come to worship it.

Apart from a brief period between 1811 and 1818, when the Cawnpore Collectorate and magistrate's courts were moved out to Bithoor to stop the squabbling between military and civil authorities, the Cawnpore residents had little contact with Bithoor. This separateness was accentuated by the arrival of the ex-Peishwa of Poona when he was sent to live in exile at Bithoor.

Towards the end of the Mahratta Wars, in June 1818, Bajee Rao, the Peishwa of Poona, the once powerful head of the Mahratta Confederacy, delivered himself up at the camp of Sir John Malcolm. For six months he had been a fugitive from Malcolm's troops, but when they had him surrounded they offered him terms for surrender. The terms and consequences of this surrender, which seemed at the time merely one incident in the conclusion of the Mahratta campaign, eventually cost the thousand English lives lost in the mutiny at Cawnpore. The terms were liberal. The Government promised to give the Peishwa an ample pension of £80,000 a year to support him and his family and to receive him with respect and honour. In return he should resign all sovereign power for himself and his successors. Bajee Rao hesitated over the offer for as long as he dared and then replied flatteringly, 'I have found you, who are my only friend, and will never leave you; would a ship-wrecked mariner, after having reached the port he desired, form a wish to leave it?'[31] He accepted what amounted to a bribe to end the fighting.

The Governor-General appointed Bithoor as the place where the ex-Peishwa should live in exile, since he was a Brahmin and it seemed appropriate that he should live in a holy city. Bajee Rao with his entourage took up residence surrounded by generals and retainers who chose to follow him into exile. While he lived there in considerable style, Government closed the civil headquarters in Bithoor and moved them back to Cawnpore.

To the British in Cawnpore, the ex-Peishwa was a subject of mystery and curiosity. They heard the Government paid him a handsome pension, which kept him in a state of absolute luxury and paid for the keep of three sets of dancing girls and a small army of retainers. Fashionable picnic parties were organised in the hope of catching a glimpse of the great man, but he was rarely seen in person. Lieutenant de Wend wrote home that 'some of the chief followers, his old generals and courtiers with their sons, in the picturesque and native dress of the Mahrattas, generally attend the public balls and large private parties in Cawnpore.'[32] Although Bajee Rao would not attend the public functions in Cawnpore, he believed in keeping up

Temple of the Holy Nail, Bithoor, c. 1930.

Procession of a Native Prince: *sketch by Captain Robert Smith, c.1828. Bajee Rao, the ex-Peishwa of Poona, rode in state into Cawnpore once a month.*

appearances by riding in state into Cawnpore once a month. The procession used to pass the bungalow of Captain Robert Smith who recorded it in his diary and also sketched the scene.

He was always preceded some distance in advance by an elephant bearing a huge drum which was beaten in intervals to announce his approach and warn everybody to make way; then followed the great man himself on a richly caparisoned one accompanied by officers and attendants, some on elephants and others on horseback surrounded by a troop of Mahratta horsemen with their long lances, dashing along and a crowd of peons or footmen scampering away and struggling to keep pace with the quick shuffling walk of the elephants. [33]

For most of the time Bajee Rao remained within the walls of his Bithoor palace. Government appointed a Commissioner-in-Chief, Captain Manson, to advise him on his affairs and provide a link between him and Government. The arrangement worked well: Manson proved a trusted and successful Commissioner and the ex-Peishwa – now known as the Maharaja – seemed satisfied with the peculiar benefits of his position.

The Cawnpore residents were impressed with the 'conspicuous fidelity' of the Maharaja and the good conduct and orderly behaviour of his people. Captain Rawlins noted in his diary that his loyalty was more than passive. 'When the war in Afghanistan in 1838–40 was going on, and money was grievously wanted, he lent the Company 5 lacs [sic] of rupees; and when afterwards our dominions were threatened by the invasion of the Seikhs he made an offer to raise and maintain 1000 horse and 1000 foot.'[34] Nevertheless, the relationship between the English and the Maharaja was in many ways an uneasy one. When any member of Government visited Bithoor, great care was taken on both sides that no offence should be given. This was necessary because the palace was rife with intrigue: much of the trouble centred round the Maharaja's adopted sons (see Appendix 4).

Bajee Rao had no sons of his own. For a high-caste Brahmin this was a terrible lack, because only a son could perform the essential funeral rites of his father. Hindu law recognised the importance of this function by conferring on an adopted son all the rights and privileges of a legitimate heir. Bajee Rao had two adopted sons, one of whom, Dundoo Pant, became known as the Nana Sahib.

As early as 1838, the Commissioner was anticipating trouble in securing the inheritance of the adopted sons on the Maharaja's death. Captain Manson wrote to the Secretary to the Governor-General, asking for instructions on how to proceed in protecting the treasure 'of which there must be a great accumulation' in the event of Bajee Rao's death during the minority of his two adopted sons.[35]

More difficulties arose over the question of the Government pension: the Maharaja himself, and the Nana after him, saw this sum as part of a perpetual contract undertaken by Government, to be paid to the Maharaja's family in return for his surrender in 1818. The Nana as adopted son expected to inherit it. But Government refused to continue the payment after Bajee Rao's death. Various historians attributed the Government decision to the British rejection of the rights of an adopted son. However, the British allowed the legality of the Nana's claims to all the private fortune of his adoptive father; what they would not concede was that the Maharaja's pension was anything but the generous response of Government to his defeat, valid for his lifetime only.

When Bajee Rao died in 1851, the Nana again petitioned for the pension, and was again refused. Despite the vast amounts of private treasure he inherited, despite the fact that Government had over the years paid out £2,500,000 to his father, he probably needed the money. The Nana had also inherited large debts; he had 15,000 retainers to keep; and he could not sell property for fear of losing face. As a result, he had a deep grievance against the Government.

His grievance did not apparently extend to individual Englishmen. Quite the reverse. Unlike his adoptive father, he welcomed European society, and took every opportunity to give European-style entertainments, though he would never accept an invitation because Government would not give him the honour of a gun salute. At balls and banquets, his manner was entirely friendly. Trevelyan described how the Nana Sahib mixed freely with his guests: 'inquired after the health of the Major's lady, congratulated the judge on his rumoured promotion to the Sudder Court; joked the assistant magistrate about his last mishap in the hunting field; and complimented the belle of the evening on the colour she had brought down from Simla.'[36]

The Nana spoke no English himself, but his 'English teacher', a man called Todd, went with him everywhere and translated for him. He took the Anglo-Indian journals, and endeared himself to that community with acts not only of extravagance – distributing diamonds and cashmere shawls – but also of kindness – lending his carriage and asking young couples to stay at his palace for a change of air.

This palace was a strange mixture of the expensively English and the primitive native: guns from Purdey, chandeliers from Birmingham, carriages from Long Acre,[37] cows wandering through the rooms, their droppings caught in silver bowls. An English guest, Lieutenant Lang, described the odd mixture displayed at dinner:

I sat down to a table twenty feet long (it had originally been the mess table of a cavalry regiment) which was covered with a damask table-cloth of European manufacture, but instead of a dinner napkin there was a bedroom towel. The soup . . . was served up in a trifle dish which has formed part of a dessert service belonging to the Ninth Lancers – but the plate into which I ladled it with a broken tea-cup was of the old willow pattern. . . . The cool claret I drank out of a richly cut champagne glass, and the beer out of an American tumbler of the very worst quality.[38]

The character of Nana Sahib, who was to cause the murder of the very people he entertained so splendidly, is difficult to determine. The assessments of his contemporaries, mostly written after the Mutiny, are violently coloured by hindsight: he was often described as having variations upon 'a look in which cruelty and sensuality strove for the mastery'. In reality he seems to have been an undistinguished-looking man of middle height, with a round, clean-shaven face marked by smallpox, and very stout. Captain Rawlins played billiards with him in 1844 when the Nana was a lad of fifteen, 'of pleasant and agreeable manners, good physique and gave promise of being a pillar of the state'.[39]

His birth was uncertain. Some said that he was really the son of a corn-seller of Poona, others that he had been born to a poor Brahmin family at a miserable little village thirty miles east of Bombay. He was educated at a school opened in Bithoor by missionaries at the request of his father's prime

Nana Sahib: bazaar painting, gouache on paper, of the 'Hero of the Indian Mutiny'.

The other face of the Nana Sahib: miniature on ivory by an unknown Indian artist.

minister. English was taught there, although he did not learn to speak it, and there he had his first real contact with Europeans.

Later he chose for his counsellor Azimoolah Khan, who played a very influential role in his life – some thought as his *éminence grise* – first as the handsome, smooth-spoken emissary to plead for the Nana's pension rights at the Court of St James, and subsequently as the Nana's right-hand man. He was shrewd and clever. He put his many years of living with Europeans to good use when advising the Nana during the Mutiny. It is interesting that both the Nana Sahib and Azimoolah Khan were influenced in their early education by well-meaning missionaries.

Azimoolah Khan was a charity boy, having been picked up together with his mother during the famine of 1837–38; they were both in a dying state from starvation. The mother being a staunch Mahomedan would not consent to her son (then quite a boy) being christened. He was educated in the Cawnpore Free School under Mr Paton, schoolmaster, and received a subsistence of Rs 3/– per month. His mother earned her own livelihood by serving as ayah or maidservant. After 10 years' study Azimoolah was raised to be a teacher in the same school, and two years after, he was made over, as a Moonshee, to Brigadier Scott, who in his turn made him over to his successor (when leaving the station) Brigadier the Hon. Ashburnham, when Azimoolah misbehaved himself and was turned out under an accusation of bribery and corruption; subsequently he attached himself to the Nana.[40]

The Nana grew up to be a popular member of the community and on good terms with the Europeans in Cawnpore. His generosity was proverbial; in the cold weather he issued frequent invitations to picnics, archery meetings, cricket matches and social evenings with *nautch* girls and fireworks to entertain the guests. On one occasion he had so enjoyed a game of billiards with a Lieutenant Daniell that he took the splendid ring off his own finger and gave it to the young man. He often made gifts of handsome shawls to the wives of senior residents, and Mrs Louisa Chalwin, newly arrived in Cawnpore, was delighted with the loan of a piano until hers arrived from Meerut.[41]   On his frequent visits to Cawnpore he patronised the shops of Messrs Greenway Bros., wines and provisions, noted for their Bass and Allsops Prime Golden Ale,[42] and regularly attended the meetings at Lodge Harmony, the Masonic Lodge that had been in existence since the 16th Lancers came to Cawnpore.[43] He even accompanied the Regiment to church, which surprised Private Metcalfe: 'I saw him riding in a beautiful phaeton, drawn by two splendid horses.'[44] Most Englishmen, including the Collector and the senior Army officers, regarded him as a jolly good fellow and almost 'one of themselves'.

Certain commentators have pictured the Nana as indulging in these pleasantries towards the British in the secret knowledge that he would have his revenge on them all. It is more likely that he was merely being pragmatic. He wanted the re-issue of his father's pension, and his best chance of gaining it was to placate, help and amuse the British, while petitioning every possible authority. As long as the British were supreme, there seemed no other course.

Scandal at the Court of Oude

Only the Ganges separated Cawnpore from the Kingdom of Oude. On one side lay the provinces ceded to the British in 1801, with Cawnpore at their boundary, governed by the scrupulously ordered procedures of Company administration. On the other was the wild, unsystematised territory under the nominal rule of the king at Lucknow. With every year of British presence in the ceded provinces, the difference between the two became more marked.

As early as 1773, when the fortunes of Oude and the Company had been first linked, the British had had a Resident at the court of Oude in Lucknow, to keep an eye on the Nawab and to give him what information and advice the Company thought fit. Successive Nawabs (in 1819 granted the title of Kings) seemed in great need of advice. Thirty years after the Cession anarchy prevailed, the ruling king was idle, his ministers were embezzling the revenue, the court was busy with intrigue, and powerful landlords were terrorising their tenants. The English likened the state of affairs to the feudalism of medieval Europe: at the court the king had unquestioned power over the lives – and deaths – of all natives not in the service of the Company; in the District the landlords on their own property were equally powerful and even more brutal.

To witness this alien and abhorrent system in operation in a state in which they had so much interest made the Company nervous. However, while Oude was a source of despair to officials, in the mind of other Europeans it took on the role of a romantic and mysterious Eastern realm, made all the more fascinating by tales of the terrible goings-on. While Beckford was writing his Eastern fantasy *Vathek* in Europe, the real thing was situated a mere forty-eight miles from the English inhabitants of Cawnpore.

Once a month it was customary for the king to give a public breakfast at his palace, and his Cawnpore guests rode over to get a glimpse of the wonders of the court, the menagerie, the collection of European clocks, the sheer extent of the palace buildings. The immediate impression gained by visitors, both in Lucknow and the surrounding country, was of the warlike appearance of the citizens. Bishop Heber commented on it when he arrived in Lucknow in 1824:

A swarm of beggars occupied every angle and the steps of every door, and all, or nearly all the remaining population were, to my surprise, as much loaded with arms as the inhabitants of the country, a circumstance which told ill for the police of the town, but added considerably to its picturesque effect. Grave men in palanquins, counting their beads and looking like Moullahs, had all two or three sword and buckler lackeys attending on them. People of more consequence, on their elephants, had each a *suwarree* of shield, spear, and gun, little inferior to that by which we were surrounded, and even the lounging people of the lower ranks in the streets and shop-doors had their shields over their shoulders, and their swords carried sheathed in one hand.[45]

OPPOSITE Ghazi-ud-din Haidar, King of Oude, Receiving Tribute: *oil by Robert Home, Lucknow c.1820. At court the King had unquestioned power over the life and death of all natives not in the service of the Company.*

At the centre of this ornamental, dangerous city was the king. An absolute monarch, whose every wish was instantly gratified, he had as much to fear from boredom as from intrigue. He searched constantly for amusement and anyone who could arouse his interest was bound to be popular at court. A certain kind of European frequently played this part. Zoffany's famous picture[46] of a cockfight depicts the Nawab Asaf-ud-Dowlah with Colonel Mordaunt,[47] who contrived endlessly to devise such entertainments. At the court of Nasir-ud-din, who ruled from 1827 to 1837, there were five Europeans of dubious background in constant attendance. The king enjoyed their company, both for the amusements they provided and for the obvious displeasure their presence and influence at court caused the British Resident. His colourful – and powerful – favourite, who held a post somewhere between minister, bodyguard and jester, was a barber named De Russett.

In much the same way as the story of George Ravenscroft's embezzlement of revenue typifies the unprincipled ways of his time, so the strange story of De Russett serves to illustrate the scandals at the court of Oude. He had come out to India as a cabin boy, set up in Calcutta as a barber, and on a visit up-country had the good fortune to work on the Resident's wig. The delighted Resident introduced him to the king. De Russett performed miracles of curls with the king's straight hair, and from that day occupied a position of power at court.

In the world outside, the barber appeared a typical quiet, well-to-do tradesman, 'a ginger whiskered Englishman, past middle age, of moderate stature and by no means remarkable'.[48] But in Lucknow his importance was second only to the king's, and he was treated accordingly. He stood between the king and his subjects, organising his entertainments, dining at his table, supplying his drink and European food, testing his wine for fear of poison. His income and personal expenditure were both fantastic. In Knighton's *Private Life of an Eastern King*,[49] which tells the story of the court through the eyes of another European favourite, De Russett is described presenting the king with his monthly bill, in the form of a scroll, which was usual at the time:

The king was in a playful humour; and the barber was always in the same mood as the king. He held the end of the roll in his hand, and threw the rest along the floor, allowing it to unroll itself as it retreated. It reached to the other side of the long apartment – a goodly array of items and figures, closely written too. The king wanted it measured. A measure was brought, and the bill was found to be four yards and a half long. I glanced at its amount; it was upwards of ninety thousand rupees, upwards of nine thousand pounds![50]

Naturally the barber was under constant attack, but it amused the king to condone his extravagance. Satires and jibes in the newspapers were so frequent that De Russett employed a clerk to answer them. At the court, too, there were complaints, particularly from the Indian officials oversha-dowed by the barber and his fellow Europeans. On one occasion the chief minister complained that De Russett and his friends came before the king with their shoes on. The king defended his favourites, asking, 'Am I greater than the king of England? These gentlemen would go into his presence with their shoes on. Do they come before me with their hats on? No, that is their way of showing respect. If you will take off your turban, I will insist that they take off their shoes.'[51]

Clearly Nasir-ud-din was not necessarily the fool he generally appeared to be. Yet his public reputation could not have been worse. Sir John Shore, writing in 1835, called him 'a profligate and a sot devoid of sense, who thinks of nothing but his own licentious pleasures, and of the indulgence of every whim. When anything annoys or vexes him he has recourse to drinking to drown thought.'[52] For the most part, his behaviour justified that descrip-tion. Every evening he got drunk over dinner before calling for his night's entertainment: there might be tumblers or conjurors, or *nautch* girls or puppet shows. Sometimes there were cockfights at the table, or fights between quails or partridges, or the snake charmer would perform. Sometimes he demanded a game of chess, and his opponent had to be sure to lose with elaborate care.

These evenings might sound like one long party, but the fun had sinister overtones. The king's enjoyment betrayed a mixture of naiveté and casual brutality. On the one hand he could be delighted for hours by two English sports introduced by the barber: leapfrog – the king and his courtiers made backs for each other up and down the garden – and snowballing: there was, of course, no snow, so they improvised by pelting each other with the heads of marigolds. On the other hand, Nasir-ud-din's caprice quickly turned to cruelty. Once an after-dinner puppet show was in progress. It occurred to the king to send for a pair of scissors, and he derived his real pleasure on that occasion by cutting down the puppets, one by one. The whole court, including the uneasy puppet-master, naturally had to join in the joke. The climax of the fun came when the king set the puppet theatre alight with a candle.

His curious humour was often directed at animals. He kept his menagerie to provide beasts for spectacular fights – elephants and tigers and buffalo: Knighton's book records the remarkable occasion when a man-eating horse defeated two tigers and three buffalo. The victims could equally well be human – particularly those people whom the king already disliked, such as his uncles, who would be summoned to dinner just so that some insult might be offered them. In one hideous episode, an old man was made thoroughly drunk and then forced to dance a reel with the barber, whirled round till he could hardly stand. His turban was knocked off and all his clothes snatched away from him, garment by garment. Another uncle suffered worse humiliation still when his moustaches were tied with twine to his chair and a firework let off under his nose. Urging the king on in these hysterical pleasures, as in everything else, was De Russett.

Disorder at court, however, had reached its peak, and with it the barber's power. In the second half of his reign Nasir-ud-din – not surprisingly – was subject to constant criticism from the Resident. The weight of universal disapproval made it clear that the barber, as the focus of the disturbance, had to go. He fled to Cawnpore where, within the Company's territories, he and his fortune were safe from the king's displeasure. All that is known of his later life is that years afterwards he came before an English bankruptcy court – heaven knows how he had spent the immense fortune he had gathered in Lucknow.

However, events showed that the king had not been entirely ill-advised in the trust he placed in his barber; only four months after De Russett departed, the king died from the effects of poison.

The Annexation of Oude

The atmosphere of degeneracy and lawlessness in Lucknow affected Cawnpore in many small and insidious ways. The road linking the two cities had, since the earliest times, been so dangerous that 'a single person will not travel alone in the night from one stage to another, on any consideration, as the thieves will murder a man for his clothes'.[53] The Company had no effective means of influencing what went on in Oude except through the Resident and he often found his position very difficult. William Sleeman, who had made his name during the campaign against thugee, served as an indefatigable Resident of Lucknow from 1849 to 1854. He reported an incident in which he was powerless to see justice done:

I have now before me a curious instance of the difficulty of getting at the truth when it is in the interest of the minister and others about this Court to prevent it. A wanton attack was made in April last by about one hundred men, led by one of the King's collectors, on a native British subject coming from Cawnpore to visit a brother in

OPPOSITE Asaf-ud-Dowlah at a Cockfight: *Company painting, watercolour by a Lucknow artist c.1830-35. The Nawab is surrounded by his courtiers and European favourites to watch the entertainment.*

Oude. The man himself received a wound, from which he some days afterwards died at Cawnpore; two of his attendants were killed and twenty thousand rupees were taken from him. I have investigated the case myself, with the aid of my assistant, Captain Hayes, and with the attendance of an assessor on the part of the King. The case is a very clear one, but they have produced about thirty witnesses to swear that no man of the poor merchant's party was hurt. [54]

In 1845 the Cawnpore residents were startled to find themselves being fired upon; several cannon balls fired by the King of Oude's soldiers from across the river fell into the Cantonment area. People were outraged and demanded that the men responsible be immediately punished. The Resident reported to Government that the king's officers 'hotly and cruelly' followed certain rebels and dacoits and 'so far forgot themselves as to openly insult a British Cantonment and endanger the lives and property of British subjects by the fire of their guns and matchlocks'. [55] In this case the king had little option but to agree to make a severe example of the leaders. He stressed, however, that his officers' fault lay in firing in the vicinity of the territories belonging to the British Government, rather than in the act itself.

Travellers passing through Cawnpore were warned to beware the numerous thieves who haunted Cawnpore from Oude. An army officer's wife, travelling to Meerut in 1850, had just such an unfortunate experience. She and her husband, tired from their journey, put up at the hotel where they slept well, only to find in the morning that all their baggage had been stolen. She confided to her diary:

14 January. Bitterly cold, no tidings of the lost goods. This place is, we found, celebrated for thieves. The inn is well situated for robbery, being in the Company's dominion, whereas the opposite side of the river is in the Kingdom of Oude's. At this time of year the river is so low the natives can wade across which they do with their booty, and are then out of this jurisdiction. There is a bridge of boats and everyone has been searched since who crossed it but to no purpose. [56]

Fugitives seeking sanctuary in the Company's jurisdiction from the more arbitrary and less predictable processes of punishment at the court of Lucknow came to settle in Cawnpore. The first of these exiles, who brought the splendour and extravagance of the court with them, was Aga Mir, [57] the deposed prime mininster of Oude. In 1831 he had crossed the river with an imposing train: ' . . . fifty-six elephants covered with crimson clothing completely embroidered with gold, and forty garees [carts] filled with gold mohurs and rupees'. The womenfolk of his zenana had preceded him and their conveyances consisted of 'nearly 400 palanquins'. [58]

There were restrictions on the purchase of houses in Cantonments, designed to protect officers from being priced out of their own quarters, but these were waived for Aga Mir's benefit, and he bought a house from a staff officer. In consequence, the two opposing ways of life, the stiffly British and the luxuriously Indian, came face to face: inevitably Aga Mir brought with him his large retinue, amounting to a small army and inevitably the British residents distrusted its presence.

In 1839 the same problem arose when another minister, Rooshun-ud-Dowlah, fled to Cawnpore with the profits of five years in office in Lucknow.[59] He wrote to Government, requesting permission to live in Cantonments (see Appendix 5). Interestingly, the house he bought for 30,000 rupees belonged to Adam Maxwell and was situated 'on the banks of the Ganges within the military cantonments and I am desirous of living in it because such a house cannot be had here'.[60] His dependants raised and drilled troops 'with the bustle and disturbance of military preparation' which the Cawnpore people found most objectionable.[61] They could not help but be aware of the lawlessness in Oude. Those who visited Lucknow reported that 'splendour was confined to the palace, while misery pervaded the streets'.[62]

In many such ways the unsystematic government in Oude affected life in Cawnpore, while successive Residents and officials visiting Lucknow deplored the conditions in Oude and urged Government to take action. In 1837 the Company had made explicit provision for a complete takeover of Oude, should urgent reforms fail to be carried out.

Year after year matters got worse and still the Company hesitated on such an extreme measure. In 1845 Sir Henry Lawrence gave his opinion in the *Calcutta Review*:

The government of the country is utterly palsied; its constitution is altogether destroyed; no hope remains. . . . It is the system that is defective, not the tools with which it has been worked. We have tried every variety of interference, we have interfered directly, and we have interfered indirectly; by omission as well as by commission, but it has invariably failed.

The solution therefore seemed to be to change the system. There were some, however, who felt that the greatest service the Company could perform for Oude was to leave it entirely alone. Sleeman, who after his extensive tour of Oude in 1849–50, knew his subject better than any other European, believed that the Company was bound to take on the administration of the state eventually, but that it must do so in a disinterested way, refusing all profits from its function:

The treaty of 1837 gives our Government ample authority to take the whole administration on ourselves, in order to secure what we have often pledged ourselves to secure to the people; but if we do this we must, in order to stand well

Wajid Ali Shah, the last King of Oude: three-quarter-length portrait in oils by an Indian artist, Lucknow c.1855. His kingdom was annexed in 1856 and he was forced to abdicate and live in exile in Calcutta.

with the rest of India, honestly and distinctly disclaim all interested motives, and appropriate the whole of the revenues for the benefit of the people and royal family of Oude. If we do this, all India will think us right, for the sufferings of the people of Oude, under the present system, have been long notorious throughout India.[63]

Sleeman was unusual in the stress he placed on *not* annexing Oude outright; other Company officials viewed annexation as the simplest and tidiest solution. In the event, the Governor-General, Lord Dalhousie, put forward several proposals for the treatment of Oude, and the East India Company Directors in London decided on annexation. In 1856, the year before the Mutiny, the annexation was announced; Cawnpore and the territories of Oude were once again united, this time under Company rule.

A treaty of abdication was drawn up but with dignity and pathos the King of Oude refused to sign it, or any other treaty with the British. His departure from Lucknow on his way to Calcutta, where he was to live in exile, was reported in the daily newspapers:

DEPARTURE OF THE KING FOR CALCUTTA

Lucknow, the 14th March 1856: The King left his Palace yesterday evening at eight o'clock on his way to Calcutta, whence he wishes to proceed to England. He has arrived this morning at Cawnpore. I was present at the time he came out of the Palace gates, and the scene which I then witnessed will ever be forcibly impressed on my mind . . . to me it was surprising, for I believed natives incapable of displaying so much feeling. The air resounded with shouts – *Badshah salamat* (greetings to thee, Oh King;) *Badshahat phir bani rahe* (May your kingdom again be established!) *Landhan se hukum a jawe* (May the order arrive from London!) (I suppose to overturn the present state of affairs) *Badshah salamat, salamat!* was heard everywhere. Then deep curses were imprecated on the heads of the *Firangis* (Europeans) and I felt anything but comfortable at that time. Indeed, I thought it prudent then to take myself off, for I thought it very possible that I might become a victim to a multitude exasperated against the Europeans. The King's wives, concubines, and female attendants crowded into the closed turrets and houses surrounding the enclosure and set up a long wail, long and continued, a wail heart-rending in the extreme. All were affected, and tears streamed down many cheeks.[64]

Like this spectator, most of the British in the now reunited Oude were astonished at the evident regret of the native population at losing a ruler and a system undeniably so incompetent and unjust. They had imagined that the natives of Oude would welcome the onset of a more equitable administration. What they overlooked was the Indian need to have amongst them a figure whom they could revere and relate to; a king in their midst, and a king from their own people, was infinitely more desirable than the faceless Government of the British. The British system might be more just, but it was less human, less colourful and less immediate.

Faces at the Court of Oude, 1855: taken by an amateur photographer, Ahmed Ali Khan. Two albums of his work were found in the ruins of the Residency. ABOVE *Mohib Ali Khan, Captain in the service of Wajid Ali Shah;* OPPOSITE, TOP LEFT *Court official, perhaps Munawar ood Doulah;* TOP RIGHT *Hajee Saheeb, Court official;* BELOW *Alixeen ood Doulah, favourite eunuch to the (Queen Mother) Begum, and Puran Chand, Chief of Police to East India Company.*

Hakeem ood Doulah
Favourite Eunuch of the Begum

The Hindu divinities comprehend both good and evil: the Hindu people were unsurprised if their gods dealt out misery and death. The Muslim population for its part had a sense of fatalism fostered by its religion and by the uncertainties of the land in which it lived. The two attitudes combined to create a high degree of tolerance of an oppressive or ineffectual ruler.

This is not to say that there had not been resentment in Oude at the mismanagement of Government: that had been widespread. However, in ordering the annexation, the Company succeeded in uniting all the old grievances of the native population against itself. Ominously, Sleeman had noted that there were 40,000 sepoys from Oude in the armies of the Company.

The Merchants of Cawnpore 1856

The office given to a young man going to India is of trifling consequence. But he that goes out an insignificant boy, in a few years returns a Nabob.[65]

Life in Cawnpore had always been closely linked with the affairs of Lucknow. Now the introduction of British rule into Oude, while ruining the landed gentry, disbanding the old native army and scattering desperate men throughout the province, offered new opportunities to the Cawnpore traders and merchants who anticipated a second boom.

That 'second circle' of Cawnpore residents – the tradesmen and shopkeepers – had by 1856 been established in Cawnpore for more than three generations (see Appendix 6). From the time of the Free School quarrel, when the residents had attempted for the first time to act for the needs of the community, they had grown ever closer and gained in influence. Their strength lay in working together. Their sense of interdependence was strengthened by the fact that their small society was closely knit by marriage. With each daughter given in marriage, business interests were extended and property acquired. Most of the alliances took place in Cawnpore itself, but strong ties of trade and kinship also existed between the residents of Cawnpore and the nearby towns, in particular with Fatehgarh.

In 1852, when making a presentation to the Collector on his transfer from Cawnpore, the merchants ordered from the leading Calcutta silversmith a handsome solid silver inkstand, fitted with two ink bottles and a pounce box set upon a drawer, and bearing the inscription: 'Presented to W. H. Morland CS Collector of Cawnpore by the grateful merchants of Cawnpore 1852'.[66]

These same merchants patronised the Cawnpore Races. The Merchants' Plate was the big event of the three-day meeting, carrying a prize of 25 gold mohurs. By signs such as these, they indicated that they now thought of themselves as a prosperous, integrated group who could, when necessary, bury their business rivalries and act for the good of all.

The merchants, their memsahibs and families, lived their working lives in India but they maintained a certain conviction that everything English was superior. They surrounded themselves with things English; their gardens were oases of England filled with as many cottage garden flowers as could be persuaded to survive in an Indian climate, a barrier between them and the 'horrid' sights and smells of the bazaar. The products they traded in and tempted their customers to buy were imported to enhance this mystique of 'home'-sickness. So effective was this illusion that even as early as 1837 Bishop Wilson was astonished how familiarly English Cawnpore looked: 'To enter it was like entering the outskirts of London. T. Harman, Tailor and Thomas Brookes, General Dealer, over the shop doors were new sights and strange to Indian eyes.'[67]

The similarity to England was made possible by the number and prosperity of the merchants. By the middle of the nineteenth century a young bride had to write home to England for very little of her trousseau and household needs: they could almost all be met in Cawnpore, with its English auctioneers, coachmakers, chemists, glovemakers, milliners, dressmakers, a piano tuner, a professor of music, watchmakers, harnessmakers, wine merchants and undertakers all settled and striving to make a good living.

From the beginning of trade in Cawnpore, when men such as Robert Bailie had studied the new market, the tradespeople had made it their business to supply whatever the buyers wanted, and adapt themselves to every opportunity. William Dickson, who ran a successful farm on the outskirts of Cawnpore, wrote in 1838 to Major-General Anbury with great resourcefulness, informing him of the dispatch by coolie of 'A Dozen of large Smoked Ox Tongues and Smoked Humps', at the same time apologising for having failed to procure a pair of buggy shafts.[68] However, he offered to have a pair made up for the General as soon as possible.

This ability to adjust to the requirements of the moment had resulted in many firms trading in more than one commodity. The leading firms of merchants built up interests as different as printing and newspapers, life assurance, indigo, travel facilities, auctioneering and the contract for the upkeep of the Bridge of Boats.

The most prominent name among the merchants was that of Greenway Bros. In 1821 Samuel Greenway had sought Government's permission to start an up-country press at Cawnpore, describing himself as a native of

Bengal who, during thirty years, had been the proprietor of successive newspapers.[69] From that beginning the Greenway family built a network of successful business interests which had connections, based on Cawnpore, with Agra, Allahabad, Meerut and Calcutta. Their most successful venture was to secure the contract for maintaining the Bridge of Boats across the Ganges linking Cawnpore with the Kingdom of Oude. It cost them Rs 10,000 a year but it was a lucrative contract, since every person, animal and vehicle crossing the Bridge of Boats had to pay toll. Every year, on the fall of the Ganges, heavy sands formed, 'where there is neither road nor track'. In 1852 Greenway Bros. obtained permission to build a tram-line across the sands that would provide a firm base for carriage wheels. This was a boon to the public, who had previously suffered great inconvenience and delay from 'the harassing nature of the drag across'.[70]

Greenway Bros. were the agents for the Lucknow Dak, which they advertised regularly:

Lucknow Dawk. W Greenway Leaves Cawnpore Post Office morning and evening at 8 o'clock and Lucknow Post Office morning at $11\frac{1}{2}$ and evening at 8 o'clock daily. Inside passenger 12 Rs. Outside passenger 8 Rs. Children under 10 $\frac{1}{2}$ fare. 8 as. extra for La Martinière or Lucknow Cantts.[71]

Greenway Bros.' greatest rival was Henry Brandon, rumoured to be a downright rogue. Brandon was the proprietor of the Cawnpore newspaper *Central Star*, described by Sleeman, the Resident of Lucknow, as a 'scurrilous affair'. He was closely associated with activities at the court in Lucknow, a friend of the chief ministers and reputedly in the pay of the king. Interestingly, one of his assistants at Brandon and Co., General Merchants, was young De Russett, the son of the barber who had been such a favourite of an earlier king. Sleeman twice had 'the mischievous Mr B' expelled from Lucknow for intriguing, and he believed him to be behind an attack on his life.

In the business world Brandon was well known for similarly ruthless conduct, competing with Greenway Bros. for every contract. While Greenways were the agent for the Lucknow Dak, Brandon was the agent for a rival concern, the North Western Dak Co., and his advertisement conveys a sense of keen competition:

N. W. Dak Co. (J. H. Allen) was established in 1852. It conveys passengers by Horse Carriage Dak and Parcels by Mail Cart – the latter at half the rate charged by the Govt. The rates of these companies varies from 2–4 annas per mile for a single passenger and double for a whole carriage.[72]

However, it was whispered that Brandon had built up his network of contacts and influence by bribery; now, with the annexation of Oude and the dispersal of his friends at court, he found himself at a disadvantage.

Most merchants were less dangerous, although no less eager to do well. From the time of the first up-country traders there had been quarrels and lawsuits between competitors, and it was usual for shop keepers to write dignified, graceful letters to their clients, requesting a testimony of character. When William Dickson found himself in the Criminal Court, defending his name against charges brought by another merchant, he wrote to his old patron, Major-General Anbury: 'I would esteem it a particular mark of favor if you would furnish me with a few lines as a Certificate of my character in regard to honesty and integrity in the various dealings I have had with you. . . '[73] Enormous faith was placed in the power of such testimonies or 'chits'. Other tradesmen advertised the patronage of eminent citizens of Cawnpore as London suppliers would display a royal patent:

Mr J. A. John. Clock and Watch Maker and General Mechanic, Bungalow No. 99 Old Grand Parade, under the patronage of Major General Sir Hugh Massy Wheeler KCB Commanding Cawnpore Division.[74]

Some merchants were noted for the novelty or excellence of their goods – the products of ingenious Victorian minds, able in the era of the Great Exhibition to meet any climate or circumstance with an appropriate invention. One firm offered patent sun-repellent overcoats. Sheridan & Co. advertised flavoured soda water – Ginger, Raspberry and Lemonade – at Rs 4.8 a dozen. Others were renowned less for their products than for their families. William Crump of the old-established firm of Crump & Co., one of five wine merchants in Cawnpore, was famous for the prettiness of his daughters.[75]

The shops from which the senior Cawnpore merchants operated were not shops facing on to the street, but spacious bungalows set back from the road in large gardens. Customers entered by a semi-circular carriageway, shaded by trees, and alighted under a porch. The Greenways' compound was near the old Customs House (closed in 1835); Brandon lived on the Mall, next to the Assembly Rooms and near the theatre; Crump & Co. had a large compound further along the Mall. At their gate was the public well, which was crowded by natives drawing water every day. Near the new canal was the estate of J. D. Hay, auctioneer, cabinet-maker, coachman and undertaker; his family firm had been established soon after the Cession of 1801. The first John Hay had conducted the sale that realised John Maxwell's property and had also auctioned George Ravenscroft's belongings.

The fortunes of the Cawnpore merchants had been uneven. Throughout

SODÀ WATER MANUFACTORY,

AND

DISPENSARY, CAWNPORE.

MESSRS. BATHGATE, PORTEOUS and Co. *Surgeons and Druggists*, have the pleasure to inform the Public, that their Mineral Water Manufactory, Cawnpore, is now in full operation under the immediate superintendance of one of their Partners. As the Apparatus employed is of the most powerful and improved construction, and the Materials used of the purest quality, Messrs. B. P. and Co. will furnish Soda, Magnesia, Cheltenham, and other Aerated Waters equal in quality, and at the same Prices as BATHGATE and Co.'s Calcutta

DOUBLE AERATED SODA WATER.

In Pints, at 5 per dozen.
¾ Pints, „ 3-8 „ „
½ Pints, „ 3 „ „

Exclusive of Bottles, which are received back at the Prices charged—Pints 2, three quarter Pints 1-8, half Pints 1.

Messrs. B. P. and Co. beg particularly to call the attention of Residents in the Upper Provinces to their DISPENSARY, where they may at all times obtain Fresh and GENUINE DRUGS and PATENT MEDICINES, as also such Medical Instruments and Apparatus as are in general use, supplies being regularly sent from their Establishment in Calcutta.

Orders from the Country will be attended to with punctuality, and despatched without loss of time either by Boat, Cooly, or by Banghy's, as directed.

Cawnpore, 1st February, 1830.

Messrs Bathgate advertisement from East India Gazette, *1 March 1830.*

the station's 'palmy days', they had flourished, but as the Company extended its territories north-westwards to the Punjab, Sind and Afghanistan, they entered on anxious times. When Cawnpore ceased to be a military frontier station, it lost the function that had first attracted traders to it. Like a sandbank left behind when the river changes its course, the town found itself suddenly isolated from the main current of trade. Financial ruin was averted by another political move. The annexation of Oude in 1856 promised the merchants the compensation of a large unexplored market on their doorstep. With the integration of Oude into Company jurisdiction, the irritating taxes and dues that had hampered trade previously were now lifted and the whole of Oude was open to business.

For years the European merchants had worked in close and friendly association with Indians. Together they set up agencies with the help of financial loans from the *shroffs* for the purchase of produce and the distribution of goods manufactured in England. The success of these enterprises was mutually beneficial and gradually, as the Indian merchants, traders and army contractors prospered, the humble mud huts of the bazaar were replaced by substantial masonry buildings round a central *chowk*.

At this time, too, the countrywide improvement in communications attracted trade to the city. The creation of the Grand Trunk Road, the great highway of commerce, brought Government bullock trains, country vehicles and passenger *dak gharries* and an enormous volume of trade. The Road was followed by a network of canals, one of which served the centre of Cawnpore.[76] Steam navigation on the Ganges was established between Calcutta and Allahabad, making transport by the slow river boats much safer, and in 1854 the electric telegraph connected Cawnpore with the outside world. The city had achieved a high level of commercial prosperity and the coming of the railway was to put the seal on its future importance.

The idea of bringing the railway to India took some time to develop. The railway had proved successful in England but people doubted if it was really suited to the sub-continent of India. The merchants discussed the advantages and disadvantages the railway would bring. The laying of the tracks was an impossible task, they argued: the terrain was too vast; floods would wash away bridges and embankments; white ants would destroy the wooden sleepers; the effective upkeep of the line would be difficult to oversee, and because caste forbade the mingling of people of different social grades, no Indian would travel by train, thereby making the experiment uneconomic. Then, what about the rolling stock? It would all have to be shipped and maintained with replacements from England. It seemed to many a foolish, impractical idea.

Yet, if it did succeed, the undoubted advantages of speedy transport of goods to the port of Calcutta and from there to Europe held out tempting possibilities. For the Cawnpore merchants much depended on where the railway line was built: it could bring disaster by diminishing the river trade if it did not link with Cawnpore. At last, in 1845, the Court of Directors made a half-hearted decision to face the costly experiment. Ten years later the first 120 miles of track between Calcutta and Benares were officially opened; by the beginning of 1856 the East Indian Railway engineers and their staff had arrived in Cawnpore to supervise the laying of the track between Allahabad and Cawnpore. A general air of excited and confident expectancy prevailed among the merchants.

Both they and the landed proprietors now had a new form of business activity. The pressure to send imported goods up-country and the need to send country produce from the interior to Calcutta and Europe created a two-way demand and flow of trade. Some firms in Cawnpore – Greenway Bros., Crump & Co., Bathgate, Campbell & Co. – were offshoots of Calcutta firms and quick to see the new possibilities. One man in particular found himself in a favourable position to co-ordinate this two-way movement: Dr David Begg, 'the planters' doctor'. Based on Calcutta, where he was in touch with men who could raise considerable capital, he moved in the circle of planters up-country, meeting men such as Hugh Maxwell.

David Begg had come out to India in the 1830s to serve as a doctor, touring the isolated estates in the Districts. He was a hospitable man, popular with his patients, and it became apparent to him that, with their goodwill, he could combine his medical duties with some trading: taking orders from the planters for indigo seed, and supplying them with wines from Calcutta. His sidelines became so profitable that he entered into partnership with the firm of Bathgate, Campbell & Co., Chemists and Druggists, who supplied the medicines he prescribed. The balance sheet for Bathgate, Campbell & Co. in 1856, reflecting Dr Begg's non-medical interests over a period of ten years, shows that they were also speculating in a range of country produce, including borax, saltpetre, hides and indigo seeds (see Appendix 7).

When Oude was annexed, Dr Begg shrewdly assessed the commercial future and in 1856 entered into two important partnerships: with Henry Christie[77] to form Begg, Christie in Cawnpore, and with Robert Dunlop and Henry Christie to form Begg, Dunlop in Calcutta. Bathgate, Campbell

OPPOSITE *Hugh Maxwell, c.1850.*

LEFT *Charlotte (Mrs Hugh) Maxwell, c.1850.* RIGHT *Peter Maxwell, c.1856. On the back of the photograph is written: 'Copied by Sammy [Sam Weller] from a photograph taken by John Jones in 1856. Peter Maxwell, killed in Massacre of the English Garrison at Cawnpore 27 June 1857.'*

& Co. continued trading under their old name but their assets were taken over by the new partnership of Begg, Christie & Co., Merchants and Commission Agents.

Hugh Maxwell, influenced by the events that determined Cawnpore's prosperity, moved back to the city in 1856 and settled at Barown Estate. This was close to Peter Maxwell at Muckanpore and enabled him to oversee the estate at Mendhi Ghat belonging to his brother David who was on long leave of absence in Scotland on account of family ill-health.[78] James, the youngest brother, had died in 1847 though not before he had married (in 1841) into the Churcher family, the well-known indigo planters of Fatehgarh.[79]

The official list of trades and professions for Cawnpore in 1856 does not include the names of the Maxwell brothers. This is probably because they were gentlemen of landed property rather than merchants. Their interests and fortunes depended on the products of the Indian soil and their main connection with Cawnpore at this time was with the firm of John Kirk, Trader in Country Produce, through whose agency they sold the produce of their estates.[80]

The prosperity of the Maxwell family was considerable. Peter Maxwell had been established for a long time at Muckanpore, where he lived Indian-style with his companion of many years, a Cashmere lady called Bebee Gulab Jaun, and a household that included '4 Brahmin women'.[81] He owned two houses in Fatehgarh: one, a pucka house with separate bungalow and offices, had belonged to the famous Colonel Gardner.[82] At Muckanpore the indigo factory was no longer in operation but the factory at Mendhi Ghat produced 1,000 pounds of indigo annually and there were factories at Auken and Bilhour and two new factories at Mypalpore and Shahpore in process of being set up. Each estate consisted of a two-storeyed dwelling house, assistants' bungalow, manufacturing house, drying house, go-downs, stabling and out-offices, besides reservoirs and many vats. There was a

Scene in the Opium Factory: *mica painting by Shiva Lal, Patna c.1850. Opium was* the *aspirin of Europe at that time. The dark sticky gum was harvested in March and at the factory pressed into cakes and packed in mangowood chests.*

LEFT *Maggie Jones, née French: London 1865. Taken at the time of the engagement.*
RIGHT *Gavin Sibbald Jones: London 1865.*

saltpetre factory at Gungagunj which made 200 maunds a day.[83] The official post of Sub-Deputy Opium Agent brought Peter Maxwell into contact with the EIC authorities and gave him considerable standing in the Cawnpore community; through his work as a planter he had a close link with the peasantry, while the revenue from thirty-one villages and rent from a number of mango *topes* all contributed to his life style as a rich man.[84]

This background of indigo planting was shared by the Maxwells and the Jones family. John Moore Jones, now the head of the family, lived in Fatehgarh, where he was both an indigo planter and a merchant trading in saltpetre, hides and indigo seed. He and Peter Maxwell were friends and business associates. By 1856 Gavin Jones had grown into a rather intense, tall, awkward young man of twenty. Prevented from enjoying a formal education in engineering he now joined John Moore Jones as a planter.[85] When Hugh Maxwell moved back to Cawnpore, another Jones brother, Edmond, and a nephew, Clinton Kemp, took over the factory at Palee. The network of marriage ties brought the two families together in powerful solidarity. It is not surprising that among the collection of Maxwell family photographs is one on the back of which is written, 'We were not merchants but Nabobs'.

The merchants were thriving, planning for future developments, though with some cautious reservations. Shrewd men of common sense, through their businesses they came into daily contact with the bazaar. Behind closed doors their clerks and contractors repeated rumours and gossip about unrest, agitation and discontent in the Bengal Army. They were aware of the troubled political background: for years many of them had said among themselves that Bentinck's liberal reforms, excellent though they were, had been introduced too quickly, that the Indian people distrusted every form of interference with their customs. However, in spite of the bazaar rumours, the merchants were confident of the power of the Company – and of their own individual capability – to deal with each difficult situation as it arose. They were none of them aware of the impending total collapse of the market, and did not foresee the extent of the disaster that was about to engulf them, destroying the fabric of social and commercial life built up over eighty years.

9
The Revolt: 1857

Causes of the Mutiny

The 'Indian Mutiny' was a calamity that filled Victorian England with horror and incredulity. It has become part of a myth, a mystery that has never been resolved and that continues to intrigue. For a conquered people to rise up against their oppressors would be true to human nature, but the Mutiny was not a national uprising. Of three Presidencies only the Presidency of Bengal was affected and within Bengal the uprising was contained within the comparatively small area of Delhi, Lucknow and Cawnpore. That an army of native sepoys might revolt against their European masters was always to be expected but a great many officers were so infatuated with a romantic vision of themselves in India and of their relationship with their sepoys that they were totally unprepared for the events that overtook them. In justification of that vision, however, it is a fact that many of the sepoys remained intensely loyal to their British officers. Both sides committed the most savage atrocities; many innocent lives were lost; tales of great endurance and courage and humanity were told. In clubs and barracks, lecture halls and drawing-rooms, the events that appeared to have led up to the outbreak of the Mutiny were analysed and discussed by people using Western logic, convinced of a clear distinction between right and wrong, and expecting that some definite answer must emerge. The Mutiny, however, continues to be an enigma.

Lord Roberts expressed the view that 'the revolt in my judgement would never have taken place had there not been a feeling of discontent and disquiet throughout that part of the country from which our Hindustani sepoys chiefly came, and had not certain influential people been thoroughly dissatisfied with our system of government'.[1] That is a very interesting statement. It does not speak of discontent in the Army, which was, after all, the instrument of mutiny, but *discontent and disquiet throughout that part of the country from which our Hindustani sepoys chiefly came* – Oude.

From every village in Oude fathers and sons, Brahmins and men of high caste, attracted by the *iqbal* of the Company, had left home for generations to serve with the Bengal Army. At first it has been an ideal relationship. The sepoys found a patriarchal system of battalions led by captains experienced in the language, customs and feelings of the troops, who gave their names to the battalions and with whom the men could closely identify. The ties that held a man to his regiment were an extension of the ties that existed between him and his family and between his family and the village. The 'star' of the Company stood high: to go to war was a jubilee and when the sepoy returned to his village it was with the greatly prized prestige and authority of the Company behind him.

This happy state of affairs came to an end with the severe defeat suffered by the Company in the First Afghan War of 1842. The disastrous retreat from Kabul was a shock to national pride, but its effect among the sepoys of the Bengal Army was to destroy for ever their illusion of the invincibility of the *Kampani Bahadur*. Disillusionment set in and with it came the discontents of the new peace.

This brought with it a change in the duties of the army. The sepoys far preferred going to war to doing guard duty at jails or attending parades and manoeuvres. The best of the officers, and those with connections in high places, found opportunities for advancement in civil duties and staff appointments. Many of the officers who remained with their regiments, however, became cynical and disheartened at the lack of advancement available to them. Young officers fresh from home suffered from a lack of discipline: they did not bother to learn the language, but swanked about, calling the sepoys 'niggers' and earning the disrespect of their troops.

Captain Rawlins[2] (who as a 'sub' had played billiards with the Nana Sahib) describes an incident which took place in Cawnpore in 1847: it illustrates the poor calibre of officer returning from civilian duties completely out of touch with the sepoys, and the resulting loss of respect and authority.

We had not been many days at Cawnpore when our new Commanding Officer arrived, a huge, bulky, flabby man, of vast proportions and of enormous latitude and longitude; he was the biggest man in India, and weighed 26st. and measured in his stockings 6ft 5 ins, with a face resembling an angry setting sun full of wrath and fury on a cold and boisterous wintry day! He had been Paymaster for many years and obtaining field rank was ineligible to preside longer over that department, and was relegated to the command of a regiment.

It was the invariable custom at the time, that men on duty at the main guard or elsewhere, were permitted to have their charpoys, or native cots, with them at their posts; the new Commanding Officer was much exercised at this unseemly and unsoldier-like display of luxury they had previously enjoyed during their 24 hours of incessant watching, and directed that in future the cots of the 44th should be removed and the men prohibited taking off their accoutrements for the whole time they were on duty, although the thermometer in the summer rose from 110 to 120 degrees of Farenheit! The other regiments were commanded by old and experienced men who had never left them for a day, and no such arbitrary order had been issued to them; our men became sullen and sulky, and a day or two afterwards their conduct culminated in supressed mutiny; one morning after parade the men refused to fall out and proceed to their lines as usual, when the Commanding Officer discovered he had to deal with 1,000 soldiers composed of very different mettle to the few abject Bengalee baboos in his pay office! He was astonished that *his* orders should be criticised or doubted, and for a moment scarcely realised the serious position in which he had placed himself; he lost his head, vacillated, issued orders and counter orders which were of no avail, rode off the parade ground and hurried to the quarters of Colonel Frederick to seek his advice and counsel; he soon returned, and found the regiment in the same excited state, but at once gave in and directed the cause of their disquiet to be removed and the cots returned! He foamed and swore and looked a sorry plight, but ever afterwards he was despised by the men and held in great contempt by all the officers; he had done the regiment more harm in a few days than it ever afterwards recovered.

In complete contrast were men of the stature of Sir Henry Lawrence, newly appointed to the important post of Commissioner of Oude. For all his

Sir Henry Lawrence, KCB, photographed at Lucknow, c. 1856. As the newly appointed Commissioner of Oude he prepared the Residency against attack but two days after the siege began he was mortally wounded by a shell which burst into his room. He asked to have 'He tried to do his duty' inscribed on his tombstone. As they carried him to his grave each soldier bent down and kissed him.

love of India and interest in its people, he was not blind to the dangers and difficulties of controlling a highly trained sepoy army, restless with discontent. He made it his business to know what the men were thinking. It was his opinion that the general dissatisfaction in the army was caused not so much by the boredom of peacetime service as recent acts of Government, which had been skilfully played upon by incendiaries.

The pension rules were a source of great grievance, but Sir Henry found the sepoys and non-commissioned officers were miserably paid. The *Soubahdars* and *Jemadars* had to be content with 67 and 24 rupees a month, ' . . . while in the Civil Department their fellows, ten or twenty years younger, enjoy five hundred, six hundred, and even a thousand rupees, and while they themselves if under a native ruler, would be Generals, if not Rajahs or Nawabs'.[3]

From 1848 to 1856 the Governor-General, Lord Dalhousie, ruthlessly pursued his 'dead level' policy. Native states were annexed with high-minded self-righteousness: the British Government would be guilty in the sight of God and man if it were any longer to aid in sustaining by its countenance an administration fraught with suffering to millions. In the native states of Satara and Nagpur the rights of adopted heirs were brushed aside as of no consequence. This applied to the ex-Peishwa at Bithoor also. Finally the annexation of Oude, the cradle of the Bengal Army, was announced. Of 200,000 sepoys in that army at the time of the outbreak of the Mutiny, 40,000 were from Oude alone. Every discontent in the state found its echo among the troops.

A newspaper report in *The Englishman* of 21 August 1857, headed 'Why the Bengal Army mutinied', expressed the view

that the annexation of Oude is the real cause of the disaffection: every officer of any experience and certainly every Adjutant, will allow with me, that the prejudice in favour of Recruiting in Oude has filled the ranks of our army with such a majority of men of one class, that the ties of kindred, ranging from father to cousin-ship and even to *bustee-wallah* [fellow villager], has prevented proper supervision. . . .

Long years of Company administration of revenue policies had ruined the families with hereditary rights, deprived the Cawnpore District of middle-class stability and created in Oude natural leaders of the disaffected soldiers.

Our bitterest foes and the sepoys' natural leaders were the smaller gentry, whom our ruthless 'dead level' system was everywhere ruining . . . it was our own fault that in Oude, at any rate, a mutiny grew up into a national rising. Even the Nana, monster as he was, notoriously had his grievance – and a very fair one in the estimation of a Hindoo.

A sad thing is that Kampani's Raj has done its best to kill out any seeds of loyalty

there might have been in the native gentlemen. Under it the trader and the ryot had protection; but the man of family was robbed of the consideration which was dearer to him than all else, 'he was dishonoured before the elders of his people'; and, with all higher civil and military offices closed against him, he was left literally without a purpose in life . . . tiger shooting and billiards with noisy 'subs' who took his fine presents and whom he despised, were all very well, but they could not fill up the life of a man who just drew breath at the good pleasure of the collector where his fathers had held more than feudal sway.[4]

The old Moghul Emperor in Delhi had been little more than a figurehead, but the Indian people acknowledged him as their king and his existence reminded them of their former glory. Now Lord Dalhousie informed the Heir Apparent that, on the death of his father, the title King of Delhi was to cease. For the first time since the Company had imposed its authority in India, the many and great differences between Hindu and Muslim people were dwarfed by their common hatred for this act of disrespect towards their traditional ruling family.

It was not only the rulers and gentry who became the leaders of growing discontent; the very influential Brahmins, the religious leaders of the people, had, since the time of Bentinck's liberal reforms, become increasingly unsettled by changes that threatened to undermine their authority.

Lord Roberts expressed his opinion of the fears of the Brahmins:

The prohibition of *sati* [suttee]; the putting a stop to female infanticide; the execution of Brahmins for capital offences; the efforts of missionaries and the protection of their converts; the removal of all sorts of legal obstacles to the re-marriage of widows; the spread of western and secular education generally; and more particularly, the attempt to introduce female education, were causes of alarm and disgust to the Brahmins, and to those Hindus of high caste whose social privileges were connected with the Brahminical religion. Even the obvious advantages to the people which the coming of the railways and the creation of canals, provided, were objects of horror to the Brahmins. On the railways people of every caste, high and low, were bound to travel together. And in order to build the canals the sacred waters of the Ganges had been diverted.[5]

Stories were whispered that the British were trying to convert all the sepoys to Christianity to break their caste. While the majority of British officers found it impossible to take such rumours seriously, a hard core of missionaries and Company men were fired with an evangelical spirit that longed to rescue the 'heathen' and 'idolater' from damnation. It was a dangerous ambition. To interfere with a man's religion was to interfere with

OPPOSITE *A group of sepoys: illustration from* Narrative of the Indian Revolt, *George Vicker, London 1858, published weekly, one penny.*

his caste. The structure of society in India was arranged by caste and a man's soul advanced up the social ladder with each reincarnation until he reached the highest level – that of a Brahmin. A Brahmin on his death could expect release from suffering, and oblivion. The threat of conversion to Christianity was therefore felt as a threat to a man's social order: to the foundation upon which family life and all he held most dear were built. Above all, it was a threat to a man's hope of personal salvation.

The discontent among the sepoys, the lax discipline among many of the army officers, the bitter dissatisfaction of the dispossessed ruling classes, the fears of the Brahmins, the rumours of enforced baptism were all part of the explosive material gathering to blow up the Company Raj. The spark that caused the explosion and ignited men of all races and religions with fervour for their common cause against the British was the matter of the greased cartridges.

A new rifle, the Enfield, had been introduced to the various musketry depots in India. The paper casing of the cartridges was heavily greased and the end had to be bitten off to enable the charge to ignite when the gun was loaded. Rumours gained ground that this grease was made from the fat of cows and pigs: the cow was sacred to the Hindu and the pig was abhorrent to the Muslim. Handling such cartridges would indeed break the caste of the sepoy. The officers, knowing how repugnant such fat would be to the faith of their men, categorically denied the rumour, but, incredibly, the authorities had indeed ordered the cartridges to be greased with animal fat.

Instructions were now given forbidding the use of animal fats in the manufacture of the cartridges but it was too late. The sepoys were thoroughly fearful and suspicious and ready to defy their officers and break out into open mutiny rather than handle the suspect cartridge and risk loss of caste.

The first regiment that refused to handle the cartridges was the 19th Native Infantry at Berhampore in Bengal. They were disbanded. A month later a Brahmin sepoy of the 34th Native Infantry called Mungal Pandy ran amok at Barrackpore, inciting his comrades to mutiny, and attacking the Adjutant and the Sergeant Major who attempted to disarm him. The situation was brought under control by Brigadier-General Hearsey. As he rode on to the parade ground someone called to him: 'Have a care; his musket is loaded.' 'Damn his musket,' was Hearsey's famous reply, and he ordered the nearest native officer, with a pistol to his head, to arrest Mungal Pandy. Seven days later, Mungal Pandy was hanged and the regiment disbanded. At an affecting parade at which the men were addressed for the last time by General Hearsey before he dismissed them, many were in tears and 'the General was seen to pass his coat sleeve several times across his eyes'.[6]

Every dismissed sepoy returning to Oude carried news of the tainted cartridges and of the two attempted mutinies. The air was full of rumours. There was even talk of a prophecy that the end of the Company Raj was at hand. A report in the *Mofussilite* stated:

It is given out says the *Friend of India* that the mutinous sepoys are fulfilling a prophesy which assigns this year as the limit to British dominion in India. The story referred to is given out by the Brahmins, and is to the effect, that the god gave possession of India to the British for a term of one hundred years certain. That on the centenary of the battle of Plassey next month the lease will determine.

Even at this stage there were people who believed the mutinous discontent could have been contained if only there had been more European troops available:

A HINT. FROM J.E.M. 10 MAY 1857 TO THE EDITOR 'MOFUSSILITE'
The disaffection of the Cartridge question is rapidly spreading, notwithstanding the recent executions at Barrackpore. What is the cause of this? The paucity of European Troops. We have not a European Force sufficient to overawe and quell the mutinous spirit which is daily gaining ground. Look at the state of the country, from Chinsurah to Lucknow, only one European Regiment. . . .

When the Mutiny broke out, the entire effective British force in India numbered only 36,000, against 257,000 native soldiers who, in Sir John Lawrence's words, 'had charge of our fortresses, arsenals, magazines, and treasuries, without adequate European control, and could not fail to gather extravagant ideas of their own importance'. The force and fury of the Mutiny was contained between the three focal points of Delhi, Lucknow and Cawnpore: Delhi, the capital of the Moghul Empire, Lucknow, the capital of Oude, the last splendid kingdom to owe allegiance to the Emperor, and Cawnpore, a cantonment town created by a game of war. Oude, however, was the heart of the matter. With roots in the earliest Hindu civilisation and ties that bound it closely to the Muslim Moghul Empire, Oude combined powerful elements within it. From the time when the Company moved troops up the Ganges basin, Oude had withstood its authority. Something of the flavour of life in Oude accompanied the majority of Brahmin sepoys serving in the Bengal Army. In many respects the Mutiny can be regarded as a military matter, but in Oude the violence of the uprising had the fervour of an attempt to overthrow the Company Raj.

News of the Mutiny Reaches Cawnpore

The citizens of Cawnpore were awoken at daybreak on New Year's Day 1857 by a salute of twenty-one guns. Later that day a Grand Cricket Match was held between HM 53rd Light Infantry and the Cawnpore Station Club, a popular event to which everybody who was anybody drove in their carriages.[7] The long-established rivalry between military and civilian society in Cawnpore was for once expressed in friendly competition.

The commandant of the Division was General Sir Hugh Wheeler.[8] He had ridden out that morning from the far eastern side of Cantonments, accompanied by his son and two daughters and several deerhounds. The General looked his best on horseback. He had the reputation of being a fine soldier, 'short, of a spare habit, very grey, with a quick and intelligent eye.'[9] These looks belied his fifty-two years' service: he had first joined the Company in 1805 when he came to Cawnpore with Lord Lake's army. He spoke Hindustani like a native and regarded his sepoys with great affection, calling them his children.

Riding through the sepoy lines, Wheeler was aware of the dangerous imbalance between European and native troops. There were 3,000 sepoys stationed at Cawnpore but only 300 English fighting men. Too few, he reckoned. Behind the sepoy lines were the huts and homes of the camp followers and bazaar wallahs: 60,000 natives at least. It was a part of Cawnpore the General never entered.

The patron of the civilian cricket team was Mr Hillersdon, the newly appointed Collector. He and his charming young wife had driven from the far western end of the station; their bungalow was at Nawabganj,[10] within sight of the high-walled Magazine. His brother, commanding the 53rd Native Infantry, expected shortly in Cawnpore, was a useful military link for the civilian patron; such common ground helped to foster a good relationship between the two teams. The cricket match was voted a huge success. Players and spectators drove home, confident and untroubled.

The first ripple to disturb this tranquil life came in the form of the mysterious circulation of chaupattis and lotus leaves. Lieutenant Mowbray Thomson of the 53rd Native Infantry (who had arrived in Cawnpore in February 1857 after a three-month march with his regiment) recalled that it was early in March that a *chowkidar* had run up to one of his comrades and given him two chaupattis: 'These are unleavened cakes, made of flour, water and salt; the mode of telegraphing by their means was for the cakes to be eaten in the presence of the giver, and fresh ones made by the newly initiated

A Gallant Brigadier General: *watercolour of General Wheeler by Lieutenant Charles D'Oyly, reproduced in* Sketches of Life in the Indian Army 1843-62.

one, who in turn distributed them to new candidates for participation in the mystery.'[11] The chaupattis were handed to civilians while lotus leaves, the emblem of war, were passed among the soldiery.

For a few days the mysterious affair of the chaupattis was the talk of every European household; it was impossible to guess what lay behind it. Then it was dismissed as just another curious native superstition. No one dreamt that the message of the chaupattis was part of a concerted plan to overthrow the British rule in India.

When news of the attempted mutinies at Berhampore and Barrackpore reached Cawnpore, General Wheeler wrote at once to his close friend General Hearsey to congratulate him on the manner in which he had dealt with Mungal Pandy. The two Generals had in common the military principle of discipline, that mutineers with arms in their hands should never be treated with or listened to. General Wheeler confided his anxiety about the general air of uneasiness in Cawnpore which had seemed to persist ever since the passing of the chaupattis:

Cawnpore. March 22nd 1857 . . . Everything is quiet here, but from what I hear there is an unquiet feeling among the men, nay, amongst the people at large. The general tenour of all the reports is that every exertion is being made, *by the orders of*

Government, to deprive the natives of their castes by making them use materials and food tainted with forbidden articles. But the way the country is left without artillery! We have guns and a European company, but no carriage for them. There should be at least a troop or battery at Cawnpore; and the Post Guns which were so injudiciously taken away by Lord Bentinck for a miserable and paltry economy, should be forthwith restored wherever there is a wing of a corps. The two sixes are invaluable in the case of an emeute or disturbance; and in India you can never be certain when either will occur.[12]

This air of uneasiness made itself felt in many different ways. Towards the end of March, on his retirement from India, Mr Morland, the same Collector who had been fêted by the Cawnpore merchants, travelled to Bithoor to bid farewell to the Nana Sahib. He found him in a great state of restlessness and anxiety. A palanquin and bearers stood ready at the palace and it transpired that the Nana was about to set out that evening, unattended, to travel to Lucknow. It struck Mr Morland as very strange that the Nana, who never moved without an impressive retinue of followers, should be travelling incognito. Lucknow in the aftermath of the annexation was seething with malcontents; there had been sinister rumours of secret meetings on dark nights. Surely his old friend the Nana Sahib was not involved with such matters? Mr Morland kept his thoughts to himself but the incident left him deeply troubled.

Outwardly people continued to live their normal lives. Mrs Louisa Chalwin, recently arrived from Meerut with her husband, who was veterinary surgeon of the 2nd Bengal Light Cavalry,[13] and her friend and companion, Miss Isabella White, counted herself immensely fortunate to be living in Cawnpore. She wrote enthusiastically to her sister in England: 'I have wonderfully improved in housekeeping since I came to Cawnpore – things are so much more easily procurable here.' She found the society in Cawnpore very pleasant and sociable. In spite of the evening temperature in the eighties, they were trying to get up monthly reunion balls: 'We are going to a ball next Wednesday, given by a *bachelor* in the Engineers, who is smitten with the eldest Miss Lindsay[14] . . . I think I shall wear my blue tarlatan. . . .'

In the evenings when the Chalwins were not entertaining, Louisa busied herself with wool work, embroidering a music stool cover. Her mornings were taken up with visiting and calling. One day she called in at one of the milliners – Cawnpore boasted three English milliners – to have a baby's bonnet copied; it was to be a christening present. Behind such simple activities as this, Louisa Chalwin kept her fears hidden, but who could help but be uneasy?

ABOVE *Mrs George Lindsay and daughters,
'perished at Cawnpore 1857': collodion
negative on glass c.1856. Left to right:
Caroline, Fanny and Alice. A note written
by one of the Misses Lindsay was found in
the Bebee Ghur. 'Entered the barracks May
21st. Cavalry left June 5th. First shot fired
June 6th. Aunt Lilly died June 17th. Uncle
Willy died June 18th. Left barracks June
27th. George died June 27th. Alice died July
9th. Mamma died July 12th.'*

LEFT *Miss White on a visit to the
Ommanney family, Lucknow: salt print by
Ahmed Ali Khan, c.1855. Probably Miss
Isabella White, friend and companion of Mrs
Louisa Chalwin. Miss White died at the
Bebee Ghur. They are both commemorated
on tablets in the church of St Mary
Magdalene, Taunton.*

[*The Mofussilite, March 1857*] Every post brings in more and more intelligence of a very unsatisfactory spirit among the Native Regular Infantry soldiery. And where are their displays and disaffection to end?

The 'unquiet feeling' gradually hardened into a general expectation that paralysed all activity. Reports came in from the Districts that crime had ceased altogether. Progress on the railway line was almost impossible; the engineers could not persuade the men to come to work. In Cawnpore the Collector noticed that although the courts and offices were open, no one came forward to transact any business. 'Only the opium eaters were constant; they came at the stated hour for their supply of the drug. They dwelt in dream land and were not interested in the troubles of real life.'[15] Before an earthquake there is sometimes an unnatural stillness; not a leaf moves on a tree, not a bird sings, not a creature stirs – all is in suspended animation awaiting the moment of shock. In Cawnpore everyone was waiting . . . waiting . . . but they had no idea for what.

Early in May news came from Lucknow that trouble had flared up over the vexed question of the greased cartridge. The 7th Oude Infantry had set fire to their *subadar*'s house and burnt down the whole lines. Sir Henry Lawrence dealt swiftly and firmly with the trouble-makers. He called all the Native regiments together and addressed them in Hindi using every persuasion at his command to hold their morale. For the moment he was successful.

On Sunday, 10 May, a sound of distant guns was heard in the evening. Uneasily the English community in Cawnpore waited to learn the official news; it took four days to reach them. But in the bazaar it was common knowledge that at Meerut eighty-five troopers of the 3rd Light Cavalry had been tried and imprisoned with fetters for refusing to handle the suspected cartridges on parade. Their comrades had risen in violent protest, setting light to Cantonment bungalows, killing every European in sight. Having freed the prisoners and murdered their officers, about 2,000 men marched the thirty miles to Delhi, where they pledged themselves to the service of the aged Moghul Emperor. The entire native garrison of Delhi had risen in sympathy and every Englishman they could hunt down had been butchered.

Even now, in spite of the evidence of their senses, men were still mesmerised into a strange inaction. They would not, or dare not, believe anything of the kind could ever happen in Cawnpore. Mr Shepherd[16] recalled: 'Everybody in the station seemed to think that something dreadful was to occur, but were unable to foresee what it was.' The native troops at

DESTRUCTION OF A BUNGALOW AT MEERUT.

Destruction of a Bungalow at Meerut: *illustration from* Narrative of the Indian Revolt. *On Sunday 10 May 1857 violence broke out; by 8 p.m. Meerut was a city of terror.*

that time appeared to be placid and quiet as usual, but yet something indefinite and alarming overshadowed the minds of all.

Official news came in the form of a Proclamation from Government:

[*The Mofussilite, 15 May 1857*] Whereas it has been ascertained that in the Districts of Meerut and in, and Immediately round Delhi, some short sighted Rebels have dared to raise resistance to the British Government, it is hereby declared that every Talookdar, Zemindar, or other owner of land, who may join in such resistance, will forfeit all rights of property, which will be confiscated and transferred in perpetuity to the faithful Talookdars and Zemindars of the same quarters, who may shew by their acts of obedience to the Government, and exertions for the maintenance of tranquility that they deserve reward and favour from the State.

The powerful British Government will in a marked manner recompense its friends, and punish its enemies.

The Indian Mutiny of 1857 had begun.

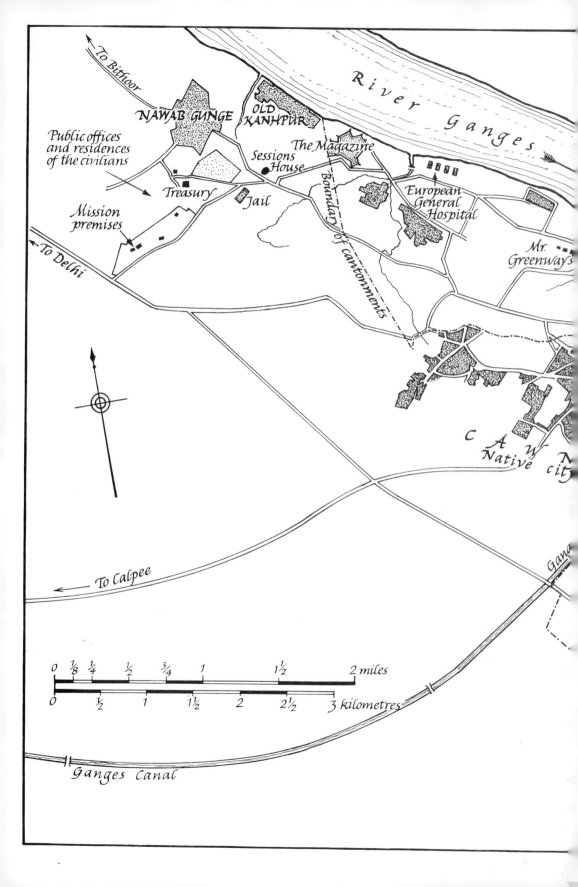

River Ganges

To Bithoor

NAWAB GUNGE

OLD KANHPUR

Public offices
and residences
of the civilians

The Magazine

Sessions
House

Treasury

Jail

Mission
premises

European
General
Hospital

Boundary of cantonments

To Delhi

Mr.
Greenway's

C A N

Native city

To Calpee

Gang

0 ⅛ ¼ ½ ¾ 1   1½   2 miles

0   ½   1   1½   2   2½   3 kilometres

Ganges Canal

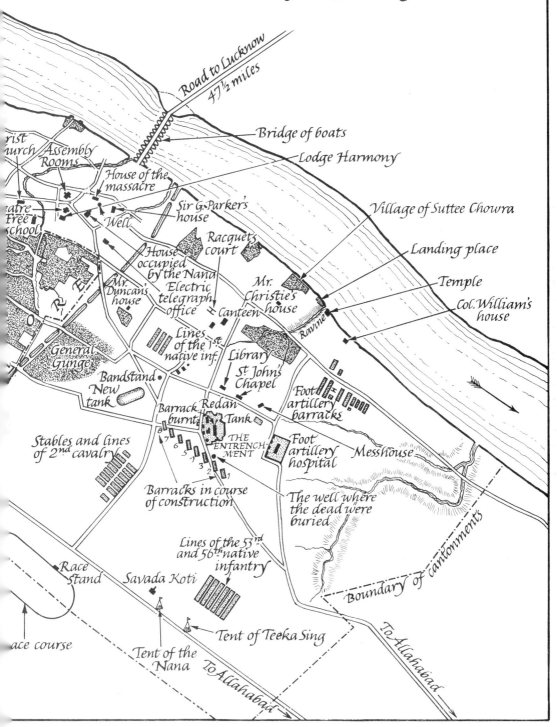

THE STATION OF CAWNPORE
At the time of the Mutiny

Road to Lucknow
47½ miles

Bridge of boats

Lodge Harmony

rist
urch
Assembly
Rooms

House of the
massacre

Sir G. Parker's
house

Well

Village of Suttee Chowra

atre
Free
school

Racquets
court

Landing place

House
occupied
by the Nana

Mr.
Duncan's
house

Electric
telegraph
office

Mr.
Christie's
house

Temple

Col. William's
house

Canteen

Ravine

Lines
of the 1st
native inf.

Library

St John's
Chapel

General
Gunge

Bandstand
New
tank

Barrack
burnt

Redan

Tank

Foot
artillery
barracks

Stables and lines
of 2nd cavalry

7 6
5 4
3 2 1

THE
ENTRENCH-
MENT

Foot
artillery
hospital

Messhouse

Barracks in course
of construction

The well where
the dead were
buried

Boundary of cantonments

Race
Stand

Lines of the 53rd
and 56th native
infantry

Savada Koti

ace course

Tent of Teeka Sing

Tent of the
Nana

To Allahabad

To Allahabad

General Wheeler's Preparation against Attack

There are two questions about the mutiny in Cawnpore that have never been satisfactorily answered: how did General Wheeler make such a fatal error of judgement in not using the Magazine as his fortress; and was the Nana Sahib the villain history has made him out to be? To some extent the two questions are bound up together since Wheeler's wife was related to the Nana Sahib.[17] It seems Wheeler did not start by assessing the danger in realistic terms. Was his judgement clouded by his intimacy with the Nana Sahib? Was the seven-mile length of Cantonments too difficult to defend? Or was there some fatal flaw in his mental processes? Once the first mistaken decision had been taken, no amount of energy or courage could save the city of Cawnpore.

In the hour of crisis the peculiar feature about Cawnpore, noted by every literary traveller – the great 'extent' of the town – was to prove a death trap. In the centre of Cawnpore, dividing it in half, was the newly constructed Ganges Canal. The authorities had recently decided to remove the entire military establishment to a site east of the Canal; new ranges of barracks were in process of being built and the sepoys were housed on open ground.

West of the Canal was the city, a warren of squalid narrow streets teeming with thousands of people. The city was fenced in to the north by the river and the gracious scattered compounds belonging to the officers and European merchants. At the extreme west, at Nawabganj, were grouped the bungalows of the senior Company servants and the public buildings – the Treasury, the Law Courts, the Jail – and close by was the huge enclosure of the Magazine, with massive turreted walls.

In Lucknow Sir Henry Lawrence prepared the Residency for a siege, and the Residency endured the siege and survived. In Cawnpore the obvious place to prepare against an attack was the Magazine. It is possible that if Cawnpore had been a closely integrated town there would never have been any question but to choose the Magazine. In the event, General Wheeler took no action whatever for ten days. Then, at the last moment, he chose to shelter the whole English population within a meagre entrenchment of earth walls thrown up hastily around two barracks. These were situated far from all means of supply, in a great sandy plain, exposed on all sides to attack, at the far eastern end of Cantonments. It was an extraordinary decision to make.

General Wheeler, it would seem, made his priority the need to maintain close contact with his troops and thereby hold their loyalty and morale. He issued instructions for all officers to sleep in the lines with their regiments. He personally went the rounds at midnight, like any subaltern, to turn out the guard. It is probable that, from the beginning, he ruled out the Magazine as a suitable rallying point because of its great distance – all of five miles – from the lines of the military. His spies were posted in the bazaars and Commissariat to bring him news of any rumours. Above all, he relied on the close family connection between his wife and the Nana Sahib for the support and friendship of an influential Indian.

The importance of maintaining a front of confident unconcern at a time of grave danger is understandable, but one of the strange aspects of the Mutiny is the number of officers who placed complete faith in the loyalty of their soldiers, beyond the bounds of all reason and credulity. In the Punjab Sir Robert Montgomery saved the situation by disarming the regiments at a dramatic early morning parade. In Lucknow Sir Henry Lawrence, while not being in a position to prevent an outbreak, had prepared his defensive position in the Residency so well that the eventual outcome was successful. While praying for the best these men prepared for the worst. Wheeler, on the other hand, made no plans for defence. It was as if he believed the best defence to be absolute trust in the loyalty of his troops.

So completely had the Nana Sahib won the confidence of the English in Cawnpore that when Mr Hillersdon, the Collector, made plans to protect the huge sums of revenue in the Treasury, his first thought was to send to the Nana Sahib for help. The Nana Sahib came 'instantly' and agreed to provide a force of 400 infantry and two guns as protection. The obvious place for the safe keeping of the treasure was the Magazine, close at hand, or, failing that, in the care of General Wheeler's troops; but it was considered unsafe to move the treasure so far. So now the Nana Sahib, in response to the Collector's invitation, took up his residence in Cawnpore.

The astonishing trust of the English in the Nana Sahib amazed an Indian lawyer called Nanak Chand. For years Nanak Chand had opposed the Nana's claims in the law courts against other members of the family for possession of Bajee Rao's personal property. He had no doubt of the true nature of the adopted heir of the ex-Peishwa:

. . . was it wise to make a *friend* of such a deadly enemy, who harboured revenge against the British for years, who was watching eagerly for an opportunity to revenge the wrongs suffered by his father, and who kept company with bad characters, and regarding whose violence numerous complaints were on record in our courts? Was it wise to authorise this man to raise armed levies at his own discretion for the protection of the people and the suppression of the mutiny? To ask a person who was every way your prisoner to protect you, was only to prove that the power of the British Government had been weakened.[18]

Daily the rumours intensified: word came through that the mutiny was spreading, Etawah and Alighur were plundered and the rebels marching towards Cawnpore. The roads were infested with robbers and unsafe for all travellers. The only communication with the outer world was by river. A boatload of bad, musty *attah* (whole-meal flour) arrived from up-country and was sold off cheaply. A wild report went round the sepoy lines that its bad flavour was due to the bones of cows and pigs ground up with the flour and that this was another trick to break their caste. In the bazaar a sergeant's wife of the 53rd, doing her shopping, was accosted by a sepoy out of uniform, saying: 'You will none of you come here much oftener; you will not be alive in another week.' Greatly alarmed, she reported this incident at headquarters, 'but it was thought advisable to discredit the tale'.[19]

Every man now took thought for the safety of his family and property. The subordinates looked to their superiors for decision and action, but with General Wheeler at the far eastern end of Cawnpore and Mr Hillersdon at the far western end, there was no united responsibility and no clear lead to follow. The first consideration should have been to send the women and children down river to Calcutta, thus freeing the men to meet whatever emergency might arise. But Lady Wheeler refused to leave her husband and the other wives decided to follow her example. The non-combatants outnumbered the fighting men two to one.

The merchants, finding no plan for defence or escape given them by the authorities, were the only body of men to maintain something of their initiative. At first they engaged boats and filled them with provisions and valuable property, ready to leave at a moment's notice. They hired as many as 25 to 30 extra men to guard their houses. Daily they met together to discuss how best to act. Many plans were proposed but at last it was decided that three or four merchants should call upon General Wheeler to ask where they might assemble to defend themselves in an emergency. The next day the deputation, headed by J. D. Hay, waited on the General. They came away far from reassured. The General was of the opinion that 'there was no immediate cause of apprehension'. He had made arrangements for the wives and families and officers of the military to take shelter in two long barracks should the need arise and he suggested that as there was no really suitable alternative for the non-official residents, they should make those same two barracks their rendezvous as well. He had no objection to the merchants arming themselves if they so wished. This suggestion did not satisfy the merchants; their homes were so scattered that in the event of an outbreak, they knew how difficult it would be to drive with their families to the far end of Cawnpore.

Mr Shepherd, a clerk in the Commissariat office, was one of the merchants who did not trust General Wheeler's plan:

However there was no help for it, and we set about arming ourselves. Mr J. D. Hay, having a good many pistols and double barrelled guns in his shop on commission sale, made them available, together with those belonging to himself and his Assistant Mr Little; many of us had our own guns and swords and it was proposed that in case of any danger, should we not find time to make to the barracks, we were to assemble in his shop, and all proceed in a body to the other place.[20]

On the morning of 21 May the whole station was seized by panic. No one knew where the rumour originated, but it was believed that an attack was imminent and everyone took to their carriages, whipping up the horses to reach the two barracks designated by General Wheeler without delay. Carriages laden with boxes and filled with terrified faces clattered through the streets. Mr Shepherd's family reached the barracks somewhat later than the main crowd and could not find anywhere to sit. Eventually space was made for them on a verandah, just big enough to sit down. 'It was a very hot day, and our infants who only half an hour ago had been enjoying the cool of *khus tatties* and punkahs, were exposed to the hot winds and almost smothered in the laps of their mothers.'[21]

Food and bedding were brought to them from their homes; they ate sitting in their carriages and at night slept on the verandah. Finding that there was no substance in the rumour and seeing how uncomfortable and totally exposed the barracks were, many families returned to their own homes. It was not until 25 May that General Wheeler gave orders for low earthworks to be thrown up round the two barracks to protect the position. These were described by Shepherd:

These barracks were single storied buildings, one of them was thatched, and both had a flat-roofed arcade with apartments and surrounded by very strong sloping verandahs made of beams and solid masonry. The walls were of brick two feet thick. Several outhouses, and only one pucca well in the centre, were attached to the buildings. Around these barracks a trench was being dug. It was commenced upon on or about the 25th May, the loose earth thus thrown up had not been beaten down nor was water sprinkled over it to make it solid. Thus the parapet which was about four feet high, was not even bullet proof at the crest, over which in many places sand bags were placed, to admit of the sentries keeping watch both day and night. Embrasures were likewise left for the guns which were in a manner almost unprotected. . . . A covering of tiles was hastily thrown over the thatched barrack to prevent its easily catching fire.[22]

Guns were positioned round the entrenchment to guard it: one twenty-four-pounder howitzer and two nine-pounders were placed to the north-east, pointing towards the Lines; three nine-pounders faced south-east; the main guard was held by a rifled piece which fired a three-pound ball, and towards the north, facing the city across the plain, the circle was completed by three more nine-pounders. Instructions were given for the barracks to be stocked with food and provisions, sufficient for twenty-five days. Dal, ghee, salt, rice, tea, sugar, rum, malt liquor and hermetically sealed provisions were ordered, but in the panic and lack of supervision that prevailed, the bulk of the stores proved to be peas and flour and in such small quantities as to be only sufficient to feed the military. The regimental messes on their own initiative sent in beers and wines and luxuries such as stores of fish, game and soup. In the event these lasted only one week.

The merchants, seeing the miserably inadequate defensive position at the barracks, pleaded once again with General Wheeler to allow the Magazine to become the fortified meeting point of all Cawnpore. They reminded the General that the Magazine was an immense walled enclosure, containing many buildings, sufficient to house the whole population with ease, whilst the two barracks were each intended to hold only 100 people. The River Ganges flowed beneath the walls of the Magazine, making communication with Allahabad and guarding the bridge of boats into Lucknow both possible; the vital water supply was certain. The Magazine was well stocked with artillery, powder and shot and if guns were positioned on the high walls they would dominate and safeguard the Treasury and jail. Near at hand were the villages of Nawabganj and Old Kanhpur which would provide fresh provisions. In every way the Magazine was the ideal place to withstand a siege should trouble break out.

The old General, while not disclosing his reasons, was adamant in refusing to consider moving into the Magazine. The one concession he made was to give an undertaking that if there was a mutiny in Cawnpore, the Magazine would be blown up[23] to prevent the ammunition falling into the hands of rebels.

Information received from spies in the bazaars was that, even if the native troops broke out, they had no intention of harming the English or the Indian Christian community. Their plan was to seize the money in the Treasury, march to Delhi to make a gift of it to the Moghul Emperor and then return to take possession of Cawnpore in his name.

To General Wheeler the one matter of overriding importance was to remain calm and confident. If the troops did march to Delhi, reinforcements from Calcutta would surely reach Cawnpore before they could possibly return. He argued so persuasively that the merchants who had sensibly prepared their boats to make good their escape reluctantly agreed to remain in Cawnpore. Perhaps the General hinted that once they had left Cawnpore, he could not protect their property from being looted.

Some said that Lady Wheeler had persuaded her husband to decide on the barrack site close to his own residence, in order to spare him at his age from exposure to the gruelling heat of the sun which long rides to the Magazine would have involved. The merchants reacted very bitterly, believing that the spot for the entrenchment had been selected because the guns of the European artillery would protect the officers' bungalows.

If the idea behind fortifying the barracks instead of moving into the Magazine was that it would suggest confidence, it did not succeed. Such scenes of panic surrounded the work going on at the hasty entrenchment that one of Sir Henry Lawrence's aides, arriving from Lucknow on a quick dawn inspection, reported that he had never witnessed

. . . so frightful a scene of confusion, fright and bad arrangement. Four guns were in position, loaded, with European artillerymen in night caps and wide-awakes and side arms on, hanging onto the guns in groups – looking like melodramatic buccaneers. People . . . of every colour, sect and profession were crowding into the barracks . . . cargoes of writers, tradesmen . . . a miscellaneous mob of every complexion from white to tawny – all in terror of the imaginary foe; ladies sitting down at the rough mess tables in the barracks, women suckling infants, ayahs and children in all directions. . . .[24]

While the preparations at the barracks were the sole responsibility of General Wheeler, the security of the city was the province of the Magistrate, Mr Hillersdon. With the Treasury guarded by the Nana Sahib's troops, Mr Hillersdon concentrated on strengthening the police guard in the city, enlisting the aid of influential native merchants and moneylenders to supply 250 extra men. Night after night he was in the bazaars, seeing that the police did their duty. Nanak Chand decided to make one last desperate attempt to warn him against the Nana Sahib:

Today (26 May) I wrote a full account of the Nana's doings on plain paper, and filed it as a petition, so as to warn the Magistrate and induce him to speak to the General so as to avoid falling into error; but the Magistrate gave no heed to my petition, and got so vexed with me that I cannot describe his anger. He said to me, 'You have all along been speaking ill of the Nana, and filing suits against him in the courts. I cannot pay attention to any representation from a person so hostile to the Nana.' I replied that those affairs had no connection with the present question, that the Nana had long harboured enmity to the Government, and a great number of rascals belonged to his party; that he (the magistrate) would remember my caution, and that I had obtained certain intelligence, as the men of the Nana's household communicated it to Chimna Apa, my Client. The Magistrate would listen to nothing. In despair, I did nothing further than keep a copy of the petition in my book. It is a hopeless case. Let us see what will be the end of all this neglect.[25]

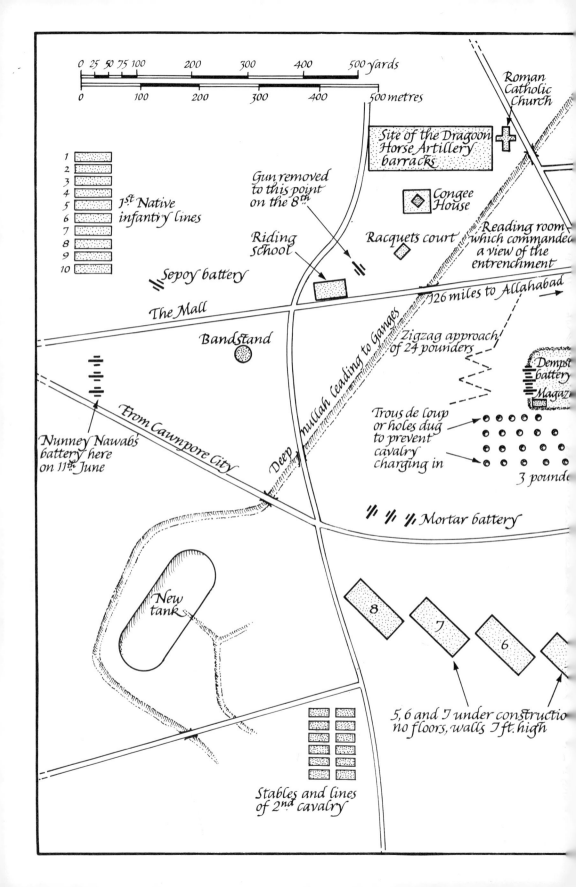

0 25 50 75 100   200   300   400   500 yards

0   100   200   300   400   500 metres

Roman Catholic Church

Site of the Dragoon Horse Artillery barracks

1
2
3
4
5   1st Native
6   infantry lines
7
8
9
10

Congee House

Gun removed to this point on the 8th

Racquets court

Reading room which commanded a view of the entrenchment

Riding school

Sepoy battery

The Mall

126 miles to Allahabad

Bandstand

Zigzag approach of 24 pounders

Dempst battery

Magaz

Trous de loup or holes dug to prevent cavalry charging in

From Cawnpore City

Nunney Nawab's battery here on 11th June

3 pounde

Deep nullah leading to Ganges

Mortar battery

New tank

8

7

6

5, 6 and 7 under constructio no floors, walls 7 ft. high

Stables and lines of 2nd cavalry

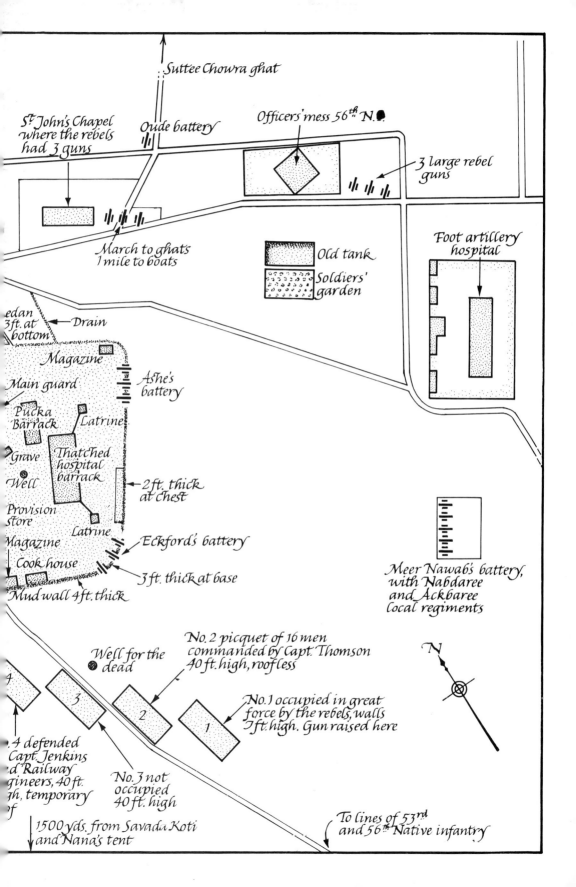

Suttee Chowra ghat

St. John's Chapel where the rebels had 3 guns

Oude battery

Officers' mess 56ᵗʰ N.

3 large rebel guns

March to ghats 1 mile to boats

Old tank

Soldiers' garden

Foot artillery hospital

edan 3 ft. at bottom

Drain

Magazine

Ashe's battery

Main guard

Pucka Barrack

Latrine

Grave

Thatched hospital barrack

Well

2 ft. thick at Chest

Provision store

Latrine

Magazine

Eckford's battery

Cook house

3 ft. thick at base

Mud wall 4 ft. thick

Meer Nawab's battery, with Nabdaree and Ackbaree local regiments

Well for the dead

No. 2 picquet of 16 men commanded by Capt. Thomson 40 ft. high, roofless

N

No.1 occupied in great force by the rebels, walls 7 ft. high. Gun raised here

4

3

2

1

.4 defended Capt. Jenkins d Railway gineers, 40 ft. h, temporary f

No. 3 not occupied 40 ft. high

1500 yds. from Savada Koti and Nana's tent

To lines of 53ʳᵈ and 56ᵗʰ Native infantry

Whatever the views of Nanak Chand, General Wheeler was apparently satisfied with the steps he had taken to prepare Cawnpore in the event of an outbreak. He telegraphed this message, published in the *Mofussilite* on 29 May:

All as well as I could wish and better than I could have expected. Mr Hillersdon informed me today, that the cool, quiet but determined manner in which the preparations were made to meet any outbreak, has completely disheartened all, and that they are sobering down. Vigilance will be necessary for some time to come. I have caused our position to be intrenched. . . .

Last Days before the Mutiny

It was 24 May and Queen Victoria's birthday, the occasion for a salute of guns and an official entertainment for the whole Cawnpore station. However, General Wheeler had forbidden any peel of bells or salute of guns for fear that it might set off trouble in the lines. Amelia Horne, a newcomer from Lucknow, where her stepfather was agent for Greenways Dak Company,[26] was alarmed by the uncanny silence of a Sunday afternoon without church bells: 'It frightened us not a little for it was something so strange allowing the day to pass unnoticed.'

On 29 May Mrs Louisa Chalwin sat down with a heavy heart to try to write a letter of condolence to her sister in England. Anxious to give comfort she wrote not one word of the daily terror all Cawnpore lived in. But on 31 May there was no longer a chance to hide the truth. In a brief postscript she dashed off a few lines to catch the post, the last one to leave Cawnpore:

P.S. 31st May 1857. We are in a great state of excitement today, for we have heard that soldiers of the regiments at Lucknow have risen, and that is only a 15 hours' march from here, and they have murdered 4 or 5 officers. . . . Everything here is quiet but however they may rise at any hour, day or night. We have returned to the house for an hour or two (but nearly all other ladies are in the barracks) as it is very near the European barrack, but we sit in fear and trembling all the time – however the heat there is dreadful. This is the third Sunday passed in this way. God grant our troubles may soon end. Everything is done here to repel the insurgents, such as guns ready, intrenchments dry and clean, but I think it a great shame all the officers are still obliged to sleep in the middle of their respective regts. as it is almost certain death if they rise. In the night even my husband goes – I can't say more now dearest Maria. My very very fondest love and 1000 kisses and hoping we may give you a better account next mail.[27]

Many were the letters written to catch the post of 31 May. Emma Cooke, the mother of Amelia Horne, wrote to a friend in Calcutta: 'Fancy us sleeping in an open verandah with men, women and children all huddled together and in momentary expectation of an attack . . . we are in a sad predicament.'[28]

A letter written to Bombay was reported in the *Mofussilite*:

I am writing to you from our intrenchment! where we have all been obliged to take refuge in a barrack. All our houses are forsaken, and we are crowded up in numbers together; the sepoys have not yet manifested their bad feeling here, but they are quite ready, although some think we have nothing to fear but from pressure from without; *every* bungalow burnt down at Lucknow last night . . . the officers have always reckoned on their fidelity hitherto, and they are now beginning to fear the truth.[29]

Colonel Ewart of the 1st Native Infantry and his wife, close friends of the Collector, Charles Hillersdon, faced the gravity of the situation. With that strength which comes with despair they found the words to express their affection for their families so far away:

[COLONEL EWART] I do not wish to write gloomily, but there is no use in disguising the fact that we are in the utmost danger; and as I have said, if the troops do mutiny, my life must almost certainly be sacrificed; but I do not think they will venture to attack the entrenched position which is held by the European troops so I hope in God that my wife and child will be saved. And now, dear A—— farewell. If under God's providence, this be the last time I am to write to you, I entreat you to forgive all I have ever done to trouble you, and to think kindly of me, I know you will be everything a mother can be to my boy. I cannot write to him this time, dear little fellow. Kiss him for me. Kind love to my brothers.

[MRS EWART] My dear child is looking very delicate. My prayer is that she may be spared much suffering. . . . It is not hard to die oneself, but to see a dear child suffer and perish, that is the hard, the bitter trial, and the cup which I must drink, should God not deem it fit that it should pass from me. My companion Mrs Hillersdon is delightful. Poor young thing, she has such a gentle spirit, so unmurmuring, so desirous to meet the trial rightly, unselfish and sweet in every way. She has two children, and we feel that our duty to our little ones demands that we should exert ourselves to keep up health and spirits as much as possible.

Such nights of anxiety, I would never have believed possible, and the days are full of excitement. Another fortnight, we expect, will decide our fate: and, whatever it may be, I trust we shall be able to bear it. If these are my last words to you, you will remember them lovingly and always bear in mind that your affection and the love we have ever had for each other is an ingredient of comfort in these bitter times.[30]

While the military and civil authorities composed themselves to meet their fate with dignity, the shopkeepers and merchants and those long resident in Cawnpore were not ready to resign themselves so easily. Many had lived in Cawnpore all their lives: with their thorough knowledge of the native language, familiarity with the geography of the town and with trusted servants and employees, they thought that in an emergency they could escape. Some, in fact, were Anglo-Indians and felt that, in disguise, they would not be discovered. Houses were secretly rented in the city in the names of servants, and plans made to remove into them under cover of darkness. Disguises were earnestly discussed with ayahs behind closed doors; simple garments of rough homespun cloth were stitched; fair hair was dyed black. Old Mr McIntosh and his son decided to play the role of *chowkidars* while Mrs McIntosh was to be the wife of a washerman with a big bundle of clothes to carry on her head.[31]

Pensioner Green, the Superintendent of the Bridge of Boats, lived with a native woman and therefore felt quite safe.[32] The Chinese shoemaker, Auchin, likewise felt that since he was neither European nor Christian, he would have nothing to fear.[33] One man prepared to die fighting; he was a discharged drummer called Cloony who, with a few Indian Christians, barricaded a small, strongly built flat-roofed house in General Gunge. They blocked the doors and took their stand on the roof with all the matchlocks they possessed.[34] The Assembly Rooms had been hired and used as a shop by a Portuguese merchant called Dagama. He devised a bizarre retreat, and had his servants place a huge chest on the flat roof of the building. It was filled with food and drink to last a week and holes were bored into it to give ventilation. Poor Dagama believed that here he would be safe.[35]

The wealthiest merchants consented to go into the entrenchment only after they had buried their treasure. Mr Crump, with the help of few servants, buried valuables and gold mohurs to the value to two lakhs in his compound. The Greenways did the same and then drove out of Cawnpore to a distance of sixteen miles, where they thought they would be unmolested at their Nudjafghur indigo factory.[36] Their rival, Mr Brandon, had much property in his compound belonging to the ex-King of Oude and believed that this would sufficiently protect his own goods. The two Jacobi brothers, one the watchmaker, the other the coachmaker, had long been established at Cawnpore. One brother agreed to go into the entrenchment, but Mr Henry Jacobi and his wife arranged to be concealed in the house of an Indian acquaintance living in Gwaltoli.[37]

Out in the District Peter Maxwell and John Moore Jones discussed what to do for the best. John Moore Jones and his young brother Gavin decided to seek protection with the other Fatehgarh residents in the Fort there. Peter Maxwell preferred to put his trust in General Wheeler. He handed over his house and estates at Muckanpore to the care of his senior Indian assistants and rode into Cawnpore to take refuge in the entrenchment. When he arrived few people recognised him, for he was so seldom in Cawnpore, but they made way for him to join them.

One of the few who left Cawnpore for Calcutta was Mrs MacDowell, the milliner. Not bothering about the £500 of uncollected money owed to her, she took her four children to safety. A few others were away from Cawnpore by chance: Dr Tresidder, the Nana Sahib's doctor,[38] was in England on leave, Hugh Maxwell by a stroke of fortune was in Calcutta, staying at Spence's Hotel; he had travelled down to meet his wife and family who were returning by ship from England.

The majority of Cawnpore society waited within the entrenchment. There was no certain knowledge of what was going on outside. Spies brought word that the greatest discontent was among the troopers of the 2nd Cavalry; secret meetings had taken place between their ringleaders and the Nana Sahib, but he kept changing his place of residence and it was difficult to follow all his movements. One evening it was known that he had talked for two hours in a boat on the river with the troopers. In the street of brothels, the prostitute Azeezun, a favourite of the cavalry,[39] boasted that her admirers would fill her house with gold mohurs; was it not known that the Nana Sahib was in command of the Magazine and Treasury and had he not agreed to be their leader?

In the darkness of early morning on 5 June, three shots from a pistol and a blaze from the riding master's bungalow as it was set alight were the signal that the 2nd Cavalry had broken out. With a bugle call they aroused the 1st Native Infantry and together they set out down the road to Nawabganj, the Nana Sahib and the Treasury. Colonel Ewart pleaded with his men in Hindi, 'My children, my children! This is not your usual conduct. Do not so great a wickedness!'[40] But it was too late to stop them.

For a few hours the officers of the 53rd and 56th Regiments held their men steady, but at daybreak they made the mistake of dismissing the men back to the tents. Messengers from the mutinous troops crept back. They whispered that until the 53rd and 56th also broke out and joined them there could be no share out of the treasure. Swayed between loyalty to their officers and greed at the thought of so much riches the men hesitated and argued. Suddenly they found themselves under gun fire; in an ill-conceived moment General Wheeler had ordered the guns from the entrenchment to open fire. At the third salvo, the men broke and fled. Literally driven away, the 53rd and 56th Regiments joined their brothers at the Treasury.

The British had trusted the Nana Sahib implicitly. Had he indeed bitterly detested the whole race who had deprived his adoptive father of a kingdom and himself of a goodly pension, and secretly plotted his own return to power? Or was he merely caught up by the fast-moving events and thrust into the position of prominence he acquired simply because the rebel cause demanded a leader? Was the Nana Sahib virtually a prisoner of the four rebellious regiments and forced to comply with their demand for loot and plunder?

It is certain that the Treasury was looted and, according to Trevelyan, the £100,000 shared among the four regiments. The Magazine was broken into and the valuable arsenal acquired for use against the British. The prisoners in the jail were set free and the civil offices and bungalows plundered and set alight. Then the insurgents marched off along the Grand Trunk Road on their way to Delhi, and the Nana Sahib rode with them.

It was alleged that he went with the rebels as their leader and that with a promise of great booty he persuaded them to turn and destroy the entrenchment before attempting to march to Delhi. It is also said that the Nana was a prisoner of the rebels, that they insisted on his accompanying them to Delhi; but seeing his reluctance they suggested instead that he return with them to capture Cawnpore first. Whatever the reality and the true motives, the Nana emerged as the leader of the insurgents and on the morning of 7 June he sent a message to General Wheeler warning him that he was about to attack. One of the survivors sadly commented, 'The Rajah of Bithore [sic] was supposed to be on our side. . . .'[41] That he found it necessary to warn General Wheeler suggests a last gesture to past friendliness and that the Nana *was* coerced into adopting the role he eventually agreed to play.

Military men assisted by every able-bodied male civilian – civil servants, merchants, railway gentlemen, clerks, drummers – went about their appointed tasks. In the entrenchments the bugles sounded the alarm, 'All hands to arms!' Gunners took up their positions beside their guns, sentries were posted, terrified women and children were herded under cover. At 10 a.m. the dreaded moment at last arrived; though for some it brought the relief of certainty and action. The Nana's guns boomed out, the first round shot fired from a nine-pounder struck the crest of the mud wall and flew over with a peculiar whizzing sound.

Thirty-five miles away, the Collector of Futtehpore was entertaining his guests to Sunday luncheon. Finding the house stuffy and hot they opened the windows and venetian blinds towards the west and sat out on the verandah. In the distance a purple haze clung heavily to the horizon and a sound of guns was distinctly heard. The Nana was attacking Wheeler's entrenchment for the first time. It was Trinity Sunday, 7 June 1857.

City of Desolation

For twenty-one days in June 1857, at the height of the hot weather, Wheeler's gallant forces withstood the attack of the Nana Sahib's army which outnumbered them twelve to one.[42] General Wheeler put Captain Moore in charge and Moore of Her Majesty's 32nd Foot, a tall Irishman with twinkling blue eyes and a full ruddy beard, carrying his arm in a sling and a revolver in his belt, inspired everyone with his own cool confidence.

The entrenchment was rectangular. On a flat open plain, burnt by the sun and treeless, a ditch and low mud wall enclosed two barrack buildings in an area of about four acres. On three sides a battery of three nine-pounders was drawn up. To the north, where there was no enemy gun to face, a triangular redan or earthwork was manned to give early warning of attack. The main guard faced the city. Moore placed each battery and face of the entrenchment under the command of a particular officer. Behind each of the batteries infantry were posted fifteen feet apart, under cover of the four-foot mud wall. 'Each man had at least three loaded muskets by his side, with bayonet fixed in case of assault; but in most instances our trained men had as many as seven and even eight muskets each. The batteries were none of them masked or fortified in any way and the gunners were, in consequence, exposed to a most murderous fire.'[43]

To the south and outside the entrenchment wall were a long range of eight half-built red brick barracks affording dangerous cover to the enemy. Barrack No. 4 was manned night and day by the railway gentlemen, with orders not to surrender. They had to leave the entrenchment and return crossing the exposed open plain. Hour after hour they stood watching for creeping figures closing up on them. Always they reserved their fire until it could be most deadly. 'Their sharp sight and accurate knowledge of distance acquired in surveying had made these gentlemen excellent marksmen.'[44] Ammunition and arms were buried in stacks in three corners of the entrenchment. Food was stored in an outhouse next to the main guard. The cookhouse stood against the back wall. Two outhouses at either end of the Thatched Barrack served as latrines for the entire establishment.

From the protective cover of the city, from ruined bungalows and compound walls, sheltering behind St John's Chapel and the Racquets Court, the heavy guns of the Nana Sahib's army pounded the entrenchment. Lieutenant Delafosse estimated that the rebels used three mortars, two twenty-four-pounders, three eighteen-pounders, one or two twelve-pounders, one or two nine-pounders and one six-pounder – all taken from

LEFT *Captain Edmund Vibart, 2nd Cavalry: daguerreotype by Baker. A fugitive from Fatehgarh, he was murdered on 10 July 1857.* RIGHT *Brigadier Jack, 'massacred at Cawnpore': photographed in civilian clothes by Surgeon John MacCosh c. 1850.*

the abandoned Magazine. Wheeler's guns were useless against the twenty-four-pounders, no nine-pound shot was available and six-pound shot was ineffectual. When darkness fell the rebels crept up close around the entrenchment. At every moment an assault was expected, no man dared close his eyes, guns were kept ready loaded, matches burning. A sentry going the round, sounding the 'All's Well' each half hour, became instantly the target for hundreds of bullets.

For the Europeans of Cawnpore the full horror of their predicament now became apparent. One thousand souls, herded into two buildings designed to hold no more than a hundred each. Women and children and invalids crowded, terrified, in whatever rooms they could find. There was nowhere to sit, nowhere to sleep, and no matter how they might barricade the rooms, there was nowhere to hide from death.* Mr Shepherd described how he and his family shared a miserable space with twenty people and passed one whole day clinging to the walls and crouching in the corners to avoid the shots. Terrible scenes were enacted around them:

*On the first day with each cannon ball that struck the buildings heart-rending shrieks and terrified wails came from the women and children. It took one day for them to learn to endure the sound of gunfire in silence.

The side rooms were crowded to suffocation, and a great many were left unwillingly under the thatch in the middle. Suddenly something struck the tiles on top with a tremendous crash, and an immense iron ball, an 18-pounder darted down, killing a handsome-looking youngster, who was held by the hand by his mother, and wounding one or two besides. Oh! the anguish of that moment! For a while fearful silence prevailed, then the heart-rending shrieks of the mother (an officer's wife) burst upon us (it still sounds in my ears while I write this). It would be impossible to describe the horrible consternation and fright, or the wild alarm and dismay which was visible upon the features of those around. All moved out of the spot, when another crash, more terrible than the first, startled every body – down came an enormous ball evidently fired from the same gun, and fell harmlessly a little further up. Some took shelter under the archway of the doors, and some against the walls. I saw several familiar faces there, but the following occurrence is most vivid in my recollection. Captain Seppings, the Officiating Deputy Pay Master of this station, was one of those under the door arches with his wife and children; he was quite calm and collected, endeavouring to encourage the ladies with him. He knelt down and offered up a very appropriate short but earnest prayer to God.

Each day the pitiless sun rose into the June heavens, driving men mad, striking them down with heat stroke and apoplexy. It was often so hot that it was impossible to touch the barrel of a gun. There was only one well for

Part of the Barracks held by General Wheeler – after the bombardment: photograph Felice Beato, 1858.

drinking water, across open ground, exposed to fire from the city and from the south. Water had to be drawn at night but the depth of the well was so great that it was hard work to draw up the leather buckets and the creaking of the tackle gave away the position and dangerously attracted the enemy's fire.[45] Water was a desperate craving. The distress of the women and children was so terrible to witness that men risked their lives to bring a drop of water to them. 'I have seen the children of my brother officers sucking the pieces of old water bags, putting scraps of canvas and leather straps into the mouth to try and get a single drop of moisture upon their parched lips. Not even a pint of water was to be had for washing from the commencement to the close of the siege.'[46]

The cooking and distribution of food was an enormous problem. After a week provisions became scarce and the garrison was reduced to a ration of split peas and a handful of flour a day. All funerals took place at night; bodies lay all day where they were killed, and at night the fatigue party came to drag them away and throw them down a well outside the entrenchment. The *Pucka* Barrack was stoutly made but when it sustained a direct hit, the falling bricks were dangerous · All the woodwork of doors and windows was soon shot away. The Thatched Barrack housed many of the women and children and was used as a makeshift hospital. When a shell set the roof on fire the whole building burned, destroying all the medical stores. Not one surgical instrument was saved. It was no longer possible to dress wounds or extract bullets; the only treatment was water to keep the wound open.

The fighting men took duty turns to stand at their exposed posts ready to repel the constant attacks twenty-four hours a day. They watched the skies anxiously: when the monsoon broke it would wash away the mud walls of the entrenchment and leave them with even less protection. On the twenty-first day of the siege a woman, barefoot and carrying a baby, was seen to approach. It was Mrs Jacobi, who had been sent with a letter offering safe passage to Allahabad to all those who laid down their arms. It was not signed but in the handwriting of Azimoolah Khan. After lengthy negotiations the terms of capitulation were agreed and the treaty returned signed by the Nana: boats to be prepared and provisioned, conveyances to the ghat provided, officers would retain their arms.[47]

The next morning the entrenchment was evacuated. The emaciated survivors, faces gaunt and wretched, their clothes tattered and stained, many without shoes or stockings, made their way slowly down to the river bank at Suttee Chowra Ghat. The level of the river was low and the boats lay flat down on sand banks with two feet of water rippling round them. Mrs Eliza Bradshaw, the widow of a musician, saw what happened:

Treachery at the boats: illustration from Mowbray Thomson's The Story of Cawnpore. *The boats, broadside on and lying in low water, stuck fast. Only two got away.*

At sunrise, on the 27th, some hackeries, three or four elephants, and three palkees were brought into the entrenchments by the sowars. The General and some officers were on elephants, Mrs. Wheeler was in a palkee, the Colonel's wife was also in a palkee, and Mrs. Kempland in the third. The ladies were on the hackeries. An artillery man wounded in the foot was placed in one of them, but the sick were left till the hackeries could return. When we reached the bridge with the white railings near Colonel Williams's house, we saw a large crowd assembled, men from the city and villagers; the sowars who were ahead, shouted out that they were to stand aside, and none to come down to the ghât; we then descended into the dry nullah leading to the river. When we got to our boat, we found that it had no bamboo flooring. Suddenly we heard firing, and the pattering of bullets, and then the roar of cannon on both sides of the river. We jumped out, the boat was between us and shore. In the water, a few paces off, by the next boat we saw the Colonel's youngest daughter. A sepoy was going to kill her with his bayonet. She said, 'My father was always kind to sepoys.' He turned away, and just then a villager struck her in the head with a club, and she fell into the water. We saw the clergyman take out a book, we did not see him read it, for a sowar rode into the water and cut him down with a blow on the neck; he then killed the Padre, and the other, who was a missionary. A sepoy killed a child with his bayonet, it was about 4 years old; another sepoy took a young child by the leg and threw it into the water. Suddenly shouts were heard, that the Nana had ordered the firing to cease; the sepoys and sowars were not to kill any more women and children; there were no European men left alive at the ghat.

Massacre Ghat: c.1926. It was from here the embarkation in the boats took place. For many years a cross marked the spot.

Lieutenant Mowbray Thomson, one of the four survivors, described his amazing escape and said that it was *Khuda-ka-mirzee* – by the grace of God – that his life was saved.

We got down to the river and into the boats without being molested in any way. Major Vibart and his family were the last to go on board, a party of his regiment, 2nd Cavalry, escorted him down and insisted on his taking all that belonged to him on board the boats but when they saw him firmly embark and us trying to get our boats away from the bank they made a signal to the boatmen who immediately left us having previously put fire in the thatched coverings of the boats which broke out instantly into a blaze. Every one who could was obliged to jump overboard. The wounded and helpless who could not perished in the flames. These cavalry men were the first to fire on us and their firing appeared to be the signal for the massacre to commence for the instant afterwards four guns opened on the forty boats which had been provided for us and about 10,000 Muskets. I was thus obliged to forsake the boat in which I had first taken shelter and swam across the river to one which I saw had escaped. Many a poor fellow I saw sink before me in that dreadful swim, some from exhaustion and others from round shot grape or shrapnel. Two poor fellows of the name of Henderson, brothers, one of them of 56th NI, were swimming with me and before we had got half over the elder brother said he was exhausted and could go no further. We tried to cheer him on but it was of no use he sunk before us and directly after a grape shot hit my only remaining companion on the hand and shattered it. He put it on my shoulder and we managed to reach the boat which had escaped. When we got over to the Oude side of the river two more guns opened upon us besides a heavy fire from some men of the 17th NI and a large number of matchlockmen. We managed to drop down the river about six miles where we stuck upon a sandbank and were obliged to get out to push the boat off (which contained both wounded women and children) The bravery here displayed by one and all is beyond my feeble power to describe. It was in efforts like this that we lost so many splendid officers and men. Here poor Moore, Ashe, Whiting, Vibart, Harrison, Quin and many others all fell, seriously wounded or killed. Lieut Delafosse 53rd NI and private Murphy of the 84th Foot although wounded were always foremost out of the boat when assistance was required. These brave acts were not of occasional accurance but had to be performed two or three times a day. At last we succeeded in getting the boat down to Nudjufghar where the sepoys came down upon us in another boat. They came closer to us than they intended and we killed a great number of them. After returning to Cawnpore I heard they were so disgusted with this affair that they returned to the Nana and told him they could not take the Feringhees unless he sent a much larger force to be despatched, four fresh companies and 150 Cavalry. After leaving Nudjufghar we dropped down to a place called Soorajpore where the boat again stranded and nothing could move her. Daylight revealed our position to the sepoys who had followed us during the night and they again opened fire upon us. We found we had got into the wrong Channel and that something must be done to get out of the shallow water we were in. Major Vibart who was very severely hit through both arms ordered me out as a last effort with Lieut Delafosse, a Sergeant of the 84th Foot and eleven men to try and beat off the rebels whilst the remainder were to try and float the boat. Our party succeeded in landing and drove the enemy back some little distance but was at last completely surrounded so I was obliged to order a retreat towards the boat which to my sorrow was nowhere to be seen. No time was to be lost so I started with the men down the stream in search of her but no boat was to be found. The enemy followed close upon our heels keeping up a very heavy fire. At last seeing how exhausted the men were becoming for they had had no food for three days and seeing how fast the enemies numbers were increasing I ordered the men to retire into a small temple which stood about 30 or 40 yards from the river's bank. I regret to say that Sergeant Grady was shot through the head whilst going into the temple. They tried every means in their power to dislodge us from this place and lost a great many men in the attempt. At last they tried to burn us out. They heaped around the temple large quantities of wood and sticks and set all on fire. The first fire we managed to bear but the second was too much for us for they threw in large quantities of powder until we were almost suffocated., There was now no alternative but to sell our lives as dearly as we could or be smothered in the place so each man seizing his musket out we rushed and gave the brutes the point of the bayonet and a volley. They broke. We saw the river before us and those who could swim jumped in. Seven got into the water the remaining six were cut up on shore, and swimming down the river we lost three more of our number killed and three wounded but still we swam on. At length to our great relief the firing grew slacker until finally it ceased altogether. Then we made for the shore to take a rest of which we were much in need, and whilst resting we heard voices on the bank above us. Immediately we struck out for the middle of

RIGHT *Lieutenant Mowbray Thomson: photographed by Bourne and Shepherd, 1874.*

BELOW *Massacre at Cawnpore: illustration from Charles Ball's* The History of the Indian Mutiny, *1857. 'When the captives from one of the boats were dragged in front of the Nana the doctor's wife refused to leave her husband. "I will not leave my husband. If he must die, I will die with him." So she ran and sat down behind her husband, clasping him round the waist. Directly she said this, the other Memsahibs said, "We also will die with our husbands." And they all sat down, each by her husband. Then their husbands said, "Go back." But they would not. Whereupon the . . . soldiers . . . pulled them away forcibly. But they could not pull away the doctor's wife, who there remained. Then the Padre . . . requested leave to read prayers before they died . . . and the Sahibs shook hands all round. Then the sepoys fired. One Sahib rolled one way, one another, as they say. But they were not dead. So they went in and finished them off with swords.' (Testimony of a native spy.)*

the stream but this time we found ourselves among friends. They turned out to be sepoys belonging to a Rajah by name Dirigbijah Singh of Moorar Mhow who was friendly to our Govt. They told us if we would only rely upon them they would take us to their Rajah who would protect us and when things were a little quiet he would send us to Allahabad. We had nothing left but to trust them. They took us to their village and fed us and after resting a short time they took us to their Rajah who received us most kindly kept us for a month in his fort and then sent us across the river to a friendly Zemindar who provided us with carriage and sent us on towards Allahabad. We met a Detachment of the 84th on its way to Cawnpore so we returned with it and related all we had gone through to General Neill.[49]

The women and children, about eighty in all, who survived the slaughter at the boats were taken prisoner, first to the Savada Koti, the house that had at one time been an SPG orphanage, and then, with the fugitives from Fatehgarh, to the Bebee Ghur. Close by, at Mohomed's Hotel, the Nana Sahib had his headquarters. At the Bebee Ghur 206 women and children were imprisoned for thirteen days. News of the approach of General Havelock's relieving forces was to be their death warrant. One day before Havelock arrived, they were all massacred.

A woman in the Nana's household, known as the Begum, used to attend at the Bebee Ghur morning and evening, but the wife of a bugler, a native Christian, did everything for the ladies. They were given one meal a day, of dal and chaupattis. There was no furniture, they slept on the ground as best they could, on coarse bamboo matting. Drummer John Fitchett of the 6th Native Infantry claimed to have been imprisoned in a small shed close by and to have witnessed the massacre.

The woman called Begum told the ladies they were to be killed by the Nana's orders. A lady went to Jemandar Usuf Khan, of the 6th regiment, who was in command of the guard over the prisoners, and said to him, that she heard they were all to be killed. I was only a few paces from him at the time; he replied, that he had not received any orders, that she was not to be afraid. Sepoy Kurm Alee said to the woman Begum, that her orders would not be obeyed, who was she to give orders. The Begum went to the Nana's house. The sepoys on guard, they were men of my corps, and I think some of the 1st regiment, took counsel and decided that they would not lift their hands against women, though they would kill every man. The sepoys were told, that if they did not carry out the Nana's order, the artillery would be sent against them; they afterwards told me, that they intended to save the ladies, in order that their own lives might be saved. The Begum returned with five men. These men were ordered to fire at the ladies. I heard from Nubbee Buksh, that they fired at the ceiling. I heard the reports, they only fired once; the five men then entered, they had swords, it was about sunset. The lady who spoke to the jemadar was at the door, she was first cut down. I saw her fall, but could not see further than the door; I heard fearful shrieks. This lasted half an hour or more. I did not see any of the women or children try to escape. The sowars were posted at the trees near the house. A Velaitee, a stout, short man, and fair, soon came out with his sword broken. I saw him go to the Nana's house and bring back another sword. This he also broke in a few minutes, and got a third from the Nana. I saw him go out to the next compound, which was the Nana's, but could not see whether he went into the house. The groans lasted all night. I was only fifteen or sixteen paces from the house.

At about 8 o'clock the next morning, the sweepers living in the compound were ordered to throw the bodies into a dry well, near the house. The bodies were dragged out, most of them by the hair of the head, those whose clothes were worth taking, were stripped. Some of the women were alive, I cannot say how many, but three could speak; they prayed for the sake of God that an end might be put to their sufferings. I remarked one very stout woman, a half caste, who was severely wounded in both arms, who entreated to be killed. She and two or three others were placed against the bank of the cut by which bullocks go down in drawing water from the well. The dead bodies were first thrown down. Application was made to the Nana about those who were alive. Three children were also alive. I do not know what orders came, but I saw one of the children thrown in alive. I believe the other children and women, who were alive, were then thrown in. There was a great crowd looking on; they were standing along the walls of the compound. They were principally city people and villagers. The children were running round the well, where else could they go to? and there was none to save them. No, none said a word, or tried to save them.[50]

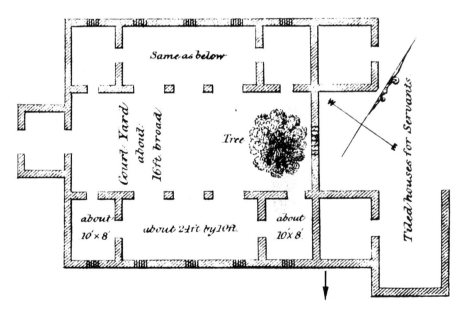

W. J. Shepherd's ground plan of the Bebee Ghur. 'The house was originally built for the reception of a native woman, the Mistress of an Officer, and was attached to the large bungalow ... since called the "Medical Depôt".' The arrow points towards the well 'about 35 or 40 feet from the building'.

The Bebee Ghur: c.1857. Photographed shortly after Sir Henry Havelock reached Cawnpore.

The day Havelock's men marched into Cawnpore the sky was clear blue, patched with small clouds, and reflecting the heat intensely. There were no human sounds, only the croaking of frogs and shrill piping of cicadas. The air was hot and damp, filled with the offensive odour of the neem trees and of death. The Nana Sahib had withdrawn to Bithoor and no one stirred in the ruined city, terrified of the inevitable reprisals that would follow. Mr Sherer[51] was one of the first to go to the desolate Bebee Ghur:

From the hotel, not a hundred yards' walk led us to the celebrated Beebeeghur. First let me say that this appellation does not mean the 'ladies house', as indicating the spot where the ladies were killed; the building had the name previous to the Mutiny. It was understood to have been a dwelling provided by a European for his Indian mistress, and was therefore constructed in the Oriental style. It was of one storey, with a court in the middle, and a tree grew in the court. Bews[52] and I were certainly among the first who saw it; but Colonel Fraser-Tytler had been there, and one or two others. But there is no question that the aspect of the place, when we entered, was entirely unchanged. It was precisely in the same condition as the first Englishmen who did see it found it to be in. The whole story was so unspeakably horrible that it would be quite wrong in any sort of way to increase the distressing circumstances which really existed. And I may say once for all that the accounts were exaggerated. The attack had evidently been made from the front entrance, and there is reason to suppose that it commenced by muskets being pushed through the

Havelock's Column attacking the mutineers before Cawnpore: illustration from Charles Ball's History of the Indian Mutiny.

venetians, and discharged. There had been a rush across the court to the opposite side, and a mass of human beings were collected in the arched chamber facing the entrance. And thither, doubtless, they were pursued by the assassins with swords. For the whole of the pavement was thickly caked with blood. Surely this is enough, without saying 'the clotted gore lay ankle deep', which, besides being most distressing, is absolutely incorrect. Then, as to what was lying about, both of us thought it wonderful that the small litter we saw could be the traces of the numbers who had been shut up there. There is no question in my mind that when the bodies were taken away the place had been tidied a little and painful objects had been removed. There were certainly a few odds and ends of clothing, some locks of hair, some little shoes, straw hats and so on. Of mutilation, in that house at least, there were no signs, nor at that time was there any writing on the walls. It is well known that there were one or two books, and in them some notes, which have long since been communicated to the public. From this dreadful place we passed down the garden to the narrow well into which many of the bodies of the victims of the assassination were thrown. I say many, because the receptacle was far too small for all, and there can be little doubt that bodies were dragged across the open space to the river, which was at no great distance. Indeed, we were told as much at the time. When we got to the coping of the well, and looked over, we saw, at no great depth, a ghastly tangle of naked limbs. I heard a low cry of pain, and saw Bews almost crouching with a sickening anguish. There is no object in saying more.[53]

The Nana was pursued to Bithoor where several regiments of his mutinous sepoys put up a spirited defence from behind earthworks. They were driven out at the point of the bayonet. The Nana escaped across the river and was never caught. His palace and temple were sacked and looted, and the wells found to contain great treasure.[54]

In Cawnpore a bridge of boats was constructed across the river and a new, strongly fortified entrenchment, the Kila or Fort, hastily built to protect it. Leaving a small force in Cawnpore, Havelock handed over command to General Neill and pressed on to relieve the besieged garrison in Lucknow.

Terrible vengeance and summary justice were carried out at General Neill's order.[55] Anyone suspected of being implicated in the uprising was hanged, but first was made to lick clean a patch of the bloody floor at the Bebee Ghur where the dried blood had been watered. Pork and beef was stuffed down his throat to break his caste. Hangings went on 'famously', the Muslims dying with *hauteur* and angry scorn, the Hindus with an indifference which astonished the English onlookers.

Cawnpore continued under military occupation. The Gwalior Contingent, Scindia's army, which had been trained and led by Company officers, and which the Maharaja had held loyal, now broke away. With Tantia Tope at their head, their numbers swollen by sepoys joining them after the fall of Delhi, they made several attacks on the small garrison at the Kila, destroyed the Assembly Rooms and were only with difficulty driven out of Cawnpore. Fighting and skirmishing continued for several months. When Lucknow was finally relieved, things gradually quietened down and it was safe once more for civilians to return to Cawnpore.

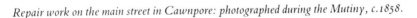

Repair work on the main street in Cawnpore: photographed during the Mutiny, c.1858.

Gallant attack of Windham's small force on the Gwalior Contingent: chromolithograph by Captain D. Sarsfield Greene, RE. Pandoo Nuddee, 26 November 1857.

Residents who were absent when the mutiny broke out in June now returned and looked at the place in bewilderment and shook their heads in sorrow. Houses, gardens, large shady trees, bazaars and huts, all had disappeared – everything to the extent of a mile all round the new fort, was being cleared away.[56]

Cawnpore was devastated. The town was reduced to a smoking blackened ruin, with hardly a building or tree left standing. Houses and shops were burnt or shattered by cannon fire.[57] The Magazine was blown up, the Assembly Rooms gutted, Christ Church twice burnt, a shell without a roof, the theatre and masonic lodge damaged but still upright. All work on the railway came to a halt; bridges were destroyed, carriages, engines and stores burnt, the track ripped up. Not until 1859 did the East Indian Railway reach Cawnpore.

No one was aware that unique opportunities for growth would follow the destruction. Many of the names appearing in advertisements, on contracts and in balance books have gathered historical associations: the majority because they figured in the accounts of the fighting and on the tablets round the church, built as a memorial to the Mutiny victims; those of Hugh Maxwell and Gavin Jones because they survived, to form the partnership and company of the Elgin Mills, the first up-country cotton mill that was to become the backbone of industrial Cawnpore and from which all future industrial progress would evolve.

Epilogue

There were only four survivors of Wheeler's fighting force: two young lieutenants, a private and a gunner.[1] The General himself was killed at Suttee Chowra Ghat. There are conflicting stories of how he met his death, but one witness stated that as he got out of his *palkee* to enter the boats, he was cut down by a sword blow to the back of his neck. Lady Wheeler and their elder daughter were killed at the Ghat. Only four days earlier young Lieutenant Wheeler, the General's son and ADC, had been killed in the entrenchment. He was sitting on a sofa, fainting from a wound he had received in the trenches; his sister was fanning him when a round shot came through the doorway and left him a headless trunk. Colonel Ewart, badly wounded by gunshot was carried in a *dhooli* down to the boats, Mrs Ewart walking in the dust beside him. Ahoodeen Pershad, a banker, was standing near the church and saw what happened. Some men from his own regiment ordered the *dhooli* to be put down, mocked him with, 'Is this not a fine parade, Colonel?' and cut them both down with swords. Mrs Louisa Chalwin died at the Ghat. Mr Hillersdon was standing talking to his wife on the verandah of the Pucka Barracks when a round shot disembowelled him and he died at her feet. Mrs Hillersdon died a few days later, killed by falling bricks dislodged by a shot. Buried beside her in the same grave was Mrs De Russett, who had gone out of her mind. Mrs De Russett was the daughter-in-law of the barber who had so delighted the King of Oude; her husband worked for Brandon & Co. Mr Gill, the schoolmaster of the Free School, was wounded when a round shot hit the building: the splinters fractured his skull. He and his wife both died when the hospital burnt down; Mrs Gill had been in labour. Mr Haycock, one of the SPG missionaries, died a raving lunatic.

Among the merchants, nineteen members of the Greenway family[2] alone were killed, together with many of their competitors. Peter Maxwell took refuge in the entrenchment and was never seen again. Conditions were so chaotic and survivors so few that no one knew if he had died in the entrenchment or at the boats. Henry Christie, whose house and saltpetre works overlooked the Ghat at Suttee Chowra, died in the entrenchment of heat exhaustion; his wife and three daughters were killed. J. D. Hay had just been to see his wife and newly born infant when he was shot through the temple and died instantly. Five members of the John Kirk family perished.

Miss Wheeler defends herself against the sepoys at Cawnpore. Illustration from Narrative of the Indian Revolt. *(See pp. 324-5.)*

BELOW LEFT *Brigadier-General James Neill in a frock coat, c.1850: calotype photograph from an album compiled by Surgeon John MacCosh c. 1848-52.* RIGHT *The Hero of Lucknow, 1857: General Sir Henry Havelock KCB seated at a table in a tent wearing a frock coat. In the background is a camp and, beyond, the city of Lucknow: mezzotint by and after A. H. Ritchie, published by* The Albion, *New York 1859.*

John Moore Jones was killed at the defence of the fort at Fatehgarh; his wife and daughter were also killed. At Palee, at the bungalow where Hugh Maxwell once lived, Edmond Jones and Clinton Kemp were breakfasting with the Collector of Mirzapore, Mr Moore, when all three were attacked and murdered.[3] W. J. Shepherd left the entrenchment in disguise shortly before the terms of the surrender had been received by General Wheeler. He was captured by the Nana's troops but survived. His wife and all his children died.[4] Miss Amelia Horne[5] and the youngest Miss Wheeler[6] were carried away from the river bank by two *sowars*, their plight and subsequent fate arousing intense speculation. Hugh Maxwell escaped almost certain death by the chance fact that he was in Calcutta. His house and factory were looted[7] and over a lakh's worth of property stolen. Young Gavin Jones,[8] after a series of astonishing adventures and escapes, survived. He reached Cawnpore, gaunt and exhausted, after weeks in hiding, to find that Havelock's relieving forces had driven off the Nana Sahib's[9] army and re-occupied the town.

The Queen's Proclamation was read in November 1858. There was a parade and the senior civilian read the document out from a carriage. The Mutiny had proved the death warrant of the East India Company. Now the administration of India passed to the direct authority of the Crown. Two days later Lord Canning, the first Viceroy, on a tour to proclaim peace, held a Durbar of great magnificence to which about a hundred loyal rajahs were invited. *Khelauts* and gifts were presented and the Rajah of Rewah and the Chikaree Rajah were singled out for special praise.

Cawnpore slowly returned to normal. At first only with great difficulty was order established. Influential men who had taken no part in the rebellion held back and it was difficult to raise a police force. The city was fined £30,000* for its too ready acceptance of the Nana's occupation, which was paid without an appeal.[10] Plundered property was strewn over an area of seventy square miles, every house had been gutted and every lane and street littered with every description of European goods. Neill threatened death as the punishment for anyone found with plundered property and quantities of goods were put out nightly into the streets.[11]

Gradually normal commercial activity began again and, once begun, it filled the gaps left by the Mutiny with amazing rapidity. 'The tradesmen, shopkeepers and labourers did not, with the exception of the very lowest classes, take part in the rising and were indeed subjected to great oppression from the soldiers raised by the Nana of Bithoor.'[12] They were joined by the

*This money was used to create the Memorial Well Gardens (now Nana Rao Park) a park surrounding the beautiful figure of an angel carved by Baron Marochetti over the Bebee Ghur well.

The Angel of the Well: c.1926. The work of Baron Marochetti inspired by a design of Lady Canning's; the Angel, holding crossed palms, has an expression of severity when viewed from one side and of gentleness from the other.

wealthy merchants and contractors who had now regained their confidence and came forward to supply money in any amount for the rebuilding of Cawnpore. Hugh Maxwell came back to save what he could and found himself the senior citizen; he was one of the few who knew anything about commercial affairs before the disaster. The problems to be faced were summed up by the Magistrate – 'the extreme difficulty of obtaining proof [of ownership of property] at this station where almost every European was murdered and records of every description destroyed'.[13]

Circumstances worked together to prevent Cawnpore from settling down to being little more than a sleepy ghost town. It was the East Indian

Memorial Well Gardens: c. 1880. A beautiful garden of some sixty acres surrounded the Gothic screen which enclosed the statue of an angel built on the site of the massacre well. At the time of Independence the entire structure was removed and re-erected in the garden of All Souls Church and a plain plinth marks the spot in what is now called Nana Rao Park.

BELOW *Ruins of the Residency, Lucknow, c. 1880. Besieged for nearly three months and twice relieved, it withstood the attack from the rebels.*

Railway that, when its goods line linked Cawnpore with Allahabad in 1859, set the seal upon the future prosperity and expansion of Cawnpore. The arrival of the first engine symbolised the importance of the event. Tremendous excitement was generated by its arrival, banners were stretched across the arches at the station with 'Welcome' and 'The Way to Prosperity, Success to the East Indian Railway' upon them. The engine, very smart in fresh paint and polish, was festooned with garlands of flowers and carried a crown of red and white in front of the funnel. On the platform

The first railway engine to reach Cawnpore: sketch by an unknown artist. It hung at the Parsonage, Kanpur, 1970.

were gathered all the senior people in their best clothes, the band played, guns fired a salute and all along the route villagers salaamed deeply as the locomotive chugged by at 30 m.p.h.[14] By 1864 Cawnpore had a direct rail link to Calcutta, bringing safe and speedy access to the port.

The flow of trade changed. Cotton, grain and oil seed, which previously had been sent by road and river channels, were now directed to Cawnpore. The Grand Trunk Road saw no more the interminable strings of thousands of carts that had in the past conveyed the merchandise of the Doab to Allahabad for shipment by steamers to the port of Calcutta. All trade now converged on the Cawnpore railhead.

Within a year of the rail link with Allahabad the civil war in America had broken out, disorganising the country's cotton trade. The Northerners blockaded the Southern ports and cotton exports from America virtually ceased. This produced a severe cotton famine in Lancashire and a sudden demand for Indian cotton. The price of cotton rose to fabulous heights, creating a boom in cotton prices and a cotton mania in India. It was the war in America that decided Cawnpore's future as a manufacturing centre.

Cawnpore was flooded with countless bales of cotton that poured in from Bundlekhand, Rohilkhand, Oudh and the Doab in huge streams beyond the carrying capacity of the Railway. The roads in the city were piled high above the roof tops, completely blocking the way. To relieve the congestion the embarrassed authorities were forced to provide storage away from the Market, the aid of the Military was called into requisition to clear away and level the mud huts that had sprung up promiscuously on Cantonment lands in the vicinity of the Railway station. Elephants were employed to push down the frail mud walls to expedite the work of demolition, to level the ground, where the piles of bales quickly grew to great heaps. A unique sight to spectators of miniature mountains of cotton raised on the broad flat level plain, which took months for the Railway to transport.[15]

Men had that sense of purpose that comes after a time of disaster. Some enterprising residents, led by Mr Buist, the Station Master, three military men, one associated with the Commissariat, and several wealthy Indian contractors, formed themselves into a committee[16] to manufacture the cotton in Cawnpore rather than send it to the port. It seemed only natural that Hugh Maxwell, backed by the stability and reputation of his family's long connection with Cawnpore, should join the Board to lend powerful support. The Elgin Cotton Spinning & Weaving Co. Limited, named after the imminent Viceroy, Lord Elgin, was launched in 1861 with a capital of three lakhs. Twenty-five acres between Permit Ghat and the ruins of the Magazine were acquired. Plans were drawn up, the mill buildings erected, machinery ordered from Platt Bros. in Oldham and in 1864 the mill began production.

Gavin Jones was in England in 1865 when he was asked to return to Cawnpore to manage the business. He brought with him something of the confidence of the economic and commercial climate of the West, and the new ideas of men such as Darwin and Marx, about which everyone was talking. It was uphill work. The workmen, with constant supervision, were gradually taught how to use the new looms. A demand for the new products had to be created, bundles of goods were given away free to encourage people to come back to buy more. Capital was locked up, stocks high and sales slow. Disagreement between the military men and the business men on

Sampling cotton: line drawing by J. Lockwood Kipling, 1872. A cotton go-down, piled high with bales of cotton.

the Board caused friction and Hugh Maxwell and Gavin Jones resigned. The pioneering attempt failed, ending in the liquidation of the mill in 1871. The goodwill, stock, buildings and the plant came up for sale in the Judge's court.

Notices of the sale had appeared in all the leading newspapers for weeks in advance but so little was the value of the industry appreciated that on the day of the auction only one bidder attended to compete for the prize. Hugh Maxwell, a small group of his personal friends and a few local people who happened by chance to be in court that day and looked on idly were the only people who came to the sale. Gavin Jones watched, fascinated.

Punctually at the hour appointed the fiat went forth from the Judge and the court chaprassi advanced to the front of the railings that fenced the Judge from the people, and with no more ceremony than the bare announcement that the Mill was offered for sale to the highest bidder, above the upset price of two lakhs, in a loud voice called for bids. The former Chairman rose from his seat and responded with, 'two lakhs and two thousand', the auctioneer sang out the bid, repeating it for a considerable time. The Judge broke the silence with, 'will no one give a higher bid?' and looked round the audience for a response. None came. Reluctantly he turned to the auctioneer and gave the order to 'knock it down', the hammer fell with a gentle tap on the rails and the solitary bidder became the fortunate owner of the Mill – 10,000 spindles and 100 looms at one-third of their cost.[17]

It was a proud moment for the Maxwell family. Hugh Maxwell, appreciating Gavin Jones's mercurial energy and technical knowledge, reinstated him and within twelve months Elgin Mills had developed into a flourishing concern, soon to become a household name throughout India for

Plan of the Cawnpore Woollen Mills: sketch which hung in the office.

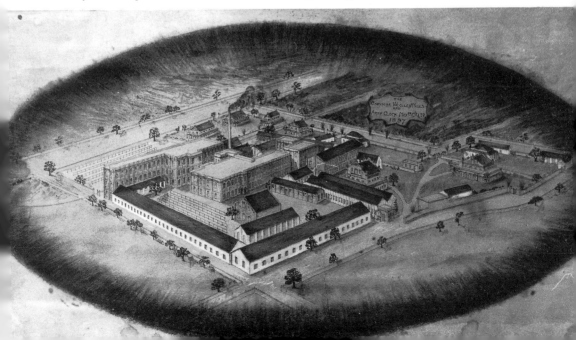

towels, khaki drill and tents. This was the first up-country cotton mill in India.[18]

To the Elgin Mills came the men from England trained in the new Western technology. Once established, they saw the possibilities ahead and, with the help of Indian finance, seized the opportunity to start their own mills. Six mills set up by British enterprise owe their parentage to the Elgin Mills, and all of them were backed by Indian finance.[19] It is significant that Montgomery's *Statistics* record that as early as 1849 there were fifty Indian banking houses in Cawnpore. This was the Indian merchants' particular and important contribution to the development of the city.[20]

Later, in 1874, after a quarrel with Hugh Maxwell, Gavin Jones set up the Muir Mills, to rival Elgin. Like many men of genius, Gavin Jones was very difficult to work with. His volatility and brilliance were so mistrusted by the partners who had financed him that they bound him with agreements from starting any other cotton mill. Frustrated in this direction, his busy mind explored new industries. First he started the Cawnpore Woollen Mills and later, with the help of George Allen and William Cooper (both later received knighthoods), set up the Government Boot and Shoe Factory. His last venture was the Empire Engineering Works.

Gavin Jones married Margaret French,[21] a sister of Lieutenant John French, then a subaltern in the 19th Hussars in Lucknow, later Commander-in-Chief of the British Forces in 1914 and Earl of Ypres. Their qualities complemented each other. Gavin Jones had a cold serenity, a silent forcefulness, a superior vitality that made people turn to him and follow his advice; at home he was quiet and gentle, leaving all decisions to his wife. She was fearless and without imagination, earning for herself the nickname La Reine. At the turn of the century, when there was hardly a factory in Cawnpore that was not his brainchild Gavin Jones proudly referred to himself as 'the Father of Cawnpore'. He finally retired in 1907, having lived to see Cawnpore hailed as the Manchester of the East. He died at Southsea on 11 January 1913. The Gavin Jones connection with Cawnpore continued through his son, Sir Tracy Gavin Jones, up to and including the time of Independence.

Hugh Maxwell was content to follow his own path. While cherishing his little kingdom at the Elgin Mills, he also went into partnership with Dr Begg. Begg Christie became Begg Maxwell & Co. and ultimately Begg, Sutherland & Co., the oldest firm of managing agents in northern India and destined to play a major role in the future. Hugh's wife Charlotte died at

OPPOSITE *Lily and Nora Maxwell with Munnee Ayah: Cawnpore 1866.*

Cawnpore Tent Club, 1866. STANDING *W.S. Halsey, officiating magistrate and collector; H.C. Barstow, assistant magistrate and collector; E.C. Buck, assistant magistrate and collector; Capt K.J.W. Coghill, brigade major; Capt T.W.R. Boisragon, 30th NI; Lieut A.J.T. Welchman, 14th Bengal Cavalry.* CENTRE ROW *A.W. Brind, executive engineer Ganges canal; F. Halsey, agent, Bank of Bengal; Capt J.T. Tovey; R.W. Maxwell, Begg, Maxwell & Co; Lieut J.R. Wilmer, RA; H. Farrell, veterinary surgeon, RA; Lieut J.T. Camilleri, 7th Dragoon Guards.* FRONT ROW *Lieut R.H. Grant, RA; H.B. Goad, officiating district superintendent of police; Cornet W.R. Truman, 7th Dragoon Guards.*

Dehra Dun in June 1865 and the family letters that survive show him to have been a kindly, considerate and affectionate Victorian father, anxious for the welfare of his large motherless family. He fulfilled his role with such dignity and good sense that his children were able to devote themselves to a delightful social life.[22] After his death at the family home in Upper Norwood, Surrey, on 5 October 1883, the business was carried on by his only son, Ralph Maxwell, and other members of the family. The Maxwell association with Cawnpore continued until 1914.

It was the unique combination of Hugh Maxwell's financial acumen, backed by his family's reputation in the District, and the brilliant and inventive mind of young Gavin Jones that set in motion amazing developments. The change that had taken place so fast in Cawnpore was summed up by a Mutiny veteran, William Forbes-Mitchell of the 93rd Sutherland Highlanders, when he revisited the city thirty-six years after the Mutiny:

On the 6 December 1857, I advanced across the Canal with *thirty-six*, well served, heavy guns [of the Gwalior Contingent] pouring shot and shell through our ranks. On the 19 August 1892 I stood on the top of the Cawnpore Woollen Mills, and counted *thirty-six* chimneys of sizes belching out smoke from more than three times that number of steam boilers. . . . I found that the European industries of Cawnpore are paying, monthly, an average of Rs 1,36,000 (£13,600) for *native* labour alone! Month after month, throughout the year, this amount of money is being expended by the European industries and European enterprise of Cawnpore, and, without a single exception, every one of these industries has been built up by independent European enterprise, and that within only the past quarter of a century.[23]

With the passing of Hugh Maxwell and Gavin Sibbald Jones, the star of their family fortunes began to wane. Now new names came into prominence to carry the development of the city further. Chief among these was Alexander MacRobert. Known for his enormous capacity for work and attention to detail, his petty meanness, his bitter quarrels, his personal loneliness, he built upon Gavin Jones's pioneering achievements and created the empire of the British India Corporation and in 1922 became Sir Alexander MacRobert, first baronet of Cawnpore and Cromar and a man of immense fortune. It was Gavin Jones himself, marvelling to see all that he had struggled and laboured with for so many years, brought to fulfilment who hailed MacRobert as the 'uncrowned king of Cawnpore'. Basking in his shadow Cawnpore was to enjoy a status it had never known before. But on that day in 1871, when the Elgin Mills came into existence, all this lay in the future.

'The Father of Cawnpore': *Gavin Sibbald Jones c.1890.*

Notes and Sources
Glossary
Appendices

Notes and Sources

INTRODUCTION

1 The legendary history is set out in *S.N. Wright's Settlement Report* BL: ISUP 40/14 and based on a Persian history compiled before the Mutiny from documents in the possession of the last Raja Sati Parshad – died a pauper in the house of Chaube Sidhari Lal who lent the manuscript to Wright.

CHAPTER ONE

1 John Carnac had come to India as a lieutenant in one of the King's Troops, the 39th Foot. (From 1754 the Company troops in India were supplemented by regiments from the regular army in England — the King's Troops.) When his regiment was ordered back to England, he transferred to the Company's service, joining as a captain in 1758. By 1760 he was in command of the army at Patna. He was aide-de-camp and secretary to Clive and so close a friend that he lived *en famille* with Clive and his wife, Margaret, when in Calcutta. In 1765 he married Elizabeth Wolleston, daughter of the chaplain in Calcutta. Two years after he had received Sujah Dowlah 'with great distinction' at Jajmau, he followed the pattern of successful Englishmen in India and returned to England where he became Member of Parliament for Leominster. As a widower of about forty-eight, he married Elizabeth Rivett, aged only eighteen. In 1776 he returned to India to serve on the Council at Bombay. He was accompanied by his wife, her sister Frances and, free of charge to the Company, the menial servants, Helena Box, Mary Baker, William Moir (his medical adviser) and Caesar, a black servant. When General Carnac stepped ashore at Bombay he was greeted with a salute of eleven guns. He remained in Bombay for the rest of his life. A monument to his memory is in St Thomas's Cathedral, Bombay.

2 Robert Clive had risen from working as a clerk in the Company warehouse on £5 a year to being the victor of Arcot and was rumoured to be the richest man in England.

3 In 1760 the total number of officers in the Company's Bengal army was 60 (See Appendix 8). 'Prior to the year 1757, the military establishment of Bengal consisted of only one company of Artillery and four or five companies of European infantry, with a few hundred Natives, armed after the manner of the country, for the protection of the several factories . . .' Williams, Captain, *Rise and Progress of the Bengal Native Infantry,* John Murray, London, 1817.

The Bengal Army Muster Roll 1716 – 1771 pt 2 lists: 'A general Return of the Land Forces in the kingdom of Bengal and Provinces of Behar under the Command of Colonel Eyre Coote, 1 November 1761.' The effective rank-and-file of European soldiers was 117 cavalry, 203 artillery and with a 'Grand Total' of infantry, 1223 (IOR).

4 Caraccioli, Charles, *Life of Robert Clive, Baron Plassey . . . wherein are delineated his military talents in the field; his maxims of government in the Cabinet, during the two last wars in the East Indies . . . With anecdotes of his private life and the particular circumstances of his death,* Bell, London, 1775.

5 IOR: P/A/6, Bengal Secret and Military Consultations 19 May 1765.

6 Broome, Arthur, *History of the Rise and Progress of the Bengal Army,* Thacker & Co., London and Calcutta, 1851.

7 IOR: P/A/6, Bengal Secret and Military Consultations 26 May 1765.

8 IOR: Mss Eur, G.37/Box 3.

9 *ibid.*

10 IOR: P/A/6, Bengal Secret and Military Consultations 21 June 1765.

11 *ibid.*

12 IOR: P/A/10, Bengal Secret Consultations 26 May 1770. Captain Gabriel Harper was appointed to the Court of Sujah Dowlah to act as intermediary between the Company and the Nawab of Oude.

13 *ibid.*

14 IOR: P/A/11 Bengal Secret Consultations 7 February 1771.

15 *ibid.*

16 IOR: P/A/12 Bengal Secret Consultations 15 April 1772.

17 Captain Robert Brooke's services against the Mahrattas were acknowledged by the Court of Directors in terms 'almost unprecedented in the case of an officer of junior rank'. Having served as Collector of Corah with commission of 2½% of the revenues, he returned to Ireland, where he tried to develop the manufacture of cotton. When this failed, he applied to the Company, who appointed him Governor of another of its territories, St Helena. He served there from 1787 until his death in 1801 (*DNB*).

18 IOR: P/A/11 Bengal Secret Consultations 1 March 1771.

19 IOR: P/A/11 Bengal Secret Consultations 30 March 1771.

20 *ibid.*

21 Heber, Reginald, Bishop of Calcutta, *Narrative of a Journey through the Upper Provinces of India, from Calcutta to Bombay, 1824-1825,* John Murray, London, 1828.

22 Warren Hastings came to India as a young Writer in 1750 and rose to become one of the Company's most able administrators, appointed in 1772 to be Governor-General of Bengal.

23 Treaty of Fyzabad 7 September 1773. See Aitchison, C.U., *Treaties, Engagements and Sanads,* vol. 2, Govt of India, Calcutta, 1930.

24 Tennant, Revd William, *Indian Recreations, Consisting Chiefly of Strictures on the Domestic and Rural Economy of the Mahomedans and Hindoos,* Longman, London, 1804.

25 A document of the 2nd Regiment, Bengal Infantry, lists the men who took part in the battle on St George's Day 1774 when the Rohillas were defeated at Babul-Nullah and their chief killed. The Nawab had promised bounty money to the brigade who had come to his assistance; the whole sum amounted to £131,250 but it was not paid until fifteen years later. The names of the men, captains, ensigns, cadets and rank-and-file are listed company by company. The men who were too sick to fight the battle were housed, in the absence of hospital buildings, in two boats, moored off Cawnpore (privately owned, now at NAM).

26 Beresford Lovett, Major-General, CB, *When and Why Did We First Take Delhi*, United Service Club, Delhi, 1899, quotes Thorn, Major, *A Memoir of the War in India . . . conducted by General Lord Lake . . . and Major General Sir Arthur Wellesley . . . from its commencement in 1803 to its termination in 1806* (no publisher given), London 1818.

27 IOR: P/2/38 Bengal Public Consultations 24 August 1780.

28 Hodges, William, *Travels in India, 1780-83*, Edwardes, London, 1793.

29 NAI : Home Dept Public 15 May 1780 no. 6.

30 NAI: Home Dept Public 20 April 1780 no. 6.

31 NAI: Home Dept Public 12 June 1784 no. 27.

32 NAI: Home Dept Public 2 August 1784 no. 21.

33 Forbes, James, *Oriental Memoirs, selected and abridged from a series of familiar letters written during seventeen years' residence in India . . .* White, Cochrane, London, 1813.

34 Tennant, *op. cit.*

35 Letter from Surgeon John Stewart to his brother William, dated 6 February 1756, Cawnpore (private collection). John Stewart, born 1756, apprenticed to Dr Graham of Stirling 1773, sailed for India on the East Indiaman *Mount Stewart*, 1778, as surgeon's mate. Died in South India (Trichanopoly?) 1794. The first member of the Stewart family, later associated with the Harness and Saddlery Factory at Cawnpore, to come to India.

36 Anglesey, Marquess of (ed.), *Sergeant Pearson's Memoirs*, Cape, London, 1968.

37 Letter from Surgeon John Stewart (private collection).

38 It is important, when considering the morals and manners of eighteenth-century Europeans in India, to compare them with those of their contemporaries in England. The zenana system was merely a copy, adapted to the circumstances of life in India, of what went on in fashionable Georgian England. The penal laws of the time were brutal. See, for example, *The Annual Register* of 1770. People were executed in public at Tyburn for theft. Horse stealing and sheep stealing carried capital convictions. Convicts were transported and often branded.

39 IOR: N/1/2 Ecclesiastical Records 1780.

40 IOR: P/2/38 Bengal Public Consultations 24 August 1780.

41 Atkinson, E.T., *United Provinces District Gazetteer, Cawnpore*, vol. 6, 1874.

42 NAI: Foreign Dept Secret 15 February 1781 no. 3. Nabob Vizier to Rajah Gobind Ram.

43 IOR: P/A/11, Bengal Secret Consultations 30 July 1771 no. 90.

44 Luce, Gay Gaer, *Body Time,* Temple Smith, London, 1971.

45 Quoted in Gardner, Brian, *The East India Company,* Hart-Davis, London, 1971.

46 IOR: E/B/98-103 Court of Directors' General Correspondence.

47 CL : Milburn's *Oriental Commerce 1802-6, Advice to the Would Be Exporter.*

48 Seton Karr, W. S., *Selections from the Calcutta Gazette 1784-1797,* Military Orphan Press, Calcutta, 1864.

49 IOR: O/5/24, Biographies.

50 Tennant, *op. cit.*

51 IOR: P/4/24, Bengal Public Consultations 9 December 1793 no. 20. This may be the same John Shepherd who established a canvas manufacture at Baypoor in 1808. Carey, W. H., *The Good Old Days of Hon'ble John Company,* R. Cambray & Co., Calcutta, 1906.

52 Private papers, 24 June 1836.

53 Private papers, 6 February 1785.

54 CL: *Calcutta Gazette* 5 May 1796.

55 IOR: O/5/26, Biographies.

56 IOR: P/3/33-42, Bengal Public Consultations for material on Robert Bailie.

57 Seton Karr, *op. cit.* Military Intelligence 21 August 1788.

58 Robert Bailie died at Cawnpore 17 March 1808 and was probably buried at Kacheri Cemetery (see Yalland, Zoë, *Kacheri Cemetery, Kanpur: A Complete List of Inscriptions . . . ,* BACSA, 1985). The sale of his effects and goods by William Preston, bazaar sergeant, under instructions from Charles Elliott, the magistrate, and auctioned by Mr Honeyman, attracted a large crowd of senior officers and civilians. John Maxwell bought panes of glass 10 × 12 inches and drawing paper, Mr Sherwood a small bottle of Florence oil and some books, Mr Foley bought brandy marked RB, Colonel Mawby bought hair powder. Others who attended were Colonel Wood, Lieutenant Parlby, the Revd Mr Ward, S.G. Evans Esq. the surgeon, Captain Wheatstone, Mr Manuel, Lala Roop Loll and Dr Armstrong. IOR: L/AG Bengal Inventories 1808.

   Four years later Mr Honeyman, the auctioneer, advertised the closure of his business in the *Calcutta Morning Post* : '. . . I have this day delivered over to Bauboo Sibnarain Mozoomdar of Cawnpore, my partner in the business, the whole of the oustanding debts . . . the whole business finally closed up to this day. H. HONEYMAN. 18 January 1812.'

CHAPTER TWO

1 John Maxwell's baptism was recorded on 25 November 1762. 'The which day Mr John Maxwell the Minister had a Son baptised named John before witnesses the Reverend Professor Lumsden (his father-in-law) and Mrs Betty Innes, The Parish of New Machar, Aberdeen.' General Register Office, Edinburgh.

2 The minister, John Maxwell, was first married in 1754 to Jean Lumsden, who died in childbirth. In 1760 he married her sister Agnes (called Nancy) Lumsden. They had six daughters and two sons: Frances born 26 July 1761, John born 24 November 1762, Anne born 1 December 1763 (died 1794), Barbara born 9 December 1764, Henry born 17 February 1768 (died 1769), Agnes born 26 May 1769, Mary born 5 March 1771 and Henrietta born 29 July 1772. (From the *Thanage of Fermartyn;* there is an inaccuracy in the record – Frances is given as Francis. In John Maxwell's will he refers to his *sister* Frances. He mentions another sister, Elizabeth, but does not mention Agnes; so perhaps, like his mother, Agnes was known by the second name of Elizabeth.)

With John Maxwell the minister are buried his infant son Henry, his daughter Anne and his widow, who died at Aberdeen on 30 December 1803.

3 Anderson, P. J., *Records of Marischal College and University,* Spalding Club, 1898.

4 Alexander Burnett (senior) married Barbara Maxwell in Mrs Maxwell's house in Aberdeen on Christmas Day 1788. Mr William Duncan, writing master at Aberdeen, was one of the witnesses. It is interesting to note that the marriage was conducted by the Revd Alexander Angus whose son John Angus was later to become Commissioner of Requests, Calcutta, and was appointed by John Maxwell to be one of his executors.

Elrick House had been the home of the Burnett family for generations. The bleak granite building rises up straight and plain with the effect of a deep, mossy moat and drawbridge to the back entrance. Here among the formal beds and yew hedges is the Fassfern rose from the villa near Rome where Prince Charles Edward Stuart had lived during his years of exile. By the stream is a dovecote for 400 pigeons, one of the finest in Scotland.

5 Anderson, *op cit.*

6 IOR: L/MAR/1 84A, Maritime Records.

7 Williamson, Captain Thomas, *The East India Vade Mecum; Complete Guide to Gentlemen Intended for the Civil, Military of Naval Service of the Hon. East India Company,* Black, Parry and Kingsbury, London, 1810.

8 Details of the voyage and the arrival in Calcutta are based on three sources: (i) Twining, Thomas, *Travels in India 100 Years Ago,* edited by W. H. G. Twining, Osgood, McIlvaine, London, 1893; (ii) Kaye, J. W., *Life and Correspondence of Henry St George Tucker, late Accountant General of Bengal and Chairman of the EIC,* Bentley, London, 1854; Tucker travelled out on the same voyage as a midshipman; (iii) IOR : MAR/184A, Maritime Records. (See Appendix 9).

9 The last P & O liner to make the round voyage to the East via the Suez Canal was the S.S. *Oronsay* in 1967. A first-class passenger paid £600 for a return ticket to Bombay.

10 Hodges, *op. cit.*

11 *East India Kalendar,* 1791. Both Maxwell and Davidson are given as 'Proprietor Europe Shop'. Hope, sister of Alexander Burnett Senior married as her first husband a James Davidson, so it is possible that Alexander Davidson was related to John Maxwell.

12 BL: *India Gazette* 12 April 1790, Burney Collection.

13 'The charge at Cawnpore for half a pint of salad oil is six shillings; and, in a camp, a two pound square jar of pickles, and a pine-cheese have sold for three pounds each – an act of extravagance in the consumer which is without any excuse, the native pickles being infinitely superior to those brought from England, and the Hissar cheeses of far better quality than the importations which are always either dry or rancid,' Roberts, Emma, *Scenes and Characteristics of Hindostan: Sketches of Anglo-Indian Society*, London, 1835.

   Pine cheese is the shortened version of pineapple cheese, a variety of Cheddar cured in net bags that mould the cheese into the shape of a pineapple. Pineapples were a novelty in England – there is mention of one from Barbados being presented to King Charles II in 1661 – and by the eighteenth century it was fashionable to have artefacts made in the shape of pineapples. (Information kindly supplied by Maggie Black, adviser to Paxton and Whitfield Cheese Club.)

14 Seton Karr, *op. cit. Extract from Mr Hastings' Memoir* 31 May 1787.

15 A few years later this site became Hamiltons, the well-known jeweller's shop.

16 Williamson, *op. cit.*

17 Seton Karr, *op. cit.*

18 Very little is known about Agnes and it is likely she died young. The baptismal entry gives 'Agnes Isabel, daughter of Mr John Maxwell, Bookseller, born 19 February 1790 at Calcutta.' Another mention is found in a list of ship's passengers: 'Agnes Isabel Maxwell aged 3 years 4 months, passenger on the *Ponsborne* accompanied by a native woman, Rose.' She landed at Gravesend on 5 July 1793, having sailed from Calcutta on 22 December 1792. Nothing more is heard of her but her ayah, Rose, retuned to India on the American ship *John* and John Maxwell writes on 22 April 1794 for a return of the Rs 280 he had paid into the EIC's Treasury as security against her return without expense to the Company.

19 Cotton, Sir Evan, W. Newman & Co., Calcutta, 1907.

20 Barns, Margarita, *The Indian Press: A History of the Growth of Public Opinion in India,* Allen & Unwin, London, 1940.

21 Richard Wellesley, Earl of Mornington (elder brother of the illustrious Wellington, who at that time was Colonel of the 33rd Regiment on the Madras establishment), took up his appointment at the age of thirty-seven. The threats posed by Napoleon's armies and the influence of the French in India gave him the excuse to conduct a policy which was both aggressive and expansionist. He set out to accomplish 'all my grand financial, political, military, naval, commercial, architectural, judicial, political reforms, and to make up a large treasure . . .' To succeed in his ambition and perform what he saw to be his public duty, he felt compelled 'to entrench myself within forms and ceremonies, to introduce much state into the whole appearance of my establishments and household, to expel all approaches of familiarity and to exercise my authority with a degree of vigour and strictness nearly amounting to severity.' Gardner, Brian, *The East India Company,* Hart-Davis, London, 1971.

22 BL: *India Gazette* 14 June 1798, Burney Collection.

23 Barns, *op. cit.*

24 IOR : P/5/4 Bengal Public Consultations 20 May 1793 no. 24.

CHAPTER THREE

1 'After a period of some twelve years, during which there was not even a titular Emperor at Delhi, the wandering heir [Shah Alam II] obtained a sort of restoration in 1771. But he was a complete dependent, at first of the Mahrattas, afterwards of a perfidious Persian Minister, until 1788, when he was blinded by a Muslim adventurer, Gulam Kadir, and afterwards held in honourable confinement by Sindhia and his European subordinates until they were driven out in 1803 by the British'. Rai Bahadur Ram Narain, MLA. *Period of Great Anarchy*. Citizen's Press, Cawnpore, 29 April 1950.

2 Forbes, *op. cit.*

3 Roberts, Field-Marshal Lord, *Forty One Years in India,* Macmillan, London, 1900, quotes Lord Wellesley, writing in 1801.

4 Henry Wellesley had accompanied the Governor-General to India as his personal assistant, He was not a servant of the Company, but such was the power of the Wellesleys that even this appointment, arrogant as it seemed, was eventually accepted by the Board of Directors in London.

5 Mr Abraham Welland joined the EIC as Writer in 1781. From the post of assistant in the Import Warehouse his career advanced in typical manner: second assistant, first assistant to the Collector of Shahabad, and in 1793 Collector of Shahabad. His last appointment before coming to Cawnpore was Judge and Magistrate of Jaunpore which he had held since October 1795. IOR: Dodwell and Miles, *Bengal Civil Servants 1780-1838.*

6 *Cawnpore Gazetteer,* vol. 6, *op. cit.*

7 Montgomery, Robert, *Statistical Account of Cawnpoor,* published by Government 1849: Welland's address to the Board of Commissioners 26 October 1802. Robert Montgomery arrived in India in 1828 aged eighteen as a Writer to the Company. After serving in the Upper Provinces at Azamgarh, Allahabad and Mirzapore, he was Collector of Cawnpore 1846-49. It was during this time that he compiled the *Statistical Account of Cawnpoor.*

8 BL: 08023 aa 7(3), Halsey, W. S., *A Report on the Question of Temporary and Permanent Settlement as Applied to the District of Cawnpore,* London (?1875). Mr Halsey, Collector of Cawnpore from 1865 to 1872, made a number of civic reforms; areas of the city still bear his name. Three main sewers were reconstructed and lined with brick and a conservancy department organised in 1866 to cart away night soil sweepings. Surseya Ghat was restored, a grain market at Collectorganj established, slaughter-houses and public latrines constructed.

9 *ibid.*

10 'Landholders' were zemindars with hereditary rights, enjoying their estates in

absolute ownership as long as they paid the government revenue . . . liable to dispossession in case of failure, by sale of their lands at public auction. Bengal Regulations VIII 1793. Wilson, H. H., *A Glossary of Judicial and Revenue Terms etc . . . of British India,* W. H. Allen & Co., EIC, 1855.

11 Montgomery, *op. cit.*

12 Doab (Dooab, Dewaub) is a Muslim word for 'the country of the two rivers' – the land that lies between the two holy rivers of the Ganges and the Jumna.

13 BL: ISUP 120 (5), Rose, H., *Report of the Settlement of Cawnpore District,* Agra, 1841, quoted by Halsey.

14 Halsey, *op. cit.*

15 *ibid.*

16 Montgomery, *op. cit.*

17 Halsey, *op. cit.*

18 Marshman, J. C., *Life and Times of Carey, Marshman and Ward,* Longman, London, 1859.

19 IOR: P/90/68 Ceded and Conquered Provinces Board of Revenue Proceedings (C P) 4 August 1803 no. 3.

20 *ibid.*

21 IOR: P/90/68 C P Revenue 11 August 1803 no. 9.

22 IOR: P/19/6 Bengal Revenue Judicial 3–31 May 1804 no. 17.

23 IOR: P/91/16 C P Revenue 25 July 1805 no. 23. Report from Colonel Nokes, Officer Commanding, Kawnpore [*sic*].

24 IOR: P/90/68 C P Revenue 22 September 1803 nos. 4 and 5.

25 IOR: P/90/16 C P Revenue 29 November 1805 no. 1.

26 CRO: Board of Trade Proceedings vol. 21, 3 January–25 March 1806 covers references to the Customs House. (See Appendix 10.)

27 *ibid.,* 25 March 1806. Translation of an *arzee* (complaint) from Gocoolchund Inderjeet and other cotton merchants.

CHAPTER FOUR

1 Deane, Mrs A., *A Tour through the Upper Provinces of Hindostan,* London, 1823.

2 Pester, Lieutenant John, *War and Sport in India 1802–1806, An Officer's Diary* (ed. J. A. Devenish), Heath, Cranton & Ouseley, London, 1913.

3 *ibid.*

4 *ibid.*

5 *ibid.*.

6 Lord Lake had served in the American and French wars. In 1800, at the age of fifty-seven, he was appointed Commander-in-Chief India, in command of the army in the north, operating against the Mahrattas. He was much loved by his men: his high standing with them derived partly from his reputation for personal bravery and partly from his evident consideration for their needs. In former campaigns the European soldiers had been obliged to sleep on the ground, but General Lake procured cots for them. He urged that the native

troops be allowed to have their packs carried for them as the Europeans did and he had great compassion for the casualties of war. After the siege of Alighur Pester returned with the General to view the scene of battle and reported: 'I never saw anyone more distressed for a moment when he entered the sortie and saw officers and men heaped on one another.'

7 Pester, *op. cit.*

8 Shipp, John, *The Path of Glory* (ed. C. J. Shanks), Chatto & Windus, London, 1969; originally published 1829.

9 *ibid.* The earliest mention of amateur theatricals at Cawnpore is in 1795 when Fireworker Sloane was killed in a duel after a quarrel at private theatricals. (Information kindly supplied by Charles Allen.)

10 'Conductors are assistants given to the commissary of the stores, to receive or deliver out stores to the army, to attend at the magazines by turns when in garrison, and to look after the ammunition wagons when in the field.' Military Dictionary, 1778.

11 Pester, *op.cit.*

12 Martyn, Revd Henry, *Journal and Letters* (ed. Revd S. Wilberforce), Seeley & Burnside, London, 1839.

13 Seton Karr, *op. cit., India Gazette.* Extract of a letter from Cawnpore, dated 14 February 1814. Colonel Tetley died in 1820, afflicted with the 'Rheumatick Gout'. He left Rs 10,000 to Chaund Bebee, mother of his three sons, and instructions for the ivory model of the 'Tajh' [*sic*], 'which cost Rs 4000/- and great trouble', to be sold carefully. In addition, he directed that '2 oyl [*sic*] paintings on copper' by Mrs Angelica Kauffmann, *Nymphs Waking of Love* and *A Sacrifice to Nature,* be left to the Nawab of Oude, 'as a small mark of the great Sence I entertain of His Excellency's condescending kindness and Friendship . . .'

14 Sherwood, Mrs, *Memoirs of Sergeant Dale,* Houlston, London, 1831.

15 Anglesey, *op. cit.*

16 *ibid.*

17 Shipp, *op. cit.*

18 *ibid.* Even as late as 1851 such executions were carried out. Private S. Willey of the 70th Surrey Regiment was 'shot' at Cawnpore on 31 May 1851. (Information kindly supplied by Raleigh Trevelyan.)

19 *ibid.*

20 'Recipe for a Fine Indigo Blue: Take indigo, soak it in water for 12 hours, grind it to a paste in a mortar, add some Terminalic citrina, pomegranate peel and alum, and mix thoroughly. Boil, put the wool into the hot bath and keep stirring till cold. Now mix in some iron filings-water and boil steadily for another two and a half hours. Wash with a beating, and dry.' Harris, H. T., *Carpet Weaving Industry of Southern India,* Madras, 1908.

21 Twining, *op. cit.*

22 No official record for the birth of Fanny Maxwell has been found but John Maxwell in his will gives 'Frances born at Aleabad in Oude on the 19th April 1803', as one of his several natural children. After her schooling in London

Fanny returned to India and in November 1821 at Cawnpore she married John Tritton, Lieutenant HM 11th Light Dragoons, by special licence from the Supreme Court. The service was taken by H. L. Williams, Chaplain of Cawnpore, and the witnesses who signed the register were Harriette Auberry, Elizabeth Grant, I. Maling and Adam Maxwell. The Trittons had associations with Cawnpore from 1804 and it is possible Fanny Maxwell and John Tritton had played together as children (see *Kacheri Cemetery, op. cit.*). Lieutenant John Tritton was the eldest son of Captain John Tritton, senior, of the 24th Dragoons who, as a widower, had married Mary Grant, natural daughter of Robert Grant, Collector of Customs Cawnpore, at Cawnpore in 1804. John Tritton, junior, joined his father's regiment January 1813, in his sixteenth year, as a cornet. Fanny Tritton died in June 1874 at Orsett Terrace, Paddington. The entry gives 'widow of John Tritton, Colonel 10th Hussars'. (Colonel Tritton's full dress uniform is on display at the National Army Museum. He fought at the siege and capture of Hattras and won medals for his part at the siege of Bhurtpore, the Battle of Sobraon and the 1842 campaign in Afghanistan.) They had four daughters and a son John, who joined Begg, Maxwell & Co. and was elected Chairman in 1863 of the recently set up Civil Municipal Committee in Cawnpore.

23 Deane, Mrs A., *op. cit.* 'As it may perhaps amuse those who have not been in India, I annexe a list of our establishment for the march. Two palankeens. Twenty-Four bearers. One *sirdah,* or head bearer, and his assistant. Two elephants with their drivers, and two attendants, one of these carried a tent. One Gig. Eight Horses. Eight grooms. Eight grass cutters for the horses. One coachman. Six *clashies,* or men to pitch tents. Three tents, with two poles in each, and double walls. Twenty coolies-(people from the bazaar, at so much per diem, to carry furniture for the tents which is all transported upon their heads.) One washerman and his family. One baker and his assistant. One *khansomer,* or house steward. Two footmen, or waiters. Two tailors, One *masalgie,* to clean knives and carry the lanthorn, go on errands etc. Two women servants. One cook and assistant. One sweeper to each tent. Seventy sheep. Thirty-five goats. Two shepherds. Nine camels. Three camel drivers. Fourteen bullocks. Five Wagons. Seven drivers. Twenty-four fowls, forty ducks, twelve geese, twelve rabbits, twelve turkeys. Two men to take care of the poultry.

'Besides the families of all these servants, with their horses, bullocks, and attendants, which may be computed upon an average of three to one, as it is customary for every individual to draw water for himself from the wells, each of them are supplied with a brass pot, called a *lota.*

'Link-boys and guides are procured at every village; so indeed are coolies, should more be required on the journey. These are relieved at the next village by others, and so on. It is also customary to apply to the head man of that village to furnish a guard for the night, which guard is paid and discharged in the morning, except a robbery is perpetrated during the night, and then (unless by *dakoity,* as they are called) the man who furnishes the guard is answerable. He also presents a kid, or a couple of fowls to you, on your arrival.'

24 Sherwood, Mrs, *A Series of Questions and Answers, Illustrative of the Church Catechism*. Houlston, Wellington, Salop, 1822.

25 Martyn, *op. cit*. In the *Journal* Martyn gives only 'Mr M. . .', but it seems likely that it was John Maxwell, son of a Minister of the Reformed Church of Scotland who was interested in discussing 'eternal things'. The Minister's predecessor at New Machar (for fifteen years) had been Thomas Reid, the famous metaphysician, and the founder of the common-sense school of Scottish philosophy.

26 Harvey Darton, E. J. (ed.), *Life and Times of Mrs Sherwood 1775–1851*, Wells Gardner, London, 1910.

27 *ibid*.

28 Sherwood, *op. cit*.

29 IOR: P/90/60 C P Revenue 13 July 1807 no. 11.

30 IOR: P/90/61 C P Revenue 15 August 1807 no. 22.

31 ARO: NWP/Sudder Board of Revenue 3 September 1814.

32 IOR: L/AG Bengal Wills 1780–1866 (see Appendix 2).

33 IOR: L/AG Bengal Inventories 1817, 1818 and 1822.

34 'Died at Cawnpore Friday 26th April 1831. Mr Joseph Samson, aged 41 years 6 months. For many years a resident of that place. He built the Roman Catholic Chapel at that Station and leaves behind a disconsolate widow.' *Government Gazette*.

35 IOR: L/AG Bengal Inventories 1817, 1818, 1822.

36 A tremendous number of religious festivals were held by both Hindus and Muslims throughout the year, and these public holidays were observed and enjoyed by everyone. The Customs House records include a reference to decking out the landing-stage with flags at the time of Dussera and until the last days of the Raj many Europeans celebrated the festival of Divali, enjoying the ritual of lighting their bungalows and compounds with *chirags*.

37 Hodges, *op. cit*.

38 Forbes, *op. cit*.

39 Nugent, Lady, *East India Journal*, privately printed, London, 1839.

40 Keene, H. G., *Servant of John Company*, Thacker Spink & Co., Calcutta, 1897.

41 IOR: P/92/15 C P Revenue 24 May 1813 no. 18.

42 Law-abiding civilians have left few records; it is the trouble-makers, men such as William Kelly, James Duhan and Thomas Tolly who came up against the authorities, whose stories can be found in the Bengal Criminal and Judicial Consultations; and O/5/25, Biographies.

43 IOR: P/91/18 C P Revenue 3 February 1818 no. 35.

44 IOR: P/92/24 C P Revenue 9 February 1814 no. 15. Tolly, in testifying against James Duhan, is described as a native of India who used to be a purser of a ship and had served Jamaica rum to sailors in the West Indies . . . (IOR: P/131/3 Bengal Criminal and Judicial Consultations 19 September 1812 no. 64.)

45 IOR: P/92/24 C P Revenue 9 February 1814 no. 15.

46 IOR: P/131/18 Bengal Criminal and Judicial Consultations 12 June 1813 nos. 68 and 70.

47 IOR: P/131/3 Bengal Criminal and Judicial Consultations 19 September 1812 no. 64.

48 James Duhan died at Lucknow in 1833. He was so heavily in debt, his property mortgaged to the Shroff Beharry Loll, that his young widow could hardly defray the funeral expenses. Dr Campbell and Dr Stevenson raised a subscription for her benefit. The firm of Duhan & Co., however, continued. In 1839 they advertised in the *Government Gazette,* 'A general stock of Eatables and Drinkables, for which orders will be faithfully executed with punctuality and dispatch'.

49 IOR: P/92/15 C P Revenue 24 May 1813 no. 18.

50 *ibid.*

51 The clash of authority between the Collector, jealous for his revenue and humane with the people he comes in contact with, and the General Commanding Cantonments, jealous for his men and his own prestige, is illustrated by the correspondence in IOR: P/91/57 C P Revenue Proceedings 28 June 1811 no. 32. It consists of some twenty-six letters written from the Collector, the Magistrate, the Brigade Major on behalf of the CO, the CO himself, the Board of Commissioners, the Commander-in-Chief, Secretary Dowdeswell and the unfortunate Daniel Clarke. Daniel O'Brien Clarke, born in Cork, Ireland, in 1797, son of Lawrence Clarke and Mary his wife (niece of Oliver Goldsmith), came to India as a young child. The family settled at Cawnpore until the row over the liquor shop drove them away. He died at Stirling Castle, Simla in 1858 and was described as a schoolmaster of sixty-one years, (Yalland, Zoë, *Guide to the Kacheri Cemetery and the Early History of Kanpur,* BACSA, 1983).

52 IOR: P/91/58 C P Revenue 30 July 1811 no. 23.

53 At the end of the Mahratta War the Peishwa of Poona, Bajee Rao, surrendered to Sir John Malcolm. In return he was offered a pension of £80,000 a year and was settled in exile at the holy spot, Bithoor (see page 203).

54 IOR: L/AG Bengal Wills 1780-1866.

55 Richard Nann was born in India in 1764 and set up shop at Calcutta in 1789 as a jeweller and engraver. Later he went up-country and settled at Cawnpore where his son John was born in 1799. He died at Delhi in 1807 and appears in the Ecclesiastical Records as 'Merchant of Agra'. It seems he was not successful as a silversmith and turned to general trading. Among his effects were '3 pairs of Cawnpore boots, 3 Cawnpore saddles with bridles complete, French claret and madeira, sugar candy wrapped in cloth, ½ Bottle of snuff, 5 pairs of spurs, 6 Umbrellas, Currie [*sic*] dishes, a Bow for arrows, Lavender Water and a painting box'. IOR: L/AG Bengal Inventories 1807, 1808.

56 Roberts, Emma, *op. cit.*

57 IOR: L/AG Bengal Inventories 1817, 1818, 1822.

58 A rice slop with small pieces of meat in it, a great favourite for nursery meals.

59 Harvey Darton, *op. cit.*

60 Dated Cawnpore 4 November 1816, addressed to 'Miss F Maxwell jun in Miss Currie's care'. A copy of the original, now believed lost, in the possession of the Maxwell family (see Appendix 1).

61 Kelly, Sophia (ed.), *Autobiography of Mrs Sherwood,* Darton, London, 1854.

62 *ibid.*

63 CL: *Government Gazette* 4 July 1831 Monday Evening. A list of drugs which appeared in an advertisement of J. Melhuish, Chemist and Druggist, Cawnpore.

64 Seton Karr, *op. cit.:* 'Advertisement. Medical Case. Thomas Martin Assistant Surgeon 2nd Battalion Artillery in defence of his professional skill.' 15 October 1789.

65 CC: De Wend, Captain J., 44th Regiment, personal papers.

66 Sherwood, *op.cit.,* gives details of home nursing.

67 A coat of arms often placed on monuments or coffins. (Information kindly supplied by Dr James Stevens Curl.)

68 Seton Karr, *op. cit.:* 'Joseph Dickson, Undertaker, Carpenter, Cabinet and Coachmaker of 41, Cossitollah near the Lall Bazar.'

69 His date of birth is incorrectly carved on the tombstone: it was 24 November 1762.

70 IOR: L/AG Bengal Wills 1780–1866.

71 IOR: L/AG Bengal Inventories 1817, 1818, 1822.

CHAPTER FIVE

1 Malcolm, Sir John, *Memoir of Central India,* Routledge, London, 1922. Sir John Malcolm was the sixteenth child of a Scottish sheep-farming family who left home at the age of twelve to join the EIC's forces as ensign. He rose to become, over a period of forty-seven years, a diplomat, statesman and administrator, friend of Wellesley and Wellington, and a renowned Persian scholar. He also founded the Oriental Club in London. His greatest gift was his humanity in relationships and his insistence on 'accessibility to all'. See Pasley, Rodney, *Send Malcolm: The Life of Major-General Sir John Malcolm 1769-1833,* BACSA, London, 1982.

2 Sleeman, Sir W. H., *Journey through the Kingdom of Oude,* Bentley, London, 1858. Sleeman's name is associated with work on the suppression of thugee. He was Resident at the Court of Oude, Lucknow, from 1849 to 1856.

3 George Ravenscroft was born in Bombay, the eldest son of Edward Ravenscroft, Senior Merchant of the Bombay Civil Service, and Frances his wife, who as Frances Rivett had accompanied her sister Mrs Elizabeth Carnac to Bombay. General John Carnac, his uncle in marriage, left him £500 in his will. He was educated at Charterhouse (London) and Christ Church, Oxford, and joined the Bengal Civil Service in 1795.

4 Louisa Benedicta Ravenscroft was the daughter of Henry Ramus, a Calcutta judge, and his wife Johanna, daughter of the late Dutch Governor at Chinsurah. Louisa married George Ravenscroft in Calcutta in 1801, where they had several children. Their younger daughter, Emma Jemima, became Lady Hereford. The Ramus family had connections with the Court of King George II. Louisa's aunt was the beautiful Benedetta Ramus, painted by Gainsborough and Romney. Louisa died

4 January 1818 aged thirty-three and is buried at the Kacheri Cemetery (see *Kacheri Guide, op.cit.*).

5 Halsey, *op. cit.*

6 IOR: P/92/21 C P Revenue 31 December 1813 no. 21.

7 IOR: P/92/23 C P Revenue 14 January 1814 no. 4.

8 Charlotte Fitzgerald became the second wife of George Ravenscroft on 16 June 1820. The ceremony was solemnised by special licence before the Collector, Robert Grant, and his wife Elizabeth, and conducted by the Revd H. L. Williams. Charlotte was the daughter of Colonel Martin Fitzgerald and his wife Barbara; her brother John was born in Cawnpore in 1796.

9 IOR: P/59/30 Bengal Revenue Consultations 6 December 1822 no. 101.

10 In all probability this was one of the portraits of the Duke of Wellington painted by Robert Home. Born in Hull, Home arrived in India in 1791 and worked in Madras and Calcutta. Eventually he travelled up-country to Lucknow where for eleven years he was Court Painter to the King of Oude. On the death of the King, Robert Home retired to Cawnpore. Emma Roberts records that '. . . he kept up a handsome establishment . . . and had been wont to exercise the most extensive hospitality to the residents of the station.' He died in 1834 at the age of eighty-two and was buried in Kacheri Cemetery. Some of Robert Home's paintings can be seen at the Victoria Memorial, Calcutta, while portaits of Richard Wellesley, the Governor-General, and his brother Arthur, the Duke of Wellington, hang in Rashtrapati Bhavan, New Delhi.

11 IOR: P/59/30 Bengal Revenue Consultations 6 December 1822 no. 52.

12 Richard Foley died 3 August 1827 (see *Kacheri Guide, op.cit.*)

13 IOR: P/59/30 Bengal Revenue Consultations 6 December 1822 no. 55.

14 IOR: P/59/30 Bengal Revenue Consultations 6 December 1822 no. 57.

15 The indigo factory was situated at Mendhi Ghat, an idyllic position overlooking the river. Years later, Fanny Maxwell, then Aunt Tritton, suggested Mendhi Ghat as a perfect spot for a honeymoon at a Maxwell wedding at Cawnpore in 1870.

16 IOR: P/59/30 Bengal Revenue Consultations 6 December 1822 no. 82.

17 IOR: P/59/30 Bengal Revenue Consultations 6 December 1822 no. 88.

18 IOR: P/59/30 Bengal Revenue Consultations 6 December 1822 no. 81.

19 IOR: P/59/30 Bengal Revenue Consultations 6 December 1822 no. 87.

20 Mr John Jones, agent of the River Insurance Co., Cawnpore, died of acute rheumatism 10 March 1825 (see *Kacheri Guide, op. cit.*)

21 IOR: P/92/21 C P Revenue 31 December 1813 no. 19. An advertisement in the *Government Gazette* dated 6 August 1821 suggests that the furore over Ravenscroft's ruin had been too much for Mr Hay. 'John Hay begs to announce . . . that owing to severe indisposition it is his determination to bring his Mercantile Concerns to a close on 30 December 1821.' This was followed on 25 March 1822 with a further announcement complaining that he was prevented from leaving India on account of collecting outstanding balances owed to him but that he was intent on retiring to Europe as he was old and infirm and had been in business for forty years. He never reached Europe but died at Vepery, Madras on 24 March 1825 aged sixty-four. 'He had taken his passage on board the *Circassia* with the intention of passing his last days in his native country . . . on the ship arriving at Madras he gave up his passage.'

. . He died but a few days later, leaving behind him a daughter surrounded by strangers.' However, other members of his family continued the business in Cawnpore and were leading merchants at the time of the Mutiny.

22 IOR: P/59/30 Bengal Revenue Consultations 6 December 1822 no. 52.

23 Montgomery, *op.cit.*

24 NAI: Foreign Political Dept 27 September 1822 no. 37.

25 NAI: Foreign Political Dept 23 May 1823 no. 63.

26 ARO: Foreign Political Dept 31 July 1823 no. 57. Eye-witnesses' testimony at the inquest on Ravenscroft.

27 Sleeman, *op. cit.*

28 IOR: P/59/30 Bengal Revenue Consultations 6 December 1822 no. 52.

29 John Maxwell's sister Elizabeth married Mr Andrew Dunn in June 1797 at Aberdeen. Andrew Dunn was Joint Rector of the Grammar School and son of the Rector. William Duncan, Writing Master, was once again (see page 297) witness. It was their son, Robert Maxwell Dunn (or Dun), accompanied by another Writing Master, William Cleugh, who joined Alexander Burnett in Cawnpore.

On 31 December 1821, Alexander Burnett's interest in Maxwell and Burnett ceased and the firm became Maxwell & Co. However, exactly a year later the position was reversed, and announced in the papers on 31 December 1822: 'The interest of Mr Adam Maxwell in the concern Maxwell & Co. has ceased, the business will hereafter be conducted by Mr Alexander Burnett, Mr Maxwell Robert Dun [*sic*] and Mr William Cleugh, under the style and firm of Burnett & Co.'

30 IOR: Mss Eur. D 279.

31 IOR: L/AG Bengal Wills 1780-1866 (Burnett's will drawn up in 1825).

32 IOR: P/60/17 Bengal Revenue Consultations 24 September 1824 no. 68. The Collector, Mr J. Wemyss, forwarded a report of the Jajmau Distillery made by Mukhan Loll *Darogah:* 'On the 18 July we were permitted to enter the Distillery for the purpose of counting and taking account of some Pipes of Rum said to contain 5827 Gallons which arrived in Boats from Coelah Ghaut, when we took the opportunity of endeavouring to ascertain if there were any stills, copper, Casks or other utensils or materials. We saw stills, a number of Pipes with some thousand Maunds of Firewood. Burnett and Co's people informed us that to the end of 1223 *Fussily,* Rum was manufactured at Jaujmao, but from 1224 FS none was made, but the Contractor had it made at Coelah Ghaut, and had it brought down to this place, the old Distillery at Jaujmao, where it was re-manufactured and coloured by adding sugar, and afterwards delivered to the Commissariat . . .'

33 Montgomery, *op. cit.,* quoting from Reade's report.

34 Burnett & Co.'s crash was followed by the failure of Fortier & Dubois at Najafgarh, whose debt to Alexander & Co., the Calcutta Agents, was said to have exceeded 26 lakhs. The indigo estate at Najafgarh had an interesting history. The *jagir* originally belonged to the sisters of Najaf Khan, an Amil under the Oude Government. They leased it to Claude Martin for Rs 12,000 who built a large indigo factory there – he had 330 vats in 13 villages and 23 wells. His nephew succeeded him and then the estate passed to Fortier & Dubois. Later a Mr Vincent farmed it for twelve years and at the time of the Mutiny it was worked by the Greenways. *Cawnpore Gazetteer,* F. M. Wright, 1881.

35 ARO: Board of Revenue Consultations 10 February 1827 nos. 11-15. Details of the crash.

36 *ibid.*

37 *ibid.*

38 IOR: Mss Eur. D 279.

39 IOR: L/AG Bengal Inventories 1829.

40 *India Gazette,* 2 December 1839, editorial on indigo planters.

41 Churcher, Emery J., *Some Reminiscences of Three-Quarters of a Century in India,* Luzac, London, 1909. This is the same Emery Churcher whose name headed the list of Directors in the Board Room of the Muir Mills Cawnpore and whose sister Ann Elizabeth married John Maxwell's youngest son, James.

42 IOR: P/96/59 Bengal Sudder Board of Revenue 12 October 1832 nos. 63-74. The long wrangle between Mr Reade, trying to bring Adam Maxwell to justice, and Adam Maxwell, trying to outwit him, can be followed in detail.

43-46 *ibid.*

47 ARO: NWP Sudder Board of Revenue 9 September 1839 no. 68. Adam Maxwell never married but a daughter Sophia Maria was born 1 January 1816 – only a few days after the death of John Maxwell. She married Edward Trant Spry, interpreter and quarter master, 24th Regiment Native Infantry at Cawnpore in 1830.

48 IOR: L/AG Bengal Inventories 1824.

CHAPTER SIX

1 Roberts, Emma, *op. cit.*

2 Lowe, Lieutenant, *Diary of an Officer of the 16th Lancers,* privately published (at Home Headquarters, 16th/5th The Queen's Royal Lancers). Lowe uses a capital letter followed by a dash for people's names; where it has been possible to check, it would appear that the initial is correct.

3 *ibid.*

4 Hastings, Marquess of, *Private Journal of the Marquess of Hastings,* edited by his daughter, the Marchioness of Bute, Allahabad, 1907. On the death of Robert Grant this announcement appeared in the *Government Gazette:* 'Died on 21st April 1830 at Massooree [*sic*] Robert Grant Esq, one of the oldest Civil Servants in Bengal . . . many years Collector of Customs at Cawnpore where his hospitality will long be remembered.'

5 To keep them out of mischief boys were encouraged to join up very young. On 4 June 1822 George Thorpe, aged twelve, and William Atkinson, aged nine, of Cawnpore entered the 1st Battalion Light Company 1st Native Infantry as drummers (Samuel Maltby mss, privately owned).

6 CRO: Committee of Public Education General Dept 1 October 1822 – 20 September 1826. Details of the Free School quarrel, the letters, reports and minutes of meetings.

7-14 *ibid.*

15 Heber, *op. cit.*

16 Parks, Mrs Fanny, *Wanderings of a Pilgrim in Search of the Picturesque,* Richardson, London, 1850.

17 Ashmore, Mrs Harriette, *Narrative of a Three Months' March in India; and a Residence in the Dooab; by the wife of an officer of the 16th Foot,* Hastings, London, 1841.

18 IOR: P/214/32 28 October 1837 no. 15. Report from Colonel Pollock, President of the Committee, Relief Society, Cawnpore.

19 Bundelas are the people from Bundelkhand, a branch of Rajputs settled in the province of Allahabad since the thirteenth century. This description was given to Fanny Parks by Lieutenant Lowe and quoted in *Wanderings of a Pilgrim in Search of the Picturesque.*

20 During the siege of Wheeler's entrenchment the Nana Sahib camped close by the Savada Koti where he held a number of Europeans prisoner. It was from the Savada Koti – the yellow house – that the fateful letter offering terms to General Wheeler of a safe passage to Allahabad was carried – some say by old Mrs Greenway, others by Mrs Jacobi.

21 A wall or two of the original Free School building are incorporated in the fabric of Christ Church School which is at present an intermediate college.

22 Roberts, Emma, *op. cit.* 'Persons newly arrived from England or Calcutta, may deem Cawnpore a semi-barbarous place, since wolves stray into the compounds, and there are bungalows in which the doors, destitute of locks or handles, will not shut: but the arrivals from out-stations, dwellers in the jungle, companions of bears and beasts (biped and quadruped), look upon it as an earthly paradise.'

23 Eden, Emily, *Up the Country: Letters Written from the Upper Provinces of India,* Richard Bentley, London, 1866.

24 *ibid.*

25 *ibid.*

26 Parks, *op. cit.*

27 Eden, *op. cit.*

28 Dunbar, Janet, *Golden Interlude: The Edens in India 1836-1842,* John Murray, London, 1955.

29 The Nawab of Oude, Ghazi ud din Haidar, had the title of King of Oude conferred on him in 1819.

30 Dunbar, *op. cit.*

31 Eden, *op. cit.*

32 *ibid.*

33 *ibid.*

CHAPTER SEVEN

1 Montgomery, *op.cit.*

2 Roberts, Emma, *op. cit.*

3 *ibid.*

4 Roberts, Emma, *Oriental Scenes: Dramatic Sketches and Tales with Other Poems,* Grant, Calcutta, 1830.

5 Roberts, Emma, *op. cit.* Emma Roberts was born in 1794, a daughter of Captain Roberts who served in the Russian Army. She accompanied her married sister to India in 1828 and spent two years in the Upper Provinces, staying at Agra, Etawah and Cawnpore. She was at Cawnpore for the opening of the Theatre for which she composed the prologue. This appears in a book of poems. Articles she wrote for the *Asiatic Journal* were republished in book form as *Scenes and Characteristics of Hindostan.* She died at Poona in 1840.

6 Letter from Lieutenant C. Beaumont Johnson, dated 2 June 1845, Cawnpore (privately owned) to Lady Johnson, his mother, 5 Cavendish Place, Bath.

7 Roberts, Emma, *op. cit.*

8 Parks, *op. cit.* Mrs Fanny Parks came out to India in 1822 as the wife of a Bengal Civil Servant (Charles Crawford Parks BCS, 1817–46). She had enormous energy and intense curiosity for everything about her and for twenty years she recorded in her journal every detail that interested her. In 1830 her husband was posted to Cawnpore as Collector of Customs and the house they rented, overlooking the river, is now the residence of the District Magistrate and historically important for Kanpur.

9 Roberts, Emma, *op. cit.* It would seem the Library referred to by Henry Martyn had ceased to exist (see page 100).

10 Johnson, *op. cit.*

11 Letter from Mrs Emma Bond dated 6 December 1838, Cawnpore, to her father, Major-General Sir T. Anbury KCB at Saugor (privately owned).

12 Roberts, Emma, *op. cit.*

13 Lowe, *op. cit.* (see page 308, note 2).

14 IOR: *Parliamentary Papers 1831-1832,* Langford Kennedy Esq. MP. Minutes of Evidence before the Select Committee.

15 Westcott, Revd, G. H. *Guide to Cawnpore,* SPG, Cawnpore, 1892.

16 Martyn, *op. cit.*

17 *Story of the Cawnpore Church Mission,* SPG, Westminster (London), 1909. Details of Henry Martyn's school given by Mrs Sherwood.

18 *ibid.*

19 Martyn, *op. cit.*

20 *ibid.* After a year preaching in Persia, Henry Martyn set out to return to England but at Tocat on 16 December 1812 he died, either from plague or the consumption which had previously troubled him. He was only thirty-two.

21 Ashmore, *op. cit.*

22 Captain Robert Smith was a Field Engineer and became ADC to Sir George Nugent, the Commander-in-Chief, whom he accompanied to Cawnpore. He also described and sketched Cawnpore in his *Pictorial Journal of Travels in Hindustan from 1828 to 1833* (Victoria and Albert Museum). He repaired various Indian monuments, including the Kutb Minar and the Juma Musjid at Delhi. Archer, Dr Mildred, *British Drawings in the India Office Library,* HMSO, London, 1969.

23 IOR: P/214/25 Agra General Proceedings, 5 August 1835-1836. Details of the acrimonious correspondence between the Bishop of Calcutta and the Commanding Officers at Cawnpore.

24–27 *ibid.*

28 Bateman, Josiah, *The Life of the Right Reverend Daniel Wilson, Bishop of Calcutta,* John Murray, London, 1860.

29 *ibid.*

CHAPTER EIGHT

1 Lord William Bentinck, Lieutenant-General and Colonel of the 11th Light Dragoons, was the second son of the Duke of Portland, a Whig Prime Minister. He had previously been Governor of Madras, in which post he succeeded Clive's son. After the mutiny at Vellore in 1806 the Company, while complimenting Bentinck on his zeal, found it expendient to remove him from office. However, two years later his reputation was vindicated when he was appointed Governor-General with a directive to cut expenditure.

His term of office, 1826-1835, was a time of humanitarian reforms: the suppression of the age-long Hindu customs of suttee, thugee, child marriage and female infanticide, and the introduction of schools and colleges to teach English – Bentinck was convinced that the English language was the key to all improvements. It replaced Persian as the official language and attempts were made to westernise society. Communications were improved and the great highway of the Grand Trunk Road was begun.

2 Gardner, Brian, *op. cit.* Macaulay quoted by Gardner.

3 Parbury, George, *Handbook for India,* W. H. Allen, London, 1841. Parbury quoted by Rai Bahadur Ram Narain, *op. cit.*

4 Diver, Maud, *The Unsung: British Services in India,* Wm Blackwood, Edinburgh, 1945. Kipling quoted by Diver.

5 Montgomery, Brian, *A Field Marshal in the Family.* Constable, London, 1973, quoting a letter to Robert Montgomery from his father.

6 There is a copy of this in the London Library which once belonged to H. St G. Tucker – the man who travelled on the *William Pitt* with John Maxwell. It is dated 1850 and was presented to the London Library in 1875. All through the book Tucker has pencilled in meticulously observed comments, picking holes and debunking at every opportunity. It would seem Montgomery was not greatly liked. On the front page Tucker wrote: 'Then I beheld all the work of God that is done under the sun; because though a man *labor* to seek it out, yet he shall not find it; yea, further. though a wise man *think* to know it, yet shall he *not be able to find it.* Ecclesiastes 8. v.17.'

7 BL: I SUP 147: Montgomery, Robert, Report on (i) The Grand Trunk Road and (ii) Thugee. The statistics of the road traffic at Cawnpore were collected by Robert Montgomery while Collector of Cawnpore. Here, at the Collector's bungalow at Nawabganj, his second son was born, who was to become Bishop Montgomery and the father of Field-Marshal Montgomery.

8 The thugs were a secret society of religious fanatics who killed and plundered their victims in honour of their goddess Bhagwan. The temple of Bhawani at Bindachun, four miles above Mirzapore, was the place where thugs met to take their vows (Parks, *op. cit.*) .

9 Grant, James, *Cassell's History of India,* Cassell, London, no date.

10 Thimble rigging is stick and garter. 'It consists of rolling up a doubled strap, the player putting a stick between any two of its convolutions, and when the ends of the strap are pulled, it unrolls, and either comes away altogether, or is held at the double by the stick, and this decides whether the player loses or wins' (Parks, *op. cit.*).

11 Fitchett, Revd W. H., *The Cornhill Magazine,* vol. 10, 1901.

12 Diver, *op. cit.*

13 IOR: P/222/58 NWP Sudder Board of Revenue 1 October 1839 nos. 68, 69.

14 Benjamin Leonard Jones, referred to in the family as John Jones, was a captain of an East Indiaman, who settled in Calcutta where he was joined by two brothers James and David, both merchants. In 1791 at his marriage to Anne Hall, a girl of fifteen, he is described as 'in the Marine Service of the East India Company, Bengal Establishment'. Shortly after the birth of his only son, John Benjamin Jones (JBJ), in 1794 he was lost at sea, presumed drowned in the treacherous Sunderbands. Anne Jones, aged only twenty, 'widow of Benjamin Leonard Jones late Master in the Pilot Service prays to receive a pension'. She was granted Rs 20/-pm on 27 May 1796.

Anne Jones was the daughter of an Englishman, Captain Hall, commander of an East Indiaman, who on one of his voyages to India married at Lisbon a Portuguese lady, Isabella Roderiques, and brought her to live in Calcutta. When Anne Jones was left a young widow she soon remarried and the care and upbringing of JBJ became the responsibility of Mrs Hall who lived in Serampore, a small Danish settlement sixteen miles above Calcutta on the other bank of the Hooghly River. The man Anne Jones married in 1798 was an older man, James Feetenby (sometimes spelt Feetonby) who was probably a cabinet-maker, prosperous and well established at Calcutta. They had a number of children all of whom died young. One son, James Mark, was accidentally killed by a musket ball in 1808 when he was six years old, perhaps in a shooting accident: a number of accidental deaths were recorded at this time, caused by people shooting at crows from their roof tops. Feetenby died in 1809 and was buried at South Park Street Cemetery. In his will he made provision for the native woman, mother of his daughter Mary, born only seven months after his marriage to Anne Jones – an indication, perhaps, of the open acceptance of the moral issues of those times.

On Feetenby's death, Anne (Jones) Feetenby, left with a sickly child, was married in 1813 for the third time to James Brown Moore, a pensioner in the EIC Marine Service and a merchant. An unfortunate mutual antipathy developed between Moore and his stepson JBJ. When Moore died, in a gesture of ill-will he left his considerable property away from JBJ, but made a bequest of Rs 500 to Sarah Anne de Rosario, 'the woman who suckled Mr John Benjamin Jones'.

15 When the first missionaries came to Calcutta the official attitude to them was so inimical that they were able to remain in India only by taking up residence at Serampore, which, being Danish, was outside the jurisdiction of the EIC. In 1801 Joshua Marshman and William Carey opened a boarding school for English and Anglo-Indian children, both boys and girls. 'Mission House School. Serampore. 1st May 1801. A School will be opened at this House, which stands in a very healthy and pleasant situation by the side of the river. Terms including board and washing, per month. Reading, Writing, Arithmetic, Bookkeeping, Geography etc Sa Rs 30/- Latin, Greek. Hebrew, Persian and Sanscrit 35/-. Regular attention will be paid to

the correct pronunciation of the English language. A Persian and Sanscrit Moonshi will be employed. Letters addressed to Mr Carey will be immediately attended to.' (Seton Karr, *Selections from the Calcutta Gazette.*)

Marshman and Carey believed fervently in the importance of educating the Indian people and in the supreme value of the message they tried to convey. They were remarkable men, learned, inspired, self-disciplined and fiery. Among other work, they translated the scriptures into the vernaculars of India and translated into English the Indian epic of the *Ramayana;* they published the first Indian vernacular newspaper and an English-language newspaper, *The Friend of India,* as vehicles for their advanced ideas.

16 Fanny Palmer was born 1798, the daughter of John Palmer and Charlotte, née Nairing. On the death of her father she inherited considerable property in Calcutta, twelve houses and land as well.

17 Family papers privately owned.

18 Roberts, Emma, *op. cit.*

19 Born at Feetenby's house on the Circular Road, Calcutta on Tuesday 22 December 1835 at 8 a.m.

20 Wilson, Mindon, *History of the Behar Indigo Factories,* Thacker Spink, Calcutta (undated). Also known as Nunkey.

21 *ibid.*

22 *ibid.*

23 Family papers, privately owned, dated 14 September 1882, Rampur. The Peppé family were Grantees at the Birdpur Estate in the Gorakhpore District, This was a grant of waste land given over by Government in a scheme to clear jungle and swamp and bring the land under cultivation. It had been held under warrant by a member of the Peppé family from 1840. The condition of the warrant was that the jungle must be cleared within a certain time. It was a hazardous, expensive and difficult undertaking. After twenty-three years of anxiety, labour and trial of all kinds, and having sunk all the family's capital without any return, the proprietor of Birdpur found himself just free of debt.

24 Wilson, *op. cit.*

25 *ibid.*

26 Roberts, Emma, *op. cit.*

27 Wilson, *op. cit.*

28 An incident that occured in the early life of our father illustrates his intrepidity and the extraordinary peculiarity of the native character. Our father when quite a young man saw a native struggling for his life in a river in Tirhoot. He instantly threw off his coat and swam out to the rescue just managing to reach him as he was sinking. With great difficulty and at much risk of his own life he succeeded in landing him, but the poor fellow was so exhausted that he succumbed shortly after reaching shore. The villagers, to evince their gratitude accused him having drowned the man and brought a charge against him of murder. The charge naturally failed and our father was acquitted and commended by the judge for his courage and humanity. (Family papers, privately owned.)

29 *ibid.*

30 For two or three years JBJ was editor of the *Benares Recorder.* In his leisure time he worked on a contemporary history of the times of Maharaja Ranjit Singh, the Lion

of Lahore, but the unpublished manuscript was destroyed in the Mutiny. Finally JBJ joined the Department of Public Works as Executive Engineer, Allahabad, where he died in 1851.

31 Grant, *op. cit.* Details of Bajee Rao's capitulation.

32 De Wend, *op. cit.*

33 V&A: Captain Robert Smith's *Pictorial Journal.*

34 CC: Rawlins, General J. S., *The Autobiography of an Old Soldier 1843-1879*, privately printed.

35 NAI: Foreign Political Department 24 April 1838 no. 12 (see Appendix 4). See also Gupta, Pratul Chandra, *The Last Peshwa and the English Commissioners 1818-1851*, Sarker & Sons, Calcutta, 1944, for good details.

36 Trevelyan, Sir George, *Cawnpore,* Macmillan, London, 1865.

37 James Purdey, gun and rifle makers, were established in 1814, later taking over the Oxford Street shop which had been the gunsmith, Manton (see 67). Purdey had many Indian customers but no actual record of guns supplied to the Nana Sahib can be traced in their ledgers. Purdey guns were available in India through Mantons and the Army and Navy Stores who were regular customers. Four Nawabs of the royal house of Oude ordered several guns and rifles in 1847, the cost varying from £45 to £63. Entries against the Nawabs' orders state 'settled by cash' so presumably the Nawabs had London agents who acted for them and perhaps placed the order in the first instance. It took twelve to eighteen months to build a gun.

Long Acre was an area of London largely inhabited by coachmakers who had been established there since 1695.

Birmingham was famous for the glass and crystal manufactured for chandeliers and in particular for the skilful patterns used in cutting the crystal into beautiful and intricate shapes and drops.

38 Lang, Lieutenant John, *Wanderings in India,* Routledge, London, 1859. Lang quoted by Trevelyan.

39 Rawlins, *op. cit.*

40 Shepherd, W. J., *A Personal Narrative of the Outbreak and Massacre at Cawnpore during the Sepoy Revolt of 1857*, privately printed, Agra, 1862. The Revd J. R. Hill, writing in the *Story of the Cawnpore Mission,* states that the son of Azimullah became a practising Christian who worked as a catechist at Banda, Karwi and Cawnpore.

41 Collier, Richard, *Sound of Fury,* Collins, London, 1963. Mrs Louisa Chalwin, wife of the veterinary surgeon of the 2nd Bengal Light Cavalry, recently arrived from Meerut, writes on 11 April 1857, 'We have had our piano returned from the tuner and I am very pleased with it and consequently every day once or twice we try over our old duets and songs' (privately owned papers).

42 Greenway Bros also advertised: 'Block Tin Dish Covers, Plate Covers, Teas of superior quality and flavour, Stationery of the newest kind, French Prunes, Candied Fruits, China Ginger, Chow Chow, Bons Bons, Cigars Nos. 1-5, Manila and Havannah shape, Sam Slick clocks, Perfumery, Shaving Brushes, Shaving Soap, Brown Windsor and Bar, Shot Powder, Gun caps, Wads, Sponges etc. Hermetically sealed Ham and Wiltshire Bacon.' Sam Slick, a wandering Yankee clockmaker, was a creation of Thomas Chandler Haliburton, the Canadian humorist and satirist (1796-1865). It seems the name Sam Slick became synonymous with a popular make of clock imported into India at this period.

43 It is interesting that Pundit Moti Lal Nehru, Nehru's father, became a member of Lodge Harmony in 1888 for one year. The craft continues to this day.

44 Tuker, Lieutenant-General Sir F. (ed.), *Chronicle of Private Henry Metcalfe of HM 32nd Regt of Foot*, Cassell, London, 1935: '1856. We arrived at Cawnpore in December and in marching into the station had the felicity of seeing that bloodthirsty scoundrel the Nana, accompanying General Wheeler, whom he subsequently betrayed and cruelly butchered at the above station. It is scarcely to be believed that the Nana accompanied the Regiment to Church on the Sunday before we left Cawnpore for Lucknow but it is a positive fact. I saw him myself riding in a beautiful phaeton drawn by two splendid grey horses.'

45 Heber, *op.cit.*

46 Zoffany's *Cockfight* was painted about 1784. It no longer exists, probably being destroyed during the fighting in Lucknow in 1857 when many of the palaces were sacked. Interesting details are given in Dr Mildred Archer's *British Portrait Painters in India 1770-1825*, Sotheby Parke Bernet, 1979.

47 Sir John Mordaunt was the natural son of the Earl of Peterborough. As a boy he was very wild, barely able to read and write. When he was sent before the Directors of the EIC to be interviewed he was accepted because of his brilliance at cribbage! In India he soon became a great favourite of the Nawab of Oude who retained him as his aide-de-camp for purposes of shooting, gambling and cockfighting. Mordaunt was a very fine shot but died in his fortieth year from a wound received in a duel. His will, written at Cawnpore in 1794, mentions a female friend, 'Bejam', and rather quaintly, seven children 'begotten on the Bodies of women Native of India'.

48 Maude, F. C. and Sherer, J. W., *Memoirs of the Mutiny*, Remington & Co., London, 1894.

49 Knighton, William, *The Private Life of an Eastern King*, ed. S.B. Smith, OUP, 1921. First published in 1855. The five English favourites were the tutor, Wright; the Librarian, Croupley; the painter and musician, Mantz; a Captain Magness and 'the hairdresser and perfumer', De Russett. Knighton based his book on detailed notes given him by a member of the King's Household, believed to have been 'the tutor'. Years later, Knighton's daughter married Dr J. H.Condon IMS, twenty-two years Brigade Surgeon at Cawnpore who joined Gavin Jones to become a founder member of the Muir Mills.

50 *ibid.*

51 *ibid.*

52 *ibid.*, quoting Sir John Shore, *Indian Affairs*, vol. 2. Shore had been Governor-General following Cornwallis in 1783.

53 NAI: Home Public Dept 1 April 1799 no. 43: Captain James Powell, Postmaster, Cawnpore.

54 Sleeman, *op. cit.*

55 NAI: Foreign Political Dept 18 April 1845 no. 90: Captain Shakespear, officiating Resident, Lucknow.

56 Unpublished journal, privately owned.

57 The Aga Mir died at Cawnpore in 1837 and is buried at the Imaumbarra on the high ground at Khalasi Lines.

58 Parks, *op. cit.*

59 Sleeman, *op. cit.* 'The salary of the prime minister, during the five years that

Roshun-od-Dowlah held the office, was twenty-five thousand rupees a month, or three lacs a year, and over and above this, he had five per cent upon the actual revenue, which made above six lacs a year. His son, as Commander-in-Chief, drew five thousand rupees a month, though he did no duty – his first wife drew five thousand rupees a month, and his second wife drew three thousand rupees a month, total eighty-eight thousand rupees a month, or ten lacs and fifty-six thousand rupees a year. These were the avowed allowances which the family received from the public treasury. The perquisites of office gave them some five lacs of rupees a year more, making full fifteen lacs a year.'

60 NAI: Home Public Dept 5 January 1839 no. 116. (See Appendix 5.)

61 *ibid.*

62 Twining, *op. cit.*

63 Sleeman, *op. cit.*

64 Hilton, E.H., *The Tourist's Guide to Lucknow,* Methodist Publishing House, Lucknow, 1911.

65 Edmund Burke's speech on Charles James Fox's East India Bill in *Works and Correspondence* ed. 1852, III 506, quoted in *Hobson's Jobson: A Glossary of Anglo-Indian Colloquial Words and Phrases,* Yule & Burnell, first published 1886; reissued Routledge & Kegan Paul, London, 1968.

66 It was John Maxwell himself who established this custom when he and 'the Principal European and Native Merchants of Cawnpore' thanked the departing Judge and Magistrate, Mr Claud Russell, for his marked support of the commerce of the Zillah. *Calcutta Morning Post* 18 September 1812. Moreover, James Wemyss BSC (who as senior civil servant had laid the foundation stone of Christ Church in 1837) was presented by the merchants with a box of plate. He valued it greatly and left instructions that it should remain in the family. (IOR: Mrs Caroline Wemyss's will, 1861.)

67 Bateman, *op. cit.*

68 Private papers: William Dickson's letter, dated 15 March 1838, was addressed to General Sir T. Anbury KCB at Saugor. Emma Roberts [*op. cit.*] wrote in 1835, 'Mr Dickson's Farm at Cawnpore is deservedly celebrated. The Vineyards attached to this establishment are the finest in India, and from their produce the proprietor has succeeded in making wine equal in richness and flavour to that of Constantia.' Things for William Dickson had not always gone well. In the *Government Gazette* of 4 March 1830 he was 'much afflicted by the failure of Palmer & Co. and asks for payment of debts to save his own failure.' He died at Cawnpore in 1845 aged fifty-one years.

69 NAI: Home Public Dept 9 February 1821 no. 41: 'I am induced in consideration of providing for a numeous and increasing family, to extend my printing concerns by the Establisment of a Branch Press at Cawnpore to facilitate the publication of matters for its Inhabitants . . . The Establishment will thus be productive of considerable advantages to Government as well as to the Mofussil Inhabitants and to yield an honest livelihood to an unfortunate individual and his numerous family, under the benevolent protection of a liberal Government.'

70 NAI: Foreign Political Dept 27 February 1852 no. 171.

71 *The Mofussilite,* Meerut 1847–75. This up-country newspaper, established at Meerut by Mr Lang in 1864, was read by most Cawnpore Europeans at that time.

72 *ibid.*

73 Dickson, *op. cit.*

74 *The Mofussilite,* 21 April 1857.

75 Lowe, *op. cit.* 'There was rather a good scene in the evening; the merit of wines got from Mr Crump, a wine merchant at Cawnpore, was under discussion. McD. . . said he knew nothing about his wines, but that there were three women in his house who he should like to kiss. T. . .with lively anxiety asked, "What, like to kiss them all?" "Yes, by heaven, all" was McD. . .'s reply. I shall never forget T. . .when he said "Why, one of them is my wife:" he had married Miss Crump.'

76 The Ganges Canal was opened in 1854. The original plan was to construct a navigational channel from end to end of the Doab to Allahabad, but it proved too difficult and an irrigational canal, which emptied into the Ganges at Cawnpore, was built instead. What was intended as a great benefit to the people brought ruin to the families of about 500 merchants who lived in General Gunge and traded as grain merchants from their go-downs at Golah Ghat. (See Appendix 11 for their petition and Government's reply).

77 Henry Christie had been in Cawnpore since the early 1840s. In 1845 he was described as assistant in Bathgate, Porteous & Co.'s Dispensary and in 1851 as chemist and druggist.

78 David Maxwell left India in 1854 on account of family ill health and settled at Blackhills, Elgin. He died in London on 13 April 1887 and is buried at Elgin. His obituary described him as 'a perfect gentleman; with rich and poor he was equally a favourite'. He married Maggie Haye Dunbar and they had five daughters and a son.

79 At the time of his marriage to Ann Elizabeth Churcher at Fatehgarh in 1841, James Maxwell is described as 'bachelor, Indigo Planter at Mendy Ghat'; the ceremony was witnessed by Thomas Churcher, Peter Maxwell and J. Mercer. James and Ann had three sons, Thomas Chardon, James Weller, and Patrick. James died at Naini Tal on 5 November 1847, where there was a memorial to his memory at St John's in the Wilderness.

80 John Kirk joined the firm of Crump & Co., wine merchants, when he was twenty-two years old, and worked for four years as manager of their depot. In 1840 he went into business on his own account and set himself up as 'the one and only member of the firm of John Kirk & Co'. On 10 October 1840 he advertised in the Bengal Hurkaru: '*Notice.* Warranted good Eatables, Drinkables and other Stores always to be had at moderate prices at our Depot.' Kirk died in 1853, leaving a widow and seven children, and is buried at the Kacheri Cemetery.

81 BL: Nanak Chand's *Narrative of Events*: Williams, Colonel G. W., *Official Report on Cawnpore Mutiny, 1859.*

82 William Gardner arrived in India about 1789 as a King's Officer and served as a soldier of fortune with the Mahratta Chieftains. He married an Indian princess of Cambay, having fallen in love with her beautiful black eyes, glimpsed through a purdah screen. He settled eventually as a zemindar in the Oude District, at Khas-gunge, but he also had property at Lucknow, Cawnpore and Fatehgarh. In 1809 he raised the famous regiment of Gardner's Horse, now 2nd Lancers, Indian Army. In the veins of his descendants flows the blood of a peer of the realm, the Moghul Emperor and the Kings of Oude (see *A Squire of Hindoostan,* Narinder Saroop, Abhinav Publications, New Delhi, 1983, distributed by BACSA, UK).

83 IOR: L/AG Bengal Wills 1780-1866.

84 There are several references to Peter Maxwell and the cultivation of opium in *Statistical Account of Cawnpoor* by Robert Montgomery, Fanny Parks also probably met him: on 2 September 1835, making her way upstream in her pinnace, *Seagull*, she anchored at Mendhi Ghat, where 'The moon was bright and brilliant . . . the night cold and clear, the stars bright and fine . . .' There, a gentleman she refers to as Mr M – escorted her to look round the ruins of the great city of Kanauj. In all probability this Mr M – was Peter Maxwell. The only time he was known to leave India was from 1 December 1845 to 31 December 1846 and it may have been during this time that he became a founder member of the Oriental Club, London.

85 There is some confusion here. Gavin Jones wrote an account of his mutiny experiences: *The Story of My Escape from Fatehgarh*, Pioneer Press (Cawnpore?), 1913. In presenting a copy of this to the British Library Tracy Gavin Jones, his son, claims that his father was on leave from the GIP railway when the outbreak occurred. Gavin Jones in his private papers says he had joined his brother John Moore Jones on his indigo estate.

A biography of Gavin Jones states that he joined Messrs Norris & Weller in 1862 as engineer in their contract for the construction of a section of the Great Indian Peninsular Railway between Jubbalpore and Hoshangabad. However, because of malaria he was forced to leave India for a while and in England worked as an engineer in the construction of a branch of the Great Eastern Railway.

CHAPTER NINE

1 Roberts, *op. cit.* Lord Roberts was born in Cawnpore in 1832, joined the Bengal Artillery in 1851 and won his VC at Khudaganj near Cawnpore, and Cawnpore society made him its particular hero. Through marriage connections Lord Roberts was related to some of the earliest families in Cawnpore: the Grants, the Trittons, the Maxwells and the Rickettses.

2 Rawlins, *op. cit.*

3 Kaye, Sir J. W., *Lives of Indian Officers*, Strahan, London, 1869, quoting Henry Lawrence.

4 On the publication of Trevelyan's *Cawnpore* a spirited attack appeared in *The Spectator* of 29 April 1865. *The Times*, in defence of Trevelyan, quoted this piece from the *Pall Mall Gazette*.

5 Roberts, *op. cit.*

6 *The Mofussilite*, Friday, 10 April 1857.

7 Until the time of Independence the New Year's Day cricket match continued to be an annual event played at Green Park, an open parade ground opposite the old Greenway bungalow. This is where the cricket Test Matches are held today. The Station Club lost by an innings and 104 runs. Mss EUR E 299/43.

8 Sir Hugh Massy Wheeler was born in Ireland in 1789. There is some mystery about his personal life. The official Lady Wheeler was Mrs Frances Oliver. whose first husband was killed in Kabul in 1841. (Miss Frances Marsden had married Thomas Oliver in Cawnpore in 1810.) When the Wheelers married in Agra, they already had three sons, one of whom was baptised at the time of the marriage, and two months

later a fourth son was born. It is believed that Lady Wheeler returned to live in Ireland and General Wheeler took an unofficial wife, an Indian lady who was a 'caste fellow' of the Nana Sahib. General Wheeler's strange decision to take his stand at the poorly protected entrenchment instead of occupying the well-stocked and defended Magazine has been attributed to his complete trust in the Nana Sahib as a family member. *Kacheri Guide, op. cit.*

9   Mowbray Thomson, Captain, *The Story of Cawnpore,* Bentley, London, 1859.

10 Sherer, J. W., *Havelock's March on Cawnpore,* Nelson, London (1910?): 'The Magistrate of Cawnpore, Mr Hillersdon, had asked us to put up with him and we stayed a day or two in his comfortable bungalow at Nawab Gunj. Mrs Hillersdon was an accomplished pianist . . . She was fond of Mendelssohn's Rondo Capriccioso, . . . and I never hear the piece without recollections of the still interior of the Cawnpore house, its accomplished mistress, her husband, her children, her brother-in-law Colonel Hillersdon, – all doomed to speedy and painful destruction.

11 Mowbray Thomson, *op. cit.* 'The 53rd Native Infantry was a fine regiment, about a thousand strong, almost all of them Oude men . . . By far the greater number of them being high caste men, they were regarded by the native populace as very aristocratic and stylish gentlemen, and yet their pay would sound to English ears as anything but compatible with the height of gentility, viz. seven rupees a man per month, out of which exorbitant sum they provided all their own food, and a suit of summer clothing . . . Thoroughly disciplined and martial in appearance, these native troops presented one memorable point of contrast with European forces – drunkenness was altogether unknown amongst them.'

12 Pearce, Colonel Hugh, *The Hearseys,* Blackwood, Edinburgh, 1905, quoting General Wheeler's letter to Sir John Hearsey.

13 Chalwin letters, privately owned.

14 When the family were in Calcutta preparing to set out for Cawnpore, the youngest daughter, Caroline, had a presentiment of approaching horror and wept most bitterly, pleading to be left behind (Lindsay family papers).

15 Sherer, *op. cit.*

16 Shepherd, *op. cit.*

17 MacMunn, Lieutenant-General Sir George, *Indian Mutiny in Perspective,* John Murray, London, 1930: 'It is common knowledge that Lady Wheeler was an Indian lady of family, those who knew said she was a Puntni, a caste fellow of the Nana.'

18 Nanak Chand, *op. cit.* For criticism of Nanak Chand's testimony see Sen, S. N., *Eighteen Fifty Seven,* Govt of India Press, Calcutta, 1958. Also see Gupta, P. C., *Nana Sahib and the Rising at Cawnpore,* OUP, 1963.

19 Mowbray Thomson, *op. cit.*

20 Shepherd, *op. cit.*

21 *ibid.*

22 *ibid.*

23 At the approach of Havelock's avenging army it was the Nana Sahib's troops that blew up the Magazine. Sherer (*op. cit.*) described how 'I suddenly saw, far in the distance, a great tongue of fire flung up towards the sky, and immediately afterwards, what looked like a vast black balloon ascended, as if in pursuit of it; showed us in dispersion, that it was smoke. Then after a perceptible pause there was the noise of a violent explosion, and at the moment I felt a pluck at my knees that made

me involuntarily sit tighter. This compression of air was the passage of the great airwave for the Cawnpore Magazine had just been blown up.'

24 Collier, *op. cit.*

25 Nanak Chand, *op. cit.*

26 NAI: Home Public 14 May 1858 no. 1.

27 Chalwin letters, *op. cit.*

28 Collier, *op. cit.*

29 16 June 1857: *From the Cawnpore Intrenchment.*

30 Trevelyan, *op. cit.*

31 McIntosh and his son were discovered hiding under the bridge near the premises of Greenway Bros and hacked to pieces. Old Mrs McIntosh was found hiding in her *dhobi*'s house and taken to the Nana Sahib and beheaded.

32 Pensioner Green, finding it impossible to remain hidden, made a dash for it and was killed on the Parade Ground.

33 Auchin was dragged in front of the Nana Sahib and pleaded he was only a poor Chinese tradesman, but he too was beheaded.

34 Cloony repulsed several attacks but under cover of darkness the house was set on fire and he was burned alive.

35 Sepoys looting the Assembly Rooms discovered Dagama; he was taken before the Nana Sahib and cut down with swords.

36 At Nudjafghur Edward Greenway, his aged mother, his wife and children and a Mr Hollings, Editor of the *Central Star,* took refuge at the indigo factory, thinking they would be safe so far out of Cawnpore, but the insurgents found them there and attacked. Mr Hollings had armed himself with double-barrel guns and ammunition and fired from the roof, keeping the attackers off all day and killing sixteen men. Next day, when his ammunition had given out, he came forward and shouted to the enemy to kill him. He was shot through the heart and fell to his death. The Greenways were taken prisoner and conveyed to the Savada Koti; a promise of a ransom of two lakhs of rupees saved their lives for the moment. Shepherd *op. cit.* commented that they were brought to the Nana on common bullock carts, with no protection from the burning sun: 'This heartless man had been all along before the mutiny on social terms with that firm – and was in the habit of frequently visiting the shop, and holding friendly intercourse with the brothers, whose hospitality he had often shared; he nevertheless treated these unoffending and good people as if they were his greatest enemies.'

37 When the houses in Gwaltoli were searched the Jacobis left at night and crossed the river but they were discovered and sent back to the Nana. Henry Jacobi died of sunstroke and Mrs Jacobi was sent a prisoner to the Savada Koti.

The Jacobi family had been settled in Cawnpore for many years. Mr Henry Jacobi, Senior, was born in Calcutta in 1785, son of J. Ludwig Jacobi, a Swiss silversmith. When he was fourteen years old John Henry Jacobi was sent to England to serve his apprenticeship with John Melvil, a London watchmaker at St James, Clerkenwell. *The Register of Apprentices to the Worshipful Company of Clockmakers 1631-1931* notes a sum of £42 was paid, possibly £6 a year for seven years' training. On his return to India Henry Jacobi, Senior, moved up-country and died at Cawnpore in 1834. His two sons, Henry, a watchmaker, and Frederick, a coach-maker, were listed among the merchants in 1856 (see *Kacheri Guide . . ., op. cit.*)

38 Dr Tresidder was civil surgeon at Cawnpore and paid an extra Rs 100 per month to

'afford medical assistance' to the Commissioner at Bithoor. This actually included attendance on Bajee Rao and the Nana Sahib. On one occasion he operated on the Nana's foot. See *Kacheri Guide . . ., op. cit.*

39 Kunhya Pershad, *Mahajan:* statement to Colonel Williams, *op. cit.* Born in 1832, left motherless when very young, Azeezun was brought up in the house of Unrao Jan Ada, the famous courtesan, at Satrangi Mahal, Lucknow. She moved to Cawnpore and when the flag was raised against the British, appeared on horseback in male attire, dressed in the uniform of her favourite regiment, armed with pistols and decorated with medals. According to an Indian journalist, Thomas Smith, after she was captured at Etawah and brought to trial, she died crying 'Nana Sahib ki Jai!'

40 Ahoodeen Pershad, banker: statement to Colonel Williams, *op. cit.*

41 BL: Add Ms 41488 Amelia Horne's ms.

42 The besieged garrison consisted of nearly a thousand people: 455 men, 225 women and 300 children. Of these the civilian residents numbered 100 men. 80 women and 100 children.

43 Mowbray Thomson, *op. cit.*

44 *ibid.*

45 John Mackillop, Joint Magistrate and Deputy Collector, was the self-appointed Captain of the Well. A tablet on the south wall of All Souls Memorial Church records: 'He nobly lost his life when bringing water from the well for the distressed women and children.' He was related to the James Mackillop who so unwisely lent Ravenscroft 'the facility of a credit which must astonish by its amount'. The family's connection with Cawnpore went back to 1788. See Yalland, *Kacheri Cemetery . . ., op. cit.,* under Sibbald.

46 Mowbray Thomson, *op. cit.*

47 Mowbray Thomson, *op. cit.:* 'The conditions were: honourable surrender of our shattered barracks and free exit under arms, with sixty rounds of ammunition per man; carriages to be provided for the conveyance of the wounded, the women and children; boats furnished with flour to be ready at the *ghaut.'*

It has never been satisfactorily established whether it was Mrs Jacobi or Mrs Greenway who carried the Nana's terms of surrender. Both had been imprisoned at the Savada Koti. Mowbray Thomson 'recognised' her as Mrs Greenway. Shepherd, who had left the entrenchment by this time, was uncertain but thought it was Mrs Jacobi. Kalka Pershad, *moonshee,* who had been employed by Thomas Greenway, giving testimony to Colonel Williams, states that it was Mrs Jacobi. Mowbray Thomson had only been in Cawnpore a couple of months and could not be expected to know all the civilians. Shepherd was told that when Mrs Jacobi was captured she spoke daringly to the Nana, shaming him for his cold-blooded murders. It seems in character that such a bold lady be chosen to convey the terms.

48 Colonel G. W. Williams examined sixty-three witnesses: Eurasian drummers and their families, a railway assistant, a few loyal sepoys, Indian merchants, and bankers associated with the Europeans in business, a few personal servants, an ayah, a prostitute, residents from the nearby districts, boatmen, and a couple of spies. It was fifteen months after the terrible events – not surprisingly dates are inconsistent, evidence is often confused and sometimes conflicting. Some witnesses were no doubt anxious to please the authorities and their stories need to be considered with caution. Taken as a whole they convey something of the true picture.

49 From the personal report of Lieutenant Mowbray Thomson (gazetted Captain

17 May 1858) to the Commander-in-Chief. Written in a fine copperplate on pale blue, heavy quality foolscap paper. The date 9 March 1858 in faded brown ink under the heading 'Cawnpore'. Courtesy of Mr John Hearsey.

50 Williams. *op. cit.* It is perhaps significant that one of the five butchers at the Bebee Ghur was a Velaitee, literally a European but in this context an Anglo-Indian. That the Velaitee bore such hatred against the English suggests the prejudice that was endured by the illegitimate Anglo-Indian children at this time from both communities and the deeply felt resentment against Englishmen taking Indian mistresses.

51 John Walter Sherer was attached as Civilian with Special Commissioner's powers to General Havelock's force on its leaving Allahabad on 6 July 1857 and accompanied it throughout the march to Cawnpore. He did not advance into Oude, being appointed Magistrate of Cawnpore. He was Magistrate during the attack on Cawnpore by the Gwalior Contingent and was shut up in the Fort until the relief by Sir Colin Campbell.

52 Bews was the brother of Lord Roberts's wife.

53 Sherer, *op. cit.*

54 Lord Roberts, then a young lieutenant, was there at the action and found a number of letters addressed to 'the treacherous Azimula Khan'. Some were from his English fiancée, others were from ladies of rank and position he had met while in England; one elderly dame called him her 'dear eastern son'. Roberts, *op. cit.*

55 Neill's order was made on 25 July. Sherer believed it was only twice put into effect. Forbes Mitchell, however, who arrived in Cawnpore on 27 October, stated that it was still operative and only ended on 3 November when Sir Colin Campbell put a stop to it as unworthy of the English and of a Christian government. The constant re-wetting of the dried blood on the floor of the Bebee Ghur may account for witnesses, even three months after the massacre, reporting finding the floor deep in gore.

It would appear that Neill based his terrible vengeance on a punishment the Indian people already understood. Sir Henry Lawrence, in his address to the native regiments at Lucknow (reported in *The Mofussilite* of 19 May 1857), urged that the Company had never harmed their religion and reminded them that under Mohammedan rule, tens of thousands of men were forcibly converted, often by having bullock's flesh crammed down their throats, and that in the Punjab, under Sikh ascendancy, pigs' blood was spilt over the tombs and mosques of the faithful.

Forbes Mitchell (*Reminiscences of the Great Mutiny, 1857-1859,* Macmillan, London, 1893) sums up the dark deeds on both sides when he describes the death on the gallows of three wretches who were captured the day before, tried that morning and found guilty. Surgeon-General Sir William Munro was there at the time examining a hook at the Bebee Ghur, covered in dried blood, on which a small child had been hung by the neck facing the wall, as evidenced by the small hand and foot prints in blood on the whitewashed wall. With tears streaming down his cheeks he cast a look of pity on the three wretches about to be hanged: 'This is horrible and unchristian to look at; but I do hope those are the same wretches who tortured the little child on the hook inside that room.'

56 Shepherd, *op. cit.*

57 Camped near the site of the Hillersdons' bungalow, Sherer (*op. cit.*) went to visit it: 'Fire had reduced the house to bare walls, and these, again, were stained by the wet

weather. I went into what had been a room; the floor was heaped with debris of the fallen roof. Amidst some broken china I found a scrap of paper. On it was printed the single word 'Spirituoso'. I thought of the music I had heard in the spring.'

EPILOGUE

1 Lieutenant Mowbray Thomson and Lieutenant Henry Delafosse, both of the 53rd Native Infantry, Private Murphy, 84th Regiment and Gunner Sullivan, Artillery, were the four survivors. After thrilling escapes they ultimately owed their lives to Rajah Dirigbijah Singh of Moorar Mhow in Oude. Sullivan died shortly after of cholera. When the Memorial Well Gardens were established Private Murphy was appointed custodian. Mowbray Thomson, with his ample ruddy beard and the bright face and laughing eyes of an undergraduate, and Delafosse, a pale wiry man, both wrote accounts of their experiences, rose to become major-generals and died full of years in England. Both took the events they had endured – events almost surpassing the most romantic adventures of fiction – in a matter-of-fact way. '[Mowbray] Thompson was once asked: When you got once more amongst all your countrymen, and the whole terrible thing was over, what on earth was the first thing you did? Did? cried he, why I went and reported myself as present and ready for duty.' (Sherer, *op. cit.*).

However calmly men seemed to react to their experiences during the Mutiny, the fact that many treasured some souvenir of those terrifying days reveals a different impression. Mowbray Thomson kept the flannel shirt from Messrs Thresher & Glenny, bright pink at the beginning of the siege and eventually the only garment he was wearing, faded and filthy. Gavin Jones preserved a faded pair of coarse handwoven cotton drawers and noted, 'This is the only clothing I escaped with when I swam for life from the boat captured by the rebels in which we attempted to escape to Cawnpore on 4 July 1857.' William Peppé had oval silver cuff-links made from the butt of the rebel pistol that wounded him and nearly cost him his life. He preserved some hairs from the tail of his horse, Watson, a faithful friend who had carried him safely through those stirring times. David Churcher, who escaped at the same time as Gavin Jones, asked when he was dying that the pocket Bible he had carried with him during his seven months as a hunted fugitive should be buried with him.

2 MacCrea, R., *Key to the Tablets in the Memorial Church, Cawnpore,* Catholic Orphan Press, Calcutta, 1898. (Names and details of the victims: MacCrea was the son of Mrs Wrixon who died at the Bebee Ghur.) Other members of the Greenway family returned, undaunted, to look after their affairs in Cawnpore. Edwin Greenway practised as a lawyer and died in Cawnpore in 1917. The Greenway bungalow became the site of the present DAV College.

3 At the annual boat *méla* at Mirzapore the ballad of the murders at Palee is still re-told. Mr Moore, according to a report in *The Englishman,* was bathing at the time of the attack; he tried to reach his horse but was shot and beheaded. He is buried at Mirzapore. Edmond Jones and Clinton Kemp were buried at Gopi Gunge where, in a small walled enclosure beside the road, their two simple crosses are kept whitewashed and often decorated with fresh marigolds.

4 W. J. Shepherd's *Narrative of the Cawnpore Massacre* went into three editions. He was granted two villages at Unao and died in Lucknow in 1891.

5 BM: Add ms 41488: Amelia Horne's ms at the British Library is in several handwritings and signed 'True Copy MacCrea Lucknow 1890' '. . . the boats were not very close to the shore and we had to wade through the water as well as we could . . . . All this time the enemy were looking on . . . taunting and mocking us. Every boat was crowded to suffocation; I sat on the roof of one alongside of my little sister with the broken leg . . . the enemy were not long in opening fire upon us, the shots fell thick and fast, two soldiers near me were most fearfully wounded, and a gentleman very horribly mutilated while wading to the boat, they made several cuts at his neck, chopped off his hands which he held up to protect his head, the swords being blunt . . . I saw him about half an hour afterwards still alive.

'Our boats had been all grounded and useless were our exertions to get them adrift. Live shells were thrown amongst us setting more than one boat on fire – the Cavalry surrounded us with drawn swords, and the Infantry came into the boats to loot . . . a few trinkets were forced away . . .

'It was just then I was beckoned to by a sowar who was on his horse alongside of my boat, the water up to his very saddle girth . . . I was of course deaf to his bidding – but what resistance could I make?

'I was taken to the shore where I found another young lady in the same painful position as myself – it was Miss Wheeler – we were made to walk alongside of the horses the riders keeping a tight hold of our hands all the time. I was drenched to the skin, and barefooted and bareheaded . . . taken to a Subadar's hut about 3 miles from the Ghaut . . . later carried before two moulvies and forcibly converted to Mohamedism.'

Several months later, when near Allahabad, the sowar, Modh. Ismail Khan of the 2nd Cavalry, let her go, using the fact that he had spared her life as the means of securing his own in the advance of British troops. Eventually she reached Calcutta where she later married William Bennett of the Railways and settled down to giving piano lessons.

A contemporary letter conveys a sense of the ordeal she endured: '. . . she is able to give a very connected account of things up to the massacre, but whenever she reaches that point she becomes mad.' NAI Home Public 14 May 1858 no. 1.

6 Miss Ulrica Wheeler, General Wheeler's younger daughter, aged about eighteen, was also carried away from the boats by a trooper of the 2nd Cavalry called Ali Khan. He was described as a Pathan, resident of Rampur, fair, with a long nose, dark eyes and wearing a beard and small moustache. A story was put out that she had killed her captor and his whole family with a sword and thrown herself into a well, but Shepherd discounted it: 'Subsequent inquiries made by our police lead to a strong conviction that this was a mere fabrication and that the poor young lady was carried away to some place of safety and afterwards accompanied the flight of the rebels and remained with her captor under a Mohamadan name.' Drummer Fitchett, who had been a prisoner at Savada Koti, gave evidence before Colonel Williams: 'I saw a European lady with the sowars' women. She was in native dress, silk pyjamas and a chudda over her head but was riding on a side saddle. The sepoys all said she was General Wheeler's daughter.' Stories of the fate of Miss Wheeler continued to excite interest. MacCrae stated in 1878 that Miss Wheeler was living in

Cawnpore. About fifty years after the Mutiny, Miss Florence Leach, a missionary doctor in Cawnpore, was called out late one night to go to the bazaar to attend a dying woman. The Roman Catholic priest, a Franciscan, was also sent for. Speaking in cultured English the woman told them she was Miss Wheeler and had married the Indian who saved her life at the ghat.

Now some new evidence in this intriguing story has come to light. A Mrs Emma Clarke and her husband settled in Cawnpore in 1880 and lived in what is now Vikramajit Singh Road. She told her daughter, Mrs Iris Shepherd née Bason, that through her ayah she got to know of an Englishwoman living in the bazaar. The carriage and the ayah were sent regularly to bring this lady discreetly to the house. On these occasions the mysterious visitor would delight in putting on European dress, which she wore under her burka. Mrs Clarke urged her to make her whereabouts, known to her family but she was too ashamed to do so and said, moreover that the man had been very kind to her.

Emma Clarke was the daughter of David Russel Crawford who had been a friend and associate in the indigo trade of Dr David Begg. Her first marriage took place in Lucknow in 1858 when she was seventeen and she was therefore a contemporary of Miss Wheeler and might even have met her in Lucknow in pre-Mutiny days. Certainly they would have had friends in common. Among the lists of files at the Cawnpore Collectorate is one headed Miss F. Leach 1902/3. Perhaps this would yield the secret of Miss Wheeler's death.

7 Cosens, Lieutenant-Colonel F. R. and Wallace, C. L., *Fatehgarh and the Mutiny*, Newul Kishore Press, Lucknow, 1933.

8 Gavin Jones, private papers. 'The fort (Fatehgarh) was held for about a fortnight against overwhelming odds – about 150 to one and when it became untenable for losses and failure of ammunition, a last effort was made to save the ladies and children by flight in boats down the river Ganges to Cawnpore. Many of the fugitives were killed on the passage but the majority reached in sight of Cawnpore and fell into the hands of the Nana, who massacred the entire party. Two only of the fugitives from the fort escaped, David Churcher and the writer who saved themselves by swimming when their boat was captured and found protection from villagers in Oudh. In all over 300 residents of Fatehgarh lost their lives at the hands of the rebels.'

Gavin Jones's knowledge and respect for the Indian people, learnt as a boy on his father's estates, probably saved his life. When he sought refuge in a village, exhausted and wounded, the Rajput headman kindly offered him dal and chaupattis in his personal *thali*. Gavin Jones, aware of the hostility this would cause among the onlookers was reluctant to accept and asked for the food to be transferred to a platter of leaves. Surprised and pleased, the headman remarked, 'The sahibs too understand our prejudices.'

9 The fate of the Nana Sahib is given in a letter from General Harris. 'I knew the Nana quite well, having been introduced to him at Cawnpore as far back as '51 . . . In November [1858] I was ordered with a detachment of three Companies, first to Byram Ghat and then to a ford on the upper Gogra, called Chilari Ghat. A small party of seventeen Royal Engineers, under Richard Harrison, presently joined me, with orders to construct a bridge, and a regiment of Pioneers, unarmed, with a Lieutenant in command, to help, I commanded the whole . . .

'Now this force was only about thirty miles from the *terai*, into which the rebel forces, with the Nana had been driven. Very shortly I found that, through my Native officers, I was thoroughly posted up in all the Nana's movements. There are, as you know, a lakh of rupees reward for him dead or alive. Two of my Subadars were always at me to allow them three or four days leave to capture him. They kept me informed of his movements like a Court Circular. I always told them, that I was on duty for a certain purpose, and it was impossible I could give any man leave. One Thursday Ram Singh came to me begging me still more strongly than before, saying the Nana was getting much worse – he was as I knew suffering from fever and ague and had an enlarged spleen – and he told me that the Nana had had his little finger cut off, and had burnt it as an offering to Kali, with a view of propitiating the goddess. Two days after this Ram Singh and the other Subadar came and said: 'No one will get the reward now! He died and was burnt yesterday.' And I feel quite sure it was true, for I had known for some weeks all about his movements.'

The *Cornhill Magazine* article in which this letter appeared was printed in the *Pioneer* about 1907. From personal papers of Colonel Morris IMS, BASCA records IOR.

This accords with Sherer (*op. cit.*): 'In the winter of 1859/60 the Nana died in the jungles of Nepaul. The event was marked by the passage through Oudh of the body of people who had been in attendance on him or supported by him.' At that time Jowala Purshad was captured. He told Sherer that although he had not been present when the Nana died, he had attended when the body was burnt.

Humphrey Peppé stated that a man named Joseph Veasy Collier, a friend of his in the UP Forest Dept, was employed by the Nepal Government as an adviser and for cutting Sal jungle and selling the timber to the railways for sleepers. While clearing the jungle some miles inside Nepal territory, in thick virgin forest, he came across the ruins of a considerable settlement, with the foundations of a large central building of European style which he was convinced at the time (about 1920) had been the Nana's hideout in Nepal.

The Peppé family also believed that the Nana's escape had been across the Birdpur Grant – their estate. After the Mutiny some of the inhabitants of Birdpur area returned to their villges and from inquiries William Peppé, Senior, was convinced that many of them had been taken by the Nana as carriers.

10 Sherer, *op. cit.*

11 NAI: Home Public Proceedings 8 January 1858 no. 278.

12 Wishart, W. S., *Commercial History of Cawnpore 1863-1902,* unpublished ms, privately owned. Mr Wishart was for many years Secretary of the Chamber of Commerce in its formative years and devoted to Cawnpore.

'The masses waited in the wings to watch the outcome. They had little choice but to accept whoever happened to be master. There was no national sentiment in the way it is understood today, even among the leaders there was constant intriguing and little agreement. [See the Foreword by Maulana Abul Kalan Azad, Minister for Education, in S. N. Sen's *Eighteen Fifty-Seven.*]

'In the puppet shows of India the little man is trampled under the elephants and cavalry of kings and queens, trounced by armies, beaten down and left for dead. But always he jumps up again as soon as the opportunity arrives. So the man in the street in Cawnpore was more concerned for his livelihood and the safety of his family than the rebel cause. It was no discredit to him. He was following the age-old pattern of survival.'

13 ARO: Cawnpore Mutiny File 655 26 July 1858 no. 12. When the Nana's army hurriedly retreated from the Cawnpore a party of sepoys lodged for the night in the English Kacheri at Nawabganj, 'which was so full of paper that all the men made up beds of it'. Statement of Mary Gilligan, widow of a drummer in the 67th Bengal Native Infantry, a captive in the rebel camp. NAI: Foreign Correspondence 29 July 1859 nos. 75-77.

14 Based on Samuel Carrington's mss at the IOR: EUR B 212.

15 Jones, G. S., *Rise and Progress of Cawnpore,* unpublished ms, privately owned.

16 Mr Buist, station master East Indian Railway, Har Chand Rae, Ramanand Goro Pershad Sukul, Muflis Rai Gunga Sahai, and Babu Nanu Mal, an employee of A. Warwick, from Hinganghat. With them were associated Captain Aitkin, afterwards Inspector General of Police, Oude, and Captains Toby and Coghill.

17 Jones, *op. cit.*

18 The first cotton mill in Bombay was established in 1854.

19 Gavin Jones was the first to leave Elgin to set up a rival mill, the Muir Mulls. John Harwood, mill manager, left in 1882 to start Cawnpore Cotton Mills a year later. Atherton West came out from Lancashire as weaving master to Elgin and left in 1886 to set up the Victoria Mills Co. Ltd, and, in 1923, the Atherton Mills. A. F. Horsman originally came out to Elgin to erect mules and left to join Atherton West at the Victoria Mills. Later he went as manager to the Cawnpore Cotton Mills until in, 1911, he established the Swadeshi Cotton Mills and the Horsman family fortune.

20 Lala Baldeodass of Farrukabad lent money to the newly established Elgin Mills to extend the mill and became their cashier – he had been introduced to them by the Collector, Mr Halsey. (See page 299, note 8.) His son Juggilal was sent to Elgin to make cash advances and pay staff and there he made friends with Atherton West and A. F. Horsman and laid the foundations of what was to become the Juggilal Kamlapat empire.

21 The marriage took place in London in 1865. She was the daughter of Captain John French RN, Deputy Lieutenant of Kent and his wife, an heiress from Renfrew. Mrs Despard, the suffragette, was one of her sisters.

22 Extract from the speech given by Mr H. A. Wilkinson, the author's father, on the occasion of the seventy-fifth anniversary of the Company: 'Business in those early days was not as strenuous and so fiercely competitive as it is today, and Mr Ralph Maxwell was able to devote himself energetically to sport, in almost every branch of which he excelled. His activities included pig sticking, shooting, steeplechasing, cricket, rackets and rowing. It was, however, as a pig sticker he was pre-eminent and at one time was considered the best pig sticker in the North of India. The Cawnpore Tent Club famous to generations of pig stickers owes its existence to Mr Ralph Maxwell who was its Hony. Secretary for 18 years from 1870 to 1888. In 1929 then 86 years of age, Mr Maxwell attending a dinner in London of the Shikar Club had the honour of being placed at the Prince of Wales's Table as the Grand Old Man of Pig Sticking. Next to pig sticking, his chief hobby, especially after his pig sticking days were over, was shooting. He was an outstanding shot – particularly at

snipe and such was his wonderful physique that right up to his 80th year he continued to enjoy his hobby on the grouse moors of Scotland.

'Mr Ralph Maxwell is the member of the family who devoted the best years of his life to building up the concern. Born in 1842, he was educated at Uppingham. He tried for the I.C.S. but failing in this he joined his father in 1863 in starting up the Pioneer Cotton Mill of Northern India. Mr Ralph Maxwell actively participated in the control of the business for some 40 years, and for a further 10 years continued to come out to Cawnpore every winter until in 1914 he finally retired from India.

'Mr Ralph Maxwell was also responsible for the raising of the Cawnpore Squadron of the United Provinces Light Horse in which he held the rank of Major. There will be one or two here this evening including myself, who remember his final retirement from India in 1914, when a guard of honour of his old command escorted him to the Station. The life of this fine old gentleman came to a close in October 1937 at the age of ninety-two.'

Percival Spear in *The Nabobs: A Study of the Social Life of the English in Eighteenth Century India*, London, 1932, comments that it was a 'unique feature of Anglo-Indian society that commerce and trade should be compatible with gentility'. Three generations of family wealth in commerce enabled Ralph Maxwell to be 'a nabob in ideal'.

23 Extract from *The Statesman and Friend of India*, 19 March 1893, quoted by Joe Lee in *The Indian Mutiny: A Narrative of the Events at Cawnpore*, Victoria Press, Cawnpore, 1893.

Mrs Emma Clarke and family: Cawnpore c.1900. It was Mrs Clarke who entertained Miss Wheeler at home. See page 324, note 6.

Lieutenant Frederick Sleigh (later Lord) Roberts, Bengal Horse Artillery, in civilian dress, 1857. Taken at the siege of Delhi. See page 318, note 1. (Reproduced by special permission of the National Army Museum.)

Glossary of Indian and Anglo-Indian Words

āmil	native collector of revenue
baba logue	children
bajrah	one of the millets
batta	field allowance
bebee, bibee, bibi	lady, wife or mistress
beoparees	pedlars, traders
bigah, beegah	measure of land, approx. 5/8 of an acre
budgerow, bujra	keel-less barge
buriah ayah	old ayah
burkandases	armed retainers or policemen
burra	senior
burra khana	dinner party
chamar	leather worker
chaprassi	office peon
chattah, chatta	sunshade, umbrella
cherbutra, chabootra	raised garden terrace
'chupper', chhappar (Hindi)	thatched roof
chick, cheek	screen of split bamboo
chirag	oil lamp
choota, chota	junior, small
'chopper cot', chhappar khat (Hindi)	bedstead with curtains
chota hazri	early breakfast
chowk	market square
chowkidar, chokedar	watchman
chowrie, chowry	ornamental fly flapper
chudder	cloth, mantle
chunam, chuna	lime plaster for cement floor or walls
circar, sircar	Indian accountant
cutcherry, kacheri	law courts
dak, dawk	post
dak gharry	mail carriage
dandies	boatment
darógah	chief native police officer
dewani, diwani	right of receiving revenue
dhooli, doli	litter

dustack, dustuck	pass or permit, literally signature
fussily, fusly	Moghul calendar
ghar, ghur	house
garh, gurh	fort
gooderie	padded cotton quilt
gunge, gunj	market place
hackery	two-wheeled bullock carriage
'iman', inam	gift, tip, reward
iqbal	prestige
jagir, jageer	hereditary assignment of land
jamader, jemadar	head officer
khansamah, khansomer	head servant, cook
khelaut	ceremonial dress of honour.
khitmatgar	servant, table waiter
khus tatties	screens of sweet-scented vetiver
kist, kisht	revenue paid by instalments
koti, kothi	mansion
lathi-wallahs	guards carrying formidable bamboo poles often tipped with iron
mahajen, mahajan	merchant
mali	gardener, garland maker
mela	festival, fair
moonshee, moonshi, munshi	clerk, writer, teacher of languages
mora, morha	stool made of reeds and string
moulvie	learned man, teacher of Urdu
nauch, natch, nautch	dance
nuzzer	ceremonial present
palkee	palanquin
pergunnah	small area of a district
rageenamah, razinamah	pass, permission, assent
rowannah	customs pass giving clearance
sanad	deed of grant
shroff, sarraf	money changer, banker, goldsmith
sowar	cavalry trooper
subadar, soubedar	chief officer
suwarree	cavalcade, cortege
tatties	grass screens
thali	metal tray
talookdar	landed gentry
terai	marshy tract in the foothills
tope	grove

John Maxwell to His Daughter Fanny Maxwell

Cawnpore 4 November 1816

My dear girl

I wrote to you twice in the early part of the year from Calcutta and I afterwards received your letter of April 1815, with which I am very well pleased – as a first production – but there are some inaccuracies – with the spelling, which I hope to see amended in your next. I conclude that you are before this time settled at Blackheath – and I hope soon to have the pleasure of hearing from you there – that you find your situation as agreeable and comfortable as you can desire – your entry for the first time among strangers may not have been pleasant but that would soon wear off, and I trust that I shall hear you are quite happy and giving satisfaction to Mrs Palmer, for whose character I entertain a very high respect, and whose good opinion I beg you will cultivate by every attention in your power. I leave to her entirely the direction of your studies. I suppose that you have already acquired all the more solid parts of female education – and that your attention will now be required to the ornamental, such as Music, Dancing and Drawing; if you find you have any talent for the latter, but without that, I think it is waste of time to try it. Do not forget what you have already learnt and let me especially request the greatest attention to your reading with propriety, writing and spelling correctly – I hope you will always keep up an intimate correspondence with your aunts, to whose kindness you have been greatly indebted. By the ship *Warren Hastings* just about to sail from Calcutta, Mrs Paton goes a passenger. She is your Godmother, an old and most particular friend of mine, she will probably call upon you at Blackheath or request Mrs Palmer to permit you to visit her in town. She is a very clever, sensible woman and I beg you will be as attentive to her as possible. Speak to her as an intimate friend of mine and she will be happy to listen to all you have to say. I do not know a kinder hearted creature on earth.

This will be forwarded to you – by your old and worthy friend Mr Martin, who you will always look up to, as your Guardian and Protector in my absence. You must know his worth before now, and that he is well deserving of your entire confidence as he has mine. Adam will write to you by this conveyance – both he and your cousin Burnett will also desire to be particularly remembered to you. Write to me often and Believe me.

Always most affectionately

Yours JOHN MAXWELL

APPENDIX 2

John Maxwell's Will

It having pleased the Almighty Dispenser of all Blessings, after Various Vicissitudes of Fortune to Crown my labours with Success, Sensible of the uncertain tenor of this life and in Order to prevent disputes about the disposal of my property after my death, being at present in good Health and of Sound Judgement. I John Maxwell of Cawnpore in the Province of Oude do make this my last Will and Testament and request my Executors herein after named to see it properly Executed,

In the first place my will is that the undermentioned property, lying and situated in the Zillah of Cawnpore Province of Oude, be all sold in the way or Manner considered most advantageous by my Executors, giving to my son Adam and Nephew Alexander Burnett a preference if they should wish to become the purchasers, and give Satisfactory Security for the payment thereof Vizt.

My house and Grounds in the Cantonment of Cawnpore at present Occupied by myself with all the Various Out Houses and Buildings for workshops, with all my Plate Furniture Books Horses Carriages, wines etc on the said Estate. My Cotton go-downs Cotton Presses Press Houses and all their appurtenances lying at Jajemow in the said Zillah of Cawnpore my Indigo Factory at Mahrajipore Pergunnah Selimpore in the aforesaid Zillah of Cawnpore with all the buildings implements of Manufacture and Stock of Every description together with the Indigo vatts Outstanding Balances and Mortgages on the Several Villages attached to the said Factory – my Indigo Factory and Bangalahs at Mokempore Pergunnah Billore together with my Bangalah and other Buildings at Kakoopore in the Pergunnah of Shurrazepore, all lying and Situated in the Zillah of Cawnpore aforesaid, and all the buildings, Implements of Manufacture, Stock of Every descrip-

tion and Outstanding Balances belonging to the said Factories at Mokempore and Kakoopore, my House Indigo Works Cloth godowns and other
Buildings my property at and near Aleabad Pergunnah Deriabad Rudoulic
[Darayadad – Barrah Banki] in the Territory of the Vizier of Oude. There
being at present a period of three years of my Contract with Government
for the Supply of Rum unexpired I request that my Executors will take
measures for carrying on the Distillery of Jajemow in the most Economical
way on account of my Estate until the Expiration of the said Contract
when my will is that the whole of the Buildings Still and worms Vatts and
Stock of every description belonging there to Shall be Sold or disposed of
in the most advantageous way for the Estate giving as before preference in
the purchase to my son Adam and Nephew Alexander Burnett provided
they can give satisfactory Security for the payment of the same.

The aforementioned property being disposed of in the manner directed
and the proceeds together with whatever Sum or Sums of Money may be
due to me at the time of my death being realised-my will is that after
payment of my just and lawful debts the sum of sixty Thousand Sicca
Rupees shall be set aside in the first instance and placed in Trust to be
divided in Equal Shares among my several Natural Children and paid to
them on their beccoming of age. Vizt, Adam born at Calcutta on the 30
October 1793, Frances born at Aleabad in Oude on the 19 April 1803 Peter
born at Cawnpore on the 25th June 1808 Hugh born at the same place on
the 9th June 1809 David born at the same place on the 9th June 1811 and
James born at the same place on the 24th February [1813] That after the
appropriation of the aforesaid Sum of Sixty Thousand Rupees a further
Sum of Sicca Rupees Ten Thousand, be invested by my Executors in the
Securities of the Hon East India Company or in Such other Securities as
my Executors may think most Eligible for the purpose intended the
Interest of which shall be paid as received to Elizabeth Nann, the daughter
of Richard Nann deceased (formerly a Silversmith at Cawnpore), the
Mother of my children Peter, Hugh, David and James, during her natural
life and at her decease, the principal to be equally divided among my
aforesaid Six Children Share and Share alike. After the appropriation of the
aforesaid Sums of Sixty Thousand Sicca Rupees and Ten Thousand Sicca
Rupees, my will is that the further sum of Fifty Thousand Sicca Rupees, if
there remain so much otherwise such sum as may remain of the proceeds
of the property (Sold and debts realised J.M.) [later interpolation] as before
directed after payment of the aforesaid Sums of Sixty Thousand and Ten
Thousand Sicca Rupees, shall be paid to my sisters Frances Barbara
Elizabeth, Mary and Henrietta in equal shares, share and share alike to be

entirely at their own disposal, but with a recommendation (which I hope they will attend to) to those of them who have no Children of their own to bequeath this Legacy to my Children in Such Manner as they may think fit.

The small House and Out offices lying and situated to the westward of my Estate in the Cantonment of Cawnpore and divided from it by the Public Road leading to the Ghaut of the River formerly the property of Richard Nann deceased, together with the Garden all the Ground and Buildings theron Erected, lying on the same Side of the Road Enclosed by a Mud wall and adjoining the said House, the whole being my property I give and bequeath to the aforesaid Elizabeth Nann, the Mother of my Children, for her residence and to be Entirely at her disposal.

If after making these dispositions any Property Shall remain unappropriated, my will is that it be further realised, and my Executors are requested to do so in Such way as they may deem most advantegeous for the Estate, the Proceeds to be divided into Equal Shares between my Several Children afore named, Share and Share alike. The Interest that will acrue on the Property devised to my Children shall be applied by their Trustees to their Maintenance and Education until they become of age, when they will be entitled ot receive the principal, my son Adam having already attained that age shall be entitled to his share as soon after my decease as the property can be realised and the amount of the Shares ascertained.

In the event of the decease of any or Either of my unmarried Sisters before my own death then my will is that the Share or Shares of such Sister or Sisters herein bequeathed shall become the property of and be paid to my Daughter Frances, upon her becoming of age, and I hereby revoke the Clauses before written in this my last will leaving my unmarried sisters at liberty to bequeath their shares to whom they think fit, and make it peremptory that they shall bequeath it to my said Daughter Frances, and that the Shares of each of my said unmarried Sisters shall become her property on their or either of their deaths.

In the Event of the death of Either of my Children herein before named, without issue lawfully begotten, then the Share or Shares of him or her so dying shall be divided among the survivors in equal Shares, but if either of the aforesaid Children shall die and leave issue lawfully begotten, then the share or Shares of such, the said Children so dying shall go to such issue for ever.

I request my worthy and Esteemed friend Martin of Lloyd's Coffee House London. Matthew Lume and John Angus of Calcutta Esquires and my Nephew Mr Alexander Burnett of Cawnpore to become Executors of this my last will and Trustees for my Children and as a Small Testimony of my Sincere regard for them, I beg of each to accept of a Ring of the Value of Five Hundred Rupees to be paid for out of the first part of my property that may be realised.

I declare this Paper written with my Own Hand at Cawnpore afore said the first day of February in the year of Our Lord One Thousand Eight hundred and fifteen, to be the true intent and meaning of my last will and to be as full and valid as the most regular will that can be drawn by a Professional Lawyer.

Signed and sealed in the presence of
THOMAS WHITE   JOHN MAXWELL

Codicil

In addition to the property herein stated and devised I hold a Bond of my Son Adam Maxwell for S. Rs 50,000 on account of the purchasing of Sundry Villages in the District of Cawnpore which Stand in his Name in the Collector's Book of the said District and which he has engaged in the event of his Death to leave by will to his Brothers Peter Hugh David and James but it is not my intention that this Bond should be put in force by my Executors or administrators unless they should deem it necessary on any particular event which they shall be the Judges of. There are three Bank Shares in the hands of John Angus of Calcutta also sundry sums amounting to about 30 or 40,000/- Rs Sa of which no mention has been made in the will but which Mr Angus will of course account for and I further give and bequeath to my Nephew Alexander Burnett a further sum of Five Thousand Rupees (Rs 5,000/-) in addition to this already divided to him through his Mother Barbara Burnett in consideration of his kindness and attention to me and I further grant to my old and Faithful Servant Manshee Bugwanna the Sum of Sa Rs 2,000/- and Sa Rs 1,000 to be divided amongst my other Servants in proportion to their wages if so much shall be remaining after the payment of the Sums already bequeathed.

Signed and sealed at Cawnpore
on the 23rd day of December in the
presence of
W. H. TIPPET
Acting Judge and Magistrate   JOHN MAXWELL

Details of oath sworn by Angus in Calcutta and Burnett in Cawnpore.

Census of Cawnpore Population, 1849

The population of the City consists of 42,491 Hindoos and 16,330 Mussalmans, and of the Cantonment 39,837 Hindoos and 10,138 Mussalmans a total of 108,796. Amongst 6,628 persons occupied in trade and professions there are:

295	Bakers	1	Cooper
109	Betel Leaf Sellers	56	Carpet Makers
19	Buttermen	198	Carders of Cotton
353	Butchers	12	Carders of Silk
412	Bankers and Money Exchangers	123	Cotton Spinners
43	Bottle Sellers	1	Comb Maker
6	Bullock Sellers	5	Cage Makers
35	Bamboo Merchants	3	Chandlers
97	Bhoosa or Chaff Sellers	3	Chintz Stampers
82	Brokers	3,769	Cultivators and Labourers
1	Bead and Necklace Seller	12	Coach Men
109	Braziers	70	Druggists
62	Burnishers	91	Dyers
21	Bonnet and Hat Makers	13	Dancers
3	Book Binders	87	Embroiderers
27	Blacksmiths	4	Ear Cleaners
47	Basketmakers	407	Fruit and Vegetable Vendors
53	Brickmakers	40	Fishermen
362	Bricklayers	56	Flour Sellers
547	Beggars	44	Flower Sellers
2	Bards	22	Firework Makers
14	Buffoons	27	Farriers
401	Barbers	1,377	Grain Sellers
249	Boatmen	292	Grain Parchers
411	Cloth Merchants	220	General Merchants
5	Cotton Merchants	333	Gold Smiths
49	Coal Merchants Charcoal	2	Gold Beaters
212	Carpenters	10	Gilders

111	Grain Grinders	13	Soap Vendors
159	Grass Cutters	70	Silverware Manufacturers
113	Haberdashers	558	Shoe Makers
3	Hookahmakers	199	Saddlers
175	Hackerymen	5	Surgeons
12	Intoxicating Drug Sellers	15	Shawl Darners
4	Ice Sellers	27	Sieve Makers
79	Inn Keepers	34	Silver Cord Manufacturers
9	Jugglers	126	Sweepers
5	Kite Makers	16	Seal Engravers
19	Liquor Manufacturers	2	Tent Makers
23	Lime Sellers	249	Tobacconists
285	Milkmen	65	Tinners
7	Mat Weavers	474	Tailors
45	Morah or Wicker Stool Makers	14	Turban Binders
21	Mill Cutters	125	Tanners
56	Muneehars	17	Torch Bearers
37	Musicians	52	Teachers
333	Oilmen	7	Tape Makers
8	Pickle and Preserve Sellers	7	Watch Makers
169	Potters	963	Weavers
40	Poultry Sellers	187	Wood Merchants
3	Picture Drawers	446	Washermen
16	Painters	220	Waterbearers
291	Pundits	34	Blanket Makers
3	Puppet Showers	12	Fowlers
420	Prostitutes	31	Fan Makers
320	Palkee Bearers	48	Pig Merchants
49	Physicians	14	Musical Instrument Makers
37	Rope Makers	29	Snake Hookah Makers
393	Spice Sellers	6,628	Servants of all kinds
298	Sweetmeat Vendors		

Extract from Robert Montgomery, *Statistical Report of Cawnpoor*, 1849

Visit to Maharaja Bajee Rao, 1838

Captain Manson and I proceeded to the Durbar on an Elephant escorted by a party of the Maharaja's mounted followers. His *burkundauz* and spears men were drawn up near and about the house in which he received us, and also the remainder of his troopers. We were met at the gate of the house yard by Soubadar Ram Chander and his sons, and taken direct to the Durbar room. The floor being covered with a white cloth, and no chairs placed, we took off our shoes as is customary. The Maharaja entered and seated himself on the guddee or throne almost immediately after our entry. He is a man of middle size, fair complexioned with well formed features having the appearance of a hale man of fifty, though he is, as he told me, 66 years of age. He understands but does not speak Oordoo, preferring to communicate through the Soubadar, principally I think as a point of dignity.

After the usual complimentary enquiries he expressed himself (in rather an emphatic manner) sincerely gratified at the Governor General's attention to him in deputing an Officer from this camp to Bithoor. He intimated the anxiety to have Captain Manson vested with Criminal powers at Bithoor and seemed pleased when I told him that Captain Manson had obtained leave to apply for them officially. He then requested that I would inform the Governor General of the satisfaction which he and his followers desired from having such a person as Captain Manson to refer to, and I may here observe that it was very gratifying to see the Commissioner appear to possess the confidence and esteem of all the persons under his charge so entirely as it seems to me Captain Manson does. The Maharaja further begged that I would let His Lordship know that he would make over the money recovered from Mr Maxwell (about Rupees 7,000) with 3,000 Rupees in addition for the purpose of giving employment to the distressed poor in making the road between Bithoor and Cawnpore, and for the construction of some Bridges required upon it. I took care to express in strong terms the gratification with which the Governor General would receive the intelligence of this act of Charity, and spoke of the credit which the Maharaja would gain thereby in the opinion of all good Men.

The above were the Chief points of conversation, great care was taken by Bajee Rao and the Soubadar to avoid all questionable matters and (to avoid the possibility of giving offences) the Maharaja's two adopted sons were seated at a distance from him to the left, and somewhat in the rear of the guddee, instead of being placed on two sides as is the uniform custom on ordinary occasions. After we had received uttur and pown the Maharaja withdrew, and we shortly afterwards followed him.

We then went to the house of the Soubadar Ram Chander – he renewed the assurances of Bajee Rao's great gratification at the deputation of an officer to him, and added much regarding his own satisfaction. He said that he had begun to fear that the British Government had forgotten him entirely. I remained some time at his house, conversing with him during the whole of which time the same delicacy was evinced in avoiding questionable topics, It was only when I was about to mount the Elephant that he asked Captain Manson, whether he might say one word about the 9 villages he lays claim to. I immediately told him that his chance of getting them was, as small as could be, but that the Governor General as a mark of favor to him had allowed Captain Manson to write to Bombay for the details of the claim which would be submitted to Government.

Bithoor is rather a large town for a place not an Emporium of any trade and the Inhabitants appear generally in good circumstances. Bajee Rao resides in the heart of the place without the boundary of his *Jageer;* he has two large houses well built, and not unhandsomely fitted up in the Mahratta style. That intriguing person Jumna Baee Gokla still resides in a large Garden at Bithoor, the entrance to which opens on the main road between Bajee Rao's, and the Soubadar's house. It seems to be very desirable that she should be directed to leave the place as her object in remaining there can be only to forment intrigues.

Memo
In the event of the Bajee Rao's demise during the minority of his two adopted sons, whether the Commissioner would be authorized in making any arrangement for the security of his Treasure, (of which here must be a great accumulation) as well as of other property in jewels &c., for the benefit of his adopted children? If so, in conjunction with whom?

Bithoor. 2nd July 1838.Sd. MANSON
Commissioner.

Captain Manson is desirous of receiving private instructions on the points noted in the Margin. As the Maharaja has an immense amount of property in jewels and treasure,and is surrounded by a considerable number of armed men who owe allegiance only to him, and in the event of their being tempted to commit outrage, having the territory of a foreign state on the opposite bank of the River to escape into, Captain Manson might be authorized to summon a sufficient force from Cawnpore for the protection of the above property on Bajee Rao's demise, until the money and effects could be sealed and entered in an inventory and delivered to the heirs. The Commissioner might be empowered to call in Soubadar Ram Chander and Bapoo Jee, or any other few of the trust worthy servants of the Maharaja to aid him in taking charge of the effects on the part of the heirs: if visited with Magisterial powers, the Commissioner might of course use his discretion in summoning troops to prevent anticipated outrage, or might even take charge of any property *Ex Officio* which he might think in danger of being plundered.

Captain Manson is further desirous of being informed whether His Lordship is disposed to allow any reward to the person who recently informed him of Jumna Baee's plot to poison him and Ram Chander. It is rather a delicate point on which to communicate with Captain Manson and I would venture to suggest that Mr Wilson the Magistrate of Cawnpore to whom the alleged Conspirators were made over for Examination, be asked, demi-officially in the first instance for his opinion of the value of the Informers services. Captain Manson might perhaps be allowed a sufficient sum to be given as from himself, should the man be considered really deserving of reward, for should Government appear to pay for informa-tion in a place like Bithoor, where there is so much intrigue going on continually gratis, plots might become more numerous than they are now, and more troublesome to investigate.

Sd/-H TORENS,
Deputy Secretary

True Copy
Sd/-

Secretary to the Govt. of India
with the Governor General.

Foreign Political Department: 4 April 1838, no. 12

Letter from Nawab Rooshun ud Dowlah, 1839

A letter to the Right Hon'ble Governor General. Received 8 March 1839.

The Circumstances of my father and myself having been long attached to the interests of the British Government will appear evident from the records of the Political Department at Calcutta, and of the Residency at Lucknow.

Adverting to the kindness evinced towards me by the British Government, I beg to state that after adjusting the affairs entrusted to me by the Court of Lucknow I took leave of the King and reached Cawnpore two months ago, since that I have been put to great inconvenience by being obliged to occupy an incommodious Bungalow. The causes which led to my removal from Lucknow must have been reported to your Lordship by the Resident to your Lordship, Colonel Low.

Three or four years ago I purchased a house belonging to a Merchant named Adam Maxwell for thirty thousand Rupees, and expended an additional sum of 40 thousand Rupees in repairing and improving the Estate, It is situated on the banks of the Ganges within the Military Cantonments and I am desirous of living in it because such a house cannot be had here but as I am unable to reside within the Cantonments without your Lordship's permission, I beg that your Lordship will graciously be pleased to issue an order to the officer commanding at Cawnpore to allow me to occupy the house in question in the same manner as permission was accorded to the late Nawab Maatmaduolah.

Reply from Mr F. H. Maddock, Secretary to the Government of India, with the Governor General. Camp at Bustee.

11 March 1839

After compliments,

The letters recently addressed by you to the Governor General and myself have duly arrived, and I hasten to apprize you of His Lordship's opinion on their contents.

His Lordship conceives that you have done well to take up your residence at Cawnpore where you are afforded the advantages of a sojourn under the equitable rule of this Government and also of protection by the actual presence of a large body of its troops. The provinces of the British Government are open to all men equally, the only thing required of their indwellers of whatever degree being due attention to the laws and regulations, whether local or general prevalent in them.

Among such regulations are certain ones, neither strict nor harsh, which have been instituted for the proper ordering of cantonment of the British Army. The Governor General is well assured that you will not attempt to do otherwise than conform to them which renders wholly unnecessary any letter form His Lordship to the General Commanding at Cawnpore. The fixed and unalterable nature indeed of these orders makes it improper that any private applications should be put in, which might be calculated to infringe the constitutions of established rules so expedient and so necessary. My friend, to conceal the real truth is neither accordant to the honesty of friendship nor the duty of public men; hence it is right that I should mention that representations have been made regarding the practices of certain of your dependents at Cawnpore in raising and drilling soldiers, a measure unnecessary in the midst of an army, and annoying to persons residing in the cantonment.

Any number of Burkundauz, or of Chokedars, whose employment is not attended with the bustle and disturbance of military preparation might be with advantage entertained, for the protection of your property, but to do more than this is unnecessary and indeed objectionable.

My friend, the wise man comprehends in a word, what the fool would not understand were it written in volumes.

NAI: Home Department Public 5 January 1839, nos. 114, 115, 116

Cawnpore 1856

CAWNPORE, (N. W. P.)
628 Miles from Calcutta

CHRIST CHURCH 800 seats, *Chaplain*, Reverend E. T. R. Moncrief, M.A.

ST. JOHN'S CHURCH, 1,000 seats

MISSION OF THE SOCIETY FOR PROPAGATING THE GOSPEL
Missionaries, Reverend H. Sell and Reverend W. H. Haycock

ROMAN CATHOLIC CHAPEL — Reverend Joseph J. Rooney

FREE SCHOOL
Director, Rev. E. T. Moncrief, M.A.

Head Master . . . M. Gill   *2nd Master* . . . Grees Chunder
3rd Master, Myaram

GOVERNMENT CHARITABLE HOSPITAL AND DISPENARY
Superintendent Assistant Surgeon, J. N. Tressider, M.D.
Sub-Assistant Surgeon, Koylas Chunder Mookerjee

RELIEF AND CHARITABLE FUND
Secretary ———

ELECTRIC TELEGRAPH OFFICE
Assistant in charge, W. Ramsay
Assistants, H. T. Goodings and H. Farmer

POST OFFICE
Post Master, J. R. Collins, *(absent)* Rs. 150
Officiating ditto, J. H. Taylor.

JUDGE'S OFFICE   *Clerk*, T. Pounce, Rs. 100

MAGISTRATE and COLLECTOR'S OFFICE
Deputy Collector & Deputy Magistrate, Nusseer Alli Khan
Deputy Collector, W. H. Stacy

Office Establishment
Head Clerk, J. O'Bricn. 153   *2nd Clerk*, W. H. Ward, 75

MAGISTRATE'S OFFICE *Head Clerk*, C. S. G. Martindell, 100

LAW OFFICERS
Principal Sudder Ameen, Moulvee Abdool Ruhman
Sudder Ameen, V. F. Berkley
Vakeels, Ahmed Alli Khan and Urjoon Singh

———

Free-Mason's Lodge, '*Harmony*' No. 611, and '*Sincerity*' No. 552, and
Royal Arch Chapter, '*Harmony with Fidelity*'

EAST INDIAN RAILWAY COMPANY
District *Engineer* Vacant
Resident Engineers, James Collett and A. M. M. Miller
Assistants Ditto, R. Hanna, W. D. La Touche and J. C. Bayne
Overseers, J. Burns, and S. Barlow
Clerks, G. M. Warden and J. Pushong

RAILWAY CONTRACTORS
J. R. Brandon and Co. *Partner*, John Rose Brandon
Line and extent of the contract is 30 Miles in the District of Cawnpore,
Purgunnah, Goonzepore, Uckburpore, Shapoor and Baitoor.
European Assistants, J. R. Virgin, John Murphy and William Ramsay

Commercial
CENTRAL STAR PRESS AND NEWSPAPER
Proprietor, J. R. Brandon
Newspaper published every Wednesday and Saturday.
Also publishes the 'Central Star Overland Summary' Bi-Monthly.
Superintendent, Printer and Publisher, Ed. A. Duel.

	TERMS OF SUBSCRIPTION	RS.	AS.	P.		TERMS OF ADVERTISING	RS.	A.	P.
In Advance	Per Annum	36	0	0		Per Line	0	3	0
"	Per Half-Year	20	0	0		Less than six Lines	1	0	0
"	Per Quarter	10	0	0					
In Arrears	Per Month	4	8	0					

N.B. All advertisements received, without specifying the number of insertions, will be
continued until countermanded — *Contract rates for Columns or Half-Columns, may be
learnt on application to the Superintendent.*
PRINTING, TYPOGRAPHIC, LITHOGRAPHIC and COPPER-PLATE Printing of
every description
executed in the neatest style; also FANCY PRINTING, in *Colors and Gold*, executed
with neatness.
AGENTS: Calcutta, R. C. LEPAGE AND CO.   Madras, PHARAOH AND CO.
Meerut, GIBBON AND CO.

CAWNPORE BANK IN LIQUIDATION
Agent, Ramchunder Dutt

DELHI BANK AGENCY
Agents, Greenway Brothers

Cawnpore Banking and General Agency: Manager H. Sheridan

Railway Hotel, on the Grand Parade, *Superintendent*, John Purdey

2nd United Service Hotel, 3rd Cawnpore Hotel and
4th Old Cawnpore Hotel, W. Marshall, manager.

Bathgate, Campbell & Co.	Chemists, Druggists &c., &c. *Partner* Henry Christie
Brandon & Co.	Merchants, Commission Agents and Railway Contractors and Agent for the North-West Dâk Company. *Partner* J.R. Brandon
Mrs. Cormody	Milliner
W. Crump and Co.	Wine Merchants &c.
I. X. Dagama	Wine Merchant and General Agent
W. Gee	Manager, Inland Transit Company
Greenway Brothers	Bankers and Merchants. *Partners,* E. Greenway and T. Greenway
J. D. Hay	Coach and Cabinet-maker, Auctioneer and Undertaker
J. Haycock	Watch and Clock Repairer, &c.
W. C. Hollings	
G. Ireland	Agent, Central India Horse Dâk and Parcel Company
F. Jacobie	Coach-builder and Undertaker
H. Jacobie	Watch-maker
J. R. Kirk	Trader in Country Produce
John Kirk and Co.	Wine Merchants
W. Kirkpatrick, Jr	Trader in Country Produce
J. H. Patten and Co.	Traders
Price and Co.	Boot and Shoe-makers
W. Probet	Manager of the Inland Transit Co.'s Yard
John Purdy	Commission Agent and Supdt. Railway Hotel
James Shearin	Commission Agent and Trader
Mesdames, Tomkins and Co.	Milliners, Dress-makers, &c.
W. Vincent	Nudjuffghur, Merchant, Indigo Planter, &c.
Wills and Co.	Auctioners, Stable-keepers, &c.
G. Read	Trader in Country Produce
Aga Jaffir	Arab Horse Dealer
Chooneelall	Central India Horse Dâk Company
Eellahi Bux	General Merchant
Goopeenath Nundie	Wine Merchant
Jyjiram	Horse Dâk to Lucknow
Rammohun and Co.	Wine Merchants
Shamchand Dass and Co.	General Merchants
Syed Ahmed	Arab Horse Dealer

Insurance Agents

Colonial Life Assurance Co.	Brandon and Co.
Universal Life Assurance Co.	H. Sheridan
River Insurance Co.	Greenway Brothers

Residents

J. M. R. Elliot, A. Miller, J. C. Schorn
Nawabs Nizamud Dowlah, Mahomed Alli Khan.
Bakur Alli Khan and Ameenuth Dowlah.
Sreenath Maharaja Dhodhopunth, Nana Sahib.
Punth Perdan Pasoah Bahodoor.

Bathgate, Campbell & Co

Dr. .... *Abstract of* BATHGATE, CAMPBELL *and Co's.,*

To losses on the following speculations:

On Cottons	20,423	15	0			
On Tincal and Borax	3,504	2	2			
On Safflower	475	8	10			
On Piece Goods	638	1	2			
On Hides and Tallow	602	0	2			
On Bottles	48	14	1			
On Sundries	1,007	11	7			
				26,700	5	0

CHARGES

Establishment, &c., &c., *viz.*:

General Merchandise	20,262	7	0						
Add Bad Indigo seed debts	6,295	15	7						
				26,558	6	7			
Deduct at credit of dustoorie account to 30th April 1855	1,738	8	8						
				24,819	13	11			
Add General Merchandise, Season 1855–56				2,597	14	5			
							27,417	12	4
Total, Rupees							54,118	1	4

Net Gain on the transaction of the ten years, appropriated thus:

The late John Campbell				17,588	13	11			
Interest to old Partners on stock purchase				56,253	7	0			
David Begg in his own right 30th April 1855	2,53,542	14	6						
His 10-16th share of 1855–56	46,239	12	5						
				2,99,782	10	11			
His 10-16th share by right of purchase from G. M. Porteous				1,21,465	15	0			
Henry Christie to 30th April 1855	1,72,057	8	6						
His 6-16th share of 1855–56	27,743	13	10						
				1,99,801	6	4			
							6,94,892	5	2
Total, Company's Rupees							7,49,010	6	6

DRAWN OUT AT CAWNPORE
The 9th September 1856

profit and loss accounts for ten years, ending 30th April 1856 .... *Cr.*

By Profits on Saltpetre Speculations:
Home Manufactured   ... 15,667 5 7
Deduct Loss in season
  1855–56 .... 1,107 11 4
  _____14,559 10 3
Home Manufacturing 10,435 9 4
Home Kooreah 12,217 1 5
  _____ 37,212 5 0

Lucknow, Gogra, and
  Ganges 51,737 3 3
Dooab including
  Futteghur 23,146 0 3
Shipments to London .. 1,852 14 4
  _____76,733 1 10
Deduct Losses on various shipments
  to London 4,226 0 7
  _____ 72,510 1 3
  _____1,09,722 6 3
By Indigo seed to 30th April 1855 .... 3,70,770 3 2
Add Profit in season 1855–56 .... 67,231 4 2
  _____4,38,001 7 4
By Dispensary and Soda Water to 30th April 1855 ... 1,06,958 7 9
Add Profits of last year 1855–56 .... 13,790 2 3
  _____1,20,748 10 0
By Insurance to 30th April 1855, Rs. 42,054-3-2, last
  season 1855–56, Rs. 357-1 ....   42,411 4 2
By Indigo to 30th April 1855, Rs. 12,983-14-8 less loss in
  season 1855–56, Rs. 4,275-6-8 ....   8,708 8 0
By Zemindary to 30th April 1853, Rs. 21,129-15-10 less
  loss in season 1855–56, Rs. 42-12-0.... ....   21,087 3 10
By Government Paper 4,832 6 11
By Gram contract 948 12 0
By Discount on Purchase of stock 1,920 12 9
By Dustoorie, season 1855–56★ ....
  ★and Rs. 1738:8:8 credited on the other side of this
  account 628 15 3

Total Company's Rupees 7,49,010 6 6

(Signed) HENRY CHRISTIE

A List of the Officers of the Bengal Army, in the Year 1760

CAPTAINS

John Gowan
Thomas Fenwick
James Spear
Christian Fisher
Martin York
Ranfur Lee Knox
Peter Carstairs
Charles Earnest Joecher
Alexander Champion

Henry Oswald
Hugh M'Kie
Thomas Robertson
Lauchlan M'Lean
Giles Stibbert
Henry Spelman
Martin White
James Tabby
Patrick Moran

CAPTAIN-LIEUTENANT

John Broadburn

LIEUTENANTS

William Turner
George Wilson
Ambrose Perry
Henry Sommers
Hugh Grant
John Nollickens
Christian Hasencliver
John Mathews
Francis Cozens

Anthony Casteel
John Price
James Treadwell
John Trevanion
Sir William Hope
Lewis Brown
John M'Dowall
William Ellerson
John Downie

George Alston
John Bourne
William Smith
Primrose Gailliez

George Morrison
Gilbert Ironside
James Morgan
John White

ENSIGNS

Anthony Polier
Richard Parry
John Mauve
Thomas Fenwick
William Glenn
Archibald Swinton
Walter Furlong
George Hay

Samuel Hampton
Maurice Roach
Benjamin Wilding
James Jones
Richard Holland
John Walkins
John Mackleron

TOTAL OFFICERS: 60

[From Williamson's *Bengal Native Infantry*]

APPENDIX 9

William Pitt, *East Indiaman*

On voyage which took John Maxwell to India

Captain £10 per month, £149 for the round voyage
Captain's mate, £5 per month
Second mate, £4
Third mate, £3
Fourth mate, £2
Fifth mate, 30/–
Purser, £2
Surgeon, £3
Five Midshipmen, 26/– per month
Carpenter, £3.10.0
Gunner, £2.15.0
Boatswain, £2.15.0
Caulker, £3
Cooper, 50/–
Sailmaker, £2
Armonour, 30/–
Ship's steward, 30/–
Captain's steward, 30/–

Ship's cook, 30/–
Captain's cook, £3
Carpenter's mate, 50/–
Carpenter's second mate, £2
Cooper's mate, 30/–
Caulker's mate, 40/–
Gunner's mate, 30/–
Boatswain's first mate, 30/–
Boatswain's second mate, 30/–
Captain's servant, 26/–
Butcher, 26/–
Seaman (82)*, 26/–
Chief mate's servant, 20/–
Second mate's servant, 18/–
Surgeon's servant, 15/–
Gunner's servant, 15/–
Carpenter's servant, 15/–
Six quartermasters, 30/–
Ordy seamen (7), 20/–

*One impressed as caulker's mate but went as seaman.

Customs House, Cawnpore, 1806

FORT WILLIAM THE 25TH MARCH, 1806

Additional Officers required for conducting the Duties of the Government Custom at Cawnpore conformably to Regulation XI, 1804

Names of Officers	Duties to Perform	Salary
	WRITERS' OFFICE	
Samuel Black	Keeper of Import and Export Register	Rs. 100
Alexander Ducas	Do. Register of Rowannahs granted at other stations and fair Copyest registers	100
Choteylaul	Amlaws for Sudder Office Persian Rowannah Navees	15
	2 Assistant Register Navees & other accounts	16
Bussentlaul	Nagree Register Navees	10
Gungapersaud	Ditto Ditto	10
	1 Duftory at present charged in contingent Bill	7
	1 Furrath Do.	3
	1 Mater Do.	3
	1 Bhistee	4
	WHARF	
Shaik Nasir	Tallashee Durrogah owing to the increase of business from the establishment of Town duty and a Wharf an increase of Safary is recommended for a head Tallashee Durrogah	10
Khodabux	Do. Musriff do. do.	3
Shaik Feyzullah	Naib Durrogah of Tallashee for Wharf	10
Suddey	Do. Do.	10
Mohubbellee	Do. Do.	10
	2 Assistant Musriffs @ 7 each	14
Dulaur	Assistant Weighman 10	
Nahaul	Do. Do. 10	20
	1 Carpenter for opening of Packages for Examination	7.8
	1 Dulwar at present charged as Extra	15

Ln Sa Rs   367.8

Cawnpore Govt. Custom House

the 18th September, 1805.–

R. GRANT   Collr.

[Board of Trade Proceedings, vol. 21, 1806]

Petition from Indian Merchants, 1851

The humble Petition of Chynesook Buxeyram, Mujlisroy, Gunga Sahoy, Gungabishoor Khemanund, Gyan Chund, Peramsook Sookhunnia Zowkaram, Ummur Sing, Mootleedhur, Jumnadoss, Dowlutram, Baldeo Sahoe, Beekhoomull, Deokeenundun Jouhare Mull Moeejeeram, and about 500 others – owners of Houses in General Gunge and Golah or Brigadier Ghaut, at the station of Cawnpore. Most respectfully Sheweth,

That your Lordship's Petitioners solicit permission with the greatest humility and respect, to lay their very hard case before your Lordship, craving at the same time your Lordship's forgiveness for this intrusion on your valuable time.

That your Lordship's Petitioners have houses to the number of upwards of 500, large as well as small, in the above mentioned place at the station of Cawnpore, from a very long time – the same having been built both for the purpose of occupying and carrying on Trade, at a cost, varying from 100 to 8,000 Rupees each. That they carry on their mercantile business to a very large extent keeping their Goods, chiefly consisting of grain to the value of lacs of Rupees in those Houses; and Goods, which come by water from different parts of the country, are landed at Golah or Brigadier Ghaut, and kept in the Houses there. In short, the two places mentioned above, viz, General Gunge and Brigadier Ghaut, are the principal marts for grain and many other articles of Trade at this station. But your Lordship's Petitioners have been exceedingly alarmed at the intelligence that a branch of the Ganges Canal is to pass through the Bazar of General Gunge to the Ghaut, where it will join the river; and that therefore all the Houses belonging to your Lordship's Petitioners must be destroyed, the occupants thereof, computed from 3000 to 4000 souls will thus become homeless. Your Lordship's Petitioners are quite incapable of expressing in adequate terms their feelings at the Threatened or impending evil, which the contemplated project is calculated to occasion: in the event of its being carried into effect, there is no doubt but it will produce most injurious, nay in some cases fatal consequences, and it will prove an utter ruin to many and a great number of poor people who have no means to repair their loss, or build new Houses, are likely to suffer extremely from grief, while the trade will meet with a most serious interruption to the great injury of the inhabitants of the station.

Your Lordship's Petitioners are aware that it is the intention of Government to allow a compensation to the owners of the Houses in question, and from what they have heard, your Lordship's Petitioners are about convinced that the amount thereof will be but a mere trifle in comparison to what the Houses have actually cost and to the loss their owners are likely to suffer. But all these evils can be avoided, if the Canal be made to run only at a mile distant on the more easternside, leaving the Bazar of General Gunge, and Brigadier Ghaut as they now stand, and this arrangement will occasion no harm to Government or obstruction to the Canal, while it will confer incalcuable benefit on the poor subjects. It may be said that the owners can remove to some other part of the station and build new Houses there; but your Lordship's Petitioners beg to assure your Lordship that many of them as already stated, have not the means to do so, and will at once be plunged into insolvency, should they be deprived of their houses. Moreover, there is no other Ghaut at the station so well adapted for the landing and storing of Goods as Brigadier Ghaut. Therefore, should the prayers of your Lordship's Petitioners be not granted, the hardship will be an unprecedented one, and most deeply felt by your Petitioners. Your Lordship's Petitioners applied to the different authorities at this station on this subject, but in vain, as they (Petitioners) were told by all of them that the plan of the proposed course of the Canal had already been approved and sanctioned by Government and that therefore nothing could be done now.

Under these circumstances, your Lordship's Petitioners, feeling assured that it is in your Lordship's power to order an alteration to be made in the course of the Canal, they have taken the liberty to represent their hard case to your Lordship, most humbly craving that your Lordship will be gracious as to take it into your favourable consideration, And render them that impartial justice for which the Enlightened British Government is so well renowned in every part of the world.

And your Lordship's Petitioners as in duty bound will ever pray. . . .

Cawnpore 14th February 1851

PS Your Lordship's Petitioners have heard a rumour in the Bazar that the British Government are going to allow the inhabitants of the above mentioned places Rupees 36,000 for their support and injury; your Lordship's Petitioners have been exceedingly astonished, and are very sorry to trouble your Lordship with their humble Petition, that if your Lordship will be so gracious as to excuse the intrusion and grant the boon herein solicited by removing the branch of Ganges Canal, be made to run only at a mile distant on the more eastern side from the above mentioned place, Your Lordship's Petitioners assuring that the British Government will save their Lacs and Lacs of Rupees by joining the Canal at the above mentioned Place and your Lordship's Petitioners also for this act of benevolence, your Lordship's Petitioners, as in duty bound, shall ever pray.

(True copy) Sd/- E C BAYLÈY Under Secy to the Govt of India with the Governor General

OFFICE MEMORANDUM   *Copy No 90 Home Department*

Camp Khyrabad 22 March 1851

Read a Petition from Chynesook Buxeeram and others, residents of Cawnpore, dated 14 February last stating that they have landed property in General Gunge, and Brigadier Ghaut – that they have been informed the branch of the Ganges Canal was to pass through the Gunge which would destroy a number of their houses and cause a great loss to them, and praying that the course of the Canal be altered.

Ordered that the Petitioners be informed in reply that the plan for connecting the Canal with the river Ganges at Cawnpore, by carrying it through the middle of Cantonments, was adopted for the comfort and salubrity of the station. Moreover the land belongs to the Government, and when it is considered that Tradesmen and others only live there by sufferance, with a primary regard to the wants and necessities of the Cantonments, the Governor-General considers that there seems to be no reason for remonstrance.

Sd/– H M ELLIOT Secretary to Govt of India
with Governor General

NAI: Home Public Dept 11 April 1851

Mrs Angelo's Diary, 1857

Lieutenant Frederick Cortlandt Angelo of the 16th Native Infantry, grand-son of an officer who had served in Warren Hastings's bodyguard, was posted to Cawnpore as Deputy Superintendent Ganges Canal on 14 May. He arrived, accompanied by his pregnant wife and two little girls, to find the Cawnpore residents moving into Wheeler's entrenchment.

Mrs Helena Angelo kept a brief diary of events:

25th May Last night the General sent word to say he expected an outbreak either that night or during the following day.

26th May Frederick has given up the boat on which we have been living. This evening we are to go into the entrenched camp.

Later This entrenched camp is a singular scene – parties of officers and ladies singing and laughing in one place – gentlemen assembled in the open air – all noise and bustle and one would imagine it some gay assembly.

27th May Fred is attached to the Battery but seems thoughtful and serious.

28th May Fred absolutely determined that I and the children should go to Calcutta with Mrs. Volk, so we are to start this evening much against my wish but he seems to wish it. I can only pray God that this step is blessed by Him and turn out beneficial to us both, yet in my opinion husband and wife should separate as little as possible. Started at 6 p.m. Oh! my God keep and protect my beloved husband.

The next entry is missing but according to family tradition they travelled to Allahabad by river, hidden at the bottom of the boat by a loyal servant.

30th May Arrived last night at 10 p.m. found the Station quite empty, everyone in the Fort. Went to Noor Mahmud's hotel, where I got a wretched hole of a room. The heat was intense, continues so to-day. Took a palkee garrée (covered trap) and drove with Mrs. Volk to the steam wharf. The steamer is to sail to-day. I cannot be ready as my woman will not go with me. I am sorry, as I think dear Fred will be disappointed. Drove to the Fort to-day to try and get apartments there, but could not find the Fort Adjt. and got back very tired. Mrs. Potts asked me into her house and dissuaded me from going to Boll's hotel – very kindly offered me half her room at the Fort – I slept there – found it very hot.

31st Sunday Still at hotel in the middle of day. Mr. Walcot came and recommended (me) to go to the Fort, so after an early dinner we all went. Major Moorhouse gave me the room next to Mrs. Potts. The heat is frightful.

1st June Monday Spent the day in the Fort, Mrs. Howard of the Artillery came to see me. There is very bad news from Lucknow, when will all this end?

2nd Still at the Fort. Nell very unwell all day. Mrs. Williams of the 6th came to see me in the evening, rather a nice person. Slept in Mrs. Newman's sitting room, quite delightful after the heat and noise of the quarters.

3rd Dr. Stuz came to see the children – a telegraphed despatch from Agra with good news of a success over the insurgents near Meerut. Engaged an extra coolie.

4th Spent the day with Mrs. Norris in cantonments, a delightfully quiet day.

5th A day of alarms, not allowed to go to cantonments. In the morning took our cabin in the steamer. In the afternoon heard it was gone to Benares for European soldiers. Benn's regt. mentioned. Sikhs and Europeans fought well and put them to flight. Received five letters from my dearest husband. Thank God all is quiet at Cawnpore. 2 guns sent down to the bridge of boats.

6th Was just in bed this evening when Mrs. Pott told me to get up and dress as there was something the matter – a great deal of musketry firing in the direction of cantonments. The 6th have mutinied and are massacring their officers and all the unit. We spent the whole of this sad night in the verandah listening to the firing and cries of the insurgents.

7th Sunday At 12 a.m. prayers in the lower verandah – 15 officers killed alas! What a sad time – no news from Cawnpore. Fires and throwing shells into the City during the day and night.

8th Monday Wuzee Khan went into the city and got us some sagee (semolina) flour and bad bread. Mrs Pott's bearer went to the station, but never came back. It is said that the Mahomedans have raised their standard in the City and called all the people to join them, daring wretches! – no news from Cawnpore.

9th Turned out of my room, and obliged to double up with Mrs Pott. Continued firing on the marauders – It is said two gentlemen came to the Fort to-day who passed Cawnpore a few days ago, where they heard firing – God grant the entrenched camp has held out, and that my beloved husband is safe.

10th Great difficulty in getting food or servants – I hired a bheesti (water carrier) to-day, and we luxuriated in a (?) in the evening he ran away – To-day it is very hot – the 15 railway people have come in, but poor Mrs. Bevis died from exhaustion and exposure to the sun.

Foraging parties out to-day – 200 sheep brought in and the Sikhs allowed to plunder – the whole district seems to have risen round the so-called standard of Mahomud. Oh! for the hour of retribution. No news from Cawnpore nor from any direction, the telegraphic wires cut in every direction and no daks (posts). Steamer not come in. Mrs. Potts intends going to Mirzápore with Mrs. Walcot. Continued firing from the fort, all last night and to-day. We have got quite accustomed to these awful sounds – It is said that this is solely a Muhamedan rise, and the Hindoos only join from fear. Mrs. (?) tells (me) there is a report that firing was heard at Cawnpore for 24 hours. Oh, what would I give to know how they have fared there – Oh my beloved husband! Where are you now!

11th Thursday Yesterday the Sikhs were allowed to loot. Brought in 200 sheep. Capt. Elgin had a sun stroke. This morning a spy caught dressed as a fakir. No news from Cawnpore. A regular struggle here to get food. Col. Neil and 40 Europeans arrived. The Col. took over command to the great joy of all who have groaned under an old woman's rule. A Frenchman arrived this morning from Cawnpore, who says the entrenched Camp was all right – the Cavalry looting the Treasury and Sir Hugh Wheeler firing away – Cantonments on fire. Bam Chuccar so very insolent that I was obliged to discharge him. Thank God the children continue in good health, notwithstanding the heat and scanty food.

12th Col. Neil commenced work this morning. 500 Sikhs and Europeans went out at gunfire (dawn) to destroy the villages close to the bridge. Guns from the battery firing all the morning. In the evening all the ladies went to the top of the barracks to see the City on fire. Very hot night.

13th A steamer arrived last night with Madras fusileers on board. More fighting this morning, only 100 Sikhs went out and were driven back – inside shelter of fort guns. No news from Cawnpore. I wish I could know what they are doing there – My darling husband. Mrs. L. came from the Colonel to say that all the ladies that could must leave by the steamer, and would be sent to Calcutta at Govt. expense.

14th Preparing all day to go on board! – what a Sunday! all noise and confusion. Went on board at ¼ 4 o'clock – In a wretched state of discomfort and great heat. I did the best I could by dividing the partition allotted to us.

15th Started very early this morning, the other steamer started before us to go and shell a village ten miles up the river – The guns commenced immediately on our departure and we plainly saw the smoke of the burning city. The heat is intense. I know not how we shall manage with the children. A curious collection of half caste people here, everyone ruined and going down to Calcutta without 1 rupee, poor creatures; And how many on board in the same state of anxiety as myself about their husbands. We arrived at Mirzapore at 4 o'clock Mrs. Volk and Vincent accompanied Mrs. Potts on shore and got her a palkee carriage to go up to the station. She sent for her baggage in the evening without even a note for me. Her promises are worth as much as other peoples.

16th Tuesday I fear we shall be kept here very late, as there was a good deal of cargo. The heat is something dreadful.

17th About 10 a.m. we started, passing Chunar at 1 p.m. – And many delightful recollections the sight of its old walls recalled – Reached Benares at sunset – Mrs. Gordon to see Mrs. Woodhouse and me. We saw to-day on the bank near Ramnaggar some European women and children, the Capt. would not stop to take them – His conduct has been reported to the Conl. by the volunteers. The French Col. from Cawnpore is on board and talked to me a great deal this evening, filling me with grievous apprehensions as to the fate of my beloved husband.

18th Mrs. Gordon sent some bread and biscuits – Left Benares at 9 a.m. Mrs. Volk tells me there is news *this* morning from Cawnpore that all are safe in the entrenched camp. God grant this may be true, but I fear I cannot hear anything until I reach Calcutta.

24th At Rajmahal to-day taking in coals. The last few days I have not written anything, the weather has been so bad, windy, cold and wet, quite a different kind of climate to what I expected. Both Helena and I have suffered slight bowel complaint – Nearly a month since I left my dear husband. God grant I have a husband yet! Ah what joy. What relief I will be in if I get news on arriving at Calcutta.

26th Friday This morning we left the Ganges and struck into the river Goorae. The channel, which is narrower and much deeper than the Ganges – the banks are beautiful. At 12 a.m. reached Camulla for coal – a sweet pretty place – the shores shut in like a lake – got very good fruit, milk.

27th All day in the same course, reached Coolice in the evening – the last station for coaling, and at the mouth of the Sundarbans. Fine pine apples, cocoa beans and good butter. Some of the gentlemen went on shore and brought news that all was right in entrenched camp up to the 15th. Thank God for this much news.

28th Sunday Entered the Sundarbans this morning. The shores are covered with dense jungle. The rain has been pouring in torrents all day – Everything cold, wet and uncomfortable. Mrs. King lead service after dinner, and gave us a good discourse on faith.

29th & 30th Monday and Tuesday We have been threading through wide and beautiful Sundarbans, chilly weather with constant head winds.

1st July We to-day passed through Diamond harbour. Very wet. Expect to reach Calcutta about five. I feel sick with apprehension about news. God in his mercy grant he may be safe and well. Arrived opposite the ghat at 5 o'clock. Mrs. O'Donahan told me that news had been received from Cawnpore where the camp was holding out bravely. No one came to meet me so went on shore with Mrs. Volk and Capt. Stace who drove me in his buggy to Cook's' where I got a palkee garri and drove to Cassipore, which we reached at ½ eight and were very kindly received by Major Angelo (her father-in-law) and Elliott (her brother-in-law).

2nd Elliott's house very small, loads of mosquitoes. No fresh news from Cawnpore. My dear Fred, I wonder whether my prayers have been answered and you spared in all these dangers!

3rd Wrote to Frederick and to Robert. Minnie very troublesome. Engaged two coolies from yesterday for the punkers.

6th The last two days I have been far from well, suffering from bowel complaints. No news yet from my own darling.

Lieutenant Frederick Angelo was wounded during the siege and killed at the ghat. A memorial to him is in the north aisle at All Souls Church. Mrs Angelo, when she reached Calcutta, was befriended by Lady Canning and it was at Government House that Lieutenant Frederick Angelo's posthumous son was born, Lord Canning standing as godfather. Mrs Angelo sailed for England in the *Nile* on 20 November with her two little girls and baby son. (Information kindly supplied by Richard Muir.)

Index